Texts in Philosophy
Volume 10

The Socratic Tradition
Questioning as Philosophy
and as Method

Volume 1
Knowledge and Belief: An Introduction to the Logic of the Two Notions
Jaakko Hintikka. Prepared by Vincent F. Hendriks and John Symons

Volume 2
Probability and Inference: Essays in Honour of Henry E. Kyburg
William Harper and Greg Wheeler, eds.

Volume 3
Monsters and Philosophy
Charles T. Wolfe, ed.

Volume 4
Computing, Philosophy and Cognition
Lorenzo Magnani and Riccardo Dossena, eds.

Volume 5
Causality and Probability in the Sciences
Federica Russo and Jon Williamson, eds.

Volume 6
A Realist Philosophy of Mathematics
Gianluigi Oliveri

Volume 7
Hugh MacColl: An Overview of his Logical Work with Anthology
Shahid Rahman and Juan Redmond

Volume 8
Bruno di Finetti: Radical Probabilist
Maria Carla Galavotti, ed.

Volume 9
Language, Knowledge, and Metaphysics. Proceedings of the First SIFA Graduate Conference
Massimiliano Carrara and Vittorio Morato eds.

Volume 10
The Socratic Tradition. Questioning as Philosophy and as Method
Matti Sintonen, ed.

Volume 11
PhiMSAMP. Philosophy of Mathematics: Sociological Aspects and Mathematical Practice
Benedikt Löwe and Thomas Müller, eds.

Texts in Philosophy Series Editors
Vincent F. Hendriks   vincent@hum.ku.dk
John Symons   jsymons@utep.edu
Dov Gabbay   dov.gabbay@kcl.ac.uk

The Socratic Tradition
Questioning as Philosophy and as Method

edited by

Matti Sintonen

© Individual author and College Publications 2009. All rights reserved.

ISBN 978-1-904987-64-2

College Publications
Scientific Director: Dov Gabbay
Managing Director: Jane Spurr
Department of Computer Science
King's College London, Strand, London WC2R 2LS, UK

http://www.collegepublications.co.uk

Original cover design by orchid creative   www.orchidcreative.co.uk
Printed by Lightning Source, Milton Keynes, UK

All rights reserved. No part of this publication may be reproduced, stored in a retrieval system or transmitted in any form, or by any means, electronic, mechanical, photocopying, recording or otherwise without prior permission, in writing, from the publisher.

TABLE OF CONTENTS

Preface vii

Jaakko Hintikka: Introduction: Questioning as Philosophical Method and
    as Philosophical Activity 1

PART I
QUESTIONING AS A PHILOSOPHICAL METHOD IN ANTIQUITY

Pierre Aubenque: Sense and Function of Aporia 15
Robin Smith: "None of the Arts that Gives Proofs about Some Nature Is
    Interrogative": Questions and Aristotle's Concept of Science................... 25
Marja-Liisa Kakkuri-Knuuttila: The Relevance of Dialectical Skills to
    Philosophical Inquiry in Aristotle 51
E. Moutsopoulos: Moderation and Kairos in the Philosophy of Socrates 89

PART II
QUESTIONING AS A PHILOSOPHICAL METHOD IN THE MIDDLE AGES

Tomás Calvo Martinez: On the Origin and Extent of Questioning in the
    Middle Ages 97
Mikko Yrjönsuuri: Commitment to Consistency 109

PART III
QUESTIONS AND QUESTIONING IN THE CONTINENTAL TRADITION

Jean-François Courtine: The Question of Being: Meaning of the Question
    and the Question of Meaning 125
Karl-Otto Apel: Questioning: The Almost Forgotten Dimension in
    Traditional Logos-Reflection and its Re-Detection by Hermeneutics....... 139

PART IV
QUESTIONING AS AN EPISTEMOLOGICAL AND SCIENTIFIC METHOD

Vladislav Lektorsky: Questions in Philosophy, Science and Education 157
Gerhard Schurz: Models of Abduction – From An Interrogative
    Viewpoint 167
Matti Sintonen: The Two Aspects of Method: Questioning Fellow
    Inquirers and Questioning Nature 193
Luc Bovens and Wlodek Rabinowicz: Democratic Answers to Complex
    Questions – An Epistemic Perspective 223
Jaakko Hintikka: Presuppositions of Questions – Presuppositions of
    Inquiry 253

PREFACE AND ACKNOWLEDGMENTS

Questioning is our default view of method, *the* most natural way of finding knowledge of the natural and social world – and indeed of ourselves. It was turned into the cornerstone of western thought in the Socratic elenchus and Aristotle's doctrine of explanation and inquiry. Aristotle's dialogical games, especially as they founded expression in *Topics*, survived in medieval dialectical games, and they had a profound and longstanding impact on practices in academic life. When the moderns began criticizing the Aristotelian views of knowledge and knowledge acquisition the target was not the question-answer idea itself but rather who – or what – the partner in the dialogue was supposed to be. The message of the new natural and experimental philosophy since Francis Bacon, Robert Boyle and the scientific revolutionaries of the 17th Century was: a true philosopher cannot confine to reading Aristotle's books, or those of any other ancient authority, but must address Nature directly. This meant reliance not only on reason and observation but, especially since the experimental turn proper, intervention in Nature's course. As Kant famously put it, Reason "must not allow itself to be kept, as it were, in nature's leading-strings". To be successful it must approach Nature not "in the character of a pupil who listens to everything that the teacher chooses to say, but of an appointed judge who compels the witnesses to answer questions which he has himself formulated." In fact, as Hans Christian Oersted, the Danish physicist and Kantian philosopher who discovered electromagnetism, observed, experiments *are* questions put to nature:

To observe is to detect the actions of nature; but we shall not advance far in this path, unless we have a notion of its character. To make experiments is to lay questions before nature; but he alone can do that beneficially who knows what he should ask. (Christian Oersted, *On the Spirit and Study of Universal Natural Philosophy*, London, 1852).

Questioning is not just a method but also a philosophy in its own right. Man not only desires to know, but wonder and perplexity are at the very heart of man's essence. As Karl-Otto Apel persuasively argues in this volume, Gadamer's *Truth and Method* was not just, or perhaps even mainly, a methodological insight into how knowledge was to be obtained. Rather, in philosophical hermeneutics questioning has a more profound standing, marking, as Apel puts it, "logos-reflection" and hence dialogue in the full sense.

This collection of essays by leading philosophers probes questioning as philosophy and as method both from a historical and a systematic perspective. Based on papers delivered at a meeting of the *International Institute of Philosophy* at Helsinki and Tarto in 2001, the volume is divides into four sections. In section Perre Aubenque, Robin Smith, Marja-Liisa Kakkuri-Knuuttila and Evanghelos Moutsopoulos examine questioning as a philosophical method in antiquity. In the second section T. Calvo Martínez and Mikko Yrjönsuuri probe the extent of questioning in the middle ages as well as the commitment to consistency in medieval dialogue games. The third section is devoted to questioning in the continental tradition, and here Jean-François Courtine and Karl-Otto Apel examine questioning in Heidegger's and Gadamer's thinking in particular. In the concluding section the focus is on questioning in epistemology and philosophy of science, with papers by Vladislav Lektorsky on science and education, by Gerhard Schurz on models of abduction, by Matti Sintonen on questions addressed to nature and to fellow inquirers, by Wlodek Rabinowicz and Luc Bovens on democratic answers to complex questions, as well as by Jaakko Hintikka on presuppositions of questions.

I wish to thank not only all the writers who contribute to the volume but also all those who were engaged in the arrangements in Tartu, Estonia, and Helsinki, Finland. My special thanks go to Ms Catherine Champniers from the *Institut International de Philosophie* (IIP) in Paris, and the then-President of IIP, Professor Jaakko Hintikka, for assistance and support during the process of preparing this volume for publication. Mrs Auli Kaipainen, kindly and skilfully as always, assisted in turning the contributions into a camera-ready form.

Helsinki, August 20, 2009

Matti Sintonen

JAAKKO HINTIKKA

INTRODUCTION: QUESTIONING AS PHILOSOPHICAL METHOD
AND AS PHILOSOPHICAL ACTIVITY

Aristotle said that knowledge begins with wonder. He might have said instead, and even more accurately, that knowledge begins with questioning. Certainly philosophical and scientific method began in the Western tradition with questioning, in the form of the Socratic *elenchus*. The remarkable subtlety and depth of Socrates' questioning method is shown by the fact that it prompts problems that are still grist to the mill of philosophers of the twenty-first century. Among them there are the following: If Socrates was right in claiming ignorance how did he know to ask the right questions so as to direct *elenchus* to the intended conclusion? It might seem that asking any question requires knowing its presupposition. So how could Socrates ask any questions at all without knowing something, at least the presuppositions of the questions he was asking? If he did not himself know anything, how could he evoke in his dialogue partner nontrivial new knowledge, as he did to Meno's slaveboy? Where did such knowledge come from?

The power of the Socratic *elenchus* impressed Plato so much that he turned it in his academy into an institutionalized technique of reasoning and of philosophical training, as described in Ryle (1971 (a) and (b)). Both what we would call deductive arguments and what we would call ampliative arguments were conducted in the form of questions and answers.

It is not hard to guess what the main focus of Aristotle's interest in Platonic questioning games was. He was as competitive as the next Greek, and hence kept a keen eye on what it takes to win a questioning game. Any experienced trial lawyer knows the answer to this question. The secret of successful cross-examination lies in the interrogator's being able to anticipate witnesses' answers to his or her questions. In studying the ins and outs of such anticipation, Aristotle came upon a momentous discovery. He discovered that in some cases one could predict the answer to a yes-or-no question with complete certainty. In the light of hindsight or perhaps rather hindlogic it is easy to guess what such answers are like. They are the answers that are in our contemporary jargon said to be implied by earlier answers. As Aristotle puts it, only an uneducated man would refuse to grant the implied answer. By studying the conditions on such predetermined answers Aristotle began to study relations of logical consequence, and thus became the first logician in our Western philosophy.

As far as the internal structure of questioning processes is concerned, Aristotle's discovery meant in effect a distinction between two kinds of steps in an interrogative process. If the answer to a question is necessitated by earlier ones, it does not matter who the interlocutor is. Such a step can be considered *ad argumentum* and not only *ad hominem*. The questioner could as well take the step on his or her own. Such steps become what have later been called logical inference moves.

This insight has a remarkable corollary. It suggests that Aristotle's theory of syllogistic logic and his theory of scientific reasoning and of the structure of science are thought of by him as aspects of a more comprehensive theory of questioning games. The two *Analytics* are quite as much part and parcel of a theory of questioning procedures as the *Topics*, admittedly with the admission that Aristotle was so enthusiastic about his new syllogistic tool of reasoning that he assigned it a disproportionate role in his theory.

I cannot argue for this interpretation fully here. Suffice it to refer you to one passage. After having carefully explained the nature of syllogistic necessity, Aristotle in *An. Post.* A6, 75a21–28 realizes that his audience is in the danger of forgetting the interrogative context of all inquiry. Speaking of incidentals, Aristotle writes:

> Yet someone might perhaps puzzle about what purpose there is in asking questions about them, if the conclusion is not necessarily the case; for one might as well ask any chance question and then state the conclusion. But we must ask not as though [the answer] were necessary because of what was asked [earlier], but because it is necessary for anyone who says them [viz. the earlier answers] to say it [the answer], and say it truly if they truly hold.

(I have modified Barnes' translation slightly.) The "conclusion" mentioned here is obviously an answer to a question. It is instructive to see how questions and answers suddenly make their appearance in the middle of a discussion of syllogistically constructed science. Aristotle might as well have expressed himself by saying that nonnecessary answers have to be judged *ad hominem,* not *ad argumentum.*

Evidence for Aristotle's reliance on an interrogative framework in the two *Analytics* can easily be multiplied. A witty example of this reliance is provided by Richard Robinson (1971).

In the middle ages, questioning games played an important role for a long time as the centerpiece of philosophical training and philosophical argumentation. They were known as *obligationes* games, and like the Platonic games they were competitive exercises.

The *obligationes* games might at first sight strike my contemporaries as arcane and of merely antiquarian interest. In reality, they prompt questions which have a great historical and topical interest and which have not yet been fully answered. Among them, there are the queries: Which one does an obligation game have as its conclusion, logical truth or a material truth? Was there a confusion between the two among the scholastics, and did they all answer this question in the same way?

Medieval questioning games slowly became extinct, unless one can consider their role as ancestors of formalized academic disputations. The viability of such uses of *obligationes* games was demonstrated in Helsinki a few years ago when one of the contributors to this volume, Mikko Yrjönsuuri, defended his dissertation. The candidate and the external examiner, who was Calvin Normore (another contributor) agreed to conduct part of the oral defense in the form of an *obligationes* dialogue which they in fact did most successfully.

Independently of the disputation tradition, questioning became a major theme in the twentieth century in the thought of R. G. Collingwood (1940) and Hans-Georg Gadamer (1960). They even spoke of the logic of questions and answers, and saw in it their main methodological tool. Collingwood paid special attention to the presuppositions of questions and sought to trace them back to the questioner's "ultimate presuppositions". Both in Collingwood and in Gadamer questioning served a hermeneutical purpose, as a means of finding out the meaning of observed facts, texts and even of other persons' behaviour.

In one direction Gadamer's "Logic of questions and answers" is very close to its Socratic precedent. In the same way as Socrates exposes through his questioning the tacit assumptions and tacit contradictions of his dialogue partner's thinking, the use of questioning Gadamer envisages serves hermeneutical and critical purposes and is above all a means of a dialogue participant's self-discovery. Independently of Collingwood and Gadamer Michel Meyer (1986) has argued for a project of philosophy as a problematological enterprise. I will not try to outline it here. It is in any case a worthy continuation of the Socratic tradition.

These uses of the questioning method are humanistic rather than logical and scientific. What Collingwood and Gadamer call "the logic of questions and answers" does not meet Tarski's or Gödel's standards for an explicitly articulated logic. But this leads straight to the question: Where do we find such a fully developed logic? The long history of the questioning method and its role as father – or at least godfather – of formal logic might lead you to expect that the interest of the questioning method has long since been exhausted by logical and philosophical analysts.

This prima facie impression is totally wrong. On the contrary, the logic of questions and answers is only now coming into its own. In particular, it is only now that we can define such concepts as the presupposition of a question and the "presupposition" (uniqueness condition) of an answer, the desideratum of a question etc. (cf. below). These concepts are crucial for any systematic theory of questions and answers. What is more, the development of a real logic of questions and answers is part and parcel of the most important recent and ongoing developments in logical theory.

What are these developments? Questions are primarily requests of information, attempts to come to know something. Their logic is therefore a part of epistemic logic (logic of knowledge) and the logical and epistemological properties of a question can be largely determined by specifying the epistemic state that the questioner wants to raise. The statement specifying it is called the desideratum of the question. For instance, consider the (direct) question:

(1)   Who murdered Roger Ackroyd?

The epistemic state of affairs that the questioner wants to reach is specified by its desideratum which is

(2)   I know who murdered Roger Ackroyd.

An equivalent formulation is clearly

(3)   There is some particular person, say x, of whom I know that x murdered Roger Ackroyd.

In a logical notation this could be abbreviated as

$$(\exists x) K_I \, (x \text{ murdered Roger Ackroyd})$$

or even more briefly

(4) $(\exists x) K_I \, M(x,r)$

Consider similarly the experimental question

(5)   How does the variable y depend on the variable x?

Its desideratum can be similarly expressed in the form

(6) $(\exists f) K_I (\forall x) \, S[x, f(x)]$

Here we must resort to a second-order quantifier (function quantifier) which is theoretically unsatisfactory. Without doing so, we cannot construct a general first-order theory of questions and answers that would among other things preserve the parity of (3) and (5).

Now it turns out in fact that (6) cannot be expressed on the first-order level by means of received epistemic logic. What is the source of this awkward state of affairs? Surely (4) and (6) are comparable and ought to be possible to handle in the same way? But what is the concrete model-theoretical meaning of (3) or (4)? One natural way of answering this question is to say that to understand (4) is to understand a certain kind of game of verification and falsification. The existential quantifier $(\exists x)$ marks a move by the verifier. He, she or it (for the player may be a computer) has to choose an individual (say b) from the appropriate domain, in this case from among persons. In other words, the epistemic operator K_d (d knows) operates like a universal quantifier ranging over the scenarios ("possible worlds") compatible with everything d knows. The order of symbols in (4) shows that the individual b has to be selected before the falsifier chooses the scenario. In order for (4) to be true, the sentence $M(b,r)$ must be true in the scenario chosen.

But this is not the only way of handling the semantics of (4). The verifier does not have to choose b *before* the falsifier chooses the scenario she hopes to disprove the epistemic claim. It suffices for her to choose it in ignorance of the falsifier's move or, as game theorists would put it, *independently* of the falsifier's move.

Now this kind of independence cannot be expressed in the received logic that goes back to Frege and Russell. (See Hintikka 1996.) Hence we have to extend our logic so as to be able to express such independence. One way of doing so is to introduce an ad hoc independence indicator / (slash). Then (4) can be rewritten as

(7) $K_I(\exists x/K_I) M(x,r)$

Lo and behold, by means of the slash we can now express also (6) on the first-order level, for instance as follows:

(8) $K_I(\forall x)(\exists y/K_I) S[x,y]$

The reason this cannot be expressed by the received logical means is that $(\forall x)$ depends on K_I and thus $(\exists y)$ depends on $(\forall x)$ but not on K_I. This makes it impossible to write the three in a linear order.

This treatment can be generalized to other questions. From any first-order sentence in a negation normal form, we can form the desideratum of a question (possibly of a multiple question) by prefixing it by K_I and then replacing a quantifier $(\exists x)$ (or more than one such quantifier) by $(\exists x/K_I)$ and/or replacing one disjunction $(S_1 \vee S_2)$ (or more than one such disjunction) by $(S_1(\vee/K_I)S_2)$.

In general logic, the introduction of the notion of independence has created a veritable revolution. (Cf. Hintikka 1996, 1998 and forthcoming (b).) The received Frege-Russell treatment has turned out to be inadequate, and our understanding of the most basic typical notions, quantifiers and propositional connectives, has to be deepened. The development of the new logic of questions and answers just outlined – or, rather, the development of the epistemic logic of which it is a part – is thus part and parcel of an extremely important breakthrough in logic in general. I suggested that logic began in the hands of Aristotle as a chapter of the logic of questioning. Today, general logic and the logic of questions and answers are still progressing hand in hand. This amounts to an impressive revitalization of the Socratic tradition in the philosophy of logic of the twenty-first century.

At the same time this tie between a satisfactory epistemic logic and the newly introduced notion of independence explains why a truly satisfactory logic of questions and answers has not been developed earlier in spite of the length and importance of the Socratic tradition.

What does the new logic of questions and answers look like? Only a few basic points can be made here. One important opportunity that it offers is to be able to define some of the basic concepts of questions and answers. For instance, the presupposition of a question is obtained from its desideratum by simply omitting all slashes $(\exists x/K_I)$ and $(\vee/K_I)$. (For a discussion of the presuppositions of questions, see my paper "Presuppositions of questions – presuppositions of inquiry", in this volume. (The desideratum is assumed to be in negation normal form.) Thus the presupposition of (1) is

(9) $K_I(\exists x)M(x,r)$

(Cf. (7).) The presupposition of (5) is likewise

(10) $K_I(\forall x)(\exists y) S[x,y]$

(Cf. (8).) These make excellent sense, except that in ordinary usage we drop the initial epistemic operator K_I when we speak of presuppositions.

The presuppositions of correct questions might seem an arcane subject without a broader practical or deeper theoretical interest. It might even seem a more fascinating question to inquire how one can beat one's opponent in a questioning game by disregarding the presuppositions of questions. Raymond Smullyan (1997) has in fact shown by means of his inimitable playful examples how such presuppositionless questions can be used to reach any end whatsoever. He envisages the beautiful but damned Scherazade who persuades her captor to answer truthfully one yes-or-no question. She asks: Will you answer *no* or spare my life? If the king says *yes*, he will have to spare her life, for he has not answered *no*. But the king cannot truthfully answer *no*, for that answer would be truthful only if he did not say *no*.

In reality presuppositions lead to important philosophical insights. Collingwood's tactic was to trace presuppositions of questions back to ultimate presuppositions. But presuppositions are not transitively ordered, and hence cannot always be traced back to a common source. Furthermore, not all questions have presuppositions, which makes such backwards reduction often impossible. Indeed, genuine yes-or-no questions do not have presuppositions. And in fact the Platonic Socrates asks mostly yes-or-no questions. It has even been claimed that he never asks any other kinds of questions, but this claim is simply not true. We can now see that Socrates relied on yes-or-no questions in order to preserve his ironic stance, for such questions do not need any presuppositions to be known before one raises them.

How come such simple presuppositionless questions suffice for the ambitious philosophical and pedagogical purposes of someone like Socrates? The answer lies in the fact that in a sense any question can be replaced by a yes-or-no question. Suppose that I have asked a complicated question with a complex presupposition and received the answer A. If so, I could as well have asked the same respondent the question "Is it the case that A or not?" Assuming a modicum of consistency on the part of the answerer, he, she or it cannot help answering "yes". Then I would have obtained the same answer by means of a simple presuppositionless yes-or-no question.

So are all other kinds of questions actually redundant? The correct answer is: yes and no. If you claim the dispensability of other questions in our example, I will have to ask you: How come you could know to ask the very question "A or not-A"? You knew to ask it only because you had already received the fact that A is an answer to another kind of question. But if so, the earlier question is not epistemically dispensable.

What we have to do here is to distinguish *definitory* or permissive rules of questioning from its *strategic* rules. It is permissible to replace any other kind of question by a yes-or-no question, but there is in general no strategic rule for doing so. In the justificatory sense of "can", questions other than yes-or-no questions can be dispensed with, but not in a strategic or epistemic sense of "can". These remarks are elaborated in my paper "Presuppositions of questions – presuppositions of inquiry" later in this volume.

The distinction between two kinds of rules can be generalized to other kinds of goal-directed activities. Applied to the "game" of deductive logic it brings out the fact that the so-called rules of inference are merely permissive rules, not strategic rules. Since these "rules of inference" play a central role in logic teaching, it is no wonder that such teaching is often experienced as useless. What is being taught is not how to reason well, but merely how to avoid fallacies.

The central role of the notion of independence in the logic of questions and answers makes this logic a part of a breakthrough development in logic. In a somewhat analogous way, the possibility of applying the strategic viewpoint to questioning opens a radically new perspective on epistemology in general. I have suggested modeling knowledge-seeking in general as a questioning process. (See Hintikka 1999.) This suggestion is not any more radical than the position Aristotle represents in his *Topica*. However, in the present-day perspective it opens interesting new vistas. Whatever else there is to be said of this suggestion, it makes it possible to study logically and epistemologically the process of scientific and more generally epistemological discovery.

This is no mean feat. It used to be customary to distinguish in epistemology contexts of discovery from contexts of justification and almost as customary to claim that only contexts of justification can be studied rationally by logical and epistemological means. But when we conceive our knowledge-seeking processes as questioning process we see that we can study discovery-oriented reasoning quite as well as – in fact more easily than – justificatory reasoning. This promises a tremendous expansion of the scope of the applications of logical and epistemological theorizing.

I cannot review the theory of questioning strategies fully here. It is in any case worth pointing out that this new theory is even in its technical incarnation hauntingly familiar from the history of the subject. Plato already conceived the questioning dialogues which served as his methodological tool as competitive games between a questioner and a responder. The most important conceptual tool of the contemporary theory of questioning processes is the mathematical theory of games founded by John von Neumann. One epistemological moral that game theory brings home to us is that in the last analysis only entire strategies can be evaluated or, as game theorists put it in their economical jargon, can be associated with utilities. Such strategies do not govern rules one by one, but the entire history of a play of the game in question.

This result has a remarkable further consequence. Since the actual scientific process that we have modeled as a questioning process involves both discovery and verification, strategies of scientific and more generally epistemological inquiry must involve both. In other words, discovery and justification must be considered and evaluated together – at least in the last instance. Not only is it not the case that justification must be studied alone, separated from the messy psychological process of discovery. Justification cannot in principle be studied in such splendid isolation.

As far as the content of the theory of interrogative strategies is concerned, suffice it to point out one interesting development. The questioning games for pure discovery there obtains a close parallelism between the use of a proposition as the input of a purely logical (deductive) move and its use as the presupposition of a question. For instance, an existential proposition $(\exists x) S[x]$ can serve either as the input of a logical move of existential instantiation whose output is of the form $S[\beta]$, where β is a "dummy name" similar to the John Does and Jane Roes of legal parlance standing for "an arbitrary individual".

Likewise, a disjunction $(S_1 \vee S_2)$ can be used deductively to start two different paths of countermodel construction with S_1 and S_2 as the two distinguishing new members. It can also be used as the presupposition of a propositional question. If an answer is available and if it is S_i (i=1 or 2), then one similar path is started. However, the question need not be asked if the questioner knows which one the answer will be. Hence in strategic planning the inquirer must consider both paths.

Furthermore, a presuppositionless yes-or-no question is in the same way analogous to the introduction of a tautological disjunction $(S_o \vee \sim S_o)$, which is the gist of such deductive rules as the cut rule or the modus ponens.

This parallelism is the full story only in the case of a game of pure discovery, that is, when all answers are true and known to be true. In such a case, it has a remarkable consequence. The parallelism shows that the rest of a deduction will be analogous to the parallel inquiry (questioning process). Hence the best way of carrying out one of these processes is parallel to the best way of carrying out the other. What this means is although we must separate sharply question-answer moves in interrogative games from logical inference moves, this distinction is merely definitory. Strategically speaking, the best guide to interrogative reasoning (as long as it aims at discovery) is deductive logic. I have illustrated this on other occasions by speaking of the Sherlock Holmes conception of logic as the secret of all good reasoning. Now we can see that Sherlock Holmes was right. In a strategic perspective, the best guide to empirical (interrogative) reasoning is after all deduction.

The strategic viewpoint illuminates also the history of questioning methods. For instance, we can finally reconcile Socrates' ironic ignorance with his skills as a master of the elenchus, his questioning method. Socrates did not need to know any answers to his questions ahead of the time, but he had to know which questions to ask. His superior knowledge was strategic rather than factual. The puzzling question – a new Socratic paradox – is how the latter knowledge was possible without the former. Or was it? Was Socrates perhaps pretending ignorance merely – merely? – for the purpose of shocking his interlocutor into realizing the epistemological significance of strategic knowledge and strategic rules?

Other aspects of the logic of questions and answers lead to other philosophical insights. Not only do questions have presuppositions; answers have them, too, although in the jargon of epistemic logic they are often called uniqueness conditions. (See here Hintikka, forthcoming (a).) What is at issue can be seen by imagining that the question (1) elicits the answer "b" whatever the name or singular noun phrase b is. Does that satisfy the questioner, that is, does it make the desideratum of (1) true? Not always. Assuming a context of pure discovery, such a response makes it true for the questioner to say

(11) $K_I M(b,r)$

But this does not entail the desideratum (7) alone, only in conjunction with the additional premise

(12) $K_I(\exists x/K_I)(b=x)$

What this means is that the questioner knows who b is. Answering (1) in this way hence involves bringing the questioner to know who b is. Once again, this sounds almost trivial, until we have a closer look at (12) and ask what kind of knowledge is expressed by the "uniqueness condition" (12). It is not difficult to see, especially by considering the case in which b is a proper name, that this knowledge is partly a priori, knowledge of what our expressions, including proper names, in fact mean.

Likewise, if an experimental question like (5) prompts a reply the function g, this reply brings about the truth of

(13) $K_I(\forall x)S[x,g(x)]$

But this entails the desideratum (6) only in conjunction with

(14) $K_I(\forall x)(\exists y/K_I)(g(x)=y)$

Here we may think of g as a "function-in-extension", that is, as being represented by a curve on a graph paper or a class of coordinated pairs of argument values and function values. Then (14) will say that the questioner knows the mathematical function that the graph represents. This knowledge is not factual but mathematical, and hence a priori.

What this amounts to is that answering a purely factual experimental question involves ("presupposes") certain a priori knowledge which is in this case mathematical rather than semantical. Thus we have reached a remarkable insight. Even in the process of answering a purely factual experimental question, we will need some purely a priori knowledge. In the case of experimental questions, this *a priori* knowledge is mathematical in character (knowledge of the identity of mathematical functions). This shows in terms of an experimentum crucis the role of mathematical a priori knowledge in experimental science.

This result and its consequences are discussed at greater length in my paper "The indispensability of mathematics and the a priori element in experimental science" (forthcoming (a)). It is hard not to see in the crucial role of *a priori* knowledge in experimental inquiry overtones of Plato's belief in *anamnesis*.

Thus we can see that the Socratic tradition is not only alive in our contemporary philosophy. It would not be much of an exaggeration to claim that it is the most vital aspect of philosophy today. It is intrinsically connected with some of the most promising current development in logic and epistemology. At the same time it is connected with the central ideas of the hermeneutical tradition. It should be a source of satisfaction for our Institute that these different developments have been prominently represented by its membership, including such distinguished philosophers as Hans-Georg Gadamer. But we have also seen that this tradition has not strayed very far from its Greek origins. In fact someone once characterized the questioning model of inquiry as the Socratic elenchus in the form in which John von Neumann would have practiced it.

The connections between topical questions and history are among other things illustrated by a certain artificiality of the dichotomy of interrogative steps vs. logical steps in inquiry. Socrates did not have it. It was in effect discovered and implemented by Aristotle, even though he did not appreciate the fact that logical (deductive) steps do not introduce new factual information into reasoning. For one thing, it is often useful to prompt an interrogative move by a question. Why is it useful, in view of the fact that the answer does not introduce any new information? By choosing a particular question to ask the questioner can guide the selection of the next logical move (deductive step). And, as was indicated above, in such selections lies the gist of one's choice of deductive strategies. Hence in purely logical reasoning, too, asking the right questions can be a way of implementing the best strategies. Meno's slaveboy's reasoning was largely logical and mathematical, and yet it was evoked entirely by the questions Socrates put to him.

Such are the questions that ought to be cultivated in teaching – not questions calculated to find out what a student knows, but designed to prompt him or her to draw the right inferences.

REFERENCES

Aristotle, 1994, *Posterior Analytics,* translation with a commentary by Jonathon Barnes, second ed., Clarendon Press, Oxford.
Collingwood, R.G., 1940, *Essay on Metaphysics*, Clarendon Press, Oxford.
Gadamer, Hans-Georg, 1960, Wahrheit und Methode, J. C. B. Mohr, Tübingen.
Hintikka, Jaakko, forthcoming (a), "The indispensability of mathematics and the a priori element in experimental science".
Hintikka, Jaakko, forthcoming (b), "Hyperclassical logic (aka IF logic) and its general implications".
Hintikka, Jaakko, 2002, "Presuppositions of questions – presuppositions of inquiry", this volume.
Hintikka, Jaakko, 1999, *Inquiry as Inquiry* (Selected Papers, vol. 5), Kluwer Academic, Dordrecht.
Hintikka, Jaakko, 1998, *Language, Truth and Logic in Mathematics* (Selected Papers, vol. 3), Kluwer Academic, Dordrecht.
Hintikka, Jaakko, 1996, "On the development of Aristotle's ideas of scientific method and the structure of science", in William Wiens, editor, *Aristotle's Philosophical Development: Problems and Prospects*, Rowman and Littlefield, Lanham, MD, pp. 83–104.
Hintikka, Jaakko, 1996, *The Principles of Mathematics Revisited*, Cambridge U.P., Cambridge.
Meyer, Michel, 1986, *De la Problématologie*, Pierre Mardaga, Paris.
Robinson, Richard, 1971, "Begging the question 1971", *Analysis*, vol. 31, 113–117.
Ryle, Gilbert, 1971 (a), "The Academy and Dialectic", in *Collected Papers,* vol. 1, Hutchinson and Co., London, pp. 89–115.
Ryle, Gilbert, 1971 (b), "Dialectic in the Academy", in *Collected Papers* vol. 1, Hutchinson and Co., London, pp.116–125.
Smullyan, Raymond, 1997, *The Riddle of Scheherazade and Other Amazing Puzzles*, Harcourt, Brace and Company, New York.
Yrjönsuuri, Mikko, 1994, *Obligationes: 14th Century Logic of Disputational Duties* (Acta Philosophica Fennica, vol. 55), Societas Philosophica Fennica, Helsinki.

Part I

Questioning as a Philosophical Method in Antiquity

Pierre Aubenque

Sense and Function of Aporia

Socrates is the founder of a tradition which could most happily be called "aporetic". This characterization, which I will try to explain and to justify, seems to me much better than "dialectical", which, especially through its Platonic and Hegelian transformations, has acquired a rather different sense, and indeed a sense opposite to the Socratic intention and practice. To Socrates, dialectic was the art of questioning, not of answering. This point is confirmed by Xenophon's and Aristotle's statements. We learn from Xenophon that Socrates was always questioning, but that he never answered [*Mem.*, IV, 4, 9–10]. Aristotle confirmed this statement and gave as the reason of Socrates' behaviour: "for he recognized that he did not know" [*Soph. Refut.*, 34, 183 b 7 sq.]. In order to answer, one must have knowledge, while it is not necessary to have knowledge to ask questions [*ibid.*, 11, 172, a 18, 30]. Even more, ignorance or "unknowledge" is the motive of inquiring curiosity.

It is Plato, and not Socrates, who defined dialectic as "the art of questioning and answering" (for example, *Cratylus*, 390 c). Thus Aristotle told us why the dialectician as such cannot give answers: he does not know. If he nevertheless goes against his mission and gives answers, impelled as he is by an irrepressible tendency, it is because he wants to "appear to know the thing in question" and, if it is his turn to argue against the interlocutor, that is, if he is defending a thesis, he can do it, in so far as he is a dialectician, only with arguments that look like true (*eikotes*, *endoxoi*, "truthlike"). Dialectic is negative by nature, that is, interrogative; if it intends to proceed not only by questions but by assertions or denials, it can only claim to have an appearance of truth. A positive dialectic is a "*Logik des Scheins*" (Kant).

Right from the beginning, the Socratic method of questioning is presented as being independent of all knowledge. Vice versa, the questioning method yields no knowledge: "No art that is a method of proving the nature of anything proceeds by asking questions (J. Barnes)]" [*Soph. Refut.*, 11, 172 a 15]. On the contrary, "the demonstrator does not ask (*erotan*) for his premiss, but lays it down (J. Barnes)" [*Anal. Pr.*, I, 1, 24 a 24].

But then, if questioning does not serve as a basis of knowledge, what can be its utility? It puts into question another person's knowledge by revealing its impossibility to answer the question. It is here that the notion of *aporia* makes its appearance. *Aporia* is not a question, but the impossibility to answer a question and the feeling of anxiety which follows it. *Aporia* is literally the lack of way, but also at the same time something that prevents the progress of thought from reaching its end. The fact that we have no answer to a question compels us to ask the same question again in another form or to ask further questions. *Aporia*, which is the lack of a result, is at the same time a motive for a further development.

Here we have Socrates' existential situation: "I am erring and I am in *aporia* (*planômai kai aporô aei*)" [*Hippias Maj.*, 304 c]. But using himself as an example, he aroused the same situation to his interlocutor: *poiei aporein*, "he makes him be in *aporia*". We are in *aporia* when we cannot give a grounded answer to a question, that is, an answer which does not prompt another question. *Aporia* is not the general case. Most questions have an answer which derives its evidence either from experience (the case of an empirically verifiable proposition) or from the totality of previous demonstrations, which come from accepted premises. It is this empirical verifiability or this demonstrative coherence that characterizes sciences, either empirical sciences or formal ones such as mathematics. In this sense, there is no *aporia* in science once it is constituted. A pupil's trouble in finding an answer of a geometrical problem, such as the slave boy's problem in the *Meno*, is not strictly speaking an *aporia*: his trouble will fade away as soon as he will be in possession of the appropriate premises, and it will not be possible to question again the solution of the problem. The search for premises is a difficult art, but it is taken over by a logic of research, by a "zetetic", not by an aporetic.

Hence there can be an *aporia* only in the following cases:
1) the answer to a question is ambiguous;
2) the answer to a question is arbitrary;
3) there are several answers to a question which are incompatible with each other.

But these three cases can be brought back to one, to the one that Aristotle named "a balance of contrary reasons":

a) If the answer is ambiguous, it is equivalent to giving simultaneously at least two distinct answers to the same question at the same time, answers between which one will have to choose.
b) If the answer is arbitrary, it amounts to saying that there would be at least as many good reasons for giving a different answer to the same question.
c) If several answers are given, it means that we impose on the interlocutor an obligation to choose between these answers.

These three cases are subsumed under what Aristotle named the "balance of contrary reasons" (*isotes enantiôn logôn*) [*Top.* VI, 6, 145 b 16–20]. *Aporia* does not lie in that balance, but in the psychological situation (confusion) which ensues from it. Aristotle distinguishes very carefully, in an *aporia*, the cause, which is the balance of contrary reasons, and the effect, the confusion which results from it in the answering person and which is communicated to the questioner in the form of dissatisfaction concerning the quality of the answer (ambiguous, arbitrary or multiple). But as this definition of *aporia* is given in a work on logic, one can gather that this distinction between the objective and the subjective is a secondary matter (the reference of the lived confusion is doubtless here an allusion to Socrates' existential situation). The possible weakness of the answering person who is in a subjective confusion calls for a pedagogical treatment, even if an objectively troublesome situation is not present. The only interesting apories are the ones which resist such a treatment because of their objectivity. Among apories of that kind there are the Socratic apories, that is, the ones in which Socrates forced on his interlocutor (*poiei aporein*)[1] and that Socrates shared, in showing the authenticity of a confusion which is neither accidental nor temporary. Such is also the confusion into which Plato's Socrates was thrusted when he discovered that he could not himself define being: "we thought that we knew up to now what we meant when we uttered the word "being", but here we are now in *aporia* (*nun d'êporêkamen*)" [*Sophist*, 244 a].

From the logical point of view, it is possible to reduce *aporia* to its objective correlate, which is also called by Aristotle *aporêma*, and to define it exactly as "a balance of contrary reasons". Another definition of *aporêma* is also given by Aristotle: *syllogismos dialektikos antiphaseôs*, "dialectical syllogism of contradiction" [*Top.*, VIII, 11, 162 a 15–17]. The most obvious meaning of that formula is that *aporêma*, if it explicates the balance of reasons which makes a choice impossible, is constituted by a couple of syllogisms that, from obviously different premises, yield two opposite propositions about a same subject[2]. The best historical example is provided by Kant's antinomies, where it is seen that the thesis and the antithesis concerning cosmological ideas are such as neither of the two, even though they contradict each other, "can enjoy a preferential claim to approval" [*KrV*, A 421]. We are captured by a "*Gedränge von Gründen und Gegengrüden*" [*Ibid.*, A 465], whose equal force makes it impossible for us "to decide" [*ibid.*]. Each of the opposed sides has "unfortunately reasons supporting its side that are no more legitimate and necessary to approve than those for the opposite side" [*ibid.*, A 422]. So we have here *isotes enantiôn logôn* mentioned by Aristotle or also *isostheneia tôn logôn* discussed later by the Skeptics [*D.L.*, IX, 61 sq.], a tradition which Kant explicitly referred to [A 425]. The conflict doubtless arises here from an appearance, but an appearance that is "natural and inevitable" [*KrV*, A 422], which removes from an aporetic situation all of its accidental character and hence gives it the status of essential *aporia*. The psychological consequences are aptly identified in the first sentence of the *Kritik der reinen Vernunft*: "*Die menschliche Vernunft [...] wird durch Fragen belästigt, die sie nicht abweisen kann [...], die sie aber auch nicht beantworten kann*" [A VII]. It would be possible to discuss the causes of this situation, but, from a formal

---

[1] For example, *Theaetetus*, 149 a ; *Meno*, 80 c ; *Gorgias*, 522 a.
[2] When there are only two possible answers inside a same genre, the contraries can be treated as contradictory. Cf. *Metaph.*, I, 1055 b 3–7.

point of view, we have here the two conditions that constitute an *aporia*: the inevitability of the question and the impossibility of a grounded, unique, and unequivocal answer.

Aporia is therefore a form of questioning. All questions are of course not aporetical, unless we agree with the Skeptics that no question allows a verifiable or demonstrable answer. On the other hand, positivism maintains that any correctly formulated question leads to a univocal answer. In that sense, Marx asserted that "humanity poses only problems that it can resolve"[3]: posing the question already presupposes that the elements of the answer are given in experience or in history. In the same way, even though for other reasons, Wittgenstein says in the *Tractatus*, 6.5: "If a question can be put at all, then it can also be answered (B. Russell)". Between these two extreme positions, which would need to be justified fully, lays the middle position represented by Aristotle: there are questions which are not aporetical (according to the strict sense given to this expression) and there are other questions which are aporetical.

This leads us to a classification of types of question:

1. There are questions which I will call "categorial", that is, questions which, within a determined category (which defines a certain kind of questioning objects), call for an answer homogeneous with the question, that is, under the condition of its relevance, checked by experience. To take again the Socratic example of the *Meno*, if I ask for "What is virtue?" and if the interlocutor answers: "It's a great thing", the answer may be true, but it is irrelevant to the question asked. But such a "category mistake" is a logical mistake, which has nothing to do with an aporia. An aporia would be present only if there were an essential doubt concerning the very sense of the question, but we would then find ourselves in the field of metalanguage or of ontology, which I will examine later.

2. There are questions that I will name "definitional". They are in fact questions concerning a category, but there is a fundamental one, which is *ti esti*. It is known that Socrates was accredited by Aristotle with the merit of having been the first to put the problem of definitions [*Metaph.*, M 4, 1078 b 18–19]. That problem is solvable in principle: if it is true that, according to the Aristotelian understanding which, on this point, does not fundamentally differ from the Platonic understanding, every thing has an essence (*ousia* or *eidos*) and if the definition is *logos tes ousias*, it must be possible to find that *logos*. In these conditions, there is no impossibility in principle to tell what the thing is. That can be difficult, but the answer is here guided by an intuition of essence (which is always at our disposal, like an object of recollection according to Plato), an intuition which concludes the search. If there therefore always is a right a definition of the thing ("real definition" is a pleonasm), the search of the correct definition is the matter of the zetetic, not of the aporetic. There are never equally strong reasons to choose between two different definitions of the same thing: there is always one

---

[3] *Einleitung zu einer Kritik der politischen Ökonomie*, 1857.

which is objectively better (*beltiôn*, *Meno*, 76 e, 77 e), more adequate, than the other.

Then where does the tradition come from that has been called "aporetical", the dialogues that focus precisely on the search of a definition? First, let us note that this term is an invention of modern interpreters[4]. They understand by that term dialogues without a definite conclusion. This inconclusiveness may be due to a shortage of time, as at the end of the *Meno* without Plato evoking an impossibility in principle of answering to the question *ti esti*. There is no *aporia* about the definition of empirical objects, or of mathematical objects, or of ideal essences (if they exist). There is only *aporia* about the definition of ethical or metaphysical objects.

Therefore there is in principle no *aporia* concerning definitions, except when the problem is an integral part of an ethical interpretation or of an ontological decision. The Platonic dialogues are the more aporetic the further they wander from the supposedly Socratic problem of the definitional.

I believe that *Charmides* and *Theaetetus* show very well how Plato proceeded from definitional research to the proper *aporia*. *Charmides* and *Theaetetus* are both focused on science. Their fundamental aporeticity might seem paradoxal if it is admitted, as I wrote earlier, that there is no *aporia* in science. But *Charmides* and *Theaetetus* do not claim to give examples of scientific research. They do not move within science, but they are discourses about science, metascientific discourses.

The case of *Charmides*, to which I shall confine myself here, is already pertinent in this respect. This dialogue does not seek directly a definition of science, but wonders how we could know science, that is, to have a science of science. That leads us to face the following *aporia*: a science cannot be known without knowing the object of this science, because all science is science of something. If such is the case, the science of some particular science is nothing else than this science itself. But the one who has a perfect command of this science does not know, as far as he has a perfect command of this science, anything else than the object of this particular science, and the science of this object is not itself its proper object, so that there is no science of science. So if there is therefore a science of science, there is no science of science. The science of science is not a science, for, if it were, it would not escape from its own question; then a science of this science will have to be admitted, and so on *ad infinitum*.

Here is an *aporia* which, in whatever way it is presented, anticipates Wittgenstein's thesis about the impossibility of a language to refer to itself: "That which expresses itself in language, we cannot express by language (B. Russell)"

---

[4] The adjective *aporêtikos* is found neither in Plato nor in Aristotle. In the literature on the latter, it qualifies men, but not texts or situations: *Aporêtikoi* is one of the names given to the Skeptics. Upon the different senses of the term *aporia* and the related terms, *Cf.* the nowadays complete survey by A. Motte et Ch. Rutten (ed.), *Aporia dans la philosophie grecque des origines à Aristote*, Louvain-la-Neuve, 2001 (Publications of the Centre d'études aristotéliciennes de l'Université de Liège).

[4.121]. I believe that the same fundamental *aporia* is at work in Heidegger's negative thesis about being: "Being of beings is not a being". If the being of beings were a being, it would be necessary to ask what the being of that being is, and so on *ad infinitum*; but if the being of beings is not a being, one cannot tell what that being is.

The definitional *aporia* (which is psychological and relative in the general case) turns therefore into the main *aporia* as soon as the object of definition does not preexist in experience or in a world of mathematical Ideas (or of Ideas in general, if their existence is admitted), but is constituted by the definition itself. All definitions of a non-empirical or a non-intuitively perceptible object (such as a mathematical object) are linked to a circle: in order to define what a thing is, its essence has to be known; but, to know its essence, one has to know first what it is. That *aporia*, which affects every attempt at a non-empirical definition, is thematised by Plato in the well-known *aporia* of the *Meno*: one cannot learn what one does not know, for one does not know what has to be learned. This *aporia* of circularity cannot be solved by examining its logical form. It can only be overcome by as it were breaking up the opposition of contrary arguments: by means of a hypothesis – here, the hypothesis of recollection – or, from a general point of view, by means of a decision.

3) I am now coming to the third kind of *aporia*. We have already met it on the way through which we have already traveled in dealing with the difficulties due to definition. They are the essential *apories*. They are not solved by a logical process and they can only be overcome by decisions. Where do we find cases of essential *aporia*?

a) The first case which is neglected by the commentators of Aristotle's logical treatises, is cited by Aristotle to illustrate "the balance of contrary arguments": it is the *aporia* that is related to the question: "What must I do?": "When, by reasoning in the two senses, all reasons appear to us equal from side to side, then we are in *aporia* about what we have to do (*aporoûmen hopoteron praxômen*)" (*Top*. VI, 6, 145 b 19–20). Here the *aporia* is linked to a choice, to a conflict regarding alternative means, that is, to a choice of the particular premise in a practical syllogism. The major premise in its generality is commonly admitted by everybody or at least most of the people; in the ethical order, it can be phrased as *bonum est faciendum*.

This premise cannot be put into question. What is nevertheless possible to question is the choice of means, or the selection of the minor, that is, what is right and good in a particular case. Let us take as an example of the *Antigone* of Sophocles. In this tragedy, everybody wants what is right. But what is right? To refuse to bury an enemy of the city or, on the other hand, to provide burial to a dead brother? Two theses are present here: one of them gives priority to the safety of the city, the other gives priority to family devotion. The arguments for the two sides balance each other: both directions are well spoken (*eu eirêtai diplôs*), comments the chorus. Therefore Creon and Antigone are both right. If one of them were right and the other wrong (as is far too easily assumed by modern readers, who are inclined to find Antigone to be right), there would be no tragedy.

At this point it is our best interest to take literally the Aristotelian definition of *aporia*, according to which the conflicting theses are opposite but not contradictory. If they contradicted each other, one of them would be true and the other false and at worst one might hesitate to acknowledge the truth of one of them. But the tragic *aporia* is actually born from a contrariness of reasons. According to a good Aristotelian logic, the contraries cannot be true, but they can both be false at the same time. There would be here a reasonable way, but not a "tragic" one, to dissolve the *aporia* by demonstrating that the protagonists are both wrong. But it would result in questioning the question, to posing another question, once the first one has been denounced as an irrelevant question, as a false problem. It is probably what the rhetor Diodoros of Sicilia (I, 37) meant when he proposed to "solve an *aporia* by *aporia*" (*aporian aporiai luein*).

Aporia is therefore dissolved by denying the question. But there are questions that cannot be avoided, and likewise in the field of practice action usually calls for a quick decision. One cannot deliberate endlessly. When a decision is unavoidable and when the reasons balance each other, when a decision cannot be entirely grounded, refusing to choose is itself a choice which belongs to the selection of the alternatives.

Is the case of a practical *decision*, in which the reasons are assumed to balance, only a metaphor, or does every *aporia* rather conduct to a decision that is not necessitated by reasons?

b) We are going to examine two fundamental theoretical apories, to which all the metaphysical apories are reduced: the *aporia* of ground and also the *aporia* of essence or of being. The *aporia* of ground or of principle can be easily expressed. A ground cannot be based on its consequences, for these consequences presuppose the principle that has to be based. More precisely, the first principle cannot be demonstrated, for any demonstration presupposes that principle itself, in the present case the principle of contradiction. Any demonstration of the first principle involves a *petitio principii*. The only relevant question is to ask oneself, not how to solve that *aporia*, but how to avoid it.

The method of analysis which is borrowed from geometricians and which means to reverse the order of reasons, to proceed from a consequence to the premise of a demonstration, i.e. the reverse way, which makes of the principle the conclusion of its consequence, is only possible inside a closed and homogeneous system, within which reasons are contemporary and their links reversible. Outside mathematics, one cannot see any field in which this homogeneity and this timelessness are given. One will therefore have to resort to a hypothesis (replacing the principle by a hypothesis which will be judged by the utility of its effects but which will always remain in question and precarious), in other words, to resort to a belief which amounts to a dialectical and even perhaps ethical disqualification of whoever denies the principle (this is the way of the Aristotelian *elenchos*).

An original way, which has been proposed by Karl-Otto Apel, consists in turning the very procedure through which a statement is established into the ground of its foundation. Foundation (*Begründung*) presupposes, by its very act, what it is trying to establish, the primacy of discourse, i.e., of rationality (*logos*). Conversely, whoever denies the principle is committing or, rather, in a positive sense, producing a performative contradiction in showing in that way the unavoidability of the principle that he is disputing, even in the absence of demonstration. By contesting this *logos*, he is confirming it (Aristotle). But this is in a way a pragmatical foundation, implying that one departs from the logic inherent in discourse in order to decide that the practised discourse has a value or a sense. The question is validated by itself precisely by its being posed. To ask oneself in discourse for the meaning of a *logos* is to assume that there exists a meaning that one can ask a question about, and therefore, in a certain manner, to answer the question. Here the *aporia* finds in itself the outcome which nevertheless does not enable us to say that the question which has been asked and which gives rise to the *aporia* has been solved. It is rather a kind of move to another level, a level that could be called transcendental because it is a condition of possibility. However that move removes nothing of its non-demonstrable nature, and therefore in the proper sense of the term, arbitrariness of the decision. The opposite decision, the one involving an attribution of nonsense, would be disastrous pragmatically, but it remains logically open.

I now come to the last and the most fundamental *aporia*, the one which was to make an appearance in the *aporia* about definition and which could be named the *aporia* of essence. It is the properly ontological *aporia*, the one which is born from the question "What is being?". For the record, I recall that this question was declared by Aristotle [*Metaph.*, Z, 1] the most aporetic of all questions in the sense that it "has no beginning and will not have an end in time": being is the *nun kai palai kai aei aporoumenon*. What could be taken as a mere pomposity has in fact here a very precise sense. The expression is borrowed from Plato who already talked of *aporia* concerning the same question [*Sophist*, 244 a], but with a distinctive emphasis: to Plato, we are now in *aporia* (*nun*) and he certainly hoped to solve it; he will do it, he thought, through the theory of the highest genera (*megista genê*). Aristotle does not have any such hope.

The ontological *aporia* lies in the fact that the being is homonymous, that is, has a plurality of senses. This homonymy is neither obvious nor consequently surmountable by a process of reduction to unity: the different senses of being are not the species of a genus that would be the being; for these multiple senses ("categories") are themselves genera, and being is not a genus (and is therefore not "their" genus). It is a unity which has to be looked for and which is beyond any generic unity. It is transcendental, and therefore, being the condition of all definability, is not itself definable. Being has no essence, since essence is one of its senses. These arguments justify the claim that being is somehow essentially homonymous: as in the similar case of Good, it is a matter of "non-accidental" homonymy, *ouk apo tyches* [*Eth. Nic.*, I, 6, 1096 b 25–27]. The homonymy of being (and of Good) therefore is certainly what Jaakko Hintikka calls a "mere ambiguity", in the sense that there is not a unique definition of the term and that its various applications (in the limit infinite) operate differently in different cases in accordance with its different senses: quantity is not quality, neither the place nor the relation, and so on ...[5]. Therefore, we certainly have here an ambiguity, but it is, if we may speak with Kant, "a natural and inevitable one".

Ambiguity is not accidental when, in the absence of a common definition, there nevertheless remains a certain community among the different senses in the form of the relation to a unique (*pros hen*) and first (*proton, arche*) term. This structure, which can be precisely applied to the case of being, is what G. E. L. Owen aptly named "focal meaning". But where is, in the case of being, the "focus"? We have no intuitive insight into it, the main reason being that in order to have such an insight and to recognize it as giving us the primary sense of being, we would already have had to decide the criteria of what counts as this primary sense. But if the primary sense is the criterion of what is fully and firstly worth the name of being, there is no criterion that allows us to recognize that primary and dominating sense.

This difficulty was recently raised under the title "inscrutability of reference", in the form of the admission that any ontology, here introduced by the term "being", is a theory of reference. A first difficulty comes here from the fact that the word "being", borrowed from natural language or from a group of (Indo-European) languages, has no determinate sense, but a multiplicity of possible senses. Admittedly, one of these senses seems predominant, but only because it is given in the lexical (and not in the syntactical use) sense of the verb "to be", in

---

[5] Therefore I cannot follow here Jaakko Hintikka ["Aristotle and The Ambiguity of Ambiguity", 1959, in *Time and Necessity*, 1973, pp. 10 sq.], who, inside the *pollachôs legomena*, is precisely distinguishing between "plurality of applications" and "properly named homonymy" (mere ambiguity), but seems to put in the same category, wrongly to my mind, properly called homonymy and homonymy *apo tyches*. In this last phrasing, which can only be found in *Eth. Nic.*, I, 6, 1096 b 27, "homonymy" is to be understood in a strict sense, as it is proved by the line 1096 b 25: they are cases in which, between the different senses of the polysemic term, "there is nothing in common coming from a unique idea". The senses of being (or of Good) are therefore certainly homonymic (to the strict sense) [*contra* Hintikka, p. 11], but they are not homonymic "by chance" (*apo tyches*). Inside the polysemy, it is necessary to distinguish three cases, and not two, as Jaakko Hintikka is doing: 1) simple variety of applications, which lets the unity of definition remain; 2) non-accidental homonymy in which Aristotle proposed several cases: by relation to a unique term, by dependence of a unique term, by analogy; 3) purely accidental homonymy. The third case is illustrated by the example, which has become well-known, of "the dog", an animal or a galaxy. The second case – middle but the most philosophically interesting – is the one of being, of good and of the One.

which "to be" is opposed to "to become" on one hand, and to "to seem, to look" on the other hand. From the point of view of natural language (the Greek language), it was therefore tempting to turn *ousia* (*étantité*, beingness) in the sense of "substance", with the lexical connotation of "permanence", into the first and fundamental sense (*proton*, *arche*) of the polysemic expression "to be". But this was not necessary. If one considers the list of categories of being, none of which can be excluded *a priori* from a claim to primacy, it is seen that each of the nine categories other than essence could likewise have been considered without absurdity as the primary one: relation, action, quantity, time, and so on. Historical examples of those possible alternative decisions could be cited: the primary sense is to the Protagoreans relation, to the Pythagoreans quantity (number), to the Heracliteans time, to the Atomists place, to the Stoics action, and so on.

There is no intrinsic necessity to choose *ousia* as the primary sense of being, or even to choose being (which suggests a primacy of *ousia*) as the general title of reference. In view of the danger of unilateral overdetermination which was inherent in the double choice by Plato and especially by Aristotle of their starting point, first in favor of being and then within being in favor of *ousia*, the Neoplatonists preferred to resort to the "One". This is less determinate than being, as the first principle of what would from there on be an "henology", but not as an ontology in a strict sense.

That there should exist a history of ontology in a wide sense, and that there should be "alternative ontologies", is therefore no accident, but rather an inevitable consequence of the underdetermination, of the inscrutability of their starting point, which requires "decisions" that are incommensurable with each other and untranslatable into the categories of another theory.

That there should not be any absoluteness in the choice of the starting point, in that it admits neither evidence nor demonstration without vicious circle, that all ontology should be linked to a decision, to a commitment, an *"engagement"*, which can have good reasons for itself, if not logical reasons, then at least pragmatical or ethical reasons, is to my mind the principal effect of the Socratic questioning. In that sense, Socrates is the true initiator of metaphysics, but of an aporetical and critical metaphysics, and insofar as it includes necessarily thinking about its own conditions of possibility, "transcendental" metaphysics[6].

---

[6] What seemed to suggest W. V. O. Quine, *Ontological Relativity and Other Essays*, 1969, at the end of chapter 2.

ROBIN SMITH

"NONE OF THE ARTS THAT GIVES PROOFS ABOUT SOME NATURE IS INTERROGATIVE": QUESTIONS AND ARISTOTLE'S CONCEPT OF SCIENCE

Modern interpreters have often regarded Aristotle's *Posterior Analytics* as a mystery, or even a bit of an embarrassment. In his treatises on natural science and ethics, Aristotle is constantly concerned to review the opinions of his predecessors and of people in general; where appropriate, he also takes note of experiential observations, some of them highly specialized. However, the traditional view of the *Posterior Analytics* is that it advances an almost Cartesian picture of sciences as deductive systems founded on intuitively evident first premises. How are these to be reconciled?

One reconciliation is to hold that the *Posterior Analytics* is not about scientific method but instead treats science in some other way: for instance, as Jonathan Barnes argues (Barnes 1981), about scientific pedagogy. Another possibility is to agree that the *Posterior Analytics* and the methodology of the treatises conflict but to explain this developmentally, as Irwin 1988 does. Others have looked in more subtle ways for methodological links between the *Analytics* and the treatises (Lennox 1987, 1994, Ferejohn 1991) or aggressively defended the innatist position (Kahn 1981). However, for modern interpreters, these approaches still leave a critical question unanswered: if Aristotle did think that sciences should have deductive structures, and if he knew (as *An. Post.* I.3 shows he did) that deductive systems must rest on first principles not themselves justified by deduction, then what alternative account of the justification of first principles did he have to offer?

Beginning with the work of G. E. L. Owen (Owen 1960, 1961), an answer to this question has been elaborated, principally by that is now nearly a matter of orthodoxy[1] In outline, it is that Aristotle thought the principles could be established by 'dialectic', which is (in Irwin's words) 'a method of arguing from common beliefs', and where these common beliefs are a collection of views held by certain classes of people. Irwin in particular argues that Aristotle came to believe a kind of dialectical argument could accomplish the task of establishing the principles of sciences after having rejected what Irwin regards as the 'pseudo-performance' of 'cognition by νοῦς' to which Aristotle appeals in *Posterior Analytics* II.19. This picture of Aristotle's method as dialectical rests on several proof texts, most critically *Topics* I.2 and *Nicomachean Ethics* VII.1, 1145b2–7, and on the observation that Aristotle often begins the treatment of a

---

[1] There are dissenters: see D. W. Hamlyn 1990 and Smith 1993, 1994, 1999.

subject with a survey of the views about it generally held or held by earlier philosophers. I have argued elsewhere that this type of interpretation rests on a conception of dialectic that is at best misleading and on unsustainable readings of certain critical texts.[2] Rather than repeat those criticisms here, I want to explore a question that arises if they are sound. For Plato, dialectic was the philosopher's method of inquiry. Aristotle, by contrast, treats dialectical and philosophical arguments as they were disjoint and explicitly says that dialectic cannot be a part of science. What has brought about this change, and what conception or conceptions of dialectic underlie each philosopher's opinions?

In brief, I shall argue that Aristotle and Plato agree on the nature of dialectic up to a point and that it is a difference in epistemology that leads to their different views of its relationship to philosophy or science. Both philosophers think of dialectic as a matter of question and answer. Plato holds that we have innate knowledge of the Forms, which are the true objects of science, and that we acquire wisdom by recovering this knowledge already within us. This leads not only to the notion that questioning can both teach and discover the truth but also to the method of Division, which both Plato and Aristotle treat as central to the philosopher's activity. Aristotle denies that we have any innate knowledge and holds that we acquire all the knowledge we have through experience. He also believes, on the basis of some rather sophisticated logical theorizing, that the indemonstrable principles on which a science rests can be extracted from a collection of truths about its subject matter. Finally, he has a dimview of the prospects for armchair science based on *a priori* theorizing, evidently because he has disillusioned by seeing it practiced. As a result of all this, question-and-answer exchange has no particular role in the philosopher's method according to Aristotle.

For Plato, the asking and answering of questions was the very lifeblood of philosophical activity, which he conceived of as essentially a form of conversation (he even characterizes thought as a dialogue of the soul with itself). For Aristotle's philosopher, the accumulation of facts from experience is much more important than the participation in dialectical exchanges, and questioning therefore takes on a far more restricted utility. Collecting the opinions of others is an important first step in any inquiry, since an analysis of the inconsistencies and problems in the received views (a process Aristotle calls διαπορεῖν, 'puzzling through') will bring to the fore where the problems lie. However, the asking of questions plays no role at all in establishing the finished stages of philosophical inquiry: "None of the arts that proves concerning any nature asks questions" (οὐδεμία τέχνη τῶν δεικνυουσῶν τινὰ φύσιν ἐρωτητική ἐστιν: *Soph. El.* 172a15–16).

---

[2] See Smith 1993 and Smith 1997, Introduction, 52–55.

1. Innate Knowledge, Forms, and Philosophical Method in Plato

For Plato, the existence of separated, suprasensible Forms was both attested to by, and necessary to explain, our cognitive abilities. In (*Phaedo* 74a–75d), he argues as follows. We often judge two sticks or stones to be equal or unequal, yet we have never perceived any two sticks, stones, or anything else that were truly equal: all the so-called 'equals' we have encountered were only approximations, falling short of equality itself. Whence, then, came the knowledge of this equality itself with which we are comparing these many approximately-equals? It cannot have come through perception, for we have never perceived such a thing. Neither can its object be a perceptible object, for all that we perceive is always subject to change, whereas our knowledge of the equal itself is knowledge of something which is always just what it is and nothing else. Instead, there must *be* an equal itself apart from the perceptible world. Moreover, since we cannot have acquired a knowledge of it through perception in this life, that knowledge must have been *innate* in us.

This argument takes our ability to understand the word 'equal' as a given and concludes that this understanding can only be explained on the suppositions both that the equal itself exists separately from the entire sensible realm and that we have innate knowledge of it. Generalizing this to other notions besides equality gives us Plato's theory of forms. We should take note here of a critical difference between Plato's concerns and the basic position of modern epistemology. Since the time of Descartes, philosophical epistemology has been motivated by the goal of responding to skeptical claims that we do not have knowledge. By contrast, Plato takes our knowledge of such things as equality for granted and asks how it is that we could have it. Answering the epistemological skeptic is not a major concern for him. I shall argue below that the same is true of Aristotle, and indeed that Aristotle's views have been distorted by a failure to realize this.

If the Forms are the objects of knowledge, and if the knowledge of Forms cannot be acquired from experience, then teaching cannot be a matter of imparting knowledge to those who do not have it: that would be, in the words of *Republic* VII, "like putting sight into blind eyes" (518c). Instead, teaching can only be a matter of reminding, of getting us to recall the knowledge already in our souls. This reminding, for Plato, is brought about by questioning in the right way.

2. Plato's Answer to Meno's Challenge

Plato argues for this picture of knowledge as recalling in the *Meno*, where Socrates is challenged by Meno with the following puzzle:

And how, Socrates, will you seek something when you don't know at all what it is? For which one of the things that you don't know will you set up as the thin you are seeking? And even if you did come across it as much as possible, how would you know that this is that thing which you didn't know? (*Meno* 80d2–5)

Meno's puzzle is about inquiry, not pedagogy: Meno's dilemma is that inquiry is either pointless or impossible. In response, Socrates says, in effect, that we already know everything, having acquired that knowledge in a prior existence, and that it only needs to be brought out through a process of reminding. As evidence for this, he undertakes to lead one of Meno's slaves, a man[3] who has never studied geometry, to recognition of the answer to a geometrical problem, using only questions. Socrates claims that he does nothing but ask the slave to answer according to his own opinions. Using this technique, he first shows the slave that his initial beliefs about the problem are false; then, when the slave has become perplexed and no longer believes he knows the answer, he elicits from him answers to a series of simple questions that end in his assent (with understanding) to the proposition "the square on the diagonal of a square is double that square". Socrates concludes that the slave really possessed this knowledge all along, or otherwise he would not have been able to answer Socrates' questions. Moreover, since he did not acquire these opinions in his present life, the slave must always have had them, and thus must always have existed. Socrates concludes:

Socrates: So, if at that time when he was not a man, there were true opinions in him which, when awakened by questioning, become knowledge, then his soul will already have learned through all of time.
Meno: So it seems.
Socrates: So them, if the truth of things is always in our soul, then our soul is immortal. So whoever does not actually know now that is, who does not recall must be brave and try to inquire that is, be reminded?
(*Meno* 86a6–b5)

Socrates' gloss of 'inquire' (ζητεῖν) with 'be reminded' shows that the subject here is really the right way to pursue philosophical inquiry, not simply pedagogy. Since the entire exchange was prompted by an argument from Meno to the effect that we cannot learn anything we do not already know, that is to be expected.

In the *Phaedo*, Plato alludes to this episode in terms that make it explicit that 'reminding' is a matter of asking questions in a certain way:

When people are being questioned, if you do the questioning well, then they will on their own state everything as it is; yet if knowledge and correct reason were not actually present in them, they would not be able to do that. (*Phaedo* 73a1–6)

---

[3] Despite the almost ubiquitous characterization of him as a 'slave boy' in the secondary literature, he is only identified as a slave, not also as a child. The word παῖς, 'boy', is quite commonly used to mean 'slave' (as indeed 'boy' was in the American south under slavery). Manuscripts of the dialogue identify this character as 'Meno's boy' (παῖς Μένωνος), and Socrates so addresses him (85b5–6). This was the standard way of referring to a slave (male or female). If we do take παῖς in that phrase to mean 'child', then the meaning becomes 'Meno's child', i.e. Meno's offspring, which is obviously not what is meant: the sense is 'Meno's slave'. He enters the dialogue when Socrates asks Meno to call 'one of these many attendants of yours' (82a8–b1: τῶν πολλῶν ἀκολούθων τωυτωνὶ τῶν σαυτοῦ ἕνα). All that we are actually told about his status is that he is Greek, speaks Greek, and was born in Meno's household.

Unfortunately, Plato does not tell us, either in the *Meno* or the *Phaedo*, what this correct way of questioning must be. Let me offer an attempt at filling that gap.

2.1 Dialectic and Refutation

Whatever the right way of questioning is, throughout his works, Plato associates the term 'dialectic' with the activity of the philosopher. Just what he means by it may change from dialogue to dialogue (Robinson suggested that we might almost take it to mean "the method of philosophy, whatever that turns out to be"). However, some generalizations are reasonably secure. To begin with, dialectic is concerned with questioning. This can be grounded in the history of the term before Plato. Aristotle named Zeno of Elea as the founder of dialectic, and both Aristotle and Plato regarded Socrates' characteristic style of interrogating people as dialectical. Two things these practices share are that they are matters of arguing by asking questions and that they aim at refutation (though in Zeno's case, the questions may be answered for a notional respondent by the arguer himself).

Now, refutation may clear the ground for further investigations or inspire a desire to learn, but it is not very promising as the whole of a method of philosophical inquiry: if all that you do is refute, how can you ever build anything up? Plato puts exactly this criticism into Meno's mouth:

Socrates, even before I met you, I heard that you were just confused yourself and mode others confused as well. And now, as it seems to me, you are bewitching me and charming me and enchanting me into the middle of a confusion. If I may joke a little, you seem to me, both in appearance and other ways, very much like the flat torpedo-fish in the sea: it too is full of numbness and makes anyone who touches it numb. I think you have just now done that to me. I am truly numb in soul and speech, and I can't answer you. However, I have given many speeches about virtue, thousands of times, in front of many people and done it quite well, as far as I'm concerned, yet now I can't even say what it is at all. (*Meno* 79e7–80b7)

Making allowances for Meno's wounded pride and Plato's ironic humor, there is a serious point here. If all that Socrates can do with his refutations is leave people confused, of what benefit is it? Socrates' answer to this, through his conversation with the slave, is twofold. First, he says that even if all he does is refute people and thereby leave them confused, he does not injure them but rather benefits them, since it is always better to know one is ignorant than to believe falsely that one knows (84a–c).

Socrates does not stop, however, with this defense of his practice of refuting people and leaving them confused. He also claims that the slave already has knowledge in him about the question at hand, and he undertakes to show this by asking him questions to help him recover that knowledge. These questions, however, do not involve any refutation. Thus, we have dialectic without refutation: it still relies on question and answer and rests on the opinions of another, but the questions are intended to awaken dormant knowledge rather than to expose unacknowledged ignorance.

In effect, the *Meno* expands the notion of dialectic beyond the practice of refutation ubiquitous in the early dialogues to obtain a positive method. This new kind of correct questioning is dialectical because it rests on questioning and expects respondents to answer in accordance with their own opinions, but it has positive, not merely negative, effects. Its end result is newly awakened knowledge. But what would a method of inquiry by asking questions look like?

2.2 Questions and the Method of Division

The simplest description of Socrates' method in his conversation with Meno's slave (*Meno* 82b–85b) is that he asks very simple questions and shows how a hard but unanswerable question can be replaced by a series of simple questions. At the beginning of the exchange, he asks the slave simple questions that determine that the slave knows what a square is and can understand how to compute the area of a square. Then, he poses one more question that the slave takes to be equally simple: "How long is the side of the double square?" The slave answers confidently but incorrectly, and Socrates refutes his answer by showing him that it leads to results that are (to him) obviously incorrect. This is repeated for the slave's other attempts, and finally he gives up and says he does not know. It is at this point that Socrates turns from refuting to 'correct questioning'. He asks short and easy questions, mostly admitting of simple yes/no answers: "If we add three more like squares around this one, is the result a square?" "If we draw a line through this square from corner to corner, does it divide the square into two equal halves?" "Do these four lines, from corner to corner in each of these four squares, form a square?" Proceeding in this way, he leads the slave to the recognition of the correct answer to the initial question: the side of the double square is the diagonal of the square.

In this example, it is hard not to suppose that Plato is relying on his audience being aware that the question "How long is the side of the double square?" is especially difficult to answer in the way the slave tries to answer it. Since the two are incommensurable, the relationship between them is, in Greek mathematical terminology, ἄρρητον – literally, 'unsayable'.

One lesson that might be taken from this example is that it is easier to choose among alternatives than to come up with a substantive answer. If we are able to replace large questions of the form "What is X?" to questions of the form "Is X Y, or is it Z?", we may find them more tractable. We may also find it easier to deal with questions that admit of yes/no answers rather than requiring more substantive responses. To oversimplify, Meno's slave can get nowhere with "What is the side of the double square?", but he does quite well with "Is this square on the four-foot line the double of the square on the two-foot line?"

Now, in the *Sophist* and *Statesman*, Plato introduces a method of 'Division' as the way to discover the essences of things. Division is a method for finding the definition of a thing. We begin by locating our subject X in a general class or γένος. We then divide this genus into two or perhaps into three or four or more, but let us ignore that here and ask ourselves, "Into which part of the Division does X fall?" Having answered this, we then divide that part again, choose one of the parts, and so on, until we have reached X all by itself. For instance, a Divider trying to determine the definition of 'human' begins by locating it in the genus 'animal', then divides this into mortal and immortal animals, and finally asks: is a human mortal or immortal? The divider chooses 'mortal', and the division proceeds from there.

The method of Division thus takes exactly the same approach to questioning as Socrates did in talking to Meno's slave: it replaces a large substantive question with simpler choices between alternatives. We may not know just what to do if asked "What is a sophist?", but we can do better with "Is a sophist a kind of hunter?" To take a more serious example, it will be easier to respond to "Is a human terrestrial or aquatic?" than to respond to "What is a human?" The method of Division, I am proposing, is the systematic reduction of large and substantive questions to small questions that ask for choices among alternatives.

Though it has been disputed, I think it is clear that Plato thought Division was genuinely a method for the pursuit of philosophical inquiry. For one thing, a concern with answering a question of the form "What is X?" is at the center of most of Plato's dialogues, from the *Euthyphro's* question "What is piety?" to the *Republic's* "What is justice?" to the *Sophist's* "What is a sophist?". Such questions are answered by definitions, and Division aims at finding definitions. External testimony also confirms the preoccupation of the early Academy with finding definitions.

Support can also be drawn from Aristotle's *Topics*. Especially in its eighth Book, Aristotle clearly takes for granted that his audience is familiar with a stylized form of debate governed by a number of rules. Each debate takes place between an answerer, who seeks to maintain some thesis, and a questioner, who seeks to refute it, i.e., to lead the answerer to concessions from which its contradictory can be concluded. The questioner is allowed only to ask questions that can be answered by 'yes' or 'no'; the answerer is only to respond affirmatively or negatively (though questioners are allowed to reject questions as ill-formed if, for instance, they implicitly ask many questions). Evidently, the principal subject-matter of these debates is definitions. This is evident in the classification of all predications into four types: those giving the genus of something, those giving its definition, those giving its 'peculiar property' (*proprium*, ἴδιον), and those giving an accident or incidental property (συμβεβηκός). As Aristotle notes (I.5, 102b27–35), this entire classification system revolves around definitions. Moreover, this system is the principle of organization of *Topics* II–VI, which discuss arguments about each of the predicables in turn. Whatever else we may conclude about the *Topics*, its focus is clearly arguments about definitions.

I will simply take it for granted that members of Plato's Academy engaged in a formalized kind of disputation by question and answer concerned primarily with definitions and that the *Topics* is intended primarily for these exchanges. To speculate a little further, these disputations might plausibly have been based on the premise that knowledge of the natures of things, being already present in us from birth, could be brought to light by an appropriate form of questioning. Debate, for Plato, was a form of scientific research. There are other reasons for supposing that Plato took philosophical inquiry to be closely, or even indissolubly, linked to debate and dialectical exchange. His expressions of distrust of writing in the *Phaedrus*, the *Statesman*, and the *Seventh Letter* are motivated in part by the view that only in an exchange between two persons is real philosophy possible.

3. Aristotle's Criticism of Division

Aristotle rarely mentions Division except to criticize it, and his criticism is severe: he complains that as a method of proof, it fails since it is little more than begging the question. As he puts it in *An. Post.* II.4:

> Nor is the route through divisions deduced, as was said in the analysis concerning the figures. For nowhere does it happen that this fact must be given that these things are; rather, it is like the person arguing inductively, who also does not demonstrate. For the conclusion should not be put as a question or be as a result of someone conceding it; instead, it should be necessary for it to be given that these are, even if the answerer denies it. "Is a human an animal or inanimate?" If he picks "animal", it still has not been deduced. Next: "Every animal is terrestrial or aquatic." He picks terrestrial, and that man is the combination, terrestrial animal, does not necessarily follow from what was said, but he assumes this as well. It makes no difference whether one does this with many cases or with a few, for it is the same thing. (91b12–23)

Aristotle's criticism, broadly speaking, is that each step in a Division depends on an answerer's choice or concession. At no time is the next step something which 'must be given that these [i.e. prior steps] are', that is, a conclusion which follows from prior steps (the phrase Aristotle uses here is taken from his definition of a 'deduction' or 'syllogism' (συλλογισμός): see *An. Pr.* I.2, *Topics* I.1, *S.E.* 1. Now, it might be objected against Aristotle that this criticism supposes that Division was intended as a mode of proof in the first place, something which (it will be urged) it need not be. Division, according to this objection, is a method of discovery for definitions, not a technique for proving them. Indeed, the objection continues, since Aristotle himself does not think that definitions in general can be proved, and since he proposes something very reminiscent of Division in *An. Post.* II.13 as a means for finding definitions, his criticism of Platonic Division is grossly unfair. Division and deduction simply aim at different results, and to complain that Division does not deduce is therefore no more sensible than to complain that deduction cannot be used to discover definitions.

I believe that this objection does not recognize how deep Aristotle's criticism goes. What he is doing is rejecting not just Plato's view on how to find definitions but also Plato's conception of how to pursue philosophical wisdom, and ultimately Plato's conception of what philosophical wisdom consists in. From this perspective, his criticisms are, I shall argue, right on the mark.

We must first see what Aristotle advances as an alternative to the Platonic picture. This is most forcefully presented in *An. Pr.* I.30 where, having finished his presentation of what he regards as the universal theory of valid argument, he announces that what he has given us is nothing less than the one true method of inquiry:

> The way is the same for everything: for philosophy as well as for any art or study whatever. That is: we must collect what belongs to each thing and what it belongs to, have as many of these available as possible, and investigate them through the three terms, establishing in this way, refuting in that (according to truth, from what has been demonstrated to belong according to truth, in dialectical deductions from premises according to opinion. ... For this reason, the principles of each science are to be provided by experience. ... thus, if the facts that obtain about anything are grasped, it is already ours to bring demonstration readily to light. For if nothing that truly is the case has been left out of the *historia*, we will be able to find the demonstration of everything that has a demonstration; and for that of which there is no demonstration, we will be able to make that evident. (46a3–30)

There is no mistaking the sweep of this declaration. Furthermore, Aristotle quite clearly intends it to supplant Plato's own method. He follows this passage immediately with a criticism of Division that repeats the main points found in *An. Post.* II.5. The "route of division through genera", he says, is only "a certain small part" of this one true method, and on its own it is only a kind of extended begging the question (46b2–19). Moreover, its partisans failed to understand even the limited usefulness that it does have. Thus, Aristotle claims, the little that is valuable about Division is already subsumed under his own grander method, and the proponents of Division did not understand the power of their own method.

What, then, is this method with which Aristotle compares Division? We might suppose that it is some better method of finding definitions. However, definitions are the goal of Division because, for Plato, definitions express the content of the philosopher's knowledge: Division is Plato's road to wisdom. Aristotle rejects this view and maintains instead that the philosopher's knowledge – science, ἐπιστήμη – consists in the possession of *demonstrations* (ἀποδείξεις). Science, he tells us in *An. Post.* I.2, is knowing the reason why something must be so, and we have such knowledge when we possess a demonstration of it, which is a deduction of it from premises giving its cause or explanation. A deduction (συλλογισμός) is simply a valid argument, that is, an argument with the property that its conclusion is necessarily true if its premises are. Now, Aristotle's fundamental complaint against Division is that nothing is ever necessitated by what has gone before. What a Division cannot do, then, is explain why anything must be the case. Aristotle's complaint is not simply with the method of Division but with the underlying supposition that science or philosophical wisdom can be expressed in definitions.

But Aristotle's criticisms of Division have as their background a comparison of Division with his own alternative method. What precisely is that method, and how is it able to accomplish what Division cannot?

One further element of Aristotelian theory makes this method possible. Aristotle believes that a relatively simple theory can be given that accounts for absolutely all valid arguments. Since his method is unintelligible apart from that theory, we need to pause for a look at it.

4. Deduction and Aristotle's Philosophical Method

Aristotle thinks that every sentence with a truth value is one of two types: either an affirmation affirming some predicate of some subject, or a denial that denies some predicate of some subject. Affirmations and denials may be further subdivided into those with individual subjects ('Socrates is human') and those with universal or general subjects ('Greeks are human'); those with general subjects may be further divided according as the predicate is affirmed or denied of all of the subject ('All Greeks are humans', 'No Greeks are humans') or of part of it ('Some Greeks are humans'). His logical theory (which we may conveniently call the 'syllogistic') is then the theory of inference for sentences of these types. Very roughly, Aristotle's logic is the 'traditional' logic of the syllogism.

It will be convenient to introduce some notation here. I represent the four types of general sentence as follows:

A holds of every B (Every B is A)	AaB
A holds of no B (No B is A)	AeB
A holds of some B (Some B is A)	AiB
A does not hold of every B (Not every B is A)	AoB

In *An. Pr.* I.1–7, Aristotle studies the valid inferences involving pairs of these sentences that share one term. This theory is the principal basis of his well-deserved reputation as one of the greatest logicians of history; since it has been thoroughly studied (see Lukasiewicz 1957, Patzig 1968), I will only note a few points here. First, Aristotle proves that all the valid syllogistic arguments can be 'reduced' to these four (I give the medieval mnemonic names for each):

$AaB, BaC \rightarrow AaC$ (*Barbara*)
$AeB, BaC \rightarrow AeC$ (*Celarent*)
$AaB, BiC \rightarrow AiC$ (*Darii*)
$AeB, BiC \rightarrow AoC$ (*Ferio*)

Second, Aristotle knows that these results follow from what he has proved:

1. A universal affirmative conclusion can only be deduced from the form *Barbara*.
2. A universal negative conclusion can only be deduced through one of these three forms:

   AeB, BaC → AeC (*Celarent*)
   AaB, AeC → BeC (*Camestres*)
   AeB, AaC → BeC (*Cesare*)

Now, suppose that we are seeking a proof for a universal affirmative proposition *AaB*. Since *Barbara* is the only syllogistic form with an *a* conclusion, our proof must end with an inference like this:

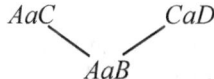

If we continue our regress by looking for true premises from which each of *AaC*, *CaD* can be deduced, we will in each case have to find another pair of true *a* propositions, e.g.:

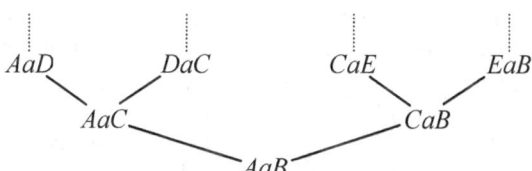

Aristotle explores the properties of such regresses in detail in *An. Post.* I. 19–22. To explain his results, it will be clearer to use diagrams representing the relationships of the terms in the propositions rather than the propositions themselves. I represent an *a* proposition *AaB* as a graph in which *A* is above *B* and an *e* proposition *AeB* by joining two terms with a line marked with *e*:

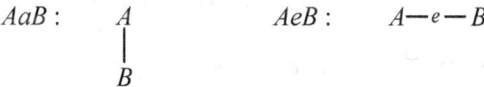

The term-chain graph for the regress for *AaB* depicted previously then looks like this (with annotations to the right showing the correspondence with the previous representation):

```
         A
         |\
         | \AaD
         D \      
         |\  \AaC
         | \DaC\
         C  \    \
         |\  \    \AaB
         | \CaE\   \
         E  \   \CaB\
         |\  \   \   \
         | \EaB\  \   \
         B
```

As this diagram shows, each stage of the regress requires the introduction of a new term *between* the terms of one of the premises reached at the preceding stage. For instance, term D is between A and C, the terms of premise AaC. This term then serves as the middle term in a proof of that premise. The regress can continue as long as another term can be found between two adjacent terms at the last stage of the regress. We may call this process 'packing' the interval AC, following Aristotle.[4] Conversely, if there is no such term, then the regress comes to a stop at that point. A premise for which this happens is 'unmiddled' (ἄμεσος)[5]. Such an unmiddled proposition cannot be deduced, in Aristotle's logic, from *any other true propositions*.

The last point is crucial: in a system governed by Aristotle's logic, there can be true propositions which cannot be deduced from any other true propositions whatever. This is a reflection of the very weak character of Aristotelian entailment. Under classical propositional logic, for instance, no proposition can have this property (any proposition p is logically equivalent to $p \wedge p$, pp, and infinitely many other propositions; so, if p is true, then so are infinitely many other propositions from which it can be deduced). By contrast, consider the set

$$\{AaB, BaC, AaC, AiC, CiA, AiB, BiA, BiC, CiB\}$$

All the propositions in this set can be deduced from the two propositions AaB and BaC; in fact, the set is simply the deductive closure of $\{AaB, BaC\}$. However, neither of these two propositions can be deduced from any combination of the remaining propositions. Consequently, each of these two sets is deductively closed:

---

[4] The Greek verb is καταπυκνοῦν, 'pack full' or 'thicken'; he uses it only once, at *An. Post.* I.14, 79a30.
[5] I prefer to avoid the potentially misleading but traditional translation 'immediate'

{AaB, AaC, AiC, CiA, AiB, BiA, BiC, CiB}
{BaC, AaC, AiC, CiA, AiB, BiA, BiC, CiB}

For Aristotle, of course, these are not facts merely about syllogistic systems, since he thought (and indeed thought that he could prove[6]) that the syllogistic was the correct theory of inference absolutely speaking.

Regresses for e propositions are somewhat more complicated. First, note that if AeB, then no chain descending from A can intersect with any chain descending from B (otherwise, we would have a proof of AiB via *Darapti*. Consequently, for any terms C and D below A and B respectively, we must have CeD:

$$A - e - B$$
$$C - e - D$$

However, two chains ascending above the terms of an e proposition may intersect, as in this configuration:

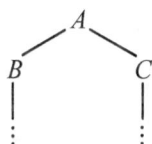

---

[6] I will not try to argue for this claim here, but the relevant texts are these: (1) at 40b17–22, when he has finished his account of the syllogistic, he says that he has shown that all 'arguments in the figures' (i.e. two-premise syllogisms in the traditional sense) are 'completed' by the first-figure forms and . He then continues, 'But that every deduction absolutely speaking is like this (ἁπλῶς πᾶς συλλογισμὸς οὕτως ἔχει) will be clear when it has been proved that all come about through one of the figures'. This is followed by an argument beginning with the claim that any proof must prove some predicate either to belong or not to belong to some subject and concluding that this must employ arguments 'in the figures'. (2) At 46b38–47a9 he summarizes what he has achieved and what remains to be done of his project. The final phase will be showing 'how we can analyze existing deductions into the aforementioned figures', and indeed what Aristotle discusses in the rest of An. Pr. is how to turn various types of argument into figured arguments. (3) In *An. Pr.* II.23, 68b8–14, Aristotle says that 'not only do dialectical and demonstrative deductions come about through these figures, but also rhetorical ones, and absolutely any kind of proof whatsoever from any discipline whatever' (ἀλλὰ καὶ οἱ ῥητορικοὶ καὶ ἁπλῶς ἡτισοῦν πίστις καὶ ἡ καθὰ ὁποιανοῦν μέθοδον). Whether Aristotle actually succeeds in proving these claims is another issue; the point is that he leaves no room for doubt that he thinks the theory of 'arguments in the figures' is the universal theory of valid arguments, without restriction.

Now consider how regresses for a universal negative proposition AeB can proceed. A deduction of AeB must have one of three forms: AeC, $CaB \rightarrow AeB$ (*Celarent*), CaA, $CeB \rightarrow AeB$ (*Camestres*), or CeA, $CaB \rightarrow AeB$ (*Cesare*). Each of these uses an a premise with one of the terms A, B as its subject and an e premise containing the other term. A continued regress for the a premise will consist of packing the interval between its terms. Continuation of the regress for the e premise will again give a and e premises. However, as the following graph shows, any additional middle term will always be either in an ascending chain above A or in an ascending chain above B:

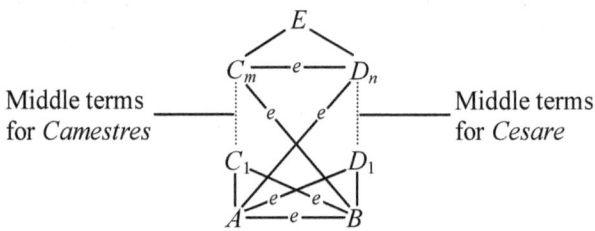

The regress thus produces ascending chains above A and B.

Now, Aristotle argues (*An. Post.* I.22) that every ascending or descending chain is finite, that is, contains only finitely many terms. From this, it follows that every premise regress for an a proposition eventually comes to a stop: an infinite regress would pack infinitely many terms into the interval between its subject and predicate, thus producing both an infinite ascending chain above the subject and an infinite descending chain below the predicate (see *An. Post.* I.20). Now consider regresses for e propositions. As shown above (and by Aristotle in *An. Post.* I.21), any such regress produces ascending chains above both subject and predicate; if every ascending chain is finite, then these must eventually stop[7].

Consider the terms at the tops of the chains above A and B in a fully packed e regress (C_m and D_n in the figure). $C_m e D_n$ will be true but unprovable (in order to prove it we would need to find a term over one of its terms and e-related to the other, but since the regress is packed there is no such term). Therefore, we have found an unmiddled e proposition. There are two ways this might happen: (1) there may be no term over C_m and no term over D_n (in this case, we may call C_m and D_n *highest terms*).(2) there may be some term E over both C_m and D_n such that the intervals EC_m, ED_n are unmiddled (I will call this an *unmiddled branch*). Aristotle is aware of both types of case[8] (*An. Post.* I.15, I.23).

---

[7] There are some complications in Aristotle's argument in *An. Post.* I.21. In particular, the text at 82b21–33 seems to be confused and may be corrupt: see Smith 1989 for discussion.

[8] There are some problems with his argument, since in I.15–I.17 he seems at times to assume that case (1) is the only possible case, though he clearly recognizes it as possible in I.23.

4.1 The Regress Argument of Posterior Analytics I

Aristotle does not argue for these results simply out of a theoretical interest in the properties of his logical system. Instead, he uses them to address a critical problem of the *Posterior Analytics*. The subject of that treatise is a certain kind of knowledge which, for lack of a better translation I shall call 'science' (ἐπιστήμη). In *An. Post.* I.2, he first characterizes science as knowing the reason why something must be as it is and then explicates this as possessing a demonstration or proof, where a demonstration is a deduction from premises that give the cause of the conclusion. He then presents a problem. Some people, he says, claim that demonstration is impossible because:

1. The premises of a demonstration must themselves be known scientifically.
2. Only what is demonstrated is known scientifically.

These opponents next ask, "How are the premises of demonstrations known?" and then present a dilemma. Either the premises are scientifically known because they are demonstrated, or they are not. But if they are demonstrated, then they must be demonstrated from others which are known scientifically, and thus, by repeating this step, we get an infinite regress of premises. On the other hand, if they are not demonstrated, then by premise 2 they are not scientifically known. Thus, it seems that scientific knowledge is impossible.

This regress argument is very often taken to be a familiar skeptical argument about the regress of justification. However, Aristotle's way of seeing it is different in an important way. Instead of asking whether the premises of a given demonstration are justified, we can ask: *are there premises from which these premises could be demonstrated?*. Now, in Aristotle's logical system this is a far more interesting question than it would be in any modern system, since Aristotle's system allows for the possibility of true propositions which are not logically derivable from any other true propositions, Thus, the answer to this question may in some cases turn out to be 'no' because there are no true premises from which the premises can even be deduced. Should this occur, then the regress 'comes to a stop' on grounds quite independent of anyone's epistemic state. Now, the advocates of the regress argument hold that there is no scientific knowledge except by demonstration, and thus they hold that if a regress comes to a stop in this way, then its premises (and consequently everything deduced from them) will not be scientifically known. Aristotle responds by in effect embracing the second horn of the dilemma but deny the opponents' second premise: he argues that *all* regresses ultimately must come to a stop in just this way. If this is the case, then every true proposition is either itself unmiddled (and thus indemonstrable) or deducible from unmiddled propositions (since reversing a regress gives us a deduction). Since unmiddled propositions are indemonstrable, scientific knowledge of them, if possible at all, must come through some means other than demonstration. Thus, a necessary condition for the possibility of science is the possibility of such a form of knowledge for these propositions. However, if every non-unmiddled proposition can be deduced from unmiddled propositions, then scientific knowledge of the unmiddled propositions would also be *sufficient* for the possibility of science overall. We thus have a precise condition for the possibility of scientific knowledge: it is possible *if and only if* (scientific) knowledge of the indemonstrable premises is possible.

Nothing in this argument appeals to any epistemological notion such as self-evidence or intuitive evidence: the unmiddled propositions are defined solely on the basis of their logical relationships to other truths. In fact, Aristotle thinks that when we begin to acquire scientific knowledge, we will not in general find the principles particularly obvious and may find them less evident than their consequences, or even less evident than falsehoods. Our task in acquiring scientific wisdom is to change our epistemic sensibilities to bring them into line with the way things are by making ourselves see the principles as more evident than anything else. As in the case of moral education, this takes time and is accomplished by a kind of habituation (this parallel is developed in *Metaphysics* Z.3, 1029b3–12).

Since Aristotle does not identify the starting points of demonstrations on the basis of epistemology, he can separate two questions: (1) how can we find the principles? (2) how can we come to know the principles?

4.2 The Road to Wisdom

The first question is answered by Aristotle's one true method. In brief, that method is a procedure for finding middle terms[9]. Aristotle spells it out in detail in *An. Pr.* I.27–29. Let us say that we want to prove some proposition. Since this is *Aristotle's* system, using Aristotle's logic, our proposition must have a predicate term A and a subject E. The method begins with the collection of three lists of terms: those which follow A (call this list B), those which it follows (list Γ), and those inconsistent with it (list Δ). For instance, if A is 'animal' and E is 'human' then B will include 'man', 'woman', 'Greek', 'American senator'; Γ will include 'mammal', 'chordate', 'primate', 'organism'; and Δ will include 'petunia', 'stone', 'integer'. Repeat the process for term E, collecting terms that follow it (list Z), terms it follows (H), and terms it excludes (Θ). When we have compiled these six lists, we can look for a middle term for our original proposition simply by looking for points of intersection between the three A-term lists and the three E-term lists. What intersections we look for, and what we do with a middle term we find, depend on the kind of proposition we started with. The details are summarized in the following figure:[10]

---

[9] Hence its usual medieval name of *inventio medii*.

[10] A figure similar to this first appears in Philoponus (*In An. Pr. Comm.*, 274). In the Middle Ages, the diagram acquired the name *pons asinorum* ('bridge of asses'). See Bochenski 1961,

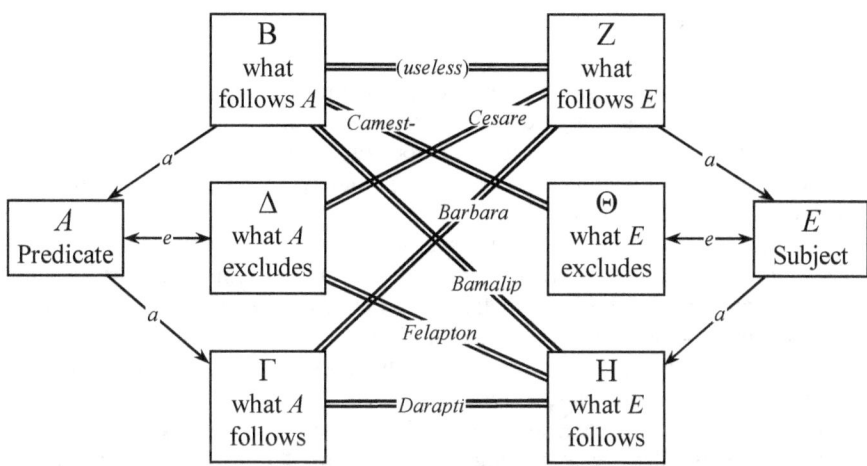

For example, if we started with *AeE*, the method tells us to look for a common term in the lists Γ and Z. If they have some term *X* in common, then *AaX* (by the definition of Γ) and *XaE* (by the definition of Z); from these, *AeE* follows (*Barbara*). On the other hand, it may be that there is *no* term common to Γ and Z. Since the method assumes that we have collected *all possible terms* for each of the six classes, this would mean that then there is no middle term to be found and that, consequently, *AeE* is unmiddled. Aristotle's one true method, then, allows us not only to find middle terms for propositions that can be demonstrated but also to find that *there are no middle terms* for other propositions, which will consequently be indemonstrable. This depends of course, on the assumption that our six term lists are truly exhaustive. Aristotle recognizes precisely this in summarizing his results:

if nothing that truly belongs to the things, according to the collected facts (*historia*), then for anything of which there is a demonstration, we will be able to find this and demonstrate it; and if there is none, then we will be able *to make that evident*[11]. (46a24–27, emphasis added)

This collection of facts is, for Aristotle, only possible through experience, as Aristotle says explicitly:

The principles concerning anything are to be provided by experience. I mean, for instance, that the principles of astronomical science are to be provided by astronomical experience (for when enough phenomena had been obtained, astronomical demonstrations were found in this way), and so it is similarly for any other art or science whatsoever. So: if the facts about anything (τὰ ὑπάρχοντα

---

pp. 219–221 and plate facing. Though no figure is found in manuscripts of Aristotle, it is quite possible that he had one in mind.

[11] οὗ δὲ μὴ πέφυκεν ἀπόδειξις, τοῦτο ποιεῖν φανερόν. I take the last phrase to mean 'to make it evident that there is no demonstration'. Other translators generally take it to mean something like 'to make that proposition evident': presumably, to make evident in some other way a proposition that cannot be demonstrated. However, Aristotle has said nothing at all about making indemonstrable propositions themselves evident.

περὶ ἕκαστον) have been obtained, then we are already prepared to reveal the demonstrations. (46a17–24)

Once the facts are collected, repeated application of it will organize the truths about any subject matter into demonstrations, since this will eventually discover not only the unmiddled (and hence indemonstrable) propositions about it but also the deductions of all other propositions, ultimately filling these in to produce deductions from indemonstrables.

Aristotle's stress on the indispensability of experience here reflects a criticism he expresses elsewhere of those who try to do philosophy without the needed experience of the facts: that: as he says in *De Gen. et Corr.* II,

Lack of experience is the cause of a diminished ability to survey the agreed facts. This is why those who have made themselves more at home in natural science are more able to suppose principles of the kind that extend to many cases, while those who are, as a result of many arguments, inexperienced with the facts, readily declare something after glimpsing at a few. cases. (*De Gen. et Corr.* II, 316a5–10)

This harsh judgment on armchair theorizing is directed at Plato. It is tempting to see here an allusion to Plato's picture in *Phaedo* 99e4–6 of "seeking the truth about things in arguments". For Aristotle, nothing can come of that but empty words. This sets the stage for the second question: by what means do we acquire an appropriate form of knowledge of exactly these indemonstrables?

5. *POSTERIOR ANALYTICS* II.19: UNIVERSALS THROUGH PERCEPTION

Aristotle claims to give us that answer in *Posterior Analytics* II.19, which he says will explain "how the principles become familiar (γνώριμοι) to us". Before we try to interpret his answer, let us review the background so that we can be certain we understand the question.

Plato thought that our possession of certain concepts proved that we had knowledge that could not have been acquired through perception. In the *Phaedo*, he argues that our ability to judge perceptible objects to be equal or unequal presupposes our acquaintance with the equal itself, something which we could not possibly have experienced through perception. This recalls Meno's argument about learning: how can we recognize what we don't know if we don't already know it? Plato's answer was that we do already know it. Even perception, for Plato, relies on this innate knowledge of Forms. In order to perceive two sticks as (approximately) equal or an object as (roughly) circular, we must call on our innate knowledge of the equal itself and the circle itself. Aristotle agrees that we already recognize universals in perception. If he is to avoid Plato's conclusions, he must explain how this is possible without an innate knowledge of Forms. In brief, his answer is that we acquire knowledge of Forms through perception because perception is the impressing of the forms of external objects on our sensibility. Forms are real, though not separable, and as such they have real causal powers, including the power to cause themselves, or copies of themselves, in our minds.

In all of this, neither Aristotle nor Plato is trying to answer skeptical arguments that attempt to undermine knowledge by undermining justification. Their concern is not whether we might be mistaken about what we believe that we know. Instead, it is how to account for the fact that we do have the knowledge which (as they take for granted) we do. Aristotle is not looking for a way in which the principles might be justified. Instead, he is trying to explain how it is possible for us to have the cognition that we do.

Near the beginning of the *Posterior Analytics*, Aristotle The problem II.19 needs to solve is the 'puzzle in the *Meno*', as Aristotle calls it near the beginning of the *Posterior Analytics* (): how can we acquire knowledge that we do not already have, if not from previously existing knowledge?

Plato takes it as given that we *do* have knowledge involving universals and argues from this that we must have that knowledge innately. Aristotle's method as presented in the *Prior Analytics* rests on a similar assumption. He takes it for granted that we do acquire knowledge from experience. Even knowledge of particular facts, however, requires that we possess knowledge of universals, since all facts for Aristotle have the structure of predications and only universals can be predicated of anything. How can we acquire these universals, which it appears that we must have even to learn individual facts from experience? We are back with the *Phaedo*'s argument that we must innately know the Forms.

Aristotle's response to this question is breathtakingly simple: we know the Forms through perception because in reality perception is of universals existing in particulars. There are Forms; there just are no *separated* Forms. The Forms in things have real causal powers, and those powers include the power to affect our sense organs and the power to cause, in us, themselves. Perception, for Aristotle, is the *acquisition* of the form of what is perceived, without its matter. Our intellect is of such a nature that it can acquire the forms of things[12], and thus we are able to acquire knowledge of forms through perception.

Let me try to show that the argument of *An. Post.* II.19 conforms to the picture I have just sketched. Aristotle begins by listing the questions that remain to be answered:

1. Is the knowledge of the 'unmiddled' principles the same as, or different from, the knowledge of other truths? [His answer: different.]
2. Is this knowledge scientific knowledge (ἐπιστήμη) or something else? [His answer: something else, namely νοῦς.]

---

[12] In the more elaborate theory of *De Anima* III, the 'passive intellect', νοῦς παθητικός, is said to have precisely the capacity to take on all forms because it has no form of its own and is a kind of pure potentiality (429b21–430a2).

3. Does the cognition of the principles "arise in us without already being present" or is it "present unnoticed"? [His answer: it arises without already being present.]

The third question is the crucial one. Its second alternative is just exactly Platonic innatism, which Aristotle dismisses quickly: how could it be that we have such knowledge and fail to notice it, he asks? However, the remaining alternative presents him with a problem. He asks, "How can we recognize them that is, learn them if not from previously existing knowledge?" The last phrase clearly recalls the assertion at the beginning of the *Posterior Analytics* that "all teaching and all rational learning arises from pre-existing knowledge". If he still accepts that claim, then Aristotle's only choice is to argue that we can *acquire* some kinds of knowledge without *learning* it, that is, without acquiring it as the result of a rational process.

That is just what he does. Knowledge of forms is caused in us by perception, and perception is not a rational process but rather one in which the mind is a passive recipient. Perception, he says, is "an inborn capacity of judging" (δύναμις συμφυτὸς κριτική) which brings the universals into us from the very beginning. "Though what we perceive is indeed particulars, perception is of the universal, e.g. of man, not of the man Kallias" (100a16–18). Repeated perception then leads to the recognition of higher and higher universals through the following process:

1. When we perceive, the forms (more precisely the *infimae species*) of external objects impress themselves on our minds.
2. Repeated perception stabilizes this recognition (the universal 'comes to rest' in the soul)
3. This process is repeated at the level of higher universals (genera)

It is intrinsic to this process that we acquire cognition of universals organized as a hierarchy. This process would lead to the recognition, not simply of universals, but also of the relationships among them: what follows what, what is followed by what, what excludes what. Thus, the materials for the classification required by Aristotle's One True Method are already available in the deliverances of perception. Since that method is capable not only of finding the premises from which to prove anything that can be proved but also of discovering which truths are not susceptible of proof and thus are principles, Aristotle can explain how all of science arises from perception.

With this interpretation in mind, we can make better sense of some otherwise baffling parts of II.19. To begin with, we can get a much more straightforward account of the three progressive stages of cognition in 100a3–9 (memory arises from perception, experience from repeated memories of the same thing, and finally principles from experience). Here is his account of the critical third stage:

From perception, then, arises memory, as we say; and from memory of the same thing occurring many times arises experience: memories many in number are a single experience. And from experience or from every universal that has come to rest in the soul (from the one besides the many that is same one thing present in all of them) comes the starting point of art and science: of art if it concerns coming to be, of science if it concerns being[13]. (100a3–9)

Repeated perception gives rise to experience, then. Is it *repeated* experience that gives rise to universals? Aristotle does not say that, and when he repeats his view a few lines later he says that we get universals from perception or repeated perception: experience is not a stage on the way to perception of the universal. Thus, what gives rise to experience *also* gives rise to universals. Aristotle does not limit this to repeated perception of sensory universals. Instead, repeated recognition of universals leads to recognition of the next higher universals—that, at any rate, seems to be the plain meaning of 100a15–b3: first man, then some species of animal, then animal, and so on.

What is this 'coming to a stop'? Here, Aristotle offers us a simile that has generally perplexed rather than helped interpreters:

As in a battle when a rout has occurred, if one man stops, another stops, then another, until it comes to the beginning. The soul is from the beginning of such a nature as to be able to undergo this. (100a12–14)

Philoponus rather liberally fleshes out Aristotle's image as follows:

Suppose, as an example in words, a hundred men engaged in war with enemies; turning, they disperse, and then the army breaks up. Next, one of those fleeing, getting up his courage, turns back from flight and stands to face the enemy. Then another of those fleeing, seeing him standing, comes to him to help him. And when each of those fleeing has done this, then the hundred too stand again in the battle that had just recently perished (John Philoponus, *In An. Post.* 436.23–31)

Though this is, to say the least, a florid elaboration, the commentary tradition follows it in spirit. But what point could Aristotle possibly be making with it? Philoponus thinks that it concerns a sort of valiant effort by the rational part of the soul to make a stand against the corrupting influence of the emotions:

For when the irrational parts of the soul – I mean spirit and appetite – have dominated the rational soul, the result is that the knowledge of the universal that is in it is corrupted. Then, when from perceiving one perception is inscribed in the imagination, and next another such, and thus when many perceptions are brought in together, many memories arise ...

But absolutely nothing in Aristotle's text concerns the emotions, and in any event Philoponus seems to be presupposing that knowledge of the universal is *already* present in the soul, which is exactly what Aristotle denies. Apart from that, the image of one brave soldier turning the tide in battle has no evident relevance to the point under discussion: are we to suppose that it is the bravery of

---

[13] ἐκ δ'ἐμπειρίας ἢ ἐκ παντὸς ἠρεμήσαντος τοῦ καθόλου ἐν τῇ ψυχῇ, τοῦ ἑνὸς παρὰ τὰ πολλά, ὃ ἂν ἐν ἅπασιν ἓν ἐνῇ ἐκείνοις τὸ αὐτό, τέχνης ἀρχὴ καὶ ἐπιστήμης, ἐὰν μὲν περὶ γένεσιν, τέχνης, ἐὰν δὲ περὶ τὸ ὄν, ἐπιστήμης. Translators usually take παντὸς ἐρεμήσαντος τοῦ καθόλου to mean something like 'from the whole universal having come to rest in the soul'. But we get a much better sense if we read it as 'from *every* universal that has come to rest in the soul'

individual perceptions, or individual experiences, that somehow turns the tide against a rout of – what?

Most recent commentators have despaired of finding an answer. McKirahan, for instance, says, 'this [simile] does nothing to make the ideas clearer' (Mckirahan 1992, p. 244). Barnes, finding no reasonable sense in talk of a 'beginning', emends the text, reading ἀλκήν rather than the ἀρχήν found in all the sources: "until a position of strength is reached" (Barnes 1994, p. 265).[14]

But there is no need to go to such lengths. Aristotle does not say that, as a result of the soldiers coming to a stop, the rout is turned and the battle saved. He does not even say that one soldier stops and turns to face the enemy. All he says is that one stops, then another, then another. There is a familiar phenomenon that fits this description. Suppose that people are running in a line and that the first person stops: in that case, the next in line will stop, and the next, and so on 'until it comes to the beginning', i.e. the other end of the line. The lead runner's stopping is sufficient to bring the whole line to a stop because each person's halting causes the halting of the next in line[15]. Especially when perceived from a distance, this can produce a striking visual effect.

---

[14] Interestingly, the phrase ἀλκὴν δυσάμενος occurs in Philoponus' explication of the image.

[15] Barnes notes that a similar figure of speech occurs twice in the pseudo-Aristotelian *Problems*. As it happens, the point it is used to illustrate there fits B19 rather well. Here are the texts:

τῶν δὲ κατὰ φύσιν ἐχόντων ὅταν στῇ πρὸς ἓν ἡ διάνοια καὶ μὴ μεταβάλλῃ πολλαχῇ, ἵσταται καὶ τὰ ἄλλα ὅσα περὶ τὸν τόπον, ὧν ἠρέμησις ὁ ὕπνος ἐστίν. ἑνὸς γὰρ κυρίου στάντος, ὥσπερ ἐν τροπῇ, καὶ τὰ ἄλλα μόρια ἵστασθαι πέφυκεν. 917a28–32

... when the thought stops at one thing and is not changed in all ways, whatever others are about the place also stop, and the calming of them is sleep. For when one governing part stops, as in a rout, then the other parts are also naturally disposed to stop.

ἐνταῦθα δὲ μένει διὰ τὸ παχύτατον εἶναι τὸν περὶ τὴν γῆν ἀέρα τοῦ χειμῶνος. ταχὺ δὲ συνίσταται καὶ ὁ ἄλλος διὰ τὸ ἔχειν ἀρχὴν καὶ ἔρεισμα, ὃ δέξεται καὶ ἀθροίσει τὸ προσιὸν καθάπερ ὄρθρος· ὥσπερ γὰρ ἐν τροπῇ ἑνὸς ἀντιστάντος καὶ οἱ ἄλλοι μένουσιν, οὕτω καὶ ἐπὶ τοῦ ἀέρος. διὸ ταχὺ καὶ ἐξαίφνης ἐνίοτε γίνεται καὶ ἐπινέφελα. *Prob.* 941a8–14

But there, it remains because the air nearer the earth is the thickest of the storm. And the other also contracts quickly because it has a starting point or fixed point, which receives and collects what comes to it, as the dawn: for just as, in a rout, when one has taken a stand, the others also stand fast, so is it with the air.

The point in the first passage occurs in an explanation why some people are made sleepy by reading: the proposed answer is that reading makes thought come to a stop, and as a result the associated parts also come to a stop because thought is the governing part (τὸ κύριον): the image is thus that of a military unit halting when its commander halts. In the second passage, what is being explained is a phenomenon of condensation of air, which the writer thinks happens more quickly once a 'starting point or fixed point' has been established. Here we do find a reference to a first soldier 'taking a stand' (ἑνὸς ἀντιστάντος: the verb literally means 'stand against' or 'stand up to'), following which the others do so as well. But if we consider the point being explained, it is the simple fact of having come to a stop that seems to be important. Evidently, air moving towards (προσιόν) some already established collecting point is supposed to be more quickly collected by it. This would be illustrated by a group of soldiers coming quickly to a stop because the one in front stopped. Neither of these passages is by Aristotle, of course. They do, however, give us some idea how Aristotle's figure of speech might be understood. What they have in common is the picture of a group of moving

Aristotle describes just such a sequence of events a few lines later:

> For when some undifferentiated universal[16] has first come to a stop in the soul (it is indeed the particular that is perceived, but perception is of the universal, e.g. of man, not of the man Kallias), it comes to a stop again in these, so long as[17] the things without parts – the universals – come to a stop (e.g. such-and-such animal so long as[18] animal), and likewise in this[19]. 100a15-3

'Undifferentiated' universals are universals without differentiae, that is, *infimae species*[20]. It would make sense to say these are 'without parts' because they are not genera with further species. As the soldiers come to a stop one by one, so do the universals, proceeding in order from least to most universal. What comes to be in the soul, then is not simply a collection of universals but universals ordered in a chain.

If I can recognize the universals A and B and also recognize that A is immediately above B, then I have all that is needed for knowing that AaB is true and that it is unmiddled. If I can recognize that C and D are immediately below B as species below a genus, then I have all that is needed for knowing that CeD is true and unmiddled. Thus, the ability to recognize universals and their positions in a chain structure of terms is all that is required for knowledge of the unmiddled premises in which all regresses terminate.

I believe this reading has several advantages. First, Aristotle is then addressing the right problem: the 'puzzle in the *Meno*'. Plato used this puzzle as an argument for our possession of innate knowledge of Forms, and Aristotle provides us here with an alternative account that avoids precisely what he wants to avoid: he explains how we can acquire knowledge of universals without being born with it and without the existence of separable Forms. Second, and following close upon this, we see that once again, Aristotle's principal target is Plato's conception of philosophy and philosophical method. Third, the solution fits closely with Aristotle's own account of the 'one road' for all forms of inquiry.

---

individuals coming to a stop because one of them has come to a stop. If we turn now to II.19, we see that that is almost all there is to what Aristotle says there.

[16] Translators generally suppose that the genitive absolute stops at ἑνὸς and that πρῶτον ... καθόλου is a verbless clause; I take the whole phrase as the genitive absolute.

[17] ἕως ἂν with subjunctive can mean either 'so long as' or 'until'; other translators generally opt for the latter.

[18] The sense of ἕως here must be the same as before if this is to be an example.

[19] στάντος γὰρ τῶν ἀδιοφόρων ἑνὸς πρῶτον ἐν μὲν τῇ ψυχῇ καθόλου (καὶ γὰρ αἰσθάνεται μὲν τὸ καθ' ἕκαστον, ἡ δ'αἴσθησις τοῦ καθόλου ἐστίν, οἷον ἀνθρώπου ἀλλ' οὐ Καλλίου ἀνθρώπου)· πάλιν ἐν τούτοις ἵσταται, ἕως ἂν τὰ ἀμερῆ στῇ καὶ τὰ καθόλου, οἷον τοιονδὶ ζῷον ἕως ζῷον, καὶ ἐν τούτοις ὡσαύτως.

[20] I am unpersuaded by Bolton's attempt to give this another, and to my mind a somewhat mysterious, sense.

6. CONCLUSIONS

What has now become of questioning, for Aristotle? It has been displaced, along with dialectic, from the central position it held in Plato's method and relegated to a purely ancillary status, useful perhaps in the preparatory stages of assembling the data for Aristotle's theory-generating method. "No science that gives proofs about any subject matter asks questions," says Aristotle in *On Sophistical Refutations* 11,

... but dialectic *is* interrogative; and if it did give proofs, then at any rate it would not make questions out of the first premises, those proper [to the sciences]: for if someone were not to concede these, it would have nothing else from which to argue any more against objections.[21] (172a15–21)

These are the words of someone who has seen too many dialectical arguments leading nowhere and who has, in consequence, become disenchanted with the notion that argument alone can establish anything significant. Reversing Plato's choice in the *Phaedo* (99d–e), Aristotle turned away from lo'goi – towards looking directly at the things themselves, taking experience as the ultimate source of knowledge.

Department of Philosophy, Texas A&M University

REFERENCES

Barnes, Jonathan, 1969, "Aristotle's Theory of Demonstration", *Phronesis* 14, 123–152.
Barnes, Jonathan, 1981, "Proof and the Syllogism", in Berti 1981, pp. 17–59.
Barnes, Jonathan, trans. & comm. 1994, *Aristotle, Posterior Analytics* (Clarendon Aristotle Series), 2 ed., Oxford University Press (first edition 1975).
Berti, Enrico, ed. 1981, *Aristotle on Science: The Posterior Analytics*, Padua, Antenore.
Bocheski, I. 1961, *A History of Formal Logic*, tr. Ivo Thomas, University of Notre Dame Press.
Ferejohn, Michael, 1991, "The Origins of Aristotelian Science", Yale University Press.
Irwin, Terence. 1988. *Aristotle's First Principles*, Oxford University Press.
Hamlyn, D. W. 1990, "Aristotle on Dialectic", *Philosophy* 65, 465–476.
Kahn, Charles, 1981, "The Role of *nous* in the Cognition of First Principles in *Posterior Analytics* II 19", in Berti 1981, pp. 385–414.
Lennox, James, 1987, "Divide and Explain: The *Posterior Analytics* in Practice", in A. Gotthelf and J. Lennox, eds., *Philosophical Issues in Aristotle's Biology*, pp. 90–119.
Lukasiewicz, J., 1957, *Aristotle's Syllogistic from the Standpoint of Modern Formal Logic*, Second edition, Oxford, Clarendon Press.
McKirahan, Richard, 1992, *Principles and Proofs*, Princeton University Press.
Owen, G. E. L., 1960, "Logic and Metaphysics in Some Earlier Works of Aristotle", in I. Düring and G. E. L. Owen, eds., *Aristotle and Plato in the Mid-Fourth Century* (Göteborg), pp. 163–190.
Owen, G. E. L., 1961, "*Tithenai ta phainomena*", in S. Mansion, ed., *Aristote et les problèmes de méthode* (Louvain), pp. 81–103.
Patzig, Günther, 1968, *Aristotle's Theory of the Syllogism*, tr. Jonathan Barnes, Dordrecht, D. Reidel.

---

[21] ὥστ' οὐδεμία τέχνη τῶν δεικνυουσῶν τινὰ φύσιν ἐρωτητική ἐστιν· οὐ γὰρ ἔξεστιν ὁποτερονοῦν τῶν μορίων δοῦναι· συλλογισμὸς γὰρ οὐ γίνεται ἐξ ἀμφοῖν. ἡ δὲ διαλεκτικὴ ἐρωτητική ἐστιν, εἰ δ' ἐδείκνυεν, εἰ καὶ μὴ πάντα, ἀλλὰ τά γε πρῶτα καὶ τὰς οἰκείας οὐκ ἂν ἠρώτα· μὴ διδόντος γὰρ οὐκ ἂν ἔτι εἶχεν ἐξ ὧν ἔτι διαλέξεται πρὸς τὴν ἔνστασιν

Smith, Robin 1989. *Aristotle's Prior Analytics* (translation with Introduction, notes, and commentary), Hackett Publishing Company.

Smith, Robin, 1993a, "Aristotle on the Uses of Dialectic", *Synthèse* 96, 335–358.

Smith, Robin, 1994, "Dialectic and the Syllogism", *Ancient Philosophy* 14 (1994: special issue), 133–151.

Smith, Robin, 1997, *Aristotle, Topics I, VIII, and Selections*, (*Clarendon Aristotle Series*), Oxford University Press.

Smith, Robin, 1999, "Dialectic and Method in Aristotle", in May Sim, ed., *From Puzzles to Principles? Essays on Aristotle's Dialectic*, pp. 39–56 (Lexington Books).

Marja-Liisa Kakkuri-Knuuttila

The Relevance of Dialectical Skills to Philosophical Inquiry in Aristotle

1. Introduction

Seeing Aristotelian dialectic as situated between casual encounters and philosophy offers an insightful perspective for investigating the extent to which the aims and the logical and epistemic tools of dialectic are shared by its two opposites.[1] As compared with everyday encounters, dialectic is obviously more formal and more sophisticated but not quite sufficient for philosophy. The usefulness of dialectical tools in daily conversations derives from the fact that, as Aristotle remarks, a dialectician does with skill what others do at random, namely, attempts to defend his own opinions, change those of others, or reveal the interlocutor's ignorance.[2] This presupposes that dialectic involves a kind of general capacity for argument,[3] but to what extent it is relevant to, or perhaps even sufficient for the cognitive goals of philosophy is the more tricky issue.

One hardly need point out that the question of the usefulness of dialectical skills for philosophy concerns inquiry rather than explanation (*apodeixis*), *i.e.*, in terms Aristotle adopts from Plato, the 'way towards the first principles' rather than the 'way from the first principles'.[4] The famous passage in the *Topics* I 2 mentions two uses of the treatise for philosophical inquiry: argument both *pro* and *con* helps to distinguish the true from the false, though the more interesting aspect concerns its use with respect to the first principles of science. Obviously, the first principles cannot be examined in their own terms, which leaves the possibility of scrutinizing them with the help of acceptable opinions (*endoxa*), a task peculiar to dialectic for Aristotle.[5] Hence the question remains of how far towards the first principles dialectical skills may bring us. While Aristotle himself offers no clear answer to this question in the *Topics* or in his other treatises, a number of suggestions have been provided by interpreters.

According to some, dialectical tools only have a negative role in criticizing prevailing views, a conception seemingly in harmony with the refutation form

---

[1] This alludes to the title "Ein Problem: die Aristotelische Dialektik zwischen Gespräch und Philosophie" in Primavesi 1996, 17.
[2] *Topics* I 2 101a27, 30–34, VIII 14 164a16–b4, *Sophistical Refutations* 11 172a34–36, *Rhetoric* I 1 1354a1–6.
[3] *Sophistical Refutations* 9 170a31–b11, Smith 1993, 339 and 1994, 145–148; for its limitations, see Brunschwig 1986, 32–34.
[4] *Analytica Posteriora* I 2 71b33–72a5, *Nicomachean Ethics* I 4 1095a28–b13, *Metaphysics* VII 3 1029a33–b12, *Physics* I 1 184a16–23.
[5] *Topics* I 2 101a34–b4, see also VIII 14 163b9–16 and *Rhetoric* I 2 1355a35. Cf. *Metaphysics* II 1 993b20–30, IV 2 1004b22–26.

(*elenchus*) of dialectical argument.⁶ The critical role of dialectic may be seen in a positive light, however, by a shift of perspective to beliefs which remain intact in the face of criticism.⁷ Others argue that, in addition to the critical task, certain forms of dialectical disputation are strong enough to justify positive knowledge claims.⁸ But there are also those who claim that dialectic itself involves methods adequate to guarantee the first principles of science.⁹

In spite of numerous outstanding recent contributions on Aristotle's dialectic, it seems that our picture of dialectic in the *Topics* is not yet clear enough to settle these issues in any conclusive manner. Therefore the goal of this paper is a more modest one, simply to clarify our notion of dialectic and the skills involved. The investigation allows, finally, to draw some conclusions concerning their relevance to Aristotle's philosophical inquiry. In the following, I shall delineate the main starting-points of this study.

While the traditional understanding of dialectic has emphasized some particular feature, such as argument relying on *endoxic* premises, recent scholarship tends to take dialectic seriously as a particular social discoursive practice in question-answer form with its own characteristic rules or, rather, a set of such practices.¹⁰ Following this line of interpretation poses special challenges for a philosopher, since the logical and epistemic moves need to be understood as embedded in a social and psychological setting. The challenges are the more demanding since dialectic, unlike rhetoric, is not a lively part of the present communication culture.

The element of competition, for instance, incorporated already in the refutation form of dialectical disputations, requiring the answerer to defend a thesis and the questioner to attack it, has generated some worry about the relevance of dialectic to serious philosophical inquiry. Another source of competition, located in the rules for the questioner in Book VIII Ch. 1 of the *Topics* for the purpose of concealing his line of argument, have led some interpreters to view dialectic as reducing to eristic, hence failing to be of use for a philosophical search for truth.¹¹ The agonistic spirit of the participants is no less reduced by the presence of an audience following the discussion.

---

⁶ Le Blond 1970, 41, and Beriger 1987, 57–62.

⁷ Evans 1978, 52, Galston 1982, Smith 1993, 354, and Witt 1992, 170.

⁸ According to Ross 1971 (1923), Bolton 1993 and 1994, dialectic yields a sufficient method for practical sciences, such as ethics. Galston 1982, 90–93 and Bolton 1990, 192–196, argue that in theoretical sciences the candidates for first principles have to be shown to have explanatory power.

⁹ Owen 1986a (1961), 244, Irwin 1978, 1981, 1987 and 1988. Cf. Bolton 1990, 186 n. 2. I shall not include here studies such as Barnes 1980 or Nussbaum 1986 Ch. 8, since they make no claim that the method of inquiry they describe has further relevance to dialectic than through the explication of the notion of *endoxa* in the *Topics*.

¹⁰ Bolton 1990, 188 and 1994, 110, Smith 1993, 337, and 1997. The rules of question-answer disputation are dealt with by Moraux 1968, 280–290, Stump 1978, 160–165, Schickert 1974, 4–14, Brunschwig 1986, Bolton 1990, 1991, 1993, 1994, and Smith 1997.

¹¹ Grote 1872, 93–106 and Cherniss 1944, 18, see Owen 1986, 221–225 and Bolton 1994, 102–103.

I shall argue that the puzzles about how to reconcile these competitive elements and inquiry after truth arise because of misconceptions concerning dialectical practice, and in particular the role of competition and the rules of concealment in it. As for the concealment rules, their proper understanding reveals most clearly a misconstrual in the traditional way of formulating the question of the relation between dialectic and philosophy. It seems to have gone unnoticed that the concealment rules are meant to apply both to fair and eristic argument[12] and that, furthermore, the answerer is provided with his own means of undermining their effect. Finally, as Aristotle himself points out when introducing the rules of concealment, they merely concern a questioner in a dialectical disputation, not a philosopher or one searching by himself, thus indicating that dialectic and philosophical inquiry are two socially and psychologically distinct fields of argument.[13] A philosopher is consequently free to adopt whatever suits his specific purposes from his dialectical skills. Therefore I fully agree with Robin Smith's insight that, instead of speaking about the relevance or use of *dialectic* in philosophical inquiry in the traditional manner, it is better to speak about the relevance or use of *dialectical skills* or *methods*, *dialectic* being reserved to the disputational practice in question-answer form while *dialectical skills/methods* refer to the logical and epistemic skills/methods involved.[14]

But how should the puzzle that a fair dialectical refutation is simultaneously competitive and cooperative be solved?[15] The answer lies in recognizing that competition and cooperation need not always exclude each other. To see this, we need to distinguish two possible kinds of competition in dialectical disputation. The first is referred to in Aristotle's criticism of quarrelsome answerers who, by not granting what they should, turn the disputation into an antagonistic and eristic one, and thus into merely apparent dialectic.[16] Another sense of competition is indicated in a passage in *Sophistical Refutations* 16 175a13–14, which points out that one of the goals of the participants is to show their disputational skills.

In seeking to clarify what the dialectical skills consist of, it will turn out that a good dialectician can take the role of both questioner and answerer, is capable of dealing with problems of any kind and partners with varying skills and character. I shall argue that, for Aristotle, the common goal of participants in a proper dialectical disputation is good argument,[17] as good as possible considering the

---

[12] *Sophistical Refutations* 15 174a26–29.
[13] *Topics* VIII 1 155b9–16.
[14] Smith 1993, 350–351, also Devereux 1990, 283–284.
[15] The opposition between the questioner and the answerer is expressed in *Topics* VIII 1 155b10, 26–28, 14 164b13–15, *Sophistical Refutations* 11 171b22–26, while the cooperative aspect is referred to in *Topics* 11 161a19–21, 37–b1.
[16] *Topics* I 1 100b23–101a4,18 108a33–37, VIII 5 159a30–37, 11 161a23–24, 37–b10, *Sophistical Refutations* 11 171b16–34, see Owen 1986, 224.
[17] See, for instance, *Topics* VIII 5 159a35, b3, 11 161a17–19, 33, b38.

problem at hand.[18] This is, obviously, carried out best by skilful dialecticians in a social context rewarding good argument.

In realizing their common goal, the participants have different tasks because of their complementary positions. While the questioner's role is to produce arguments, as good as the particular situation allows, the answerer's primary duty is to check that the arguments are good ones. This allows scope for a non-zero-sum type of game in which one's gain is not another's loss, both partners can simultaneously perform well or poorly, and the quality of argument is up to both.[19] Hence competition about dialectical skills supports good argument, instead of being a hindrance to it.

Furthermore, I shall emphasize that the few references to the truth of propositions in the *Topics* should be taken at their face value. This involves a further modification to the traditional conception of dialectic while undermining the core idea of dialectical argument as one with acceptable premises (*endoxa*).[20] However, Aristotle's remark on truth via *pro* and *con* argument in *Topics* I 2, indicates that he does not consider a singular line of argument to be a strong means of distinguishing the true from the false, but prefers a complex of arguments with the logical structure of debate.[21] Moreover, the dialectical means for conceptual clarification and qualification of excessive generalizations form an important vehicle for qualifying the merely partial truths included in the knowledge basis for dialectical arguments.

The main purpose of the following examination of the rules for dialectical disputations in *Topics* Book I and VIII is to offer a systematization which best reveals their epistemic, logical, and psychological peculiarities.[22] I shall argue, firstly, that those I shall call *constitutive rules* offer a framework for both good and bad, fair and unfair argumentative discourse in question-answer form. The second aim is to demonstrate that those to be called *strategic rules* yield logical and epistemic moves to enhance good argument and the search for justified truth claims through debate. While the main responsibility in constructing arguments lies with the questioner, the main responsibility in guaranteeing good argument is imposed on the answerer. It will be shown, among other things, that the rules for the questioner to conceal his argument strategy form no hindrance to this goal, but merely a source of psychological complications to be counterbalanced by a set of rules for the answerer.

---

[18] *Topics* VIII 11 161b34–162a11.

[19] Brunschwig explicitly denies the possibility of combining competition with a common objective in spite of his emphasis on a good gymnastic discussion according to its rules (1986, 37, 39). Bolton sees gymnastic discussions as competitive in contrast to those for the sake of examination and inquiry (1994, 104).

[20] Cf. Reeve 2001, 243.

[21] By the logical structure of debate I mean a complex including arguments *pro* and *con* the premisses and inference relations of given arguments.

[22] I will sometimes refer to the *Sophistical Refutations* as well.

In explicating the disputation rules, I shall thus deviate from their order of presentation in the *Topics* by elaborating them in pairs to get an insight into how the complementary tasks of the questioner and answerer tend to enhance good argument and truth. I shall first lay out the constitutive rules, then the strategic rules, beginning with the notion of *topos* and certain logical requirements derived from the notion of syllogism and refutation (*elenchus*), continuing with the epistemic conditions of argument and then turning to the rules serving the goal of truth more directly.

Whether there was a practice of scoring the participants' performance, Aristotle does not inform us and it does not bear on my main aim. At any rate, he makes it apparent that those following exercise and examination disputations did assess the interlocutors' performance by taking into account their skills and competitive spirit as well as the difficulty of the problem. Most important of all, the criteria Aristotle offers for assessing arguments as separated from the disputation context are precisely those for good argument we find underlying the strategic rules for the answerer.

As it thus turns out that the rules for dialectical discussion offer logical and epistemic moves important for any serious pursuit of justified truth claims, participating in such discussions obviously helps to develop skills relevant to Aristotelian philosophical inquiry understood as *saving the appearances*.[23] Whether Aristotle at some point believed that his dialectic offers definite criteria for identifying the truth through debate is a complex issue not to be touched upon here, however.[24] In any case the dialectical methods as formulated in the *Topics* and *Sophistical Refutations* do not yield the highest guarantee of truth, since saving the appearances involves further forms of argument not included in them. One's dialectical skills may, however, be of great help in trying to reveal candidates for first principles as well, but they are not sufficient to distinguish the first principles of a philosophical field from its other truths conclusively. This follows chiefly from the fact that dialectical disputations focus on distinct problems, while philosophical inquiry aims at systematic knowledge, capable of saving and explaining the appearances of a whole field of research.[25]

---

[23] *Nicomachean Ethics* VII 1 1145b2–7, *Eudemian Ethics* VII 2 1235b13–18, *Metaphysics* III 1 995a24–27, see Lloyd 1968, Owen 1986a, Barnes 1980, and Nussbaum 1986 Ch. 8, Witt 1992.

[24] Bolton argues for two different criteria, one on the basis of dialectic as inquiry ('dialectical irrefutability', 1990 and 1991) and another grounded in dialectic as examination (1993 and 1994). Both appear to yield foundationalist epistemology. Irwin (1998) identifies 'pure dialectic' with coherence theory, while his 'strong dialectic' relies on particularly strong premisses.

[25] For the limitations of dialectic for philosophy, see Galston 1982, Irwin 1977, 1987, Bolton 1990, 1991, Freeland 1990, and Kakkuri-Knuuttila 1993.

2. CONSTITUTIVE RULES OF DIALECTICAL DISPUTATIONS

a. Opening moves and goals

To attain a better grasp of the social practices Aristotle counts as belonging to dialectic, we may distinguish *constitutive*, or *definitory*, and *strategic rules* among those presented in the *Topics* and *Sophistical Refutations*. The former *define* the nature of dialectical disputations by describing how *proper* dialectical communication is carried out, while the latter offer an insight into how a dialectical interchange is carried out *well*.[26] The first explications of such a classification can be traced to the *Treatise on Obligations* by the fourteenth century logician Walter Burley, dealing with obligational disputations, closely related to dialectical conversations. The title adopted by Burley for the rules constituting the particular practices of obligational disputations is *essential rules* (*de esse*) and that for those guaranteeing that the art is practised well is *useful rules* (*utiles*).[27] But we may also find hints about such a distinction, for instance, when Aristotle speaks about 'one who syllogizes well (*kalôs*)' as distinct from one simply syllogizing (drawing inferences),[28] thus guaranteeing its application to sharpening questions to be posed on the textbooks of dialectic without fear of anachronism.

While Aristotle codifies the rules of dialectic keeping in mind those already familiar with its varied practices, he naturally presupposes that his readers are acquainted with them, whereas we are not in such a favourable position.[29] Luckily, we may profit from the dialogues of Plato to nourish our imaginative capacities at critical points. To give a relatively trivial example, one of the most essential rules of dialectical disputations, stating that the answerer should accept a proposition implied by propositions previously conceded, is not, somewhat surprisingly, given in its general form.[30]

The task of the constitutive rules is apparently to explicate the opening moves and goals, as well as the essential means of dialectical conversations. The opening words of the *Topics* already reveal that for Aristotle a dialectical interchange

---

[26] Hintikka and Bachman 1991, 32–33. Another distinction, less prominent here, is between *regulative* and *constitutive rules*. The former tell us *that* certain things ought to or may be done, and the latter tell us *how* certain acts are performed (von Wright 1971, 151, Searle 1999, 122–124). An example of a regulative rule, accepted by ancient Athenians, states that one is allowed to participate in dialectical disputations. The constitutive rules then explicate how the dialectical activity is performed.

[27] Burley 1963, see Yrjönsuuri 1994, 44.

[28] See, for instance, *Topics* VIII 4 159a17–18, 5 159a35, b3, b8, 11 161a17–19, 33, b38.

[29] Smith 1997, xii and xxi. Though 'dialectic' and 'Socratic dialogue' are popular titles in contemporary management consultation literature, for instance, the intended forms of communication are not dialectical in the limited sense of Aristotle's *Topics*, Cf. Kessels 2001.

[30] This is, however, discussed in connection with induction in *Topics* VIII 2 157a34–b8.

is to have the refutation form (*elenchus*),[31] much discussed in connection with the Socratic dialogues of Plato.[32]

> The goal of this study is to find a method with which we shall be able to construct syllogisms from acceptable premises concerning any problem that is proposed and – when submitting to argument ourselves – will not say anything inconsistent. (*Topics* I 1 100a18–21)[33]

The passage makes room for two different roles in the interchange, that of the questioner whose task is 'to construct syllogisms from acceptable premises concerning any problem proposed' as the topic of disputation, and another one of the answerer whose task is to avoid saying 'anything inconsistent'.

Hence the first moves will consist of the questioner laying out the initial *problem*[34] as an option for the answerer to choose a proposition or its contradiction, and the latter choosing either one as the *thesis* he is to defend.[35] The selection of the topic for discussion thus belongs to a preparation phase.[36]

Constitutive rules for the opening moves:
The questioner puts forward a *problem* for the answerer, *i.e.* an option to choose between two contradictory *propositions*.
The answerer chooses one of the contradictories as his *thesis*.

---

[31] 'A refutation (*elenchus*) is a syllogism to the contradictory of the given conclusion' (*Sophistical Refutations* 1 165a2–3, also 6 168a34–37, 10 171a2–7). Smith (1997, xiii–xx) distinguishes dialectic in the broad and narrow sense, only the latter having the refutation form. For epistemological reasons the translation 'refutation', typically used for *elenchus*, is somewhat misleading, since no refutation needs to result.

[32] Bolton 1993 is an interesting contribution showing how a particular species of dialectical disputation parallels Socratic *elenchus* in Plato's *Gorgias*, aiming to justify his own belief concerning justice.

[33] In spite of the fact that *sullogismos* here is to be understood in a wider sense than the more familiar three-term two-premiss inference of the *Prior Analytics*, I prefer the translation 'syllogism' to 'deduction', because not each deductive inference counts as a *sullogismos* for Aristotle. Cf. *Topics* I 1 100a25–27, *Prior Analytics* I 1 24b18–20, *Sophistical Refutations* 1 164b27–165a2, and *Rhetoric* I 2 1356b15–18. See Bolton 1994, 108ff. and Section 3b.

[34] A dialectical *problem* differs from a dialectical *protasis* (premiss/question) by its form: 'For stated in this way: "Is it the case that two-footed terrestrial animal is the definition of man?" ... it is a premiss; but stated in this way: "Whether a two-footed terrestrial animal is the definition of man or not", it becomes a problem[.]' (*Topics* I 4 101b28–33). A dialectical problem may concern both purely theoretical and practical matters. A point about which everyone agrees cannot form a problem, but one about which people have no opinion, or there is disagreement between the majority and the wise or within these groups, or one about which there are arguments *pro* and *con* (*Topics* I 11 104b1–17, 10 104a5–7, 14 105b19–29).

[35] A *thesis* in the narrow sense of the term is a belief of a philosopher contrary to majority opinion or one for which it is possible to present an argument, while in the broad sense a thesis is either part of a problem (*Topics* I 11 104b19–105a2). Sometimes Aristotle distinguishes thesis and definition (*Topics* VIII 9 160b14).

[36] *Sophistical Refutations* 12 172b10 ff. deals with how to lead a companion to suitable topics in less formal encounters.

The trouble with the above passage is that it would allow the answerer not to accept a premiss whenever he anticipates a contradiction will follow, which would make eristics a proper form of dialectic, contrary to Aristotle's explicit statements.[37] As indicated in the following passage, the goals associated with the two roles, though contrary to some respect, are not fully incompatible, but are even complementary:[38]

> Now, the job of the questioner is to lead the argument so as to make the answerer state the most unacceptable of the consequences made necessary as a result of the thesis, while the job of the answerer is to make it appear that it is not because of him that anything impossible or contrary to opinion results, but because of the thesis (for conceding at first what one should not is probably a different mistake from failing to defend that concession properly). (*Topics* VIII 4 159a18–24)

It is worth adding that in spite of the wording of this passage not all elenctic arguments are of the *reductio ad absurdum* type. Aristotle himself favours direct argument strategies to inferences through the impossible for the reason that, in the first case, the contradiction of the thesis is more obvious and the answerer cannot so easily escape accepting it.[39]

Even though the stated aim of this passage is to explicate the tasks of the good answerer and the good questioner,[40] the remark about two kinds of mistake the answerer may commit seem to hold for dialectic in general. Failing to defend the chosen thesis properly, as required by the constitutive rules, changes the nature of the discussion into merely apparent dialectic. Such mutual compatibility of the goals of the questioner and answerer is a most relevant issue for our understanding of the role of dialectical skills in philosophical inquiry and in pursuit of truth more generally. For it implies that if there is an element of competition, and Aristotle claims that there typically is,[41] genuine dialectic does not reduce to a zero-sum game about achieving or avoiding an inconsistency. We should not, however, have too narrow a notion of competition. Referring to the *Sophistical Refutations* passage already mentioned (16 175a13–14), I suggest that the proper way of competing in genuine dialectic concerns the *dialectical skills* of the partners. The questioner shows his dialectical skills by trying to secure suitable premisses from the answerer which finally imply the contradiction of the answerer's initial thesis, and the answerer shows his skills by granting such premisses as required by further rules of the disputation. This allows both the questioner and answerer to succeed in a disputation simultaneously, or for instance, the questioner to perform properly even without reaching the contradictory conclusion when the answerer is guilty of not accepting what he should. Understanding the competitive element as concerning the mastery of the art of

---

[37] *Topics* I 1 100b23–101a4, VIII 11 161a17–24, 33–b10, *Sophistical Refutations* 1 165a19–37, 2 165b7–11, 8 169b20–29, 11 171b6–172b8.

[38] Smith 1997, 128.

[39] *Topics* VIII 2 157b34–158a2. The impossibility typically is an obvious falsehood, and not a logical contradiction as in modern logic (Smith 1997, 119–120).

[40] *Topics* VIII 4 159a17–18.

[41] *Topics* VIII 1, 155b26–28.

dialectic also seems to be in harmony with Aristotle's brief remarks on the various species of dialectic including exercise (*gumnastikê*), examination (*peirastikê*), and conversations for the sake of inquiry (*skepsis*), though I shall not go into the details here.[42]

Since the rules concerning the goals characterize a social communication practice rather than a system of logic, they are not to be formulated in terms of objective relations of implication.

Constitutive rules for the goals:
The goal of the questioner is to show his dialectical skills by securing from the answerer premises which would lead the latter to state the contradiction of his thesis, and such as required by the rules of dialectic.
The goal of the answerer is to show his dialectical skills by conceding such premises and conclusions as required by the rules of dialectic.

b. Means

The most important aspects concerning the means of genuine dialectical disputations involve the logical structure of questions available to the questioner and the epistemic nature of propositions the answerer should accept as premises.[43] As for the logical structure, Aristotle points out that questions such as 'What is a human?' or 'In how many ways is "good" said?' are not dialectical premises. This conveys a part of the questioner's responsibility in inventing the premises, since why-questions do not count as dialectical moves, but only questions of yes-or-no form. Consequently, instead of posing questions of this kind, the questioner has to put his own proposal for a definition of 'human', or distinctions of 'good'.[44] As we shall see later, this is not all the questioner is allowed to do, nor does this imply that the answerer is reduced to a 'yes-or-no' man on the whole. The strategic rules allow both a larger set of moves and, simultaneously, more responsibility concerning the nature of reasoning, revealing that the basis for *cooperation* consists of rules advising the questioner to propose as premises propositions with an epistemic nature such that the answerer is bound to accept them. The *competitive* element is saved in that the answerer is not the one re-

---

[42] For characterizations of these species of dialectic see *Topics* VIII 5 159a25ff., 11 161a24–33, 14 163a29ff., *Sophistical Refutations* 2 165a38–b7, 8 169b23–27, 9 170b8–11, 11 171b3–6, 172a21–b1, 34 183a37–b1.

[43] The translation 'premiss' for *protasis* simplifies matters in this context, since in dialectic it is used for the question by which the questioner attempts to secure a premiss for the intended conclusion (*Topics* I 4 101b28–32, *Prior Analytics* I 1 24a24–25). A dialectical *protasis* is also the conclusion of previously conceded premises posed as a question, at least in the case of induction (*Topics* VIII 2 157b31–33).

[44] *Topics* VIII 2 158a14–22, see also *Sophistical Refutations* 10 171a18–20. This rule is qualified in *Topics* VIII 2 158a22–24. By 'how many?' Aristotle means that determinations should also be given (*Topics* I 15 106a1–8).

sponsible for inventing premises against his thesis, this being left to the questioner.

As the opening words of the *Topics* suggest, one chief task of the questioner is to try to secure for his part that the premisses the answerer concedes are *acceptable* opinions, *i.e.*, in Aristotle's technical terminology, that they belong to *endoxa*. That Aristotle intends a dialectical disputation to rely on acceptable premisses, at least in its typical form, is seen both in the notion of dialectical syllogism and dialectical premiss. A dialectical syllogism is one with *endoxic* premisses of a certain kind.[45] Etymologically, *endoxa* consists of the opinions of reputable persons. These include, according to Aristotle, things 'which seem so to everyone, or to most people, or to the wise – to all of them, or to most, or to the most famous and esteemed' (*Topics* I 1 100a29–30).[46] In a later passage, Aristotle includes as dialectical premisses opinions derived from established arts, things similar to what is acceptable, as well as negations and contraries of contraries of acceptable opinions. However, not simply any *endoxon* counts as a dialectical premiss but, only those which are not paradoxical, *i.e.*, not contrary to majority opinion. Clearly, a proposition accepted by no-one cannot function as a dialectical premiss.[47]

Interestingly enough, the condition that the inferences be *arguments* in the sense that the premisses are initially more acceptable than the conclusion is not a constitutive rule of dialectic.[48] Such a requirement characterizes good dialectic, as Aristotle points out himself, and hence forms one of the strategic rules. We may thus formulate the rules for the questioner and answerer concerning the means available to them as follows.

Constitutive rules for posing questions and accepting premisses:
The questioner tries to secure dialectical premisses (propositions which are acceptable, similar to what is acceptable, negations and contraries of contraries of acceptable opinions, which are not contrary to majority opinion and propositions derived from established acts) in the form of yes-or-no questions which have the contradiction of the answerer's thesis as a consequence.

---

[45] For the notion of dialectical syllogism *Topics* I 1 100a25–30, *Sophistical Refutations* 2 165b1–4, *Prior Analytics* I 1 24a22–25, *Posterior Analytics* I 19 81b18–23, see Smith 1993, 335–336.

[46] For the notion of *endoxa* Le Blond 1939, 9–19, Barnes 1981, 498ff., and Smith 1993, 343–347.

[47] *Topics* I 10 104a5–37. See note 35. Cf. Reeve 2001, 238–241.

[48] The term 'argument' is often used in the wider sense of 'inference'. See the translations of *logos*, for instance, in *Topics* I 1 100a25 by Pickard-Cambridge in *The Complete Works of Aristotle: The Revised Oxford Translation* 1984 and Smith 1997. In the narrow sense applied here an argument is an inference with the particular pragmatic aim to raise the degree of acceptability of the conclusion.

The answerer concedes dialectical premises, as well as the consequences of propositions he has already conceded. Not conceding the proposition put by the questioner implies that the negation can be taken as a premiss.[49]

Here we may note a typical Aristotelian move, since these rules may be said to characterize dialectical disputations without qualification (*haplôs*). No less than four ways of qualifying them can be pointed out. For instance, if an unskilled answerer errs as to what counts as an *endoxon* or a proper dialectical premiss, the disputation does not turn into eristic, or what he calls 'apparent dialectic'. It just turns into poor dialectic, and the piece of reasoning is a poor one,[50] since the difference between dialectic and eristic lies in the motivation.[51] Ch. 5 introduces us subspecies of dialectical examinations where the answerer has to represent his own personal opinions, or the views of some philosopher. Strangely enough, the answerer is sometimes bound to grant unacceptable premisses as well.[52] To these issues we shall return in Section 6.

The constitutive rules of dialectical disputations hence involve a general framework for reasoning practice in question-answer form. They do not yet, however, include rules for argumentative discussions, and hence cannot be said to encourage either good or poor argument. In elaborating the strategic rules, our main task is to explore the extent to which they enhance good argument, and truth *via* good argument.

3. STRATEGIC RULES: THE NOTION AND CHOICE OF *TOPOS*

a. The topos

At the beginning of Book VIII Aristotle says he is taking up the matter of how to pose questions. Accordingly, Chs. 1–3 deal with strategic advice mainly for the questioner, Ch. 4 notes the tasks of the good questioner and answerer cited

---

[49] *Topics* VIII 1 156b4–9, *Sophistical Refutations* 15 174a30–32.

[50] *Topics* VIII 12 162b27–30.

[51] 'For just as unfairness in a wrestling match takes a certain form – that is, it is a kind of "dirty fighting" – so the contentious art (*eristikê*) is "dirty fighting" in disputations. For in the former case, those who choose to win at all costs use every kind of hold, and so in the latter case do the contentious. Now, those who behave like this for the sake of winning itself – these seem to be the contentious fellows and the lovers of strife; but those who do it for the sake of a reputation that gets them money are sophistical (for sophistry (*sophistikê*) is, as we said, a way of making money from apparent wisdom). This is why they aim at *apparent* refutation. Lovers of strife and sophists are men of the same arguments, but not for the same purposes, and the same argument will be both sophistical and contentious, but not in the same respect: insofar as it is for the sake of apparent victory it is contentious, but insofar as it is for the sake of apparent wisdom it is sophistical (for sophistry too is a kind of apparent but not real wisdom).' (*Sophistical Refutations* 11 171b22–34) See also *Topics* VIII 11 161a17–24, 33–b10, and *Rhetoric* I 1 1355b15–21.

[52] *Topics* VIII 5 159a38–b27.

above, while beginning from Ch. 5 the advice is mainly directed at the answerer. The questioner's task at the outset of the disputation is clarified as follows:

> First, then, the person who is going to be devising questions must find the location (*topos*) from which to attack; second, he must devise the questions, and arrange them individually, to himself; and only third and last does he ask these of someone else. Now, up to the point of finding the location, the philosopher's inquiry and the dialectician's proceed alike, but actually arranging these things and devising questions is unique to the dialectician. For all that is directed at someone else. (*Topics* VIII 1 155b4–10)

In this Section we shall concern ourselves with the notion and choice of *topos*, and in the next with the arrangement of the questions. The lists of locations which form the matter of Books II–VII of the *Topics*, include mainly *strategic rules* to help the questioner to *invent* suitable premisses for a given conclusion which, to start with, is the contradictory of the answerer's thesis or the paradoxical proposition the questioner has chosen as his aim. A location alone is evidently not sufficient for constructing an argument, because it only offers a general model of an inference. One needs, in addition, empirical knowledge about the matter in question, for which purpose Aristotle offers the advice of memorizing lists of *endoxa*, and ordering them according to subject matter, and school or type of person.[53]

Aristotle seems to assume his audience is familiar with the idea of the *topos*, since he takes no steps to define it. To illustrate, let us analyse one of the typical inferential *topoi* relying on the conceptual properties of the predicables, *i.e.*, 'definition', 'genus', 'differentia', 'property', and 'accident'.[54] In the following the inference is based on the logic of the concepts 'genus' and 'species':

> If, then, a genus is suggested for something that is, first take a look at all objects which belong to the same genus as the thing mentioned, and see whether the genus suggested is not predicated of some of them, as in the case of accident: *e.g.* if good be laid down as the genus of pleasure, see whether some pleasure is not good; for, if so, clearly good is not the genus of pleasure; for the genus is predicated of all the members of the same species. (*Topics* IV 1 120b15–20)

The example given offers as a thesis to be refuted 'good' is the genus of 'pleasure', and the following is a possible argument against it with the general principle expressed as a premiss:

The genus of a species is predicated of all the members of the same species.
Excessive drinking is not good.
<u>Excessive drinking is a pleasure.</u>
'Good' is not the genus of 'pleasure'.[55]

---

[53] *Topics* I 14 105b12–15, II 4 111b12–16, VIII 14 163b20–33, see Smith 1997 xxiii–xxiv.

[54] *Topics* I 4, 101b17–25.

[55] This already involves a notion of logical form (Smith 1997, xxv–xxvi). To illustrate how the inferential *topoi* may have helped to develop the formal syllogistics of the *Prior Analytics*, we may reduce this piece of reasoning to the following standard three-term two-premiss syllogism by leaving out the predicable term and the general premiss:

Our example *topos* can thus be said to be constituted of following three components: (1) a general form of the *intended conclusion*, understood as the denial of the answerer's thesis, (2) *advice* to seek premisses of a certain kind for the given conclusion, (3) a *general principle*, which guarantees the step from the premisses to the intended conclusion.

Because Aristotle's manner of presenting the locations varies, sometimes more and sometimes fewer parts being given, the scholars have disputed whether the inferential locations consist merely of the heuristic advice for inventing arguments or rather of the general principles.[56] My suggested solution is to interpret the notion of *topos* with the help of the *Metaphysics* I 1 conception of the master of a *technê*, who distinguishes himself from the experienced craftsman by being able to teach, which is said to involve the capacity to *explain*, *i.e.*, to offer the reason why.[57] Applied to the art of dialectic, this implies that an inferential *topos* consists of all the three components (1)–(3) mentioned above.[58] An example, if one is supplied, is not part of the location itself, its task being to illustrate the use of the location.[59] The role of the general principle is to offer an account of why the instruction to seek for premisses of a certain kind is a good one: since the syllogism is what the questioner needs to lead the answerer to refute his initial thesis, the general principle explains why this is likely to be achieved by the suggested means. The general principle, often being a necessary truth, hence offers the questioner a good reason to expect the answerer to grant the desired proposition, having conceded certain other propositions. The fact that sometimes only the advice and sometimes only the principle is presented, need not cause serious problems, since the reader can always add the missing factor.[60]

b. Topos and the syllogism

It is important to note that the inferential locations yield inferences which satisfy the several conditions of the syllogism. This is more important, since Aristotle's definition of syllogism is not tailored with a formal logical system in mind, but

---

Excessive drinking is not good.
Excessive drinking is a pleasure.
Not every pleasure is good.

[56] Among ancient scholars, the *topos* as advice is accepted by Alexander Aphrodisias and *topos* as a principle by Theophrastus (Stump 1978, 167–168). Of the contemporary interpreters, Stump (1978, 170, 173–174) favours the former view, de Pater (1965, 101–117, 140–148, 1968, 165) and Slomkowski (1997, 45ff.) the latter.

[57] Kakkuri-Knuuttila 1993, Chs. 2 and 3. The *Metaphysics* I 1 981a24–b13 model of *technê* has close affinities with that of Plato in the *Gorgias* 465a, 500e–501a.

[58] Green-Pedersen (1984, 21), Primavesi (1996, 82 ff.) and Smith (1997, xxiv–xxviii) also adopt the view that the *topos* includes both the advice and the general principle.

[59] This resembles the role of examples as evidence in *Rhetoric* II 20 1393a10–16.

[60] Aristotle seems to be simply following a principle similar to his notion of *enthymêma* as an efficient way of presenting an argument in a rhetorical context (*Rhetoric* I 2 1357a16–21, Burnyeat 1994, 21–24, 1996, 99–101).

to serve certain discoursal purposes. This can be seen most clearly in its characterization in the *Sophistical Refutations*:[61]

The syllogism arises from certain things which have been set down in such a way that it is necessary to affirm (*legein*) something different from the things laid down because of the things laid down. (1 164b27–165a2)

This brief elaboration imposes four conditions on an inference to count as a syllogism, seldom recognized. Since the necessary relation between the premisses and conclusion need not be confined to logical validity in any formal system, as illustrated by the example *topos* in the preceding sub-section, it covers valid inferences *in a broader sense* including conceptual relations.[62] However, not every general principle functions as a good reason for the questioner to expect affirmation in a dialectical exchange: no answerer can foresee all the logical consequences of any set of propositions conceded by him. The *topoi* of dialectic, or rhetoric just as well, need to yield inference relations *obvious* to most people without intermediate steps.[63] Part of the goal of dialectical exercises is precisely to improve in the skills of quickly producing and identifying such inferences.[64]

The requirement for the conclusion to be affirmed *because of* the things laid down excludes inferences with redundant premisses not needed for the conclusion to follow. The further condition that the conclusion be *different* from the premisses excludes *petitio principii* fallacies, implying that the inference has the potential to increase one's knowledge, and may thus function as an argument or an explanation.[65]

Clearly, most of the inferential locations of the *Topics* satisfy these four conditions of the syllogism, as well as the further requirement derived from the notion of *elenchus* as a refutation of a given proposition, since they are applicable both in *pro* and *con* arguments. The significance of all these five conditions in Aristotle's dialectic, though seldom recognized, is to be seen in the fact that the *Sophistical Refutations* was written mainly to offer solutions to various kinds of fallacies which follow because of breaking the definition of syllogism or *elenchus*.[66]

In addition to the four conditions characterizing the syllogism, Aristotle appears sometimes, however, to have a tendency to think of inferences in epistemic terms even in a deeper sense. For, the first criterion for assessing arguments in Ch. 11 rules out as a genuine piece of reasoning one where all or most of the premisses are either false or unacceptable.[67] One important exception to these

---

[61] Bolton 1994, 109–110. See note 33.
[62] Sorabji 1972, 206–208, Green-Pedersen 1984, 26.
[63] Primavesi 1996, 81–82.
[64] Bolton 1994, 128. Improvement in speed is one of the chief aims of dialectical argument (*Sophistical Refutations* 16, 175a20–26, 18 177a6–8).
[65] Bolton 1994, 110–112.
[66] *Sophistical Refutations* 6 168a17–20, 34–37, 10 171a1–11, 5 167a21–27, Bolton 1994, 109.
[67] *Topics* VIII 11 161b19–22.

four conditions is the requirement of necessity, since not all inferences generated by the locations listed in the *Topics* are deductive. This has often been ignored, perhaps, for the reason that Aristotle himself does not mention it in the textbooks of dialectic, though he treats the issue quite sufficiently in the *Rhetoric*.[68] Examples of non-deductive locations are, among others:

> Things the generations of which are good/bad, are themselves good/bad.
> The generations of good/bad things are good/bad.[69]
> If a predicate belongs/does not belong to a subject, then it also belongs/does not belong to another subject to which it is more likely to belong to.
> If a predicate belongs/does not belong to a subject, then it does not belong/belongs to another subject to which it is less likely to belong to.[70]

In addition to the syllogism, induction and analogy are included as relevant forms of reasoning in dialectic, though their role is confined to support premisses of the main syllogism.[71] No doubt Aristotle recognizes their non-deductive nature here as well.

c. Non-inferential topoi

A few of the locations, which may be called non-inferential *topoi*, offer strategies for other purposes than constructing inferences. They are, obviously, meant to help the questioner to carry through his argument strategy, as can be seen in the following example:

Moreover, it is well to alter a term into one more familiar, e.g. to substitute 'clear' for 'precise' in describing a conception, and 'meddling' for 'officious'; for when the expression is made more familiar, the thesis becomes easier to attack. This location also is available for both purposes alike, both for establishing and for overthrowing a view. (*Topics* II 4 111a8–13)

We may note that, along with the illustrative example, this *topos* includes three similar elements as the inferential *topoi*: (1) an intended goal, (2) advice on how to achieve it, and (3) an explanation of why the advice is good in a dialectical exchange. Interestingly enough, the distinction between the questioner's task of refuting a positive view (*anaskeuazein*) and establishing one (*kataskeuazein*) also

---

[68] *Rhetoric* I 2 1356b16–18 and 1357a27–28 also includes for the most part inferences as rhetorical syllogisms.

[69] *Topics* II 9 114b18–22, also III 2 117b4–9, III 6 119b8–13, IV 4 124a20–30, VII 1 152a1–4, Green-Pedersen 1984, 27.

[70] *Topics* II 10 115a7–11, also III 6 119b17–30, IV 6 127b26–27, V 8 137b15–27, VI 7 146a4–11, see Green-Pedersen 1984, 27.

[71] For induction as a second kind of inference in dialectic in addition to syllogism, see *Topics* I 12 105a11–16, as a *topos*, see II 2 109b13–29, III 6 120a32–b6. The strategic rules for induction are given in VIII 2 157a18–b33 and 8 160b10–12. Analogical reasoning is mentioned in I 17, VIII 1 156b10–17 and discussed as a form of hypothetical reasoning in I 18 108b7–19.

appears here, which accords with the idea that the answerer may adopt either a positive view or its negation as his thesis.[72]

d. Strategic rules concerning the topoi

It is easy to see how the mastery of the *topoi*, though not easy to achieve, can promote the discovery of arguments as compared with memorizing particular arguments.[73] Like the mnemonic techniques, developed and widely used by the Greeks and later applied by the Romans to store and recall items one wants to remember, the lists of *topoi* can be used again and again to produce particular arguments of a certain kind.[74] To enhance their feasibility, Aristotle lists the *topoi* according to the predicables, with the exception of those dealing with values and choice given in Book III Chs. 1–4.

We thus obtain the following strategic rule for the questioner:

Strategic rule for the questioner for inventing arguments:
The questioner should appeal to the inferential *topoi* to invent arguments for given conclusions and non-inferential *topoi* to guarantee that the answerer concedes the premises.

A corresponding advice for the answerer is given in Book VIII Ch. 9 160b14–16, noting that in order to be ready to oppose the questioner's arguments, the answerer should first work out an attack on it himself:

Strategic rule for the answerer for preparing to defend his thesis:
To prepare himself to defend his thesis, the answerer should first work out an attack on it himself.

4. STRATEGIC RULES FOR COMPETITION AND SHOWING ONE'S SKILFULNESS

a. Means of concealing the questioner's argument strategy

The rules for the questioner to conceal his argument strategy are most important to our main aim concerning the relevance of dialectical skills in philosophical inquiry.[75] As already mentioned, some interpreters have taken these as evidence

---

[72] Green-Pedersen 1984, 25. Aristotle is not fully systematic in the use of this terminology, Slomkowski 1997, 18.

[73] *Sophistical Refutations* 34 183b34–184b8. However, Aristotle advises memorizing arguments as well in *Topics* VIII 14 163a36–b22, 164a3–11, b16–19.

[74] Stump 1978, 6, Sorabji 1972, 22–26.

[75] One may ask whether all the advice for the questioner on how to elicit the desired response from the answerer should be called *topoi* or only those given in Books II–VII. Why not call the strategic rules for concealing one's argument strategy offered in Book VIII Ch. 1 of the *Topics topoi*, if the rule for changing an unfamiliar term to a more familiar one is so called? Aristotle may not have

that there is, after all, no essential difference between dialectical and eristic disputation, and that dialectic thus has no role in an honest quest for truth. Such views reveal misconceptions concerning the role and nature of the rules of concealment, however. Aristotle's remark in *Topics* VIII 1 155b10–16 that the rules concerning the way questions are posed are useful only for the dialectician and neither for the philosopher, nor for one inquiring by himself seems to have gone unnoticed. It clearly indicates that he regarded dialectic and philosophy as separate social activities, sharing some, though not all means. The goals of their practitioners are contrary in that the philosopher aims at developing scientific syllogisms with premises, as intelligible and as close to the conclusion as possible, while the dialectician typically needs to take some extra measures not to make his intended argument immediately transparent,[76] because, as Aristotle points out, dialectic always involves another party.[77] Taking the other party into consideration is necessary for the dialectician for several reasons, and in general, as a social activity a dialectical discussion needs to be interesting and enjoyable to each party involved in a manner different from solitary inquiry to which Aristotle compares philosophical activity.[78]

The basic concealment strategy offered for the questioner is to lengthen the series of questions by arguments for the premises of the main argument, called necessary premises,[79] then present the questions in a mixed rather than a logical order, and finally jump to the final conclusion by leaving out the intermediate argument steps. By these means the final conclusion comes as a surprise to the answerer as well as to the audience in case there is one:

Speaking generally, the person who is getting answers in a concealed manner must ask in such a way that when the whole argument has been presented in questions and he has stated his conclusion, the reason why is to be sought. But this will best come about if we argue in the way just stated. For if only the last conclusion is stated, it will not be clear how it follows, because the answerer will not foresee what premises it follows from if the syllogisms were not spelt out previously. (*Topics* VIII 1 156a13–19)

The concealment rules hence provide an important means to catch the attention of the audience.

In laying out a similar list of concealment tricks in the *Sophistical Refutations* 15 174a26–29 Aristotle makes it clear that such means are neutral with respect to genuine and merely apparent dialectic: they can be applied both in fair and unfair argument. The rules themselves do not cause the argument to turn into a fallacious one, but do permit the intellectual amusement from which the dialectical

---

found this a matter of great significance, and neither is it for our concerns. The non-inferential *topoi* may be regarded as strategic rules on the same footing as the rules for concealment, for instance.

[76] In this respect the aim of the dialectician is contrary to that of the rhetorician as well (*Rhetoric* II 2 1357a3–4, 10–12).

[77] For different interpretations of *pros heteron* in *Topics* VIII 1 155b10, 26–27 see the translation in Barnes 1984, Brunschwig 1986, 37, and Bolton 1994, 102.

[78] Devereux 1994, 270 n. 12.

[79] *Topics* VIII 1 155b17–20.

practice takes its nourishment. This also holds for the means of adding irrelevant premisses, even though Aristotle notes that they may in particular confuse the answerer into granting propositions he would not otherwise concede, thus making eristic arguments pass more easily.[80] Somewhat earlier he suggests, however, using these rules to encourage an honest reply.[81]

It may be noted that in addition to logical and linguistic matters some of the following list of rules for concealment take into account also psychological characteristics of the answerer.

Strategic rules for the questioner for concealing his argument strategy:
1. The questioner should not put the necessary premisses, *i.e.*, the premisses of the main argument directly; but should develop a line of argument for the premisses of the main argument.[82]
2. The questioner should leave the premisses of the final argument unarticulated.[83]
3. The questioner should present the questions in a mixed, instead of a logical, order.[84]
4. The questioner should ask for acceptance for propositions irrelevant to the conclusion.[85]
5. The questioner should not pose the final conclusion in the form of a question.[86]
6. In formulating the question, the questioner should state the definitions for co-ordinates instead of stating them for the terms themselves.[87]
7. The questioner should formulate his questions so that it remains open whether he wants a 'Yes' or a 'No' answer.[88]
8. The questioner should sometimes bring an objection against himself.[89]
9. The questioner should sometimes formulate the question by adding 'It is generally held that ...' or 'It is commonly said that ...'.[90]
10. The questioner should not be insistent.[91]
11. The questioner should sometimes formulate a question as if it were a mere illustration.[92]

---

[80] *Topics* VIII 1 157a1–5. Another reason is that it is too obvious for the conclusion (Smith 1997, 114).
[81] *Topics* VIII 1 156b8–9.
[82] *Topics* VIII 1 155b29–156a11, 156b27–30, *Sophistical Refutations* 15 174a16.
[83] *Topics* VIII 1 156a11–13, 16–22.
[84] *Topics* VIII 1 156a23–26, *Sophistical Refutations* 15 174a22–26.
[85] *Topics* VIII 1 157a1–3. For an illustrative example, see VIII 11 162a24–34.
[86] *Topics* VIII 2 158a7–13, *Sophistical Refutations* 15 174b8–11.
[87] *Topics* VIII 1 156a27–b3.
[88] *Topics* VIII 1 156b4–9, *Sophistical Refutations* 15 174a30–33. For competitive purposes it is sometimes useful to formulate the question in terms of contraries instead of negations (174a40–b7).
[89] *Topics* VIII 1 156b18–20.
[90] *Topics* VIII 1 156b20–23.
[91] *Topics* VIII 1 156b23–25.

12. The questioner should usually ask the most important premiss last; when arguing with ill-tempered people, or with people who consider themselves smart at answering, the most important premiss should be put first.[93]

The main purpose of the concealment tricks is, obviously, to make it more difficult for the answerer to foresee (*prooran*) the questioner's argument strategy, and to find objections to the premisses.[94] Hence they open up new possibilities both for the questioner and the answerer to show their skills in dialectical argument.

b. *Means of showing the redundancy of propositions*

The most intriguing thing in this connection is that rule 4 above has its counterpart in Ch. 6 in the strategic rules for the answerer to be on the lookout for the relevance of the premisses for the conclusion. The link is indicated, for instance, by the fact that the term 'foresee' used in connection with the rules of concealment (155b13, 156a18), also appears here (VIII 6 160b12). By taking a look at this pair of rules we gain a more informative picture of what competition about dialectical skills meant for the ancient Greeks.

The somewhat artificial way of marking out the redundant propositions from the relevant ones clearly indicates that the rules do not characterize everyday encounters, but are meant for formal disputations. The basic idea is that the answerer concedes all propositions not relevant to the conclusion, and for the relevant ones states their degree of acceptance, but says that they are too close to the conclusion and the thesis is refuted if they are granted.[95] In addition to acceptable and unacceptable propositions, the relevance rules take into account the middle position in which the proposition is neither acceptable nor unacceptable, a possibility mentioned in the preceding Chapter and to be discussed here in Section 6.

Strategic rules for the answerer to mark redundant propositions:
The answerer should concede all propositions irrelevant to the conclusion proposed by the questioner and state whether they are acceptable or unacceptable, but not add anything if they are neither.
As to propositions relevant to the conclusion, the answerer should state whether they are acceptable, unacceptable, or neither, and that the thesis is refuted if they are granted.

Interpreting the concealment rules in the light of the relevance rules for the answerer form a clear vindication of the main thesis of this paper. First, this pair

---

[92] *Topics* VIII 1 156b25–27.
[93] *Topics* VIII 1 156b30–157a1.
[94] *Topics* VIII 9 160b14–16.
[95] *Topics* VIII 6 159b39–160a11, cf. II 5 112a7–16.

of rules offers efficient means for competing about dialectical skills. The answerer can manifest his skilfulness by showing that he can anticipate the questioner's argument strategy and distinguish the relevant from the irrelevant propositions,[96] while the latter gains credit only if the extra propositions were stated on purpose. As Aristotle remarks himself, apparently making a reference to the complementary roles of the answerer and questioner described in *Topics* VIII 4 159a20–24:[97]

> [I]n this way, not only will the answerer appear not to suffer anything through his own fault, if he concedes each premiss foreseeing [what will follow], but also the questioner will get his syllogism[.] (*Topics* VIII 6 160a11–13)

The deeper purpose of the pair of concealment and relevance rules is, however, to develop skills of good reasoning, necessary in a dialectical search for truth (*skepsis*). While the concealment rules may help the answerer to elicit his true opinion, the relevance rules remove his motivation to state the contrary. Furthermore, the latter are important in guaranteeing that the inference is a genuine syllogism with no premisses irrelevant to the conclusion, since the propositions marked as redundant are not to be taken as premisses.[98] These rules help, likewise, to check that the questioner has not introduced redundant premisses by mistake.

5. Strategic Rules for a Proper Syllogism: Petitio Principii and Contrary Premisses

Among the rules for those assessing a dialectical disputation in Chs. 11 and 13 Aristotle discusses two ways of posing poor questions which appear to yield strategic rules both for the questioner and the answerer. While the questioner should avoid begging the final conclusion and asking contrary premisses, the answerer should correspondingly watch out for such premisses to reject them when found. It was perhaps considered a merit in the latter if he also pointed out the reason for the rejection. The reasons do in fact derive from the defining characteristics of the syllogism, requiring that the conclusion be different from the premisses and that the given premisses be the reason why the conclusion follows. The first requirement is broken by begging the question and the latter by asking contrary premisses.

Aristotle offers an interesting list of five ways of *petitio principii*:

Strategic rule for the questioner to avoid begging the final conclusion:
The questioner should not ask premisses of the following kind:

---

[96] Slomkowski 1997, 37, Smith 1997, 133.

[97] Important devices in competition are that 'among competitors, the questioner must at all costs appear to be inflicting something on the answerer, while the answerer must appear not to be affected' (*Topics* VIII 5 159a 30–32). See *Sophistical Refutations* 15 174a19–22.

[98] *Topics* II 5 112a9–11, Cf. *Sophistical Refutations* 17 176a21–27.

(i) the final conclusion either in the same or different terms
   (ii) a universal proposition of which the final conclusion is a particular case
   (iii) a particular proposition of which the final conclusion is an inductive generalization
   (iv) two propositions of which the final conclusion is a conjunct
   (v) a proposition equivalent to the conclusion.[99]

Strategic rule for the answerer to object to begging the final conclusion:
The answerer should reject a proposition which begs the final conclusion aimed at by the questioner in one of the ways mentioned in the strategic rule for the questioner.

Cases (ii)–(iv) have been the cause of puzzlement, since they are not included in the treatment of the matter in *Prior Analytics* II 16.[100] The problem disappears as soon as one interprets their role in the context of dialectical disputations. Having an inductive generalization, an application of a universal to a particular, or an inference to a conjunction as the main argument to the desired conclusion would certainly make a dialectical disputation quite pointless: the necessary distance from the conclusion would be lost and it would be too easy for the answerer to state his objections, indeed, all the fun would be spoiled by the whole interchange being over as soon as it began.[101] However, none of these are forbidden moves at an earlier stage of the discussion. Obviously, no syllogism derives in the case of (i) and (v) because of the requirement that the conclusion needs to be different from the premises, which explains why only these two cases are mentioned in the *Prior Analytics*.[102]

The following pair of rules states the ways of asking for contrary premises listed by Aristotle:[103]

Strategic rule for the questioner to avoid asking contrary premises:
The questioner should not ask premises of the following kind:
   (i) a proposition and its denial
   (ii) a proposition and its contrary
   (iii) a universal proposition and a denial of one of its cases
   (iv) a particular proposition and its universal denial
   (v) a proposition contrary to a consequence of propositions already conceded

---

[99] *Topics* VIII 13 162b34–163a13, also 11 161b11–18.
[100] For the different solutions suggested, see Smith 1997, 150–151.
[101] *Sophistical Refutations* 7 169b12–17, see Bolton 1994, 110–114, Smith 1997, 151. Note that Aristotle uses the same example of applying a universal to a particular case in both *Topics* VIII 1 155b30–34 and VIII 13 163a2–3.
[102] See *Topics* VIII 13 162a31–33 and *Prior Analytics* II 16 65a35–37.
[103] *Topics* VIII 13 163a14–28, see also 11 161b11–15.

(vi) propositions from which contraries follow.

Strategic rule for the answerer to object to contrary premisses:
The answerer should reject a proposition which is contrary to a proposition already conceded by him in one of the ways mentioned in the strategic rule for the questioner.

Both of these sets of rules support the main contention of this paper by demanding logically neat and genuine inferences. An inference with contrary premisses is not a good one and, for Aristotle, not even a syllogism, since one of the contraries is not needed for the conclusion to follow. Clearly, the *petitio principii* rules imposing stricter demands than necessary for philosophical research form no objection to the relevance of dialectical skills in philosophical inquiry.

6. STRATEGIC RULES FOR THE ANSWERER FOR GRANTING PREMISSES

The constitutive rule for the answerer for accepting premisses (Section 2.b) does not guarantee that an inference is an *argument*, one precondition of which is that, in addition to being acceptable, the premisses are initially more acceptable than the conclusion so that, at least in the case of deductive reasoning, the acceptance of the inference raises the degree of acceptability of the conclusion. An argument thus has the potentiality to affect the acceptability of the conclusion. Aristotle is, to be sure, aware of the significance of this condition, although, in the passage most extensively devoted to this question he surprises us by abandoning the requirement that the premisses need to be dialectical by allowing unacceptable premisses. Having made the distinction between three epistemic statuses of the theses, acceptable, unacceptable, and neither acceptable nor unacceptable, he states what appears to be a condition for arguments:

[W]hoever deduces well (*kalôs*) deduces the problem [here the desired conclusion] assigned from more acceptable and more familiar things[.] (*Topics* VIII 5 159b8–9)[104]

He postulates simultaneously three situations: if the thesis of the answerer is unacceptable, the conclusion intended by the questioner is acceptable; if the thesis is acceptable, the conclusion is unacceptable; if the thesis is neither acceptable nor unacceptable, the conclusion is also neither. Since the above criterion demands that, in each case, the premisses are more acceptable and more familiar than the conclusion, the acceptance of the inference does raise the degree of acceptability of the conclusion, though, in the second and third cases, not up to the level of acceptability. For, if the conclusion is generally rejected, some

---

[104] Also in *Topics* VIII 3 159a8–9, 6 160a13–16. 'More familiar things' here means premisses for which it is easier to produce arguments than for the conclusion (*Topics* VIII 3 159a10–11).

of the premisses may also be generally rejected.[105] If such inferences are to be considered arguments at all, they will be arguments merely in *a weak sense*.

One may wonder why the answerer would not rather choose the opposite of an unacceptable proposition, thus conceding a dialectical premiss, particularly if he can foresee that it is irrelevant to the conclusion. It seems that a great deal of cooperative will is needed from the answerer were he to defend an acceptable thesis by granting unacceptable premisses. However, as we have seen, he may rely on the relevance rules to manifest his capacity to anticipate the questioner's line of argument, and thus save face.

Aristotle also offers a further classification of premisses in Ch. 5 by distinguishing degrees of acceptance *without qualification* and *conditionally*. By the latter he means acceptability to a particular person or school, the answerer himself, or a particular philosopher, such as Heraclitus. The guiding principle here is that in conceding premisses the answerer should follow the same criterion as in choosing his initial thesis.[106]

The following rule hence qualifies the constitutive rule for the answerer for accepting propositions by posing restrictions on the degree of acceptability as well as by allowing non-dialectical premisses:

Strategic rule for the answerer for accepting premisses:
The answerer should accept propositions proposed by the questioner which are more acceptable or at least less unacceptable than the conclusion aimed at by the questioner so that, if the thesis is acceptable, unacceptable, or neither without qualification/conditionally, the answerer should make his concessions without qualification/conditionally.

This strategic advice is given immediately after Aristotle promises to turn to issues concerning how an answerer should defend his thesis well in disputations for the purpose of training (*gymnastikê*), testing (*peirastikê*), and inquiry (*skepsis*) in contradistinction to competitive discussions, for which effective strategies, evidently, have been codified.[107] One should ask, however, whether the above rules apply to each of the three purposes. The idea of accepting *adoxic* premisses seems to be out of place in testing arguments, for to convince an interlocutor that he does not know a certain proposition, or merely that his beliefs are inconsistent, the premisses have to be acceptable rather than unacceptable to him.[108] However, in serious inquiry for truth, poor argument with some *adoxic* premiss advanced for the sake of argument can be useful for distinguishing acceptable

---

[105] *Topics* VIII 5 159a38–b23.
[106] *Topics* VIII 5 159a39–b1, 23–35. Cf. Vlastos 1983.
[107] *Topics* VIII 5 159a25–37.
[108] Smith 1997, 131. For peirastic arguments, see *Topics* VIII 10 161a24–36, *Sophistical Refutations* 2 165b4–7, 8 169b24–25, 11 171b4–6, 172a21–32. Cf. Bolton 1990, 1993, 1994.

from unacceptable propositions, and the true from the false.[109] This appears to be a good reason to practice such moves in training arguments, even though Aristotle remarks in Ch. 3 that a proposition put by the questioner 'should be conceded by someone practising if it only appears true (*alêthes monon fainêtai*)' (*Topics* VIII 3 159a12), obviously referring to one not well familiar with what counts as an *endoxon*.

7. STRATEGIC RULES FOR GOOD ARGUMENT TOWARDS TRUTH

a. Induction

Book VIII of the *Topics* includes three pairs of rules for good argument which deal directly with truth, imposing severe demands on the answerer to control the quality of the argument. Moreover, the answerer is granted powers similar to those of the questioner by being allowed to pose arguments against the premises and conclusions put to him. This implies that, within a single *elenchus*, the argument may turn into a debate; in particular as the questioner seems to be entitled to make his own objections to the answerer's counter-arguments.

A natural place for the answerer to be on the lookout for weaknesses in reasoning is inductive as well as analogical reasoning, neither of which is deductively valid. Induction is dealt with from the point of view of the questioner in Ch. 2 and from the point of view of the answerer in Ch. 8 which also mentions analogy. As became evident in the rules concerning begging the question, induction cannot form the main argument for the final conclusion, but only auxiliary arguments for its premises.[110] Furthermore, Aristotle advices to use induction with inexperienced interlocutors and syllogism with more experienced ones.[111]

The guiding principle here offers the questioner a proper chance to proceed, but what is more important, it neatly supports good argument as a means toward truth: the answerer should concede the particular cases if they are *true and acceptable*, and the universal as well, if he cannot put forward any objection.[112] Likewise with the general background assumption in analogical inferences.[113] Otherwise the answerer is to be considered a quarrelsome person preventing the common goal which, as we can see, is good argument.[114]

As soon as the questioner asks the respondent to concede several similar cases, the latter can anticipate that either a universal generalization or a further

---

[109] Bolton 1994, 107 and Smith 1997, 140. Cf. *Topics* VIII 9 160b21–22, 12 162b16–27. For a discussion of this, see 7.c. on 'solution'. The remark that the degree of acceptability of the conclusion is the mean of the degrees of the premisses (*Topics* VIII 11 161b19–22, 162a19–23) is not, however, in harmony with Aristotle's views in *Posterior Analytics* I 2–3 (Smith 1997, 144–145).

[110] *Topics* VIII 8 160a35–39.

[111] *Topics* VIII 2 157a18–20, 14 164a12–13, I 12 105a16–19.

[112] *Topics* VIII 8 160a39–b13. Cf. *Sophistical Refutations* 15 174a34–38.

[113] *Topics* VIII 8 160a38, 1 156b10–17.

[114] *Topics* VIII 8 160b2–13, see 11 161a21–b10, Smith 1997, 135.

case will be offered in one of the next moves, and thus he should prepare himself with a counter-example or counter-argument against the conclusion. The questioner's interrogative powers are likewise expanded, since he may require the answerer to state his objections where the latter refuses to accept a generalization on the basis of several instances. This involves, in fact, the right to pose a wh-question.[115]

The disputation need not change its course completely as a result of the answerer's objections, since the questioner is allowed to qualify the generalization so as to make it immune to the criticism.[116] Aristotle refers to truth again in pointing out that the place for such qualifying moves are universals which are only partly true, thus noting the role of the rules of induction in the search for truth through the refinement of given *endoxic* beliefs.[117]

Since the main responsibility of good argument lies with the answerer, the moves around induction are easier to grasp if we begin with those for the answerer.

Strategic rules for the answerer for induction:
The answerer should concede all particulars, if true and acceptable, but should try to bring an objection against the universal either in the form of
  (ii) a negative instance or
  (iii) a counter-argument.
The answerer should concede the universal supported by many instances if he has no objection to bring against it.

Strategic rules for the questioner for induction:
The questioner should ask for objections to a universal refused by the answerer when the answerer has conceded the particulars in its support.
The questioner should modify the universal to meet the objections raised by the answerer.

Evidently the answerer need not always know whether the *endoxic* particulars proposed by the questioner are true or false, specially since the particulars proposed as premisses are not singular cases but generalizations.[118] This may, per-

---

[115] *Topics* VIII 2 157a34–b2.
[116] *Topics* VIII 2 157b8–33.
[117] *Topics* VIII 2 157b28–31. Qualifying generalizations accords well with Aristotle's understanding of induction as reasoning with three terms, which deviates from our two-term notion of induction. As indicated in *Topics* I 12 105a13–16, VIII 2 157a21–33, the goal of induction may be to discover the general term, the *major* in the language of the syllogistic logic of the *Analytics*, while in the so-called *inductive syllogism* the discovery concerns the middle term (*Prior Analytics* II 23 68b15–37, see Hintikka 1980, Kakkuri-Knuuttila and Knuuttila 1990). The inductive syllogism may, however, be used for justification, an example of which is the support through particular virtues for the definition of virtue as a stable capacity to hit the mean (see *Nicomachean Ethics* II 7 1107a28–32).
[118] Kakkuri-Knuuttila and Knuuttila 1990.

haps, be expected from the real expert with refined judgemental capacities as a result of long training in dialectical practices. In any case, the treatment of induction reveals that, instead of being excluded from dialectic, considerations of truth have a central role in it.

b. Ambiguous Terms

Aristotle also offers a pair of rules concerning ambiguous terms, in Ch. 2 for the questioner and in Ch. 7 for the answerer. Like the rules for induction, these involve qualification of partial truths.[119] They hence serve the purpose of truth *via* good argument by offering means of avoiding fallacies of equivocation, most useful for the purpose of competition about argumentative skills, as well as for an Aristotelian philosophical inquiry. Here, too, the answerer is primarily responsible for good argument, and may manifest his dialectical abilities by distinguishing the several senses of ambiguous terms.

In Ch. 7 Aristotle states that the answerer not only has the right to ask for clarification of ambiguous terms, but also the right to qualify propositions he accepts as premisses.[120]

Strategic rules for the answerer concerning the meanings of the terms:
If the terms are simple and clear, the answerer should say 'Yes' if he concedes the statement and 'No' if he rejects it.
If the sense of at least one of the terms is unfamiliar to the answerer, he should say 'I do not understand'.
If at least one of the terms is ambiguous and all of the senses are familiar to the answerer, then
  (i) if he concedes the proposition in all of its senses, he should say 'Yes', and if he rejects it in all of its senses, he should say 'No',[121] and
  (ii) if he concedes the proposition in one sense and not in the other, he should say In which sense he concedes it and in which sense not.[122]
If at least one of the terms is ambiguous and the answerer has conceded or rejected the proposition without realizing it, and if he later realizes the ambiguity, he may correct the earlier statement and say in which sense he concedes it and in which sense he rejects it.

---

[119] *Topics* VIII 7 160a26–28, see also VIII 2 157b2–8. See *Topics* I 13 105a23–24, 15 106a1–107b37.

[120] *Topics* VIII 7 160a24–34. Examples of Socrates' moves of this kind are to be found in Plato's *Euthydemus* 293b, 295b, e, 296a, b.

[121] In *Sophistical Refutations* 17 176a9–18 Aristotle proposes a different practice: always to point out an ambiguity in order to avoid giving a single answer to two questions.

[122] This is called one of the ways of giving a solution to a false syllogism in *Sophistical Refutations* 18 176b36.

Aristotle points out, furthermore, that where the answerer refuses to accept any of the definitions or distinctions suggested by the questioner, the latter is allowed to require the answerer's own specifications by posing the question in wh-form.[123]

Strategic rule for the questioner for posing questions concerning the meanings of the terms:
If the answerer does not accept definitions or distinctions presented by the questioner, the questioner should require the answerer to explicate his own definition or distinctions.

c. Solution

In spite of the fact that perhaps the most intricate move in *Topics* VIII is the treatment of solution (*lusis*) in Ch. 10, involving a shift from an emphasis on *endoxa* to an emphasis on truth, this passage has gone almost unnoticed.[124] This discussion offers further evidence for the claims that dialectic can aim at good argument and truth, that the main responsibility for the quality of argument lies with the answerer, and that the exchange may involve logical debating moves. The means listed are, for some reason, said to be the ways to hinder, or at least to impede an argument from coming to its conclusion.[125] However, most of the strategic rules for the answerer may likewise be counted as ways of causing difficulties for the questioner in reaching the intended conclusion.

As already repeatedly pointed out, a proper dialectical argument relies on *endoxic* premisses, no matter whether they are true or false,[126] except when the conclusion is *adoxic*, in which case some premiss may be *adoxic* as well. However, in Ch. 10 the answerer is required to present a solution to an argument with a false conclusion and, more, to identify the cause of the falsity.

Hence the proper solution to an argument with a false conclusion is to reject the premiss on which the falsity depends. Though, the best way of manifesting one's dialectical skills is to put a counter-argument against that premiss, as this reveals that one knows the cause of the falsity:

Now, the person who rejects that because of which the falsehood comes about has certainly solved the argument, but it is the person who knows that the argument is by means of this who knows the solution. For it is not enough to object, not even if what is rejected is false, but he must also demon-

---

[123] *Topics* VIII 2 158a22–24.
[124] Bolton 1991 and Kakkuri-Knuuttila 1993 Chs. 3 and 5 discuss the *akrasia* argument in the *Nicomachean Ethics* VIII 3 as an example of *lusis*. Also Bolton 1994, 107.
[125] *Topics* VIII 10 161a1, 13–15.
[126] *Topics* VIII 11 162a8–10, 12 162b27–28, *Posterior Analytics* I 19 81b18–22.

strate why it is false: this is how it will be evident whether or not he makes his objection with foresight. (*Topics* VIII 10 160b33–39)[127]

Even if solution is here characterized for the case where the argument has been brought to its conclusion, the same procedure can also be applied during the disputation. This gives more credit to the answerer, because it shows he has anticipated the questioner's argument strategy. A similar idea is expressed in the *Sophistical Refutations*:

> Whenever one foresees any question coming, one should put in one's objection and have one's say beforehand; for by doing so one is likely to hinder the questioner most effectually. (*Sophistical Refutations* 17, 176b26–28)

The next chapter adds three further forms of solution as a means of solving false or apparent reasoning: an argument with a true conclusion and a false premiss is solved, likewise, by rejecting the false premiss, an argument with a false conclusion can also be solved by a counter-argument against the conclusion, and an argument which merely appears to reason is solved by drawing distinctions.[128]

Topics VIII 10 also includes a practical remark that an objection to a false premiss should not be such that arguing against it would take more time than allowed for the discussion.[129] This involves another reference to the possibility that certain dialectical discussions may turn into debates between the participants, as the answerer may produce counter-arguments against the premises which the questioner then attacks.

This gives us the following rules:

Strategic rules for the answerer for stating objections:
The answerer should solve arguments leading to a false conclusion by rejecting the premiss on which the falsity of the conclusion depends, and advance a counter-argument against it, or advance a counter-argument against the conclusion.
The answerer should solve arguments with a false premiss and a true conclusion by rejecting the false premiss, and produce a counter-argument against it.

---

[127] See also *Topics* VIII 12 162b11–15 and *Sophistical Refutations* 18 176b38–40. Judging by the example adjoined, the appropriate solution is to object to a premiss such that the same solution applies to other cases as well. For instance, if one infers from the premisses 'He who sits, writes' and 'Socrates is sitting' the conclusion 'Socrates is writing', the cause of the falsity is, as Aristotle points out, the general premiss, even though the second may also be false (*Topics* VIII 10 160b25–33). However, in purely competitive, *i.e.*, eristic disputations, the answerer should try to suggest purely apparent solutions (*Sophistical Refutations* 17 175a31 ff.).

[128] *Sophistical Refutations* 18 176b29–177a2. For uses of *lusis* in this sense see, for instance, *Physics* I 2 185a5–10, *De Anima* II 11 422b19–30, and *Politics* VIII 6 1340b40–1341a5.

[129] *Topics* VIII 10 161a9–12. Aristotle evidently has in mind arguments, such as paradoxes of Zeno, which would impose on the questioner a task more difficult to deal with than the original one (*Topics* VIII 8 160b6–10, 3 159a4–14).

The answerer should solve arguments that fail to reason by making distinctions.
If the answerer does not succeed in doing this during the disputation, he should do it after it is concluded.
The answerer's objection should be such that arguing against it would not take more time than allowed for the discussion.

If the only way of solving fallacious inferences given is by making distinctions, this indicates that Aristotle fails to consider non-deductive syllogisms in the textbooks of dialectic. Here we may, however, refer to the treatment of the refutation of probabilities in *Rhetoric* II 25 where he notes that arguments from probabilities cannot be refuted through an objection, since it shows merely that the inference is not a necessary one. They have to be refuted, instead, by showing that the contrary is more probable.[130]

Strategic rule for the questioner for stating objections:
The questioner should try to solve arguments the answerer advances as solutions.

As Aristotle points out later, syllogisms leading to false conclusions are sometimes produced on purpose, and sometimes not, in which case the questioner is to be blamed for not having noticed the false premisses. However, in both cases the arguments are useful if their solutions help to identify false premisses.[131]

The rules discussed in this Section, those concerning solution in particular, seem to presuppose that, after all, truth is within the reach of the participants in some species of dialectic, at least. Why then care about the social epistemic status of the premisses and conclusion at all, *i.e.*, their degree of acceptability within one group or another? Aristotle's approach here, like in rhetoric and philosophy, seems to be that, though not all *endoxa* are true, it is, nevertheless, all we have to start with. By way of argument and debate we may proceed towards truth in a manner peculiar to each of these communicative fields. As concerns the relevant kind of dialectical disputation, one may suggest that *skepsis* is meant to be the one with a special focus on truth. For instance, such complicated concerns as are brought into play by solution seem to go beyond the task of revealing the ignorance of one who pretends to know, which forms the goal of examination arguments.[132] As for training arguments, such moves could be practiced only at a fairly advanced level.

---

[130] *Rhetoric* II 25 1402b22–1403a2.
[131] *Topics* VIII 12 162b16–22.
[132] Cf. *Topics* VIII 11 161a24–33.

8. STRATEGIC RULES FOR CRITICIZING AN OPPONENT AND ABANDONING THE DISCUSSION

In Ch. 2 Aristotle deals briefly with poor disputation, following as a result of too much time spent on presenting a single argument.[133] In such situations, the other party should either criticize the faulty one, or perhaps even abandon the discussion. The latter possibility indicates that if the discussion stops being dialectical, the participants have the right to withdraw. The fault lies with the questioner, if he fails to reason or merely rambles because of repeating the same question, or posing too many questions without drawing the (inductive or analogical) conclusion. The remark that the answerer is to be blamed if he does not answer, could be expanded by later comments on cantankerous opponents who cause problems by not conceding even what is obvious, granting only the contrary of what the questioner proposes, or by claiming not to understand, thus exploiting the strategic rules concerning ambiguous terms.[134] By refusing to continue, the questioner can thus prevent the disputation from turning into an eristic one.

Hence we have the following rules for attacking the opponent:

Strategic rules for criticizing the opponent and abandoning the discussion:
The questioner should criticize the answerer or abandon the discussion if he fails to answer as he should.
The answerer should criticize the questioner or abandon the discussion if he fails to draw conclusions.

9. CRITICISM OF A DISPUTATION

Aristotle's treatment of criticism (*epitimêsis*) of dialectical disputations in Chs. 11–13 offers further support for the relevance of dialectical skills to philosophical inquiry.[135] Though the position here is of those following an exercise or examination, ready to express their evaluation after the argument is concluded, we need not infer that the disputants themselves were not allowed to perform similar tasks. Inquiry (*skepsis*) is not mentioned here for the obvious reason that it belongs to a social context in which the assessment of the participants' performance is less under focus than the evaluation of the arguments in themselves. This is not sufficient in training and examination, for the adversaries may find it hard to suppress their competitive desires, thus turning the discussion into an eristic one.[136] At any rate, in pointing out the consequences of the cooperative nature of

---

[133] *Topics* VIII 2 158a25. Aristotle also refers to a time limit in VIII 10 161a10–12; see Moraux 1968, 285, Sorabji 1972, 27, and Ryle 1966, 105, 196; see Stump 1978, 163–164 for their criticism.
[134] *Topics* VIII 2 158a25–30, 10 161a2–4, 11 161a21–24.
[135] The verb *epitimân* is used in legal contexts for the assessment of penalties (Smith 1997, 138).
[136] *Topics* VIII 11 161a23–24, 37–b10.

the dialectical enterprise, Aristotle emphasizes that the goal is good dialectical argument:

> A criticism of an argument just as an argument in itself is not the same as criticism of it when it is put as questions. For the person questioned is often at fault for the argument not being argued well, because he will not agree to the premises from which it would be possible to argue well against the thesis. For it is not in the power of one participant alone to see that their common work is well accomplished. (*Topics* VIII 11 161a16–21)

One's lack of capacity to identify what counts as an *endoxon* or a genuine syllogism may be another cause of poor argument. A further reason may be the problem at issue, as the conclusion may be simply such that it is not possible to put good arguments for it.[137] Hence the questioner is said to have argued well if he has brought the discussion to a conclusion from the most acceptable premises possible regarding the difficulty of the conclusion, as well as the skills and mood of the answerer.[138] This I see as the ground for Aristotle to characterize dialectic as argument with premises as acceptable as possible.[139]

Aristotle also offers criteria for judging arguments themselves, *i.e.*, as separated from the context of dialectical disputations. The criteria are based on the notions of syllogism and *elenchus* in a manner we are already acquainted with, and the epistemic requirements that the premises be more acceptable and more familiar than the conclusion, included in the strategic rules for the answerer. Only two additional conditions are given, both needing a comment.

One of these is the statement that nothing is concluded (*mê sumperainêtai*) at all if all or most of the premises are false or unacceptable.[140] This imposes a stronger restriction on the strategic rule for the answerer for accepting propositions than the ones in Ch. 5, and indicates that for Aristotle the notion of drawing conclusions in the dialectical context includes an epistemic aspect not explicated in his definition of a syllogism. The message is clear, however. An inference with premises all or most of which are either false or unacceptable cannot have epistemic value in a search for truth via *pro* and *con* argument. Such an argument is thus a poor one as judged by itself, though not necessarily a failure in the particular situation.

Another additional condition is what Aristotle calls 'argument through the appropriate method' (*kata tên oikeian methodon* in Ch. 12 162b8). I shall use this idea to interpret the mysterious contrast between dialectical and eristic argument in Ch. 11 161a33–36 where the former is compared with geometrical proof. In the *Sophistical Refutations* Aristotle claims that reasoning should rely on starting points (*arkhai*, 9 170a34) peculiar to the field in question (*kata tên technên*,

---

[137] *Topics* VIII 11 161b34–162a11.
[138] *Topics* VIII 11 161b37–38.
[139] 'Our programme was, then, to discover some faculty of reasoning about any theme put before us from the most acceptable premises that there are ... in defending an argument we shall defend our thesis in the same manner by means of views as reputable as possible.' (*Sophistical Refutations* 34 183a37–b6, also *Topics* VIII 11 161b37–38.) Cf. Bolton 1993, 144, 1994, 107.
[140] *Topics* VIII 11 161b19–22.

170a33). Geometry and medicine should argue on the basis of geometrical and medical starting points, respectively, no matter whether the conclusions are true or false. The peculiar feature of dialectic as compared with the particular sciences is that its *topoi* (170a35) are common (*koinoi*, 170a36) to all sciences and capacities.[141] To illustrate, an attempted proof on the basis of a false diagram is called a fallacy in geometry, while a denial 'that it is better to take a walk after dinner by means of Zeno's argument' (172a8–9) is said not to be a medical, but a dialectical or eristic argument. This can be grasped on the basis of Aristotle's wider notion of logical form and validity pointed out in the discussion of inferential *topoi*, for, while the latter refers to the common notion of 'motion', the former depends on geometrical notions and axioms.[142] This allows Aristotle to say that dialectic offers a general theory of argument, and does not deal with any particular genus, because it deals with all.[143]

The following list consists of Aristotle's criteria for good dialectical argument which he offers for criticizing the performance of the questioner and answerer in an exercise or examination disputation.[144]

The criteria of good dialectical argument:
  (i)   The premisses necessarily imply a conclusion.[145]
  (ii) The premisses imply the intended conclusion.[146]
  (iii) No premiss is left out.[147]
  (iv) There are no redundant premisses, *e.g.*, no contrary premisses.[148]
  (v)   The conclusion is different from the premisses, *i.e.*, the questions do not beg the intended conclusion.[149]
  (vi) Most of the premisses are true and *endoxa*.[150]
  (vii) The premisses are more acceptable than the conclusion.[151]

---

[141] Dialectical arguments are often said to be *logikos* in contrast to *oikeios* (*Posterior Analytics* I 24 86a22, *Physics* III 5 204b4, *De Caelo* I 7 275b12, *Generation of Animals* II 8 747b28–29, *Metaphysics* VII 4 1029b13, 1030a27, 17 1041a28, XII 1 1069a28, *Eudemian Ethics* I 8 1217b17, 21), or in contrast to *physikos* (*Nicomachean Ethics* VII 3 1147a24, *Generation and Corruption* I 2 316a5–14, *Physics* III 5 204b4ff.). See Charles 1984, 128 n. 27, Irwin 1988 Ch. 2 n. 48, 49 and Ch. 7 n. 15.

[142] Cf. *Topics* VIII 14 164a7–11.

[143] *Sophistical Refutations* 11 171b6–22, 34–172b4. See also 9 170a31–b11, and Smith 1993, 339, 1994, 145–148. Aristotle's contrast between common and peculiar (*idion*) in 11 172a5, 25, 38 resembles the distinction between common and peculiar *topoi* in *Rhetoric* I 2 1358a10ff., II 22 1396b8–10, 27ff. In line 172a25 *idion* refers to principles of geometry in harmony with *Rhetoric* I 2 1358a22–26. Comp. Bolton's reading of *ta koina* in his interpretation of examination in 1994, 129–131.

[144] Cf. Smith 1997, 141–142. I take the description of clarity in *Topics* 12 162a35–b2 to concern how the argument is expressed, thus helping to capture its components. Cf. Smith 1997, 146–147.

[145] *Topics* VIII 11 161b22–24, also 12 162b3–5, 25–26.

[146] *Topics* VIII 11 161b20–21, 24–26, also 12 162b5–7.

[147] *Topics* VIII 11 161b23–24, also 12 162a35–37.

[148] *Topics* VIII 11 161b22–24, 28–30, 161b11–18.

[149] *Topics* VIII 11 161b11–15.

[150] *Topics* VIII 11 161b19–22.

[151] *Topics* VIII 11 161b26–28, 30–31.

(viii) The premises are more familiar than the conclusion, *i.e.*, they are not more difficult to argue for than the conclusion.[152]

(ix) The method of argument is appropriate to the field in question, *e.g.*, in dialectic a syllogism relies on a general proposition such as those included in the inferential *topoi*.[153]

Conditions 1–5 are logical in their nature, condition 2 being derived from the definition of *elenchus* and the others from the definition of syllogism, which were shown to be satisfied by the strategic rule for the questioner to employ the inferential locations (Section 3.b). Those numbered 6–8 are epistemic conditions included in the strategic rules for the answerer. Clearly, conditions 1–8 are relevant to philosophical inquiry. To what extent condition 9 needs to be refined for such a pursuit is an issue for further research.[154] We may conclude that the criteria Aristotle offers for assessing arguments in themselves in dialectical disputations accord with the strategic rules for the questioner and answerer. These criteria are, however, epistemically weaker than those concerning induction and solution, since they do not require the premises to be true or that the 'false' syllogisms are solved. This may be seen to justify the interpretation that the solution moves belong properly to inquiry type of dialectic, and that truth is not typically to be found in single arguments, but through *pro* and *con* argument.

10. CONCLUSION

The purpose of this paper has been to explicate the basic features of dialectic as presented in Aristotle's *Topics* in order to build a firmer basis for assessing the relevance of dialectic for philosophical inquiry and the pursuit of truth in general. Since dialectic and philosophy are for him two distinct social communication practices with their peculiar goals, dialectic forms no part of philosophy as such. One may, nevertheless, pose the question of whether dialectical skills are relevant for the argument strategies in an Aristotelian philosophical inquiry. To proceed in this task, I have explored the notion of the *topos* underlying the advice for finding arguments presented in Books II–VII, and the rules for the questioner and answerer to be found in Book VIII. In order to reveal their logical, epistemic, and psychological roles, I have divided the rules into constitutive and strategic ones, classified them into systematic groups, ordered into pairs to illuminate the complementary tasks of the discussants and, finally, investigated their relation to the criteria for assessing dialectical disputations. I have also made some remarks concerning the kinds of dialectical disputation, but this matter has

---

[152] *Topics* VIII 11 161b31–33.
[153] *Topics* VIII 11 161b33–36, 12 162b7–11.
[154] Nussbaum 1978, 108–113 discusses the relevance of the appropriateness criterion to philosophical inquiry in some of Aristotle's works. See also Freeland 1990.

not been systematically dealt with. Neither have I studied Aristotle's comments on dialectic in his other treatises.

The investigation shows that the aim of proper dialectic is good argument, in which the truth of propositions plays an eminent role. It turns out that Aristotle does not regard a single line of argument as a strong means of guaranteeing the truth of its conclusion. The limits and possibilities of dialectical argument are clarified rather by the insight that the strategic rules delineate dialectic as a continuum of *pro* and *con* moves in argument as suggested by his methodological remark in *Topics* I 2 101a34–36.

Unfortunately, Aristotle himself is not very informative about how truth is to be achieved through *pro* and *con* argument. It may even seem that at the time of writing the *Topics* he took it as an easy task – at least to those naturally gifted – to identify the true from the false as soon as the debate is carried far enough.[155]

There remains, however, the danger of the disputation turning into an agonistic and eristic one with the questioner using all his techniques to reach the contradictory of the answerer's thesis and the latter refusing to concede premises leading to the contradiction. The clue to the strategic rules is to soften this opposition built into the logic of the *elenchus* itself by establishing a social structure for a higher-level competition about dialectical skills, and hence towards good argument and truth. This holds true in an interesting way of the rules for the questioner to conceal his argument strategy, applicable both to eristic purposes and competition about skills, as well as of the corresponding rules for the answerer to mark redundant premises. The role of the audience is obviously decisive here, motivating either good or poor argument.

These results allow us to draw some conclusions concerning the different interpretations of the relevance of dialectic to philosophy in Aristotle. While the critical role of the dialectical skills is to a large extent based on the refutation form (*elenchus*) of dialectical disputations, the argument against the initial thesis has simultaneously a positive role in being and argument for its negation. Moreover, the strategic rules concerning conceptual clarification and qualification of excessive generalizations have a constructive role in generating more exact positive views. Since philosophical inquiry for Aristotle as *saving the appearances* consists of criticism, clarification and systematization of given conceptions (*endoxa*) on the matter under investigation, dialectical practice forms a good progymnastic for it, not the least because of requiring acquaintance with the very same knowledge basis. And yet, dialectical skills are not sufficient for systematizing knowledge and belief in a whole field of research. The detailed study of these issues, including argument moves available to philosophical inquiry and not belonging to dialectic, such as those allowing one to distinguish between first principles and other truths, will be left for later research.

---

[155] *Topics* VIII 14 163b9–16.

Acknowledgements

I would like to express my gratitude to the following scholars for discussions on these subjects: Lesley Brown, David Charles, Kei Chiba, Jaakko Hintikka, Martin Kusch, Martha Craven Nussbaum, Jukka Mäkinen, Pauliina Remes, Juha Sihvola, Robin Smith, Miira Tuominen, Thomas Wallgren, Charlotte Witt, and Mikko Yrjönsuuri.

References

Barnes, Jonathan, 1980, "Aristotle and the Methods of Ethics", *Revue Internationale de Philosophie* 133-134, 490-511.
Barnes, Jonathan (ed.), 1984, *The Complete Works of Aristotle*, Vol. I and II (Bollingen Series LXXI 1 and 2), Princeton University Press, Princeton/New Jersey.
Beriger, Andreas, 1989, *Die aristotelische Dialektik: Ihre Darstellung in der 'Topik' und in den 'Sophistischen Widerlegungen' und ihre Anwendung in der 'Metaphysik' M 1–3*, Carl Winter Universitätsverlag, Heidelberg.
Bolton, Robert, 1990, "The Epistemological Basis of Aristotelian Dialectic", in Daniel Devereux and Pierre Pellegrin (eds.), *Biologie, Logique et Metaphysique chez Aristote*, Éditions du CNRS, Paris, 185-236.
Bolton, Robert, 1991, "Aristotle on the Objectivity of Ethics", in John P. Anton and Anthony Preuls (eds.), *Aristotle's Ethics (Essays in Ancient Greek Philosophy IV)*, State University of New York Press, Albany, 7-28.
Bolton, Robert, 1993, "Aristotle's Account of the Socratic Elenchus", *Oxford Studies in Ancient Philosophy* 11, 121-152.
Bolton, Robert, 1994, "The Problem of Dialectical Reasoning *Sullogismos* in Aristotle", *Ancient Philosophy* 14, 99-132.
Brunschwig, Jacques, 1967, *Aristote: Topiques I–IV*, Éditions Les Belles Lettres, Paris.
Brunschwig, Jacques, 1986, "Aristotle on Arguments without Winners or Losers", *Wissenschaftskolleg* 1984/1985, Berlin, 31-40.
Burley, Walter, 1963, *Tractatus de Obligationibus*, in R. Green (ed.), *The Logical Treatise 'De Obligationibus': An Introduction with Critical Texts of William of Sherwood (?) and Walter Burley*, Ph. D. Thesis, Louvain.
Burnyeat, M. F., 1994, "Enthymeme: Aristotle on the Logic of Persuasion", in D. J. Furley and A. Nehamas (eds.), *Aristotle's Rhetoric (Proceedings of the Twelfth Symposium Aristotelicum)*, Princeton University Press, Princeton, 3-55.
Burnyeat, M. F., 1996, "Enthymeme: Aristotle on the Rationality of Rhetoric", in A. O. Rorty (ed.), *Essays on Aristotle's Rhetoric*, University of California Press, Berkeley/Los Angeles/London, 88-115.
Charles, David, 1984, *Aristotle's Philosophy of Action*, Duckworth, London.
Cherniss, H., 1944, *Aristotle's Criticism of Plato and the Academy I*, John Hopkins Press, Baltimore.
De Pater, Walter A., 1968, "La Fonction du lieu et de l'instrument dans les *Topiques*", in G. E. L. Owen (ed.), *Aristotle on Dialectic: The Topics* (Proceedings of the Third Symposium Aristotelicum), Clarendon Press, Oxford, 164-188.
Devereux, Daniel, 1990, "Comments on Robert Bolton's "The Epistemological Basis of Aristotelian Dialectic"", in Daniel Devereux and Pierre Pellegrin (eds.), *Biologie, Logique et Metaphysique chez Aristote*, Éditions du CNRS, Paris, pp. 263-286.
Evans, J. D. G., 1978, *Aristotle's Concept of Dialectic*, Cambridge University Press, Cambridge. (First ed. 1977.)
Freeland, Cynthia, 1990, "Scientific Explanation and Empirical Data in Aristotle's *Meteorology*", *Oxford Studies in Ancient Philosophy* 8, 67-102.
Green-Pedersen, Niels Jørgen, 1984, *The Tradition of the Topics in the Middle Ages: The Commentaries on Aristotle's and Boethius' "Topics"* (Philosophia), München/Wien.
Grote, G., 1872, *Aristotle II*, Alexander Bain and G. C. Robertson (eds.), London.

Hintikka, Jaakko, 1980, "Aristotelean Induction", *Revue Internationale de Philosophie* 34, 422–439.
Hintikka, J. and Bachman, J., 1991, *What If...? – Toward Excellence in Reasoning*, Mayfield Publ. Co., Mountain View Ca.
Irwin, Terence H., 1978, "First Principles in Aristotle's Ethics", in Peter A. French, Theodore E. Uehling, Jr. and Howard K. Wettstein (eds.), *Studies in Ethical Theory* (Midwest Studies in Philosophy III), University of Minnesota, Morris, 252–272.
Irwin, Terence H., 1981, "Aristotle's Methods of Ethics", in Dominic J. O'Meara (ed.), *Studies in Aristotle (Studies in Philosophy and the History of Philosophy 9)*, Washington, 193–223.
Irwin, Terence H., 1987, "Ways to First Principles: Aristotle's Methods of Discovery", *Philosophical Topics* 15, 109–134.
Irwin, Terence H., 1988, *Aristotle's First Principles*, Clarendon Press, Oxford.
Kakkuri-Knuuttila, M.-L., 1993, *Dialectic and Inquiry in Aristotle*, Helsinki School of Economics, Helsinki. Dissertation at the Department of Philosophy at the University of Helsinki.
Kakkuri-Knuuttila, Marja-Liisa and Knuuttila, Simo, 1990, "Induction and Conceptual Analysis in Aristotle", *Language, Knowledge and Intentionality: Perspectives on the Philosophy of Jaakko Hintikka (Acta Philosophica Fennica 49)*, 294–303.
Kessels, J., 2001, "Socrates Comes to Market", *Reason in Practice* 1/1, 49–71.
Le Blond, J.-M., 1970, *Logique et Méthode chez Aristote: Étude sur la recherche des principes dans la Physique aristotélicienne*, Paris. (1939)
Lloyd, G. E. R., 1968, *Aristotle: The Growth and Structure of his Thought*, Cambridge University Press, Cambridge.
Moraux, Paul, 1968, "La joute dialectique d'après le huitième livre des *Topiques*", in G. E. L. Owen (ed.), *Aristotle on Dialectic: The Topics (Proceedings of the Third Symposium Aristotelicum)*, Clarendon Press, Oxford, 277–311.
Nussbaum, Martha Craven, 1978, *Aristotle's De Motu Animalium: Text with Translation, Commentary and Interpretive Essays*, Princeton University Press, Princeton.
Nussbaum, Martha Craven, 1986, *The Fragility of Goodness: Luck and Ethics in Greek Tragedy and Philosophy*, Cambridge University Press, Cambridge.
Owen, G. E. L., 1986, "Dialectic and Eristic in the Treatment of Forms", in G. E. L. Owen, *Logic, Science and Dialectic. Collected Papers in Greek Philosophy*, Martha Craven Nussbaum (ed.), Duckworth, London, 221–238. (Orig. 1968.)
Owen, G. E. L., 1986, "Tithenai ta Phainomena", in G. E. L. Owen, *Logic, Science and Dialectic. Collected Papers in Greek Philosophy*, Martha Craven Nussbaum (ed.), Duckworth, London, pp. 239–251. (Orig. 1961.)
Plato, 1953, *The Dialogues of Plato*, B. Jowett (transl., anal., intr.), Vol. I–II, Clarendon Press, Oxford.
Primavesi, O., 1996, *Die Aristotelische Topik: Ein Interpretationsmodell und seine Erprobung am Beispiel von Topik B. (Zetemata: Monographien zur klassischen Altertumswissenschaft Heft 94)*, C. H. Beck'sche Verlagsbuchhandlung, München.
Reeve, C. D. C., 2001, "Dialectic and Philosophy in Aristotle", in Jyl Gentzler (ed.), *Method in Ancient Philosophy*, Clarendon Press, Oxford.
Ross, W. D., 1971, *Aristotle*, Methuen, London. (First ed. 1923.)
Ryle, Gilbert, 1966, *Plato's Progress*, Cambridge University Press, Cambridge.
Searle, J., 1999, *Mind, Language and Society: Philosophy in the Real World*, Basic Books, New York.
Schickert, Klaus, 1974, *Die Form der Widerlegung beim frühen Aristoteles*. Dissertation, Kiel.
Slomkowski, P., 1997, *Aristotle's Topics (Philosophia Antiqua: A Series of Studies on Ancient Philosophy Vol. LXXIV)*, Brill, Leiden/New York/Köln.
Smith, Robin, 1993, "Aristotle on the Uses of Dialectic", *Synthèse* 96, 335–358.
Smith, Robin, 1994, "Dialectic and the Syllogism", *Ancient Philosophy* Vol. XIV, 133–151.
Smith, Robin, 1997, *Aristotle: Topics Books I and VIII with Excerpts from Related Texts*, R. Smith (transl. and comm.), Clarendon Press, Oxford.
Sorabji, Richard, 1972, *Aristotle on Memory*, Duckworth, London.

Stump, Eleonore, 1978, *Boethius's De topicis differentiis*. Translated, with notes and essays on the text, Cornell University Press, Ithaca/London.
Vlastos, Gregory, 1983, The Socratic *Elenchus*, in *Oxford Studies in Ancient Philosophy I*, 27–58.
von Wright, Georg Henrik, 1971, *Explanation and Understanding*, Routledge & Kegan Paul, London.
Witt, Charlotte, 1992, "Dialectic, Motion, and Perception: *De Anima* Book I", in Martha Craven Nussbaum and Amélie Oksenberg Rorty (eds.), *Essays in Aristotle's "De Anima"*, Clarendon Press, Oxford, 169–183.
Yrjönsuuri, Mikko, 1994, *Obligations: 14th Century Logic of Disputational Duties* (*Acta Philosophica Fennica* Vol. 55), Helsinki.

E. MOUTSOPOULOS

MODERATION AND KAIROS IN THE PHILOSOPHY OF SOCRATES

Writing in the mid-20th century, the author of the most substantial monograph on Socrates, V. de Magalhães Vilhena, came to the conclusion that "none of the witnesses [to Socrates] can truly be called historical", and that "we do not have Socrates as he was"[1]. Nothing could be more true. After Aristophanes[2] and Xenophon there is Plato, who provides us with first-hand information about Socrates, even if it is information that does not enable one clearly to detect what is due to Plato and what is due to his great teacher. The picture in Xenophon's *Memorabilia* is of a Socrates preoccupied with questions of ethics[3]. Aristotle echoes Xenophon in refusing to allow Socrates a penchant for any kind of philosophical debate other than ethical, even as he recognizes Socrates as the parent of the method of induction in investigating the common elements qualifying the mutually comparable specific instances with which intellect must begin its work of unearthing the essence of a problem[4].

These contradictory conceptions, already advanced in antiquity, necessarily cast their long shadow over the diverging views of 19th-century students of Socratic philosophy. This is notoriously the case with the older German scholars. August Döring, for example, sees Xenophon's as the authentic image of Socrates, so that Plato will have appealed to Socrates purely in order to lend more weight to his own theses[5]. Karl Joel, on the other hand, will have none of the

---

[1] Magalhães Vilhena, V. de, *Le problème de Socrate. Le Socrate historique et la Socrate de Platon*, 1952, P.U.F., Paris, pp. 453 and 455; *Socrate et la légende platonicienne*, 1952, P.U.F., Paris. Cf. Dupréel, E., *La légende de Socrate et les sources de Platon*, 1922, Brussels, pp. 55 ff.; Monnier, M., *La légende de Socrate*, 1926, Paris. Cf. Robin, L., "Les Mémorables de Xenophon et notre connaissance de la philosophie de Socrate", *La pensée grecque*, 1923, Paris, p.81; Kafka, G., *Sokrates, Plato und der sokratische Kreis*, 1921; Schrempf, K., *Sokrates*, 1928; Moutsopoulos, E., *Philosophes de l'Égée*, 1991, Aegean Foundation, Athens, pp. 80–81. See also the analytical study by Fouillée, A., *La philosophie de Socrate*, 2 vols., 1874, Paris; and Brailas-Arménis, P., *La philosophie de Socrate selon A. Fouillée*, 1875, Corfu. The latter work appears in Moutsopoulos, E. & Anastassopoulou, Th. (edd.), *Pétros Brailas-Arménis Œuvres philosophiques*, vol. 5, 1978, Foundation for Research and Editions of Modern Greek Philosophy, Athens, pp.129–250 (CPGR [Corpus Philosophorum Graecorum Recentiorum], published under the direction of E. Moutsopoulos). See also Brun, J., *Socrate*, 1973, P.U.F., Paris (5th ed.), pp.114–115.
[2] Cf. Anghélopoulos, E.I., *Aristophane et ses idées sur Socrate*, 1933, Athens, pp. 37–48. Cf. Thiercy, P., *Aristophane, et l'ancienne comédie*, 1999, P.U.F., Paris, pp. 26–33.
[3] Cf. Strauss, H., *Xenophon's Socrates*, 1972; Luccioni, M., *Xénophon et le socratisme*, 1953, Paris.
[4] Cf. Deman, T., *Le témoignage d'Aristote sur Socrate*, 1942, Les Belles-Lettres, Paris, pp. 17 ff.
[5] Döring, A., *Die Lehre des Sokrates als soziales Reformsystem. Neuer Versuch zur Lösung des Problemes der sokratischen Philosophie*, 1895, Beck, Munich, pp. 33 ff.

idea that Socrates' portrait from Xenophon's brush is the only true one[6]. English scholars of the first half of the 20th century, notably J. Burnet[7], and A. E. Taylor[8], are in opposition to the preceding German tradition in taking the portrait of Socrates presented by Plato in the "Socratic" dialogues, and hence the continuity of Socrates' presence in Plato's works, as the truth. The German thinker H. Maier, a near contemporary of Burnet and Taylor, only partly espouses their view: whereas he is in agreement with them about accepting that Socrates' thought made a huge contribution to the evolution of human thought (albeit with Plato as middleman), he parts company with them when it comes to admitting the specific character that they ascribe to Socrates' contribution[9].

If all that mattered was how to evaluate what this contribution has meant to philosophy, we would be obliged to stress the innovative way in which Socrates managed to exploit the possibilities of human intelligence as he perceived them. That he introduced a new view of life is hardly deniable. *Per se*, his thesis (the authority of which remains unchallenged to this day) that "the unexamined life is not worth living"[10], reflecting the need for consciousness to maintain ceaseless vigilance when faced with day-to-day problems and, a fortiori, philosophical problems, is Socrates' way of defining a new attitude to existence. Plato has a reprise of the structure of this phrase, further on in time, in his *Statesman*: all he does is to modify its variables so as to make it applicable to a philosophy of art founded on real life. "A life not embellished with art" (he writes) "would not be worth living"[11].

Socrates was trying in his own way to introduce philosophical reasoning into a new world dominated by a respect for knowledge, a respect stemming from recognition of how important the principle of freedom is. The Presocratics had built up a corpus of knowledge about the nature of the cosmos and of human reality. Socrates, the sworn foe of the Sophists and their dispensation, for a fee, of ready-made knowledge, nevertheless kept company with them in so far as he shared the object of their concern, namely, human consciousness. And indeed, we can point to three moments in the history of philosophy when there occurred a change of target of this kind, from the external to the internal world. The first involved the Sophists and Socrates; the second, Kant; and the third, Husserl and

---

[6] Cf. Joel, K., *Der echte und der xenophontischer Sokrates*, 3 vols., 1893–1901, Berlin, vol.1, p. 33 ff.

[7] Cf. Burnet, J, *The Socratic Doctrine of the Soul*, 1916, London; *Platonism*, 1928, California Univ. Press, Berkeley (Sather Classical Lectures, vol.5); *Early Greek Philosophy*, 1930 (reissued 1948, London), chs. XII and XV.

[8] Cf. Taylor, A. E., Plato, *The Man and his Work*, new edition, with a foreword by E. Moutsopoulos, 1991, Easton Press, Norwood (Conn.), esp. pp. 24–25; cf. Taylor, A. E., *Varia socratica*, 1911, Oxford; *Socrates*, 1932, Davies, London.

[9] Cf. Maier, H., *Sokrates. Sein Werk und seine geschichtliche Stellung*, 1913, Mohr, Tübingen, pp. 73 ff. Cf. Siegel, C., *Platon und Sokrates*, 1920, Meiner, Leipzig, pp. 25–29.

[10] *Apology*, 38 a.

[11] *Statesman*, 299 e.

the tradition that began with him[12]. On further scrutiny, however, Socrates the son of Phainarete the midwife (to whom he owed his maieutic technique) is clearly differentiated from the Sophists. On Plato's showing, the latter had a knack of transforming "a weak argument into a strong argument"[13]. Socrates, however, founded his arguments on feigned ignorance, and ultimately on a single firm piece of knowledge: "the one thing that I know is that I know nothing"[14], before pursuing his path with common sense as his exclusive criterion (which is the essence of Socratic irony).

Seen in this light, the specific nature of Socrates' teaching is of signal importance. He rejects ready-made knowledge. Rather than make elaborate set speeches, he puts questions, often embarrassing ones, that unlock replies calling forth new questions; until his interlocutor, exhausted and without further recourse, is obliged to give up. The style of this type of teaching can only be understood in the context of the dialogue form, which allows the midwife technique to be applied to absolutely any enquiry whatever. It will bring the interlocutor face to face with an aporia, a dead end, and will deprive him of the chance to continue doggedly with the line of argument he has been forced into, even as he is led to choose a succession of criteria. Socrates pretends to go along with him and give him help, but in so doing he makes this quite plain to the other – perfectly aware of what is at stake each time, much like Heraclitus' infant chess-player[15], carrying out his grand strategy after each tactical move, in a spirit of intentional enjoyment of kairos. That is why Socrates has to be the central figure of every dialogue, the person pulling the strings. He can do this because his thinking is consistent: it is based on open and ceaseless recourse to the power of pure intellect. The result is an explicit recognition of the principles of reason that mark out the function field of a system of logical possibilities.

The Sophists too, to be sure, used the power of the intellect. But they did so in order to demonstrate, as and when possible, the seeming validity of both of two opposing positions; and here they were making use of a form in which the primitive mentality clothes such principles as identity and causality[16]. Socrates, by contrast, starts out from a methodical scepticism, and arrives quite deliberately at a rationalism that is, in the best sense of the word, dogmatic. For him,

---

[12] Cf. Moutsopoulos, E., *L'itinéraire de l'esprit*, vol.1: *Les êtres*, 1974, Hermes, Athens, p. 15; *Philosophes de l'Égée*, p. 84.

[13] *Apology*, 18 b: τον ηττω λογον κρειττω.

[14] *Ibid.*, 29 b: ουκ ειδως...ουτω και οιομαι ουκ ειδεναι. Cf. Reale, G., *Socrate. Alla scoperta della sapienza umana*, 2000, Rizzoli, Milano, pp. 159–161.

[15] Cf. Heraclitus, fr. B 52 D.K.16, I.162.5; *Plato, Gorgias*, 450 d; *Rep.*, 487 b–c; *Phaedrus*, 274 d; *Statesman*, 299 e; *Laws*, 820 c–e; 903 e. Cf. Moutsopoulos, E., "L'art de vivre selon Épicure: petteia et kairos", *Philosophia* 27–28 (1997–1998), pp.19–25.

[16] Cf. Lévy-Bruhl, L., *La mentalité primitive*, 1922, Alcan, Paris, republished (15th ed.) 1960, P.U.F, Paris, pp. 57–63; *Le surnaturel et la nature dans la mentalité primitive*, 1933, Alcan, Paris, new edition 1963, P.U.F, Paris, pp.13–20. Cf. Lévi-Strauss, *La pensée sauvage*, 1964, Plon, Paris, vol.1, pp. 23–29; Cazeneuve, J., *La pensée archaïque*, 1961, A.Colin, Paris, pp. 11 ff; Moutsopoulos, E., *Philosophes de l'Égée*, pp. 18–20.

any argument that is properly conducted will serve for knowledge; not just any knowledge, but knowledge related to the entire content of consciousness, in other words, the whole of the aspects of existence and human life. When things go wrong, this is because of deviation from the single road that leads to a problem's correct solution. The deviation will be out of carelessness, since "no one errs voluntarily"[17]. This is the watchword of Socratic rationalism. To insistently follow the path of philosophical investigation: that should be the philosopher's constant care. Far from being impervious to the end result, he will assign prior importance to the accidents which are in the full sense a constant guarantee that the dialogue is running along the right lines. Moreover, the majority of the dialogues written in Plato's early days, (those same "Socratic" dialogues, so called because they are thought accurately to reproduce the Master's teaching style, "are in point of fact aporetic"[18]; that is, they lead Socrates' interlocutor (as I have already pointed out) to an aporia or cul-de-sac. The most obvious thing about these dialogues is that they make clear what deviating pathway the interlocutor has been obliged to take in order to arrive at the opinion (or belief)[19] that he reckons to be true.

To grasp an object of thought properly one needs, first and foremost, exact knowledge of the range of themes in which the object under consideration (most often a specific notion) is embodied. This proper grasp is attainable only if one clearly defines the notion in play; and the definition must also take into account not only the notion's specific nature but its relation to that other notion whose particular instance it is. Its authentic sense will be revealed in return for a comparison between these two terms, using as axes the "gender and difference" which define its essence: εκ γενους και διαφορων, as Aristotle will later put it[20].

The dialectical opposition of contraries is resolved not by overriding them (the Hegelian *Aufhebung*), but by making appeal to their moderation, most often expressed as a mediety. In Plato's *Symposium*, for example, it is Diotima's teaching (which Socrates is thought to have reproduced) which overcomes the opposi-

---

[17] *Apology*, 37 a: εκων...μηδενα αδικειν. Cf. *Protag.*, 345 a, 358 c; Rep., 589 c; *Tim.*, 86 e: (κακος εκων ουδεις); *Laws* VII, 731 c; VIII, 832 e; IX, 860 c. Cf. Moutsopoulos, E., *La pensée et l'erreur*, 1961, Athens, p. 42; *La connaissance et la science*, 1972, Athens University Editions, Athens, p. 136; and by extension, see also Moutsopoulos, E., "L'homme méchant par nature: Kant contre Rousseau", *L'année 1793. Kant sur la politique et la religion (Actes du Premier Congrès de la Société Kantienne de Langue Française*, 1993), 1995, Vrin, Paris, pp.195–197.

[18] Cf. Goldschmidt, V., *Les dialogues de Platon. Structure et méthode dialectique*, 1947, P.U.F., Paris, pp. 15 –30.

[19] Cf. Lafrance, Y., *La théorie platonicienne de la Doxa*, 1981, Les Belles-Lettres & Bellarmin, Paris & Montréal, reviewed by E. Moutsopoulos, *Diotima*, 12 (1984), pp. 217–219. Cf. Moutsopoulos, E., La notion de croyance chez Platon , *Diotima*, 23 (1995), pp.143–151.

[20] Aristotle, *Topica*, A8, 103 b15: ο ορισμος εκ γενους και διαφορων εστι. Cf. *Topica*, Z4, 141 b 2; 153 b14. Cf. *Metaph.* I 7, 1057 b 7: (εκ του γενους και διαφορων τα ειδη), 1042b32 (τα γενη των διαφορων), 1030b5 (ο πρωτως και απλως ορισμος ο του τι ην ειναι των ουσιων εστι) and 1031a12 (εστιν ο ορισμος και το τι ην ειναι λογος), with *A.Po.* IV.13, 97, 26 (του καθολου και του ειδους ο ορισμος). Cp. also *Metaph.* 1036a29, 987b3, and 1087b31. Cf. also *Metaph.* A6, 987 b 3; Z11, 1036 a 29; M4, 1087 b 31.

tion between human and divine by having recourse to the notion of daimôn[21]. Although these speculations foreshadow the hallmark of Plato's doctrine of the mixed[22], it is equally true that they express certain typically Socratic considerations that may apply just as much to the domain of epistemology as to the domain of ethics and ontology. In Socrates' philosophy, virtue appears as very particularly the outcome both of exact knowledge and of a moderation, also kairic in nature, in the subject's attitude to life – a reduction of extremes of behaviour and a sort of rigorousness in the act of avoiding any excesses. For Socrates, then, moderation is not a pure form, but a genuine and essential quality that consciousness must fit with if it is to attain its purpose. What is more, moderation, under the aspect of mediety, is one of the means that consciousness uses to this end. Looked at from this angle, Socrates has tried to find the best possible reply to the attitude of most of the Sophists, whose attachment to relativism is illustrated in the extremism of their thesis. Gorgias, for instance, made no bones about recommending that the canonical proportions for sculpture should be altered so that forms seen in perspective would have a modicum of verisimilitude. Socrates was no less of an anthropocentrist than Protagoras; but his own position was that human beings are free because they are able to be consistent with themselves, and this to some extent stimulates them to train themselves in virtue[23].

Moderation as recourse to the essential quality of mediety[24], and indeed measure, and (when all is said and done) the kairos[25], freedom within the bounds of consistency, ceaseless investigation of right action in knowledge as well as conduct: these are, historically, the principal contributions of Socratic thought to philosophy. To take Socrates as par excellence the lasting model of the philosopher is no mere invention. He remains the lover of wisdom as well as of life, proceeding to teach people by jolting up people, and by offering himself as an example of the consistency in virtue that let him face death with unconcern and disdain.

---

[21] *Symposium*, 202 d ff. Cf. *Apol.*, 27 d, *Phaedo*, 107 d, *Phaedrus*, 240 b. Cf. also Moutsopoulos, E., "Sur l'idée de médiété ontologique", *Les corps intermediaires* (IVe Colloque d'Athènes), 1986, Piraeus School of Higher Studies in Industry, Athens, pp. 296–301.

[22] Cf. Boussoulas, N. I., *L'être et la composition des mixtes dans le Philèbe de Platon*, 1952, P.U.F., Paris, pp. 19–27 and 75–77; "L'esthétique platonicienne", *Actes du IVe Congrès International d'Esthétique*, 1960, Athens, pp. 749–754.

[23] *Phaedo*, 93 e: η...αρετη αρμονια...ειη; *Gorgias*, 479 d, 504 e, 506 d; *Rep.*, 403 d, 407 a, 444 d, 554 e, 613a; *Philebus*, 64 e: (μετριοτης...και ξυμμετρια καλλος δηπου και αρετη πανταχου ξυμβαινει γιγνεσθαι); *Laws*, X, 886 b, 903 b.

[24] Cf. Moutsopoulos, E., "Sur l'idée de médété ontologique", pp. 296–301.

[25] Cf. Moutsopoulos, E., "Kairos ou l'humanisation du temps", *Diotima*, 16 (1988), pp. 129–131.

Part II

Questioning as a Philosophical Method in the Middle Ages

TOMÁS CALVO MARTINEZ

ON THE ORIGIN AND EXTENT OF QUESTIONING
IN THE MIDDLE AGES

I

It is well known that *quaestio* makes the most characteristic part of philosophical and theological methodology in the Middle Ages. And it is also generally acknowledged that the interweaving of *quaestio* and *disputatio* (of question and dispute) in the form of *quaestio disputata* (disputed question) developed naturally and gradually as an academic device in schools and universities through the Middle Ages. The starting point of this development – both logically and chronologically – was the *lectio*, that is, the *reading of texts* in order to understand and to assimilate their meaning. Of course, the reader of a written text can stumble, and frequently does, on passages that are obscure and difficult to understand. In such a case the *lectio* gives rise to an aporetic situation, to a *quaestio* whose solution requires *disputatio*, argumentation.

This brief opening statement on the origin and development of the medieval *quaestio* as a method is, to my mind, historically adequate and can be easily proved to be so. Therefore, I will neither accumulate textual evidences as proof nor adduce erudite details or quotations.[1] However, I would like to emphasize an

---

[1] There are many good works available on the medieval methods of teaching, and specifically on *lectio, quaestio* and *disputatio*. The following books and articles include interesting information and discussion on our topic: M. D. Chenu, *Introduction a l'étude de Saint Thomas D'Aquin*. Paris, Vrin, 1954 (cf. particularly ch.2: "Les œvres. Leur genres littéraires"); P. Glorieux, "L'enseignement au moyen age. Techniques et méthodes", *Archives d'histoire doctrinal et littéraire du moyen age*, 1968, 65–186; G. Paré, A. Brunet, P. Temblay, *La renaissance du XIIe siècle. Les écoles et l'enseignement*. Paris–Otawa, 1933 (cf. particularly ch. 3: "Matières et procédés d'enseignement"); N. Kretzmann, A. Kenny, J. Pinborg ed., The Cambridge *History of Later Medieval Philosophy*, Cambridge, Cambridge Univ. Press 1982 (with extensive bibliography); D. L. Wagner ed., *The seven Liberal Arts in the Middle Ages*, Indiana Univ. Press 1986; E.Stump, "Dialectics", D.L. Wagner ed., *o.c.*, pp. 125–46; *Les genres littéraires dans les sources théologiques et philosophiques médiévales (Actes du Colloque intenational de Louvain-la-Neuve 25–27 mai 1981)*, particularly the articles by P. Hadot, "La préhistoire des genres littéraires philosophiques médiévaux dans l'antiquité (pp. 1–10), by C. Viola, "Manières personelles et impersonelles d'aborder un problème: Saint Augustin et le XIIe siècle. Contribution a l'histoire de la quaestio" (pp.11–30), and by B. C. Bazan, "La *quaestio disputata*" (pp. 31–50); O. Weijers, L. Holtz ed., *L'enseignement des disciplines à la Faculté des arts. Paris et Oxford, XIIIe–XVe siècles*. Brepols 1997: see the articles by A. H. G. Draakhuis, "Logica modernorum as a discipline" (pp. 129–145), A. Maierù, "Les cours: *lectio* et *lectio cursoria*" (pp. 373–391) and O. Weijers, "La disputatio" (pp.393–404); L. Bianchi, E. Randi, *Filosofi e teologi. La ricerca e l'insegnamento nell'università medievale*. Bergamo, 1989 (in pp. 109–143 there is an Italian version of the article by J. Pingborg, A. Kenny, "La letteratura filosofica medievale", from *The Cambridge History of Later Medieval Philosophy*).

aspect of the whole issue that I consider to be essential in order to understand the scope and the extent of the medieval *quaestio* as a methodological and didactical practice.

The point I want to stress is that the medieval *quaestio* originates in *lectio*, that is, *in reading*. This important fact clarifies what the intellectual horizon of the Middle Ages was – *the written text*. Indeed, the most important text was the Sacred Book (*pagina sacra*), i.e. the Bible. But besides the Bible, and in addition to it, other texts were accepted as authoritative, such as the writings of the Fathers of the Church, as well as the Greco-Latin writings transmitted either directly from the very beginning or later in translations from the 12th Century on. The Medieval thinkers, then, can be said to assume that *truth has to be found in the written texts* and, therefore, that research fundamentally consists of *the hermeneutical search for meaning*. Of course, this does not mean that questions and arguments do not go beyond the texts. Discussing texts always implies discussing the problems dealt within them. But it certainly means that problems become discussed within the framework of their textual transmitted embodiment. On the other hand, and in connection to this, it is important to take into account that the Medieval Thinkers are inheritors of a hermeneutical tradition initiated by the Fathers of the Church who had already offered a theory of meaning, of the plurality of meanings in the Holy Scripture. This theory was assumed, elaborated on and systematically applied from the beginning of the Middle Ages.[2]

II

The basic intellectual attitude that dominates medieval thought in its whole is *the search for the meaning of texts*. However, we have to recognize that there is *no substantial originality* at this point. This kind of search constitutes a basic intellectual attitude which is not originally from this historical period, but belongs to a hermeneutical option widely shared among the Christian thinkers from the Patristic days. Maybe the most fortunate expression of such an attitude in the Middle Ages can be found in the famous formula by Saint Anselm "fides

---

[2] Thus, Saint Bede the Venerable distinguishes four fundamental and eight allegoric meanings: "Allegoria verbi sive operis aliquando *historicam* rem (facti), aliquando *typicam* (spiritualis), aliquando *tropologicam*, id est moralem rationem, aliquando *anagogen*, hoc est sensum ad superiora ducentem figurate denunciat" (PL 90, 175). Like Saint Bede, Rabanus Maurus distinguishes two main meanings, the literal and the figurative: "Sunt autem signa propria vel translata. Propria dicuntur signa cum his rebus significandis adhibentur propter quod sunt instituta... Translata sunt, cum et ipsae res quas propriis verbis significamus, ad aliquid aliud significandum usurpantur" In turn, the figurative meaning is threefold: *allegorical* (which unveils supernatural truths and corresponds to Bede's typical meaning), *tropological* (which moves us to virtuous life) and *anagogical* (which unveils the meaning of our own existence): "*Historia* namque perfectorum exempla quae narrat, legentem ad imitationem sanctitatis excitat; *allegoria* in fidei revelatione ad cognitionem veritatis; *tropologia* in instructione morum ad amorem virtutis; *anagogia* in manifestatione sempiternorum ad desiderium aeternae felicitatis" (*Allegoriae in universam sacram scripturam*, PL 107, 384). This classification will be accepted and explained by Aquinas. *Cf. Summa Theol.* I, a. 1, q. 10.

quaerens intellectum", i.e. the faith that *looks for (quaerere)* intelligence, the faith that searches for and tries to find understanding. However, as is well known, this formula is inspired in Saint Augustine who tries to justify the search for intellectual clarification on part of the believer by referring to some sentences in the Bible.[3] This Anselmian proposal, which is the Augustinian one, is the *attitude adopted by the (moderate) "dialecticians" against the "antidialecticians"* in the 11th Century. Saint Augustine refers to "dialectics" in the following text, often quoted, from his essay *On Christian Doctrine*: *"the discipline of disputing is highly suitable to delve into and resolve all kinds of questions that can be found in the Holy Scriptures"*.[4] The reader of the Bible, then, finds himself often confronted with questions, and tries to find out an answer through dialectical discussion.

This general picture of medieval questioning rests on the broadest meaning of the verb *quaerere* and the noun *quaestio*. As we all know, these words have two meanings in Latin that our languages also have of the verb and noun ("to question" and "a question"). In the first place and in its widest meaning, *quaerere* is to look for, to inquire about, and *quaestio* is the search, the inquiry in order to find a solution to a problem, as well as the problem itself whose solution is sought. In the second place, and in a more restricted and specific sense, *quaerere* is to "ask a question" and to discuss, and *quaestio* is a question and a discussion. We could say that search or inquiry takes the form of a *quaestio* in its more restricted sense, i.e. as "asking questions", when the search takes place in a dialogical context or situation. No doubt, the most characteristic medieval *quaestio*, the disputed *quaestio*, takes place in a dialogical context.

As far as *quaestio disputata* is concerned, I think we should introduce a further distinction: on the one hand, *quaestio disputata* is an oral *exercise of discussion* between masters and bachelors, or masters and disciples at schools and at universities; on the other hand, it is a specific *literary-philosophical genre* which arose from the oral disputations themselves.

This distinction brings us to the literary-philosophical genres. The literary genre closer to living dialogue is, of course, the dialogue form. Three circum-

---

[3] Thus, for example, the passage from Isaiah 1, 18 that says *"venite ad me et disputate, dicit Dominus"* – the Vulgate translates *"venite et arguite me"* – or the passage from Mathew 7, 7: *"quaerite et invenietis"* that could be translated as "search, or try to find, and you will find". This is St. Augustine's text: "Nam si sapientia et veritas non totis animi viribus concupiscatur inveniri nullo pacto potest. At si illa quaeratur, ut dignum est, subtrahere sese atque abscondere a suis dilectoribus non potest. Hinc est illud, quod in ore habere etiam vos soletis, quod ait: *petite et accipietis; quaerite et invenietis; pulsate et aperietur vobis* (Matth. 7,7)... Amore petitur, amore quaeritur...", etc. (*Contra academicos* I, c.17).

[4] "Sed disputationis disciplina ad omnia genera quaestionum, quae in litteris sanctis sunt, penetranda et dissolvenda plurimum valet" (*De doctrina christiana* (II, 31, 48). This "discipline of disputing" (*disputationis disciplina*) is dialectics. Saint Augustine himself names dialectics *disputatoria*, a word which is no more than a translation to Latin of the Greek word διαλεκτικʺ (*Cf. Contra Cresconium*, PL 43, 4559).

stances are worthy of mentioning in connection to this. Firstly, the word *quaestio* in its plural: *Quaestiones*, was familiar as a title for written texts from antiquity to the Middle Ages. Secondly, these *Quaestiones* were often presented in dialogue form, by question and answer. Thus, Saint Augustine wrote dialogues with this title in the late Antiquity,[5] as did Saint Isidorus and Alcuin also in the early Middle Ages. Thirdly and finally, one has to take into account that the medieval writers of dialogues were inheritors of a long tradition leading back to Greek philosophic literature: also in Greek we find these kinds of texts, some of them written under the title ζητήματα, which literally means *Quaestiones*. It certainly would be interesting to work out a systematic *typology* of different kinds of philosophical dialogues, for example, by distinguishing the "heuristic" dialogues from the "didactic" ones; or the disciple questions from the ones where the master is the one questioning; or the dialogues about topics from the ones about texts (remember that Porphyry's *Isagoge* is written in dialogue-form), etc. In any case, *dialogue as a literary genre reflects the traditional practice of dialogue in philosophical education.*

Not only the written dialogues, but all the main medieval literary-philosophical genres can be said to reflect the current educational practices.[6] Thus, the genre "Commentary" reflects the practice of *expositio*, i.e. the explanation of the text along with the reading of it. And the *Quaestio*, as a literary genre, reflects, in turn, the oral disputation on questions. Some written *Quaestiones* were surely close to the corresponding oral disputations, since they originated in notes taken by attendants to them. They were named *Reportationes*. Other *Quaestiones* were not the outcome of actual disputations. Nevertheless, they also reflected the logical structure of the oral exercise of disputation. As for the historical origin of the practice of Commentary and Disputation, one has to take into account that also they both belong to a long tradition originated in Greek educational practices. The dialectical structure and rules of *disputatio* were transmitted to the Middle Ages, either directly or indirectly, from Aristotle.[7]

---

[5] On the genre *Quaestiones* in Saint Augustine, and on his influence in the Middle Ages, cf.. C. Viola, *art.cit.* The author distinguishes the *Quaestiones* written in a personal form (*De diversis quaestionibus ad Simplicianum, De VIII quaestionibus Dulcitii*) from the ones written in an impersonal form.

[6] On the relation of literary-philosophical genres to the school practice in Medieval Ages, cf. M. D. Chenu, *o.c.*, pp. 67–83. Further historical references to antiquity can be found in P. Hadot's quoted article.

[7] Some scholars have conjectured that medieval *disputatio* stems *directly* from Aristotle. According to them, it would have originated as a *direct* application of the Aristotelian "aporetic" method (such as it is applied, for example, in the *Nic. Eth.* VII,1). To my mind, there are not significant evidences or reasons for this conjecture. Other scholars locate the origin of medieval *disputatio* in the spreading of the knowledge of the rules proposed by Aristotle in the *Topics*. These rules appear exposed and commented in J.Salisbury's *Metalogicon* (book III), indeed. Nevertheless, the essentials of medieval *disputatio* seem to be earlier than the spreading of Aristotles's *Topics*, as can be seen from Abelardus' *Sic et Non* which is meant to supply a useful instrument for the *already existing* practice of disputing questions. Other scholars have emphasized the influence of the hermeneutic

III

Let us go on to the structure and methodology of the medieval *quaestio* and questioning. Let us start by pointing out that the formulation and development of any question must be submitted to some suitable logical and methodological rules in order to find an appropriate answer to it. In the Middle Ages the rules and logical instruments were provided by dialectics, by the *disputandi disciplina*.

To my mind, the following two statements can be accepted to be historically true about the place and importance of dialectics in the shaping of medieval method and thinking: (1) Firstly, that the medieval conception of dialectics is a complicated one, its complexity reflecting, in turn, the complexity acquired by this notion from Plato until the late Greek commentators; (2) secondly, that the dialectic instruments involved in the medieval *quaestio* and *disputatio* were available to the medieval thinkers from the very beginning of the Middle Ages. Therefore, they were available before Aristotle's works became completely translated and known in the XII and XIII centuries. Thus, literary masterpieces such as Abelardus' *Sic et non*, as well as the *Sententiae* by Petrus Lombardus, or even the articulation of the *quaestiones* (*articuli*) in Theological Summae (such as the one by Aquinas) seem not to owe anything substantial to the so-called *logica nova* whose influence appears to have moved in some specific directions.

1. As I have pointed out, the notion of dialectics transmitted to the Middle Ages is rather intricate and many-faced. Historically, its complexity came from an attempt to harmonize the different uses and meanings of the word "dialectics" from the time of Plato and Aristotle. As we all know, the concept of dialectics is linked originally to dialogue (to διαλἰγεσθαι). In the *Cratylus* Plato defines the dialectician as "the one who knows how to question and answer" (390A). However, Plato himself – even if he did not completely abandon the connection of dialectics with dialogue – spread the use of the word "dialectic" to name a method that included both uniting and dividing as the main logical procedures. (Cf. specially the *Phaedrus* and the *Sofist*). He also referred to a set of specific rules for testing statements by means of other statements either deduced from them or belonging to a higher theoretical level. (Cf. particularly, the *Phaedo* and the *Republic*). In the *Republic*, dialectics comes to be considered both as logic and as ontology, i.e. both as a method and as a science. It is the highest knowledge, science par excellence. This conception can be found in Saint Augustine, for example, when he defines (perfect) dialectics as *scientia veritatis*, as *"Science of the Truth"*. So, referring to this Platonic conception of dialectics, Saint

---

methodology of jurists. (Cf. J. Pinborg, A. Kenny, *art.cit.*, pp.122–123. On the juridical "questions", cf. infra, n. 20).

Augustine says that "it is either wisdom itself or something without which wisdom can not be achieved at all".[8]

Aristotle, on the other hand, rejected this Platonic epistemic and ontological proposal. He returned dialectics to the context of dialogue, to the discussion on debatable questions belonging to the realm of opinion. In this context, Aristotle insists on *two features* of dialectics: its necessary resource to commonly accepted opinions, i.e. to those opinions which are worthy of credit (τὰ ἔνδοξα) and its ability to argue in favor of a given thesis and of its contradictory statement. Both features of dialectics will make up essential elements in the medieval method of *quaestio*: the systematic displaying of opposed authoritative "sentences" (*sententiae*) as well as the practice of arguing in favor of the two alternative answers to the disputed question.

One could still mention other ancient conceptions of dialectics such as the ones by Diodorus Cronus, by the skeptic academic Arcesilaos, and very specially that of the Stoics. The Stoics worked with a broad concept of logic that not only included what we call today "logic", but also grammar and rhetoric insofar as all of these three disciplines deal with *logos*, with language. More specifically, they defined dialectics as "*the science of correct discussion in regard to discourses conducted by question and answer*" and also as "*the science of what is true and false, and neither <of these>*" (Diog. Laert. 7,42).

The attempt to systematize all of these conceptions of dialectics lead to conceiving it as "logic" in the broadest sense of the word *logic*. The latter alexandrine commentators of Aristotle and Porphyry assigned four fundamental methods to it: division, definition, demonstration and analysis.[9] Before them, the middle-platonist Albinus (or Alcinoos) had systematized these four devices as instruments for knowledge. According to Albinus, the knowledge of a thing can either refer to its essence (to what it is) or to its properties. In relation to essence, the search can proceed either upward or downward: if it proceeds downward, the proper method is *division* that would lead into *definition*; if it proceeds upwards, we are left with *analysis* or resolution. As for the knowledge of properties, the suitable instrument is *demonstration*.[10]

The systematic ordering of these dialectical instruments in late antiquity came sometimes to reduce them to only the first three (i.e. to division, definition and demonstration), leaving analysis aside. This is the case with Porphyry who

---

[8] "Igitur Plato, adiiciens lepori subtilitatique socraticae, quam in moralibus habuit, naturalium divinarumque rerum peritiam, quam ab eis quos memorabi diligenter acceperat subiungensque quasi formatricem illarum partium iudicemque dialecticam, *quae aut ipsa esset aut sine qua omnino sapientia esse non posset*, perfectam dicitur composuisse philosophiae disciplinam, de qua nunc disserere tempus non est" (*Contra Academicos* III, 12, 36).

[9] This quaternary classification can be found, for example, in David Armenius (*In Porphyrii isagogen commentarium*, 88.9) as well as in Ammonius Hermias (*In Porphyrii isagogen sive quinque voces*, 34.17).

[10] Cf. Albinus (Alcinoos), *Didaskalikós*, c. 5, 1.

refers only to the three mentioned devices in his *Eisagoge*.[11] And this is also the case with Boethius for whom "*logic, which is the skill in arguing* (peritia disserendi), *deals with definition, division, and reasoning* (*or demonstration*: collectio)". (*In topica Ciceronis*. PL 64, 1045). This very same tripartite classification can be found also in Saint Augustine for whom dialectics works "by defining, distributing, reasoning" *(definiendo, distribuendo, colligendo*: *De ordine* II, 12, 36. Cf. also *Soliloquia* 11, 20).

This is the way dialectics and its methods were mainly transmitted to the Middle Ages. Nevertheless, one can find some exceptions to it. One notable exception can be found in John Eriugena who assumes the more complex classification we found in Albinus together with the corresponding Greek terminology: *diairetiké, horistiké, apodiktiké, analytiké*.[12] His book *De divina praedestinatione* – his well known contribution to the dispute about dual predestination – constitutes an early medieval example of the argumentative powers of these dialectical procedures.[13]

2. Within the framework of the *trivium* (of the three arts of language) dialectics was transmitted, then, as logic in its broadest sense, as well as the specific *art of discussing or disputing*. Saint Isidorus' definition conveys this idea clearly and explicitly. As opposed to rhetoric – which is the art or science of speaking well (*bene dicendi*) –, dialectics is the art of "arguing well" (*bene disputandi*): "*dialectics is a skill that was invented to discuss the causes of things. It is that part of philosophy known as logic, that is, as rational, capable of defining, of inquiring* (quaerendi) *and of arguing* (disserendi). *It does, in effect, teach how to distinguish what is true from what is false by means of discussion in several kinds of questions*".[14] Its usefulness, therefore, becomes specifically linked to *quaerere* (as it is characterized as *quaerendi potens*, and can be applied *in pluribus generi*-

---

[11] According to R. E. Witt (*Albinus and the History of Middle Platonism*, Cambridge, 1937, p. 36 ss.), this tripartite classification of logical methods originated in Antiochus of Ascalon. This suggestion has been accepted by P. Hadot (*Marius Victorinus*, Paris, 1971, p. 120).

[12] "Conficitur inde veram esse philosophiam veram religionem, conversimque veram religionem esse veram philosophiam. Quae dum multifariam, diversisque modis dividatur, *bis binas partes principales ad omnem quaestionem solvendam necessarias habere dignoscitur*, quas graecis placuit nominare διαιρετικ˝, ὁριστικ˝, ἀποδεικψικ˝, ἀναλυτικ˝, easque latialiter possumus dicere: divisoriam, definitivam, demonstrativam, resolutivam..." The title of this chapter is worthy of quoting: "Quadrivio regularum totius philosophiae quattuor omnem quaestionem solvi" (*Liber de praedestinatione* I, I: PL 122, 357–358).

[13] An analysis of this book can be found in G. D'Onofrio, *Fons Scientiae. La dialettica nell'Occidente tardo-antico*. Napoli, Lignori ed., 1986, 275–320.

[14] "Dialectica est disciplina ad disserendas rerum causas inventa. Ipsa est philosophiae species quae logica dicitur, id est, rationalis, *definiendi, quaerendi et disserendi potens*. Docet enim in pluribus generibus quaestionum quemadmodum disputando vera et falsa diiudicentur" (*Etym*. l.II). Alcuinus follows this definition almost *ad pedem litterae*: "Dialectica est disciplina rationalis quaerendi, diffiniendi et disserendi, etiam vera a falsis discernendi potens" (*De dialectica*, PL 101, col. 952–953).

bus quaestionum), and together with *quaerere,* it becomes linked to *disputare.* So, Saint Isidorus, after introducing the seven liberal arts, refers to dialectics with the following words: *"the third one, also called logic, distinguishes what is true from what is false by means of subtle argumentation"*.[15]

IV

In order to develop any question properly and skilfully it is not enough to have the logical, *formal* instruments available. No doubt they are necessary, but insufficient. In addition to them, it is also necessary to possess some rules or *criteria to discover the most appropriate arguments*. Once again, Aristotle had offered a fundamental key and guideline to this point. On the one hand, Aristotle emphasizes the affinity between dialectic and rhetoric ways of arguing. On the other hand, he proposes a general theory of topics, of the *topoi,* i.e., of the suitable places to find arguments in both arts. In his *Rhetoric* he says the following: *"I say, therefore, that dialectical and rhetorical syllogisms are those about which we propose common places. And all of these refer to matters of justice, physics, politics, and a multitude of issues specifically different as happens for example with the common place of more or less..."*.[16] Thanks to this Aristotelian link between dialectics and rhetoric, the topics (i.e. the places where arguments lie and can be found: *sedes argumentorum*) had a broader opportunity to become a relevant part of the medieval heritage. Thus, they came with rhetoric, through Cicero and the commentaries by Marius Victorinus and by Boethius on the Ciceronian *Topica* and *De inventione,* as well as Boethius' *De topicis differentiis.*

Boethius' role was fundamental, no doubt, in the assimilation and integration of the topics.[17] Boethius interpreted topics in two ways. On the one hand, the topics are "maximal propositions" (*maximae propositiones*), "common conceptions" (*animi communes conceptiones,* i.e. the Greek κοιναὶ ἔννοιαι). They are universal and evident statements, "propositions that everyone agrees with when they hear them" (*enuntiatio quam quisque probat auditam*). Arguments rest upon them and take their strength from them. On the other hand, the maximal propositions, many as they are, can be gathered and classified into different categories. These universal categories or headings under which maximal propositions can be grouped are named also *topics.* Boethius insisted also on the usefulness of the

---

[15] "Tertia dialectica cognomento logica, quae disputationibus subtilissimis vera secernit a falsis". (*Etim.* 1,2, 1–3). On the use of the terms *logica* and *dialectica* in the Middle Ages, cf. P. Michaud-Quantin, *Etudes sur le vocabulaire philosophique du Moyen Age.* Roma, ed. Dell' Ateneo, 1970, pp. 59–72.

[16] λέγω γὰρ διαλεκτικούς τε καὶ ητορικοὺς συλλογισμοὺς εἶναι περὶ ὧν τοὺς τόπους λέγομεν· οὗτοι δ' εἰσὶν οἱ κοινοὶ περὶ δικαίων καὶ φυσικῶν καὶ περὶ πολιτικῶν καὶ περὶ πολλῶν διαφερόντων εἴδει, οἷον ὁ τοῦ μᾶλλον καὶ ἧττον τόπος (*Rhet.* I 2, 1358a11–14).

[17] E. Stump has pointed out that we know at least fifteen commentaries on Boethius' *De topicis differentiis* written in the 12th Century (cf. *art.cit.*, D. L. Wagner ed., *The Seven Liberal Arts in the Middle Ages,* p. 139).

topics for demonstrative, not only for dialectic arguments. Demonstrative reasoning rests on necessary arguments (on *rationes necessariae*), while dialectic arguing deals with probable arguments (with *rationes probabiles*). Nevertheless, there are arguments which are both, necessary and probable. Therefore, *"when the places of probable arguments are explained, it happens that also the places of the necessary ones become taught"*.[18]

Rhetoric contributed to the medieval *quaestio* in another aspect that, in my opinion, is also worthy of mentioning. I mean the interesting distinction established in handbooks of rhetoric between *quaestio finita* and *quaestio infinita*. An infinite question (called various ways: *propositum* by Cicero himself[19], as well as by Boethius, an after them by Saint Isidore, etc.) is a question proposed in the most general way by leaving out any reference to particular persons, places, time, etc., while finite questions are limited to particular cases. Now, finite questions belong to oratory, whereas *infinite questions are more of a philosophic nature*, given their generality. Even more, in the context of the handbooks of rhetoric, there is a strong tendency to call a finite question *causa*, reserving the word *quaestio* for "philosophic", infinite questions.[20]

V

These are the fundamental dialectic tools transmitted from late antiquity to the Middle Ages. These tools were used from the beginning in medieval controversies, even before the academic ordinance of *quaestio disputata*. In turn, the development of these instruments made it possible for the disputed questions to become formally instituted. This was carried out systematically by gathering together the authoritative sentences, by opposing them, by finding and developing dialectic arguments for and against the opposed sentences, and by making a final magisterial decision.

---

[18] "Sed quoniam (ut dictum est) probabilium argumentorum alia sunt necessaria, alia non necessaria, cum loci probabilium argumentorum ducuntur, evenit ut necessariorum quoque doceantur. Quo fit ut oratoribus quidem ac dialecticis haec principaliter facultas paretur, secundo vero loco philosophis" (*De top. diff.* L.II (PL 64, 1182). Cf. also John of Salisbury's *Metalogicon* III, 5 (PL 199, 902).

[19] "Quaestionum duo sunt genera: alterum infinitum, alterum definitum: Definitum est quod ὑπόθεσιν Graeci, nos *causam*. Infinitum, quod θέσιν illi appelant, nos *propositum* possumus nominare". (*Topica*, 21. Cf. also *De inventione* I, 6, *Partitiones oratoriae* 18, and *Orator* 14). The same distinction and terminology can be found in Boethius' *De differentiis topicis* I (PL 64, 1177) and later on in John of Salisbury's *Metalogicus* II, 12 (PL 122, 869).

[20] Rhetoric contributed to medieval methodology in other important ways. Thus, one should take into account the juridical technique of questioning related to the *genus legale*. This "oratorial" genus deals with the interpretation of laws when interpreters find themselves confronted with a "conflict of rules". Rhetoricians used to distinguish four kinds of hermeneutic problems concerning the right interpretation of laws: *scriptum et voluntas, leges contrariae, syllogismus* and *ambiguitas*. (Cf. H. Lausberg, *Handbuch der literarischer Rhetoric. Eine Grundlegung der Literaturwischenschaft*. München, Max Hueber Verlag, 1960, par. 193–223).

These are, in my mind, the main historic-philosophical facts about the medieval *quaestio* and questioning as a method. From this panoramic view, I would like to go one step further offering some brief philosophical comments on this. My comments will start in the form of a question (which is, in reality, a meta-question, as it is a question about the medieval question): What teachings can *we* get from the medieval *quaestio* concerning its philosophical relevance?

1. In the first place, I would say that the origin and development of the medieval *quaestio* make it clear that *questions always arise within some specific given framework*. It is the framework that makes them not only relevant, but even possible to arise. Professor Quine wrote that "there is no cosmic exile". I would say that *there is no cultural historical exile* either.

As I have stated in the beginning of my contribution, *the general framework within which the questions arise in the Middle Ages is the textual legacy,* texts transmitted through the years, and very specially, the Bible. It is true that many of the cultural improvements achieved in the Middle Ages did not come about from needs directly related to the understanding of the sacred texts. So, the Carolingian Renaissance and the creation of the palatine schools arose from the practical need to have better-educated and competent clerks. Again, neither the increase of the knowledge of Greek and Arabic texts nor the founding of universities had an immediate relationship with hermeneutic necessities of Christianity. This is all well and good, but it is just as certain that these cultural improvements became incorporated into the established intellectual framework.

But if the intellectual framework is the textual heritage, *the corresponding fundamental belief is that truth has to be sought in the texts*. I use the word "belief" not in any psychological or epistemological meaning, but in a more functional and hermeneutic sense. I use it in a sense closer to the meaning Ortega y Gasset gave it when he contrasted ideas ("ideas") and beliefs ("creencias"). Ortega y Gasset said *"las ideas se tienen, en las creencias se está"*, that is, "one has ideas, one stays on beliefs". Ideas are thought about, questioned and discussed. Beliefs constitute the *non-questioned ground by which we are supported* and staying on which we produce ideas and, eventually, question them.[21]

---

[21] Modern Science and Philosophy originated together with the abandoning of this medieval belief. The following text by R.Descartes unequivocally shows that the medieval intellectual frame has been definitively left behind: "C'est pourquoi, sitôt que l'âge me permit de sortir de la sujétion de mes précepteurs, je quittai entièrment l'étude des lettres. Et me résolvant de ne chercher plus d'autre science, que celle qui se pourrait trouver en moi-même, ou bien dans le grand livre du monde, j'employai le reste de ma jeunesse à voyager..." (*Discours de la Méthode* I). In his well known commentary on this work E.Gilson emphasizes: "Descartes knows by personal experience that science is not to be found in books. Therefore, he does not give up reading, but believing that reading can be an effective method to discover the truth" (E. Gilson, *René Descartes. Discours de la Méthode*. Paris, Vrin, 1976, 5 éd., p. 142).

2. In so far as these are the medieval beliefs and intellectual framework, the questions will naturally emerge from the text or about the text. This can happen in several different ways. Sometimes the text has left a question explicitly open without making any unequivocal decision on it. This was the case, for example, of the famous dispute on universals in the 11th Century, to quote a more strictly philosophical question. As is well known, both Porphyry's text and Boethius' commentary on it did not make any decision on the ontological status of genres and species. In other cases, a quaestio arises when there are different or opposite qualified interpretations for the same text.[22] Hence the importance of bringing forward these qualified opinions or "sentences" and of discussing them, and hence also the importance of the final magisterial "decision" (determinatio) that closes up the whole disputation. Finally, there can be cases in which a quaestio or controversy arises when different authoritative texts bring along doctrines which appear to be inconsistent with each other.

3. This last situation – i.e. the incompatibility between doctrines proposed in different texts – became, in my opinion, of special importance in the development of philosophical thought in the Middle Ages. In the first place, we may remember the renewal of theological controversies on the resurrection of Christ and on the virginity of Mary. These controversies took place in the 11th Century, before the formal establishment of the quaestio. They arose from the inconsistency between these Christian beliefs and some "necessary reasons" (rationes necessariae), such as si natus est morietur (if one is born, he will die) or si peperit, cum viro concubuit (if she gave birth, she had sexual relations with a man). These rationes necessariae were connected with "maximal propositions" in handbooks of rhetoric. So, they had a textual support. And all of it gave rise to further dispute and philosophical arguments on necessity and probability. Secondly, from a different historical point of view, particularly from the 12th Century on, the incorporation of previously unknown philosophical texts increased the conflicts between texts. The Averroism constitutes the most remarkable instance, although it was not the only one.[23] As for the rest, these conflicts make

---

[22] This is explicitly emphasized by Abelardus in the Prologue to his *Sic et non*: "his autem praelibatis, placet, ut instituimus, diversa Sanctorum Patrum dicta colligere, quando nostrae ocurrerint memoriae *aliqua ex dissonantia, quam habere videntur, quaestionem contrahentia*, quae teneros lectores ad maximum inquirendae veritatis exercitium provocent et acutiores ex inquisitione reddant. *Haec quippe prima sapientiae clavis definitur, assidua scilicet seu frequens interrogatio...Dubitando enim ad inquisitionem venimus; inquirendo veritatem percipimus*; juxta quod et veritas ipsa: quaerite, inquit, et invenietis, pulsate et aperietur vobis (Matth.VII)" (PL 178, 1349).

[23] One could mention the new conception of "nature" that developed in the 12th Century: nature became considered as something to be physically explained (as *causarum series*), instead of as a "sacred book" to be allegorically interpreted. This new conception of "nature" arose from the reading of Greek and Arab texts newly translated (such as the writings of Ptolomy, Galen, Albumasar, Alfarghani, Alfarabi and Avicenna, among others). Cf. T. Gregory, "La nouvelle idée de nature au XII siècle", J. E. Murdoch and E. D. Sylla, ed., *The Cultural Context of Medieval Learning*, Dordrecht-Boston, 1975, pp. 193–218.

evident, in my opinion, that new questions did not come from the discovery of newly observed facts, but from the knowledge of new texts. And they also show the medieval links between thought, teaching and lectio: what was prohibited in Paris was the reading of the averroist texts.

4. However, one has to agree that in the moment of its greatest strength the medieval thinking managed to "separate" the posing and discussing of questions from the reading of texts. In this way questioning acquired autonomy as quaestio disputata in the 13th Century.[24] Postponing important questions for more detailed discussion might have been the intermediate step between the dispute of questions along with the reading of texts and the independent proposal and discussion of them. In relation to this we can also remember the famous quaestiones quodlibetales or quaestiones de quolibet, which were questions about any issue considered of current interest by anyone and/or by the master himself who proposed the quaestio. It was in this kind of academic exercises that quaestio became institutionally independent. Nevertheless, also these quaestiones quodlibetales were formally regulated by the established methodology. As any other quaestio, they were conducted by proposing the opposite qualified sentences and by arguing dialectically about them.

---

[24] In the Prologue to his *Summa Theologica* Aquinas mentions some difficulties to which new students are confronted. One of these comes from the diversity of methodological approaches: "partim etiam quia ea quae sunt necessaria talibus [i.e. novitiis] ad sciendum, non traduntur secundum ordinem disciplinae, sed secundum quod requirebat *librorum expositio*, vel secundum quod se praebebat *occasio disputandi*...". This text shows that *lectio* (librorum expositio) and *disputatio* were different and separated didactic instruments.

B. C. Bazán has suggested three factors which could have favoured the autonomy of *quaestio disputata*: (1) the existence of masters who understood that their activity had to be creative and not merely repetitive, (2) the *Sentences* as a literary genre in so far as the systematic ordering of sentences was independent from their literary context, (3) and a more comprehensive knowledge of the aristotelian logic, mainly those parts which are related to demonstration and sophistic arguments. (Cf. B. C. Bazán, "La *quaestio disputata*", *Les genres littéraires dans les souces théologiques et philosophiques médiévales. (Actes du Colloque international de Louvain-la-Neuve, 25–27 mai 1981)*, Louvain-la-Neuve, 1982, p. 34).

Mikko Yrjönsuuri

Commitment to Consistency

The aim of this paper is to look at the general and quite natural duty of avoiding contradictions. Any respondent engaging in any dialectical disputation seems to be committed to it. If this was not so, there might be no other external and clear way of telling when someone loses a dispute. It seems clear that whatever one admits in a disputation, one should always be on guard against contradictions. But it is not as clear from whence such contradictions come and why it is not always possible to avoid them. What is a contradiction? This paper takes up some medieval discussions of such problems and shows how the concepts of consistency and possibility are distinguished in them.

Obligationes as Study of Inconsistency

Albert the Great distinguishes in his commentary on Aristotle's *Topics* two duties that the respondent of a dialectical disputation has.[1] The primary commitment, according to Albert, is that the respondent must grant anything that follows from his thesis and deny anything incompatible (*repugnans*) with it. This duty must always be observed. There are no sensible disputations where the respondent could be relieved from such logical commitments. The duty to concede the sentences "that seem to be true" is not as widely applicable. It is perhaps so that in all truth-seeking disputations one must be truthful in this way, Albert emphasizes, but in other cases, like in exercises, there is no such need. Indeed, Albert recognizes that there is a technique called "false thesis" (*positio falsa*) that is based on the idea that the respondent is required only to keep his first mentioned commitment of being logical. Within the context of such a technique, the duty to be truthful need not be observed in any such general way. Albert is just one among many medieval authors to discuss such a technique, though towards the fourteenth century it became more customary to use the title "obligations" (*obligationes*) instead of Albert's choice of *positio falsa*.

In essence, the respondent of an "obligational disputation" as discussed under this title and employing the kind of technique presented by Albert is partly relieved from the commitment to the truth but not from the commitment to consistency. Modern commentators have, for good reason, wondered what could be the real point of such a technique. It is clear that medieval scholars were deeply interested in such disputations, and the reason for this interest cannot be anything marginal. They must have considered the issue to be of central importance to logic in general. Nevertheless, the technique seems to have no analogues in twentieth century logic, unlike most other branches of medieval logic.[2]

---

[1] Albertus Magnus 1890, esp. p. 506.
[2] For modern discussions of the technique see, e.g., Ashworth 1981, Spade 1992 and 1993; Stump 1989 and Yrjönsuuri 2001.

Here I want to make the suggestion that the original problem addressed by the medieval logicians developing this technique was simply to explore what it is to be inconsistent and how and when do sentences granted by a respondent in a dialectical disputation cohere as a consistent whole. I will, also, point out certain interesting and innovative dimensions into which this original problem led its explorers.

Shortly put, the core of the technique of obligations can be more exactly described as follows. There is an opponent and a respondent who act in ways familiar from the Aristotelian dialectical disputations. The two participants agree on a thesis, which is taken as the ground for the disputation. In the standard case, the thesis is known to be false. Then the respondent must answer the questions put forward by the opponent one by one. He must always grant what follows and what is repugnant to his false thesis. *And* he must avoid granting contradictions. Thus, the core of the technique is really that a false thesis is laid down, and then it is checked whether it entails contradictions – or, in other words, whether it is inconsistent.

One of the first topics to emerge from this context was the study of paradoxes. It was generally assumed – following Aristotle – that a possible sentence does not yield contradictions. In certain cases it turned out, however, that this seems to happen no matter how skilled the defence. Among the foremost examples, we have the thesis "the thesis is false", and other similar variations of the so-called Liar's paradox. These paradoxes soon became an independent object of study discussed under the title "*insolubilia*".[3]

Although a false but possible sentence does not normally entail contradictions alone, it is clear that if it is connected with actual facts, contradictions may arise. It is the borderlines of these contradictions that become the main interest of authors working with obligations. Let me take an example familiar from several obligations treatises to show what I have in mind. Let us look at two sentences:

(1) Marcus is running
(2) Tullius is not running

It is not at the first sight clear whether we should judge them to be inconsistent. If we allow for the fact that both "Marcus" and "Tullius" refer to the same person, Cicero, the sentences are inconsistent. But should we? There may of course be other people with those names, and if Marcus is a different person than Tullius, there is no contradiction.

I will not here solve this particular puzzle. Instead, let me point out that the specific underlying logical problem can quite naturally be taken under discussion by using a special technique. The disputation can be regulated so that the respondent should, for example, grant (1) but deny (2) if and only if it is taken to be

---

[3] Cf., e.g., Martin 2001 and the references therein.

inconsistent with (1). In this way, the question of consistency becomes a question of whether a certain sentence should be granted on the basis of a given thesis, or not. And indeed, the main idea of the obligations rules is exactly this. Their usual setting is such that sentences which carry a logical connection to the thesis are evaluated following different criteria than those which do not have such a connection, technically called irrelevant. Relevant sentences are evaluated in accordance with logical connections, while irrelevant sentences are evaluated in accordance with the assumed truth-values. It is the cutting edge of the rules to demarcate the two different domains so that their contrasts become as visible as possible.

I rephrase my point. A false but possible sentence does not as such yield contradictions. (1) is not contradictory alone. Combining it with truths or other possibilities – like perhaps (2) – may however yield contradictions, and this is a crucial issue studied in the obligations rules. In the typical obligations rules, the respondent is required to admit a false thesis (*positum*) and to grant it and anything following logically from it. It is generally assumed that this will not force him to accept contradictions. Furthermore, he is required to grant true sentences and deny false sentences that are logically independent (*impertinens verum*; *impertinens falsum*) of the thesis. In effect he has two competing criteria for evaluation, and contradictions may arise if the two criteria are allowed to mingle in uncontrolled ways.[4]

The topic is often discussed in obligations treatises from the early times onwards in terms of the rules for conjunctions. Let us schematize a bit. Let the false thesis be "*A*" and some almost arbitrary true sentence "*B*". Now, the conjunction "*A & B*" combines the false thesis with a truth. The conjunction does not follow from the thesis alone, nor is it true. In terms of the standard obligations rules, "*A*" may have to be granted because it is the thesis. Also, "*B*" may have to be granted because it is true and there is no particular reason to deny it. However, there is no reason to grant the conjunction "*A & B*" – if we do not allow the separate and mutually inconsistent domains of the thesis and the truth to be combined. Thus, it may appear that the respondent would have to grant both parts of a conjunction that he should deny. This, however, is almost as clear a case of contradiction as granting and denying the same sentence.[5]

Most treatises on the technique of obligations discuss this particular example. I think that it is because it lies at the core of the technique. The issue is to determine how contradictions come about when sentences are drawn from different contexts. Bringing the two domains together in a conjunction makes the point in an express way. Here we need not bother with the details of the essentially simple different ways of keeping consistency. It may, nevertheless, be worthwhile to mention two general alternatives.

---

[4] The obligations rules are presented and discussed in detail in Yrjönsuuri 1994 and somewhat more shortly in Yrjönsuuri 2001. See also Spade 1982.

[5] For further discussion and references on the conjunction rules, see, e.g., Yrjönsuuri 1998.

All thirteenth century treatises and probably the majority of later treatises of obligations make it clear that the respondent should care only for the formal kind of consistency here, and not follow the duty of being truthful. On the thesis that he is in Rome he may have to grant that he is a bishop as well – or almost anything else whatsoever, with the sole limitation of coherence. They make it clear that the respondent should not care how far from the truth he becomes carried away by his answers. The point of the obligational practice is not to explore the truth, but to explore consistency.

Certain fourteenth century treatises on obligations show another kind of consideration. I will come back to it more closely below, but for now let me just point out that in these texts the problem is connected to semantic interpretations of the domains and not just to syntactic structures of the sentences. From an anonymous treatise, we even find an example considering the conjunction "you are sitting and you are standing" so that the respondent stands up between the opponent's pronouncing of the parts. Thus, each part is true when pronounced although they are mutually inconsistent. Such a case may, of course, bring inconsistencies into the disputation, but only in an innocent way. The attention is here turned to how the domain of discourse switches from one situation to another, changed situation.[6]

TIME, MODALITY AND CONSISTENCY

At this point, it is time to turn to problems of time. For simplicity, let us stick to the simple case where the sentences evaluated by the respondent are in the present tense. Thus, they seem to refer to one single instant and – if interpreted semantically – form a description of the situation obtaining at that instant. Now, according to the modal conceptions prevailing in the thirteenth century, the present is necessary. If modality is understood in terms of the possible being realized at some time, it is clear that all possibilities concerning the present have been realized and thus whatever is true is necessarily true. If, on the other hand, modality is understood in terms of natural powers, it is equally clear that the present cannot be changed further. All unrealized possibilities must – according to both modal models – be projected into the future.[7]

The central idea of the obligations technique is to lay down a false thesis as something that will have to be granted, and the standard practice was to use the present tense for it. Nevertheless, most thirteenth-century discussions give the rule that one should not grant that it is the present instant. They thought that given the falsity of thesis, it would be inconsistent to maintain that the time is exactly what it really is. If a presently false sentence is to be defended, it should

---

[6] The topic comes up in the anonymous *De arte obligatoria* edited in Kretzmann and Stump 1985.
[7] For discussion of the relevant modal conceptions, see Knuuttila 1993.

not be defended in respect to the present – except in a special way as an impossible thesis.

Interestingly enough, already the early thirteenth-century *Emmeran Treatise on False Positio* contains an argument showing that given the standard detailed rules of the technique it turns out as being impossible to give any specific time as the instant within which the thesis would be possible.[8] Any exact time may have to be denied. This result does not apparently bother the author much. He admits that it shows that given a possible thesis, the respondent may have to accept sentences which are "accidentally" (*per accidens*) impossible in the sense of violating the necessity of the present. Indeed, if we look at how the answers are given, they respectively refer to different times as the present. In his discussion the anonymous author in effect recognizes that consistency does not guarantee possibility. As it seems to me, the concept of consistency is here developed in distinction from the then prevailing notions of possibility and in contrast with them. The set of answers is not understood in terms of a situation that could in any sense obtain, but as a set of assertions that hangs together. Thus, we speak of the consistency of a set of sentences, not of the coherence of the description of an assumed situation.

John Duns Scotus is well known for his revolutionary approach to the modal concepts.[9] In the context of the obligational technique, his innovation is to abolish the rule concerning the present instant.[10] Thus, Scotus advises the respondent to give all the answers in respect to the same, present instant. This opens more space for reading the set of answers as a description of a possible or imaginable situation. The concepts of consistency and possibility come closer to each other in Scotus' modal semantics – which was widely adopted in the fourteenth century, and as a consequence of this also the obligational technique develops into new directions.

The new modal conception was based on the traditional idea that God can do anything that does not include contradictions. Using non-contradiction as the criterion of possibility is, of course, very interesting from the viewpoint of the technique of obligations. Whatever the consistent set of sentences resulting from a successful disputation is, it can retrospectively be taken to describe a situation that could have been realized by God. From the viewpoint of such modal concepts, all consistent sets of sentences describe situations that are genuine alternatives to the actual world in an interesting sense. This makes it possible to see also obligational disputations as constructing descriptions of possible situations. This aim is nothing other than the traditional aim of avoiding inconsistency – but understood in a new way.

Recent historians of science have paid considerable attention to the so-called "*secundum imaginationem*" method, which became widely used in early four-

---

[8] Anonymous 2001, pp. 209–210.
[9] See esp. Knuuttila 1996 and Normore 1996.
[10] See, e.g., Yrjönsuuri 1994, pp. 64–75.

teenth-century science. Historians of science have been rather impressed with the scope of the results achieved through this method, especially in the area of mechanics. The leading idea of the method becomes most clear through an example from Richard Kilvington's *Sophismata*. Assume that Socrates begins to move for the following hour. Assume further that he can cease to move at any instant of the hour. Now, consider the sentence "Socrates will as quickly cease to move as he will move."[11] Could it be true? The point of the discussion is to determine whether we can consistently say that anything ceases to move at the same instant as it begins to move. Is it really so that Socrates can cease to move also at the first instant of the hour, as our second assumption seems to imply? Or rather, should we say that an amount of time, perhaps indefinitely small, must elapse before he can stop after starting to move?

It is easy to see that this example is characteristically obligational. We are dealing with a problem where consistency is problematic. However, if we look at the case from another angle, we are dealing with a thought-experiment, where an unrealized situation is imagined, and the assignments of truth-values in this situation are at stake. Thus, the technique of obligations works as a methodology of thought experiments.

There seems to be no doubt that Kilvington thought that the respondent serving in disputations like his *Sophismata* must obey rules of obligations. The way in which he refers to obligations in the sophisma 47 clearly assumes that. However, it is noteworthy that Kilvington thinks that a revision of the rules is necessary. Instead of considering only formally valid inferences, one should recognize also counterfactual conditionals. As he sees it, in a thought experiment the respondent should grant everything that would be true if the assumed thesis was true.

As it soon turned out, Kilvington's revision of the rules would have required a major revision of the technique, and it was not accepted. His suggestion seems, nevertheless, natural if we take into account that he understood the thesis laid down in the beginning as introducing a situation that is assumed as the basis for truth-values during the disputation. In a Kilvingtonian obligational disputation, the respondent ought to imagine how the world would lie if the assumed thesis was true, and then give all his answers in accordance with those truth-values.

It seems that many modern interpreters of the obligational technique have made a similar mistake about the technique as Kilvington. They have understood the respondent's defence of the false thesis in a too serious way as opposed to the mere play with words. This seems to be particularly true of Paul Spade's suggestion that obligations should be seen as theories of counterfactual conditionals (see Spade 1982), and of Henrik Lagerlund's and Erik J. Olsson's recent revision of this suggestion reading obligations as belief revision models (Lagerlund and Olsson 2001). Formally, both these interpretations seem to provide relatively

---

[11] Kilvington 1990a and 1990b, sophisma 19.

accurate interpretations of what is going on in obligational disputations. However, the suggested philosophical interpretations are misleading.

Later fourteenth-century authors in the tradition took it to be important that the answers with a false thesis are not given through semantic considerations.[12] The respondent of an obligational disputation was not required to take the false thesis as true in the sense of believing or as-if-believing it, but only in the sense of admitting it in his answers.[13] As it was, the point of the technique was not to describe an imaginable situation, but to construct a consistent set of sentences. The respondent was to look at relations between sentences, not at truth-values – be they actual or imagined. The issue was primarily consistency, and the idea that the answers form a description of an imaginable situation came only afterwards, if at all. Consistency was not to be determined in the Kilvingtonian manner through imagining how the facts would lie if the thesis were true. Rather, the respondent of an obligational disputation was to play with the sentences and look at their relations to each other.

The medieval critics of Kilvington's obligational rules emphasized the use of formally valid inferences. As they saw it, inconsistency is a property that belongs to sets of sentences, not primarily to descriptions of situations. Inconsistency can be reliably revealed only through considerations of the formal consequences of the members of the examined set. A set of sentences can be proclaimed consistent only through analysing whether its members formally entail contradictions. Thus, only formal consequences can be used in obligational disputations as inferential principles.

CONSISTENCY AS RELATIONS BETWEEN SENTENCES

Let us now stop for a moment to look at how far we have got. We have been looking at the obligational disputation as a process. The respondent's answers have been taken as a set of sentences that is collected step by step. For the most part, we have ignored their truth-values – both actual and possible ones. Our interest here has been focussed on the idea that we expect the answers to cohere in an important way. The obligational respondent is not committed to truth but to consistency.

Looking at the case where the respondent's duty to grant what seems to be true is relaxed, we have seen that the commitment to consistency could not be spelled out by the prevailing modal concepts available in the thirteenth century.

---

[12] This is the approach in Swyneshed (see Spade 1977), Fland (see Spade 1980), Lavenham (see Spade 1978), and in fact all the later texts that I know of (see Yrjönsuuri 2001, p. 23).

[13] Some medieval scholars writing on obligations (e.g. Burley, see Green 1963) suggested a related method "*sit verum*" where the respondent should answer as if he knew the thesis to be true and ignore the fact that it really was false. No author ever developed detailed rules for such a belief-revision model. They were thought to be close to but distinct from the real obligational rules. In the standard technique, the admittance of the thesis was limited to giving an affirmative answer during the technical part of the disputation.

Consistency as required in obligational disputations was distinct from possibility and keeping the commitment to consistency could not guarantee that all answers based on a possible thesis would remain possible. While possibility was looked at from the point of view of the situation talked about, the obligational consistency was looked at from the point of view of the sentences used and the relations between them.

In effect, obligational disputations were thus developing a concept concerning relations between sentences that was sometimes called "compossibility" (*compossibilitas*) as distinct from possibility proper.[14] It was recognized in the thirteenth century obligations treatises that if something is not compossible, it could not be accepted in any case. In fact, already since the eleventh century it had been recognized that not even God can realize contradictions.[15] If some combination is possible, it is compossible as well. But in the other direction no implication follows. If some combination is compossible, there is no guarantee that it would be possible too. Possibility cannot be decided merely on the basis of the relations between the sentences used in describing the issue, because it depends on whether the described situation is realizable. In this sense, alternative descriptions of the past, for example, seemed to the medieval mind compossible, but surely not possible. Past cannot be changed anymore, but we surely can give consistent false stories about it. Thus, the concept of compossibility looks from our viewpoint more like the combinatorial concept of logical possibility – which we take to be distinct from natural possibility, for example.

Admittedly, after having been made in the obligational context the distinction between these two concepts did not remain clear very long. Towards the fourteenth century, modal concepts had developed to include a new sense of possibility that could perhaps be reduced to consistency. I cannot here go into the historical details. For the present purposes, it suffices to point out Duns Scotus with his concept of logical possibility (*possibilitas logica*). Many twentieth-century scholars take Scotus to have been a radical innovator in this respect.[16] Nevertheless, consistency still did not become exactly the same as conceivability or possibility.

As we saw, fourteenth century scholars writing on obligations generally still did not allow that the commitment to consistency would have been best kept through sticking to one imagined situation and giving one's answers in accordance with it. Consistency was not to be reduced to imaginability. Rather, they required objectively determinable criteria of when the set of answers coheres and when it does not. Such criteria can naturally be found only through looking at the logical relations between the sentences at issue. Rejecting the idea that the set of answers should be taken as a one big conjunction whose possibility or conceivability is at issue, they thought that consistency is best determined through rela-

---

[14] I have discussed this further in Yrjönsuuri 1998.
[15] See, e.g., Holopainen 1996.
[16] See Knuuttila 1993 and 1996 and Normore 1996 and references in these works.

tions between different answers. This is, indeed, the natural way to go if the issue is that of combinatorial consistency and not so much semantic possibility.

Now, what are the particular relations between sentences that determine their consistency? The length of a sentence, for example, clearly does not contribute anything to a matter like this. Rather, it is the logical properties of sentences that are relevant. But what are they? What kinds of specific issues do we find from the medieval treatises on obligations? The literature is of course large enough to offer a large number of different kinds of factors relevant to the logical connections between sentences, but let me look at some of them here.

We already noted problems of reference. In keeping his commitment to consistency the respondent must be very clear about the references of the terms he is using. As we saw, the two sentences "Marcus is running" and "Tullius is running" are consistent if we allow that "Marcus" and "Tullius" may refer to different persons. Analogous problems of reference do not arise only in connection to proper names, but also with common names.

A second topic that I have already mentioned is sentential logic. As we saw, most obligations treatises discussed conjunction and disjunction, and the way in which they combine the sentences used in them. Also the relation of equivalence belonged to the standard topics. Given that in a single disputation one may often need to speak of different possibilities and sometimes even allow for change in the actual reality, it is important to keep track of the interconnections among the atomic parts of such molecular sentences.

Thirdly, sentential predicates and their logic were often discussed in obligations treatises. Here I have in mind the relations between pairs of such sentences as

"It is known that the king is seated"
"The king is seated"

or

"'You are a bishop' is false"
"You are a bishop"

or further

"No grammarian exists"
"A grammarian grants that God exists".

As it turns out, the obligations treatises raise several interesting issues concerning the logical relations obtaining between such sentences. The respondent has to keep well in mind the different dimensions included in the conceptual or logical content of the sentential predicates in order to defend the thesis consistently.

We also find the obligations treatises to discuss cases where sentences are mentioned by proper or common names, thus bringing problems of object- and metalanguage under discussion. One of the most interesting topics of discussion is "the thesis is false" (*positum est falsum*; the Latin does not have the article, neither definite nor indefinite). According to Walter Burley, for example, when the thesis is in fact false, one can consistently grant that the thesis is false since this implies no contradiction with the thesis itself.[17] If the *positum* is "You are in Rome", you may grant that the *positum* is false without thereby being forced to deny that you are in Rome.

All the considerations I have mentioned so far fall relatively nicely under the concept of formal logic. From this viewpoint, it seems natural to say that the concept of consistency was, in obligations treatises, spelled out in terms of formal logic. Thus, it may seem surprising that problems of syllogistic systems would be almost completely missing. Indeed, we do not find many syllogisms within the standard obligations treatises.

It seems to me that the reason for this fact is that most medieval scholars thought that the kind of logical relation found in syllogisms is – at least in optimal cases – different from the above cases. While the kinds of logical relations between sentences, discussed above, work with syntactic structures, syllogisms are based on conceptual relations, at least in the ideal cases. Take, for example, the standard Barbara:

All B are A
All C are B
Therefore, All C are A

This syllogism is valid because the term B includes A and is included by C. Because of these conceptual relations, A is also included by C. Thus, the validity of the syllogism derives from the conceptual content of the terms at issue and not so much from the actual syntactic structure of the sentences used in formulating it.

Now, issues of conceptual content are, in fact, taken up within the obligations treatises. As William Ockham points out, the particular species of obligations called "impossible thesis" (*positio impossibilis*) is particularly useful in studying "conceptual distinctions and their structures" (*distinctio terminorum et ordo eorum*).[18] The point is just that the simplest way to discuss problems of conceptual inconsistency is to lay down a conceptually impossible thesis and look at how it can be defended.

---

[17] See, e.g., Burley 1963, p. 62.
[18] Ockham 1974, p. 741.

Let us look at an example. Let us lay down the thesis "Man is not an animal". Given that being an animal belongs essentially to what it is to be a man, this thesis violates a basic conceptual necessity, and thus there is no way in which it could be true. Usually it was also admitted that in a sense this thesis entails contradictions and is inconsistent. Being an animal is included in being a man, and thus the thesis claims that an animal is not an animal. However, if we simply give up this conceptual link and allow no inferences based on it, the thesis turns out to be consistently defensible. The respondent cannot be forced to grant any further inconsistencies.

An unknown master whose name probably begins with a W claims in his late thirteenth-century obligations treatise that in considering the thesis "Man is not an animal" we should think of a person who misuses the concept of man.[19] In a somewhat similar vein, Ockham tells us that when the thesis is impossible, we cannot take into account all logically valid inferences. Rather, we must rely only on rules and principles that are known as such (*per se*), and to every understanding. He takes the view that inferences based on conceptual content are logically valid, but not always evidently so.[20]

That conceptual impossibilities can be consistently discussed shows that the kind of consistency based merely on syntactic structures is, in a sense, stricter than the one taking also conceptual relations into account. Even a respondent who fails in conceptual consistency can limit his failure and block it from spreading further.

Here, however, we owe an interesting remark to William Ockham's younger contemporary, Walter Chatton. He points out that if we require conceptual connections from all the inferences used in an obligational disputation, we can also block a syntactic kind of inconsistency from spreading further. Suppose that the thesis is "No man is an animal and some man is an animal". Now, if conceptual connection is required of all inferences, we cannot deduce "a donkey is an animal" or its opposite. The contradiction will not spread any further than the concepts of the original thesis.[21] Thus, Chatton's argument seems to show that we cannot univocally think that conceptual inconsistencies are weaker than syntactic ones. The two criteria work distinctly, and with suitable examples we can show how their effects differ.

I started this paper by asking what a contradiction is. Now we have looked at the medieval theory of obligations as a genre of logic dedicated to this issue. We have seen first how consistency and possibility come up as two distinct concepts, which of course bear distinct relations to each other and even were assimilated by some later medieval authors. In the conceptual scheme that we have mapped, consistency depends on whether certain sentences cohere. It has strictly speaking

---

[19] The authorship of this treatise is discussed by Spade and Stump 1983. It is edited in Green 1963, see esp. p. 24.
[20] Ockham 1974, pp. 739–740.
[21] Chatton 1989, p. 154 (prol. q. 3, a. 1).

nothing to do with how the world lies. For its part, possibility requires that the world could accord with the sentences describing it. Possibility does not directly depend on the relations between the sentences themselves. Also, we have seen how obligations treatises studied the concept of consistency through studying the particular relations between sentences that are relevant to it – ignoring truth and to some extent also ignoring possibility. In effect, we have thus found a medieval logical genre that studied the different ways in which a logical contradiction may arise in combinations of sentences. This is an issue that is separate but related to the problem of demarcating the borders of what is conceivable and what kinds of counterfactual or counterpossible hypotheses we can entertain as genuine alternatives of the actual situation. Consistency and possibility can be dealt with as distinct concepts.

University of Jyväskylä

REFERENCES

Albertus Magnus 1890, *Commentarii in Aristotelis Topiciis*, (ed.) Borgnet, *Opera Omnia*, vol. II, Paris, 233–524.
Anonymous 2001, "The Emmeran treatise on false *positio*", in M. Yrjönsuuri (ed.), *Medieval Formal Logic: Obligations Insolubles and Consequences*, (New Synthese Historical Library, vol. 49), Kluwer, Dordrecht, 199–215.
Ashworth, E. J., 1981, "The problems of Relevance and Order in Obligational Disputations: Some Late Fourteenth Century Views," *Medioevo* 7, 175–193.
Chatton, Walter, 1989, *Reportatio et Lectura super Sententias: Collatio ad Librum Primum et Prologus*, ed. J. C. Wey, (Studies and Texts, vol. 90), Pontifical Institute of Mediaeval Studies, Toronto.
Green, Romuald, 1963, *The Logical Treatise 'De obligationibus': An Introduction with Critical Texts of William of Sherwood (?) and Walter Burley*, Ph. D. Thesis, Louvain.
Holopainen, Toivo J., 1996, *Dialectic and Theology in the Eleventh Century*, (Studien und Texte zur Geistesgeschichte des Mittelalters, vol. 54), E. J. Brill, Leiden.
Kilvington, Richard, 1990a, *The Sophismata of Richard Kilvington*, ed. N. Kretzmann and B. E. Kretzmann, (Auctores Britannici Medii Aevi, vol. XII), Oxford, British Academy, Oxford University Press.
Kilvington, Richard, 1990b, *The Sophismata of Richard Kilvington*, introduction, translation and commentary by N. Kretzmann and B. E. Kretzmann, Cambridge, Cambridge University Press.
Knuuttila, Simo, 1993, *Modalities in Medieval Philosophy*, London, Routledge.
Knuuttila, Simo, 1996, "Duns Scotus and the Foundations of Modalities", in Honnefelder, Ludger, Wood, Rega, and Machthild, Dreyer (eds.), *John Duns Scotus: Metaphysics and Ethics*, (Studien und Texte zur Geistesgeschichte des Mittelalters, vol. 53), E. J. Brill, Leiden, 127–144.
Kretzmann, Norman, and Stump, Eleonore, 1985, "The Anonymous *De arte obligatoria* in Merton College MS 306," in E. P. Bos (ed.), *Medieval Semantics and Metaphysics. Studies dedicated to L. M. de Rijk on the occasion of his 60th birthday*, (Artistarium Supplementa 2), Nijmegen, Ingenium Publishers, 239–280.
Lagerlund, Henrik, and Olsson, Erik J., 2001, "Disputation and change of belief: Burley's theory of obligationes as a theory of belief revision", in M. Yrjönsuuri (ed.), *Medieval Formal Logic: Obligations Insolubles and Consequences*, (New Synthese Historical Library, vol. 49), Kluwer, Dordrecht, 35–62.

Martin, Christopher J., 2001, "Obligations and Liars", in M. Yrjönsuuri (ed.), *Medieval Formal Logic: Obligations Insolubles and Consequences*, (New Synthese Historical Library, vol. 49), Kluwer, Dordrecht, 63–94.

Normore, Calvin, 1996, "Scotus, Modality, Instants of Nature and the Contingency of the Present", in Honnefelder, Ludger, Wood, Rega, and Machthild, Dreyer (eds.), *John Duns Scotus: Metaphysics and Ethics*, (Studien und Texte zur Geistesgeschichte des Mittelalters, vol. 53), E. J. Brill, Leiden, 161–174.

Ockham, William, 1974, *Summa Logicae*, (eds.) P. Boehner, G. Gál, S. Brown, *Opera Philosophica*, vol. I, St. Bonaventure, N. Y., The Franciscan Institute.

Spade, Paul V., 1977, "Roger Swyneshed's *Obligationes*: Edition and Comments," *Archives d'histoire doctrinale et littéraire du moyen âge* 44, 243–85.

Spade, Paul V., 1978, "Richard Lavenham's *Obligationes*," *Rivista critica di Storia della Filosofia* 33, 225–242.

Spade, Paul V., 1980, "Robert Fland's *Obligationes*: An Edition," *Mediaeval Studies* 42, 41–60.

Spade, Paul V., 1982, "Three Theories of *Obligationes*: Burley, Kilvington and Swyneshed on Counterfactual Reasoning," *History and Philosophy of Logic* 3, 1–32.

Spade, Paul V., 1992, "If *Obligationes* were Counterfactuals," *Philosophical Topics* 20, 171–188.

Spade, Paul V., 1993, "Opposing and Responding: a New Look at 'positio,'" *Medioevo* 19, 233–270.

Spade, Paul V., and Stump, Eleonore, 1983, "Walter Burley and the *Obligationes* Attributed to William of Sherwood," *History and Philosophy of Logic* 4, 9–26.

Stump, Eleonore, 1989, *Dialectic and its Place in the Development of Medieval Logic*, London, Cornell University Press.

Yrjönsuuri, Mikko, 1994, *Obligationes: 14th Century Logic of Disputational Duties*, (Acta Philosophica Fennica 55), Helsinki, Societas Philosophica Fennica.

Yrjönsuuri, Mikko, 1998, "The Compossibility of Impossibilities and *Ars Obligatoria*," *History and Philosophy of Logic* 19, 235–248.

Yrjönsuuri, Mikko, 2001, "Duties, Rules and Interpretations in Obligational Disputations", in M. Yrjönsuuri (ed.), *Medieval Formal Logic: Obligations Insolubles and Consequences*, (New Synthese Historical Library, vol. 49), Kluwer, Dordrecht, 3–34.

PART III

QUESTIONS AND QUESTIONING IN THE CONTINENTAL TRADITION

JEAN-FRANÇOIS COURTINE

THE QUESTION OF BEING:
MEANING OF THE QUESTION AND THE QUESTION OF MEANING

One would, no doubt, consider it fairly incongruous, or even somewhat provocative, to introduce Heidegger and the so called *Seinsfrage* within the framework of these *Entretiens* devoted to the Socratic tradition. Not only does Heidegger never (or nearly never: I shall come back to the "exception" shortly) refer to the figure of Socrates – as is the custom, albeit by way of polite academic respect – nor to the Socratic invention of philosophizing communally and dialogically, and even less to the ethico-political question of virtue (*arétè*), but one could also underline the fact that Heidegger's reading of Plato seems to provide the most evident illustration of the hermeneutic "violence" that characterises so often the work of the Master of Freiburg: one would only have to think of the essay of 1930–31 *Platons Lehre von der Wahrheit*, and of his thesis (which has, however, occasioned numerous "retractiones") of the "subjugation" of the idea of truth, in its original sense of *alètheia*, which finds itself therefore reduced to *orthotès*[1].

It is almost as if – at least in the first stage of his thought – Heidegger adopted a Brentanian position, if not a neo-scholastic one, which parades as the symmetrical inverse of the neo-Kantian inspiration of Natorp in his *Platons Ideenlehre*: for Heidegger it would therefore not be a question of putting forward the Plato of the doctrine of Ideas and the dialectic against the Aristotelian dogmatism, but to bring out, in a positive way, the figure of a phenomenological and ontological Aristotle against the dialectic.

Yet, such an opposition in reality turns out to be quite caricatured, since Heidegger envisages at the time of *Sein und Zeit*, the time with which we are concerned here, still a unitary, almost indissociable, Platonic-Aristotelian complex. But before pursuing this point, I come back for a moment to the only reference to Socrates to be found in the published works, i.e. in the lectures of 1951–1952: *Was heißt Denken?*[2] It is a "transitional" passage devoted reflexively – the point

---

[1] M. Heidegger, *Vom Wesen der Wahrheit. Zu Platons Höhlengleichnes und Theätet*, Gesamtausgabe, Bd. 34, Klostermann, Francfort 1988.
[2] M. Heidegger, *Was heißt Denken?*, Max Niemeyer Verlag, Tübingen 1961, pp. 51–52 : "Ein Schreinerlehrling z. B., jemand, der Schreine bauen lernt und ähnliche Dinge, übt beim Lernen nicht nur die Fertigkeit in der Verwendung der Werkzeuge. Er macht sich auch nicht nur mit den gebräuchlichen Formen der Dinge, die er zu bauen hat, bekannt. Er bringt sich, wenn er ein echter Schreiner wird, vor allem zu den verschiedenen Arten des Holzes und zu den darin schlafenden Gestalten in die Entsprechung, zum Holz, wie es mit der verborgenen Fülle seines Wesens in das Wohnen des Menschen hereinragt. [...] Dieser Bezug zum Holz trägt das ganze Handwerk. [...] Ob ein Schreinlehrling jedoch beim Lernen in die Entsprechung zum Holz und zu den hölzernen Dinge gelangt oder nicht, hängt offensichtlich davon ab, daß einer da ist, der den Lehrling solches lernt. [...] Das Lehren

is evidently significant – to teaching and learning. The passage is well known, but I quote the essence of it, because its movement explains the striking mention of the name of Socrates which follows immediately afterwards. The question, then, is about learning: What is learning? What is teaching? What does the person do that teaches (the *Lehrer*, in the original text)?

"Learning", remarks Heidegger in the first place, in a style that is more phenomenological than dialogical or Socratic, is to see to it that "what we do or leave" (*das Tun und Lassen*) responds, or rather, corresponds to that which in each case addresses itself to us in its essential content (*was sich jeweils an Wesenhaftem uns zuspricht*). Learning should always model itself on the matter in question and its particular requirements. "It is every time according to the nature of this essential, according to the domain from which this appeal (*Zuspruch*)", that the response is matched and that, at the same time, the nature of learning is to be specified.

Then comes a very "Socratic" example:

An apprentice carpenter, for example, someone that learns to build cupboards and similar things, practises in the process of learning not only the skill of using the tools. Neither does he only acquire knowledge on the customary forms of the things that he has to build. When he wants to become a real carpenter, he tunes himself in to the different kinds of wood and to the forms dormant in it, to the wood itself, in the way in which it penetrates the dwelling of humans by the hidden fullness of its essence.

The learning of the *technitès*, understood in this way, is everything but technical, in the modern sense of the word: it is less a question of rules of know-how or of procedures than of a "relation to the wood", learned, as we say in English, "on the job": This relation to the wood is the support of the entire craft.

After the apprentice joiner comes the person that teaches now to the foreground:

---

ist noch schwieriger als das Lernen. [...] Weshalb ist das Lehren schwerer als das Lernen? Nicht deshalb, weil der Lehrer die größere Summe von Kenntnissen besitzen und sie jederzeit bereit haben muß. Das Lehren ist darum schwerer als das Lernen, weil Lernen heißt: lernen lassen. Der eigentliche Lehrer läßt sogar nichts anderes lernen als – das Lernen. Deshalb erweckt sein Tun oft auch den Eindruck, daß man bei ihm eigentlich nichts lernt, sofern man jetzt unversehens unter "lernen" nur die Beschaffung nutzbarer Kenntnisse versteht. Der Lehrer ist den Lehrlingen einzig darin voraus, daß er noch weit mehr zu lernen hat als sie, nämlich: das Lernen-lassen. Der Lehrer muß es vermögen, belehrbarer zu sein als die Lehrlinge. [...] Der Lehrer ist seiner Sache weit weniger sicher als die Lernden der ihrigen. Darum kommt bei dem Verhältnis von Lehrer und Lernenden, wenn es ein wahres ist, niemals die Autorität des Viel-Wissers ... ins Spiel." Wir versuchen hier das Denken zu lernen. Vielleicht ist das Denken auch nur dergleichen wie das Bauen an einem Schrein. Es ist jedenfalls ein Hand-Werk. [...] Sokrates hat zeit seines Lebens, bis in seinen Tod hinein, nichts anders getan, als sich in den Zugwind dieses Zuges zu stellen und darin sich zu halten. Darum ist er der reinste Denker des Abendlandes. Deshalb hat er nichts geschrieben. Denn wer aus dem Denken zu schreiben beginnt, muß unweigerlich den Menschen gleichen, die vor allzu starkem Zugwind in den Windschatten flüchten. Es bleibt das Geheimnis einer noch verborgenen Geschichte, daß alle Denker des Abendlandes nach Sokrates, unbeschadet ihrer Größe, solche Flüchtlinge sein mußten." (Trans. Fred D. Wieck and J. Glenn Day (New York, Harper & Row, 1972).

If the apprentice carpenter succeeds in learning how to meet the wood and wooden things or not, is clearly dependant on the presence of someone that teaches the apprentice these things.

The example, hackneyed as it may be, is interesting because it will take us imperceptibly from Greece to ... the Black Forest: there is nothing maieutic to teaching (the word isn't used) and it definitely requires no *logos*, argumentation, question, response:

> Teaching is still harder than learning. [...] Why is teaching harder than learning? Not because of the fact that the teacher disposes of greater knowledge which he must have at his disposition at all times. Teaching is harder than learning, because teaching means: letting learn. The true teacher lets really nothing else be learnt than – learning. That is why his actions create often the impression that one learns actually nothing from him, that is, in so far as one considers "learning" thoughtlessly to be only the acquisition of useful knowledge. The teacher surpasses the learner only by the fact that he still has more to learn, namely, the letting learn. The teacher must be capable of being more teachable than the learners.

I emphasise again the feature which is a lot more phenomenological than dialectical: the apprentice joiner is less at the school of the master than ... of the wood, to which the master relates in his turn in a more docile way, according to a more attentive "correspondence" (*Entsprechung*):

> The teacher is much less sure of his matter than the learners of theirs. That is why the authority of the know-it-all never makes part of the relationship between the teacher and the learner, when it is a real relationship...

The paradigm of the *technè* is equally valid in the case of thought: "We try here to learn how to think. Perhaps thinking is merely like the making of a cupboard. It is, in any case, hand-work."

Learning thought is, therefore, also in the first place to turn yourself to that which gives itself to be thought over: yet that which gives the most to be thought turns itself away from us. This is the fundamental "thesis" of the lectures *Was heißt Denken?*, which is, however, perfectly in accordance with the Heideggerian definition of the concept "phenomenon" in the phenomenological sense (*SuZ*, § 7): the phenomenon is precisely that which in the first instance and for the most part does not show itself, but is in constant retreat. This is exactly why there is a need for phenomenology – to pull the phenomena out of their retreat, out of their obscuration. Hence the definition in the lectures of the 50's: thinking is "being in movement towards that which retracts itself." And I cite again the passage where Socrates is named:

> Socrates did nothing his whole life long up to his death, than to enter and to keep himself in the wind of the movement. That is why he is the purest of the Western thinkers. That is why he never wrote anything. Because whoever starts to write from out of his thought, must unquestionably resemble those people who flee to the windshelter when the wind blows too strongly. It remains the mystery of a still hidden story, that all the Western thinkers after Socrates had to be, their greatness despite, such refugees.

One sees that the tribute paid to Socrates has a double cutting edge or rather a double thrust. It constitutes also one of the severest attacks against him who, having denounced writing in the *Phaedro,* has handed down to us in his *Dialogues* the teaching, which one would, following Heidegger, call almost silent, of the "purest thinker". It's a strange figure of a Socrates who is at this point detached form his context: the sophistic and the dialogical game of argumentation on the agora, even more than in the joiner's workshop!

After these introductory considerations, I turn to my subject, which is more direct and quite limited in its intention: the question for me, here and now, is not to contribute to the study of the "genesis" of *Sein und Zeit* in general, and still less an attempt to follow step by step the rich and complex history of the thought of the young Heidegger from 1919 to 1927 or 1929[3]. I would simply like to show, in a much more simple and concrete way, how the subject of *Sein und Zeit*, which is also its initial section, its declared intention, joins directly and literally the Platonic-Aristotelian line of questioning, right at its metaphysical and ontological pinnacle, that is to say also, and in a much preciser sense, its *semantic* dimension: the line of questioning, defined as "philosophical", which is henceforth expressly about the "meaning", following the main theme of a guiding question which would be expressed not so much in the Socratic form: *ti esti?* but much rather under the title of *ti sémainei?*

I don't know if the question which is thus formulated, in its nature as question, is "Socratic" (one could doubt it); it is in any case the way in which Heidegger characterises the Platonic-Aristotelian institution of philosophising, which is exactly what he intends to repeat at the threshold of *Sein und Zeit*. It is, then, on the exact nature of this "repetition" that I would like to concentrate firstly, before considering if and to what extent this repetition remains faithful to the Platonic-Aristotelian institution or to see if the repetition submits the institution to a radical transformation of which the effects and consequences will then have to be established. But let's begin at the beginning, or rather, at the question of the beginning.

Where and how does the work of 1927 really begin? To attempt to answer this question it is important in the first place to emphasise a typographical or editorial particularity which has not always been remarked sufficiently: the work has, after its dedication to Edmund Husserl and after a *Vorbemerkung* which appears with the seventh edition in 1953, a table of contents, following the Germanic custom, a first page, numbered 1, but without any title, just before § 1 of the Introduction which provides a heading for the chapter ("Exposition of the question of the meaning of being"), so much so that this page 1 isn't listed in the Table of contents. We shall consider in what follows this page as the "epigraph" of *Sein und Zeit*.

---

[3] Cf. the valuable research of Theodore Kisiel, *The Genesis of Heidegger's* Being & Time, University of California Press, 1993. See also John Van Buren, *The Young Heidegger, Rumor of the Hidden King*, Indiana University Press, 1944.

Let's start then from this (of which the function is everything but merely decorative) constituted by a citation of the *Sophist*, 244 a [4]:

> ...dèlon gar hôs humeis men tauta (ti boulesthé sèmainein hopotan on phthengèsthe) palai gignôskete, hèmeis de pro tou men ôiometha, nun d'èporèkamen.

Literally then the book starts before the exposition of its guiding question in the Introduction, which is also the methodology, by a passage from Plato's *Sophist*, a passage which Heidegger cites in Greek, before providing it with a clarifying translation. This citation is at the same time that which allows for "making a start" (according to Hegel's formula at the threshold of the *Science of Logic*) and that which defines programmatically what is at stake in the work.

On the question as to where exactly and truly *Sein und Zeit* starts, one therefore has to answer: "right in the middle of one of Plato's *Dialogues*"! This is an answer which, as we shall see, is and isn't relevant.

Let's examine in more detail this page 1 (without a title: neither *Vorrede*, nor *Vorwort*); I translate the translation that Heidegger gives of the Greek that he has just cited:

> For manifestly you have long been aware of what you mean when you use the expression *"being"*. We, however, who used to think we understood it, have now become perplexed.

The citation is immediately followed by an "announcement" of the necessity of a repetition and an elaboration of the question of the meaning of "being". Before coming back to this announcement, I would like to recall very briefly – the text is well know – the context from which the citation is drawn: the Stranger from Elea addresses a Theaetetus here, but actually he turns to those ("you", *hymeis*) who have been characterised as people who try to establish "how many and of what nature the beings are" (242C). In the eyes of the Stranger it seems, moreover, that Parmenides himself should be counted amongst those who, in high spirits (*eukolôs*), speak to us and reason by rushing into this enterprise of distinguishing "how many" and "of what nature" ("what") (*épi krisin ... tou ta onta diorisasthai posa te kai poîa estin*) beings are.

Of what consists the "rush" that is denounced here? That is what the Stranger had just declared, when he indicated to Theaetetus the method to be followed, the way that should be taken if we want to refute Parmenides' thesis, formulated in 237 a (it's the famous fragment 7 of the *Poem*):

> Keep your mind from this way of enquiry,
> for never will you show that not-being is.

What, then, is this method, or rather this way (*hodos*), that is to be followed with a view to refute Parmenides' thesis, a thesis that is so ruinous when the question is to differentiate between the sophist and the philosopher?

---

[4] John Sallis has offered a very stimulating analysis of this passage in *Delimitations, Phenomenology and the End of Metaphysics*, ch. 8: "Were does *Being and Time* begin?", pp. 98–118, Bloomington, Indiana University Press, 1986; an analysis to which I owe a lot.

It is precisely the way of the *question*, of *questioning* or of a rigorous elaboration of the question, the way that guides (242 B–C):

to consider, first of all, the points which at present are regarded as self-evident, lest we may have fallen into some confusion, and be too ready to assent to one another, fancying that we are quite clear about them.

With reference to this requirement of examining thoroughly that which seemed obvious at the outset – the requirement of interrogating that which presents itself straightaway or in the first place as a valid domain of understanding – it appears that those people (our predecessors, one might call them anachronistically Pre-Socratics) seem to be telling us stories (*mython ... diègeisthai*) as one does to children. In fact, they tell how beings come into existence out of other beings and how they are metamorphosed.

It is also to this passage that Heidegger refers very clearly in § 2 of *Sein und Zeit*:

If we are to understand the problem of Being, our first philosophical step consist in not *mython tina diègesthai*, in not "telling a story" – that is to say, in not defining entities as entities by tracing them back in their origin to some other entities, as if Being had the character of some possible entity [5]

The Stranger remarked to those people (e.g. those who claim that the Whole *is* the hot-and-the-cold) we ask:

"Come", we will say, "Ye, who affirm that hot and cold or any other two principles are the universe, what is this term which you apply to both of them, and what do you mean when you say that both and each of them "are"?" [6]

What is this "is" that is added to the two other terms? Let's say that henceforth there are three terms and not only two: "hot and cold", or the "Whole" that is "hot-and-cold" (Heidegger adds the gloss: "as if Being [*Sein, einai*] had the character of some possible entity.")

It is, therefore, to these people and their way of speaking about beings (and also about non-being [7]) that the Stranger addresses himself just before the passage cited in the epigraph of *SuZ*. As far as they limit themselves to telling their stories, they don't even get to enter the aporia concerning the meaning of "is" or of *einai*.

---

[5] *SuZ*, p. 6; translated by John Macquarrie & Edward Robinson, Oxford, Blackwell, 1978, p. 26.

[6] Trans. B. Jowett. The Dialogues of Plato. Translated into English with analyses and introductions by B. Jowett. Oxford: Clarendon Press, 1892.

[7] I refer to the fact that, just before the passage that we are examining and that serves as the epigraph of *SuZ*, in 243b, the Stranger has formulated for a first time the "aporia", this time, concerning the *mè on*: "I mean to say, that when they talk of one, two, or more elements, which are or have become or are becoming, or again of heat mingling with cold, assuming in some other part of their works separations and mixtures,-tell me, Theaetetus, do you understand what they mean by these expressions? When I was a younger man, I used to fancy that I understood quite well what was meant by the term "not-being," (*to mè on*) which is our present subject of dispute; and now you see in what a fix we are about it."

At the risk of lapsing into micrology, I believe it to be useful to examine very closely the rest of the first page of *SuZ*, because the play with quotation marks and italics is particularly interesting in the resumption and the announcement. I quote:

Haben wir heute eine Antwort auf die Frage nach dem, was wir mit dem Wort "seiend" eigentlich meinen? [I emphasise: the question is firstly about the sense or the meaning of the little word, in Greek *on* that Heidegger renders here very literally by "seiend" (the word is in quotation marks in the text)].

Keineswegs. "We have absolutely no answer, we can answer in no way"[8].

Und so gilt es denn, die Frage nach dem Sinn von Sein <*italics in the text*> *erneut zu stellen;* because neither do we today have an answer to the question of the Stranger, because we are not much further advanced than him, it is therefore a matter of stating again, to reconsider, in a re-elaboration of the question, the problem of the meaning (*Sinn*) of "to be".

"Sinn von Sein": the phrase takes up the preceding formulation quite naturally: strictly speaking, what do we aim at (*meinen – sémainein*), what do we understand, what do we try to say, when we use the little word: "being", *seiend*? It seems to me that this corresponds completely with the kind of questions posed by the Stranger, e.g. in 244 B:

And what about the assertors of the oneness of the all (*oi légontes hen to pân*), – must we not endeavour to ascertain from them "what they mean by being"? (*ti pote legousi to on..., ti hègountai to on..., hoi legontes dèloun auto,* 243 d4 f.). Hence the question: *ti dé? On kaleite ti*? (which, I think, A. Diès [9] translates very well in French as: "Eh bien, *sous le nom d'être,* entendez-vous quelque chose?")

I insist here on the importance of translating *Sinn von Sein* by the meaning of "to be", even if it means to add the quotation marks – but in English (as in French) it is difficult to do otherwise. This is immediately confirmed by the following sentence of the text that seizes our attention:

Sind wir denn heute auch nur in der Verlegenheit, den Ausdruck "Sein" nicht zu verstehen? Keineswegs.

I leave aside here the interpretation of the text. What is clear in any case is that the question is, in the *Sophist* as in the programmed re-elaboration here, to know if and how we understand these "words", these "terms" or these expressions: "being", "to be", "is". There is, at this point of the analysis, no space to present the differences in the meaning of these three terms. What is questioned is, speaking generally, the meaning of the verb "to be" (as we say today), the meaning of its function in the economy of language and especially in the apophantic proposition. This is (and we shall come back to it) the question of the *Sophist,* Plato's Dialogue, as well.

---

[8] We don't have an answer and, as we shall see, we don't have a question either! For us the question doesn't pose itself! We have not even entered the dilemma. Hence, in *SuZ,* the questions of paragraph 1 and the highlighting of the prejudices that bar the way to *posing* the question.

[9] Platon, Le *Sophiste,* édition des Universités de France (Les Belles-Lettres), Paris, 1950.

Are we nowadays again even in the dilemma, or rather the "a-poria" (*in der Verlegenheit sein* translates here precisely the Greek *aporéô*, perfect *èporèka* (*èporèkamen* the Stranger would have said)) because we don't understand the expression "to be"? Not at all!

Und so gilt es denn vordem, allererst wieder ein Verständnis für den Sinn dieser Frage zu wecken. "It is, therefore, important, first of all to reawaken, to reactivate our understanding to the meaning of this question!"

Because, it is equally the question itself that has, *to us*, ceased making sense, having sense, showing its impact or showing that there is genuinely something at stake. We can of course recognise an interrogative position by its question mark, but taken on its own, a question mark is not enough to constitute an authentic question. We will have to rediscover the meaning of the interrogation, of the Platonic or, just as well, the Platonic-Aristotelian problem, we will have to re-light, as Heidegger says a few pages further, the "gigantomachy" (*gigantomakhia peri tès ousias*). This is, once again, with a new reference to the *Sophist*, one of the first quotations of § 1. But let us also say in anticipation that it is in § 1 that the slide from the question of the meaning of "to be" to the question of being (*Die Frage nach dem Sein, die Seinsfrage*, § 1, last paragraph, p. 4), takes place. Be it as it may on this important point, in this last paragraph, Heidegger recapitulates the first given of the pre-beginning: we not only lack the answer to the question, but it is the question itself which is obscure; it has become "richtungslos" for us; we don't have any direction, orientation or guide (*Leitfaden*) any more with which to approach the question; we neither know how to set about, nor that which is to be found out by the asking (*das Erfragte*) is about. Hence the requirement imposed on us to re-elaborate at last, and as if for the first time, sufficiently, the *posing*-of-the-question: "die Frage*stellung* ausarbeiten" – Heidegger underlines *stellung,* in "Fragestellung": let's then pose the question again, let's problematise the question once more.

Let's return to the pre-beginning (to the epigraph):

Die konkrete Ausarbeitung der Frage nach dem Sinn von "Sein" ist die Absicht der folgenden Abhandlung. "To elaborate in concrete terms the question of the meaning of "to be" is the aim, the intention of the present work, of the present treatise."

Here again I emphasise: *to be*, or rather *meaning of "to be"*, and the term "to be" is at the same time written in quotation marks (in German) and, as if that is still not enough, in italics. What does the double "mark" indicate? Again very clearly, it seems to me that the point of departure of the question, within its Platonic reference, is truly "semantic", namely: what is the meaning of the word "to be" ("is", "being")? The following sentence brings us to the greatest difficulties of the book, and I shall not linger on its range or content. I simply remark that in this sentence the expression *Seinsverständnis* means quite naturally, and in the light of what precedes, "understanding of "to be"".

Die Interpretation der Zeit *als des möglichen Horizontes eines jeden Seinsverständnisses überhaubt ist ihr vorläufiges Ziel.* [...] "Our provisional aim is the Interpretation of time as the possible horizon for any understanding whatsoever of Being." [Translation, p. 19.]

The passage from the Sophist (224 A) that we have examined, had already been quoted by Heidegger in his summer lectures of 1925[10]. These lectures are also very important for our purposes, due to its object and structure: the very long preparatory section (182 pages) is in fact devoted to the genesis and the breakthrough of phenomenological research: the main theme of the analysis here is intentionality in its relation to the conscience (*Bewußtsein*). The latter is defined from the *Ideen* of 1913 as "pure being", "absolute being", "absolutely given being". Now, it is at this precise point where Heidegger inserted his most direct critique of the absence of the question of the meaning of "being" in Husserl, by deploring a double deficiency, a double negligence (*Versäumnis*, § 13): *Versäumnis der Frage nach dem Sinn von Sein selbst und nach dem Sein des Menschen in der Phänomenologie*. (Negligence pertaining to the question of the meaning of "to be" itself and to the being of human beings in phenomenology.) It is then in this highly problematical and critical context that the reference to the *Sophist* appears. Of course, one finds this reference (244 A) again in the lectures of the preceding semester [11] (GA. 19, *Sophistes*, pp. 435–499), which were specially devoted to a study of this Dialogue of Plato. We shall come back to it in a while, but before that, let's follow again for a moment the movement of *SuZ* at its start.

After a first "positive" moment – which corresponds with the epigraph and with its explication: repeating the question, relighting the *gigantomachy*, rediscovering the meaning of the aporia – comes a critical moment: what Plato and Aristotle have discovered (and that, in exemplary fashion in their critique of the "Pre-Socratics" [12], through the "patricide" committed by the Stranger on Parmenides) has been recovered; it has fallen into oblivion, which is, thus, an oblivion which sends out its roots right up to the ancient ontology itself. This is what

---

[10] Ga., 20, *Prolegomena zur Geschichte des Zeitbegriffs*, p. 179. – Th. Kisiel, *History of the Concept of Time : Prolegomena*, Bloomington, Indiana University Press, 1985.

[11] Ga., 19, *Sophistes*, pp. 435–499; trad. Richard Rojcewicz and André Schuwer, Bloomington, Indiana University Press, 1997 (translation addapted).

[12] We should keep in mind the fact that the so-called Pre-Socratics don't play any particular role in the economy of the first Heidegger's though (that is, until '29–'30). The beginning of the philosphical tradition is clearly Platonic-Aristotelian, or even, if you like, "Socratic". Cf. *Grundprobleme der antiken Philosophie*. It is this Platonic-Aristotelian beginning that has defined itself in its debate with the Pre-Socratics. – If we have to pose the question of the meaning of "to be" newly today, it is at the same time, following the example of Plato / the Stranger, against those who "tell stories" rather than to turn to the thing itself (*to pragma auto* – Plato, *Letter* VII), but it is also in debate with Plato and Aristotle, with their answers. – We shall follow here the valuable indications of W. F. von Herrmann, *Hermeneutische Phänomenologie des Daseins. Eine Erlaüterung von "Sein und Zeit"*, Klostermann, Francfort, 1987, p. 10 : "Heidegger stellt an den Anfang von *SuZ* das Platon-Zitat, um damit zu bekunden, daß seine Frage nach dem Sinn von Sein keine neue und originelle Frage des abendländische Denken ist. Die Frage nach dem Sinn von Sein versteht sich geschichtlich als ein Wiederaufgreifen dieser ältesten, schon in die vorplatonische Zeit hineinreichende Frage. Allein, mit dieser selben Frage greift er nicht auf dieselbe Art der Fragestellung Platons und der Griechen auf. Dieselbe Frage wird neu gestellt in der Weise einer radikal gewandelten Fragestellung und Fragerichtung." It is the last point that deserves our attention.

makes the requirement for the repetition and the transformation of the question and of its structure as question: it is a matter (I summarise drastically) of substituting the question "who?" with the question "what?" (*SuZ*, § 12, p. 54; trans. 79), of restricting the range of Aristotelian categories (those of the *Vorhandenheit*) and to identify the existentials that correspond with being and with the mode of being of this being that we ourselves are: being-there, *Dasein*. The transformation of the question or rather, of the Frage*stellung*, that wants itself to be radical, consists in finding another "ground" and another "main theme" for its elaboration. That is why the repetition implies necessarily also a moment of destruction (*Destruktion, Abbau*): the confrontation with the "prejudices" that have had as effect the obscuration of the "questionability" of the question. As we know, Heidegger examined three prejudices very swiftly and in an almost programmatic way:

1) the generality of the concept of being; being defined as "transcendent"; the analogical unity of being;
2) the indefinableness of the concept of being;
3) the average evidence of the concept of being, before he started, in § 2, the examination of the formal structure of all questions in general, and the specific structure of the question of "to be".

But already here in § 1, that exposes the prejudices that bar access to the reconsideration of the question of being (*SuZ*, 5, trans. p. 25), one picks up the same ambiguities that have already been pointed out in the epigraph and its commentary. Heidegger notes, in fact:

Der Sinn von Sein muß uns ... schon in gewisser Weise verfügbar sein. Angedeutet wird: wir bewegen uns immer schon in einem Seinsverständnis. Aus hier heraus erwächst die ausdrückliche Frage nach dem Sinn von Sein und die Tendenz zu dessen Begriff. Wir wissen nicht, was "Sein" besagt. Aber schon wenn wir fragen: "Was ist 'Sein'?", halten wir uns in einem Verständnis des "ist", ohne daß wir begrifflich fixieren können, was das "ist" bedeutet. Wir kennen nicht einmal den Horizont, aus dem her wir den Sinn fassen und fixieren sollten. Dieses durchschnittliche und vage Selbstverständnis ist ein Faktum [13].

So the meaning of Being must already be available to us in some way. As we have intimated, we always conduct our activities in an understanding of Being. Out of this understanding arise both the explicit question of the meaning of Being and the tendency that leads us towards its conception. We do no know what 'Being' means. But even if we ask, "What is "Being"?", we keep within an understanding the 'is', though we are unable to fix conceptually what that 'is' signifies. We do not even know the horizon in terms of which that meaning is to be grasped and fixed. But this vague average understanding of Being is still a Fact [Translation, p. 25].

These lines are evidently decisive for our intentions, because one sees in them clearly how the transition from *Sinn von Sein* to *Seinsverständnis* is carried

---

[13] Cf. also Ga. 20, 194 : "Von diesem "Sein" als unbestimmter Bedeutung und Begriff machen wir ständig Gebrauch, so weitgehend, daß wir gar nicht wissen, daß wir "Sein" in unbestimmter Bedeutung gebrauchen. So steht es auch im folgenden, bei der Ausarbeitung des Fragens : Was "*ist*" zu seinem "*Sein*" gehörig? Wir *leben immer schon in einem Verständnis des "ist"*, ohne daß wir genauer sagen könnten, was das eigentlich bedeutet. Damit ist angezeigt, daß das Verständnis von "Sein" und ein gewisser Begriff von "Sein" immer schon da ist."

out, even though Heidegger maintains the point of the question as a question of "is" (of the copula). Since Heidegger departs in this way (something that happens often in what follows in *SuZ* and in his *œuvre* in general) from the term, from the verb "is" in its multiple uses, one is tempted to believe that he, thus, states that in every understanding in the form of language, in every proposition, an understanding is to be found present, albeit implicitly, of being, of "to be", in accordance with that which Aristotle maintained in *Metaphysics* Delta, 7, 1017 a 23–30:

> the categories are categories of being, of which the meaning, the senses, are distributed according to the multiplicity of categories: *hosakhôs gar légetai <ta skhèmata tès kategorias>, tosautakhôs to einai sèmainei*. [Aristotle continues]: "to each of the categories corresponds a meaning of being", and that is the same thing to say that "the man is feeling well" and "the man feels well", "the man is walking" and "the man walks".

But – and this is the origin of all the difficulty or ambiguity of his position – Heidegger's thesis is also that the understanding of being exceeds greatly the understanding of language, understanding in the form of language or linguistic understanding. Being is understood well beyond language or the *logos* defined as *logos apophantikos:* to pose the "question of being" in a new way, means precisely to abandon the Platonic main theme of the *logos*.

When one says: being or the meaning of being is understood well beyond language, it should, of course, be made clear that we are speaking here of *Sprache*, understood as *logos* and *apophansis*, because we know that Heidegger will also make of language "the house of the truth of being [14]". Or again, at the end of the *Letter:* "The language <for the thought to come> is the language of being, like the clouds are the clouds of the sky [15]". But be it as it may on this point, I believe that one could raise an objection here, and a strong one at that, one formulated several times by Ernst Tugendhat [16]: Tugendhat notes, in fact, that even in the framework of this second sense of the thesis that being goes beyond language, the point remains that Heidegger stays always, and necessarily has to stay, orientated on the "is" (one sees it notably in the lectures of 1941, *Grundbegriffe,* that presents a long variation on the theme [17]); it is, in fact, the "is" that constitutes the element that carries all understanding in the form of language, in general, as well as the understanding of this or that proposition. On what else should you then orientate yourself when you want to understand being? But Heidegger goes one step further: he states that all understanding, even un-

---

[14] *Brief über den "Humanismus",* Ga., 9, *Wegmarken*, p. 318.

[15] Ibid., p. 364.

[16] Ernst Tugendhat, "Die Seinsfrage und ihre sprachliche Grundlage", "Heideggs Seinsfrage", in *Philosophische Aufsätze*, Suhrkamp, 1992; and earlier in *Vorlesungen Zur Einführung in die sprachanalytische Philosophie*, lectures 5 and 6, Suhrkamp, 1976.

[17] Cf. Ga., 51, p. 30 : "We say "this man is from Swabia"; "this book is yours"; "the enemy is on the retreat"; "this is deep red"; "God is"; "there are floods in China"; "the cup is silver"; "the soldier is at war"; "the insect is in the field"; "the conference is in auditorium 5"; "On all the summits / is rest" …"

derstanding outside of language, is understanding of being. The difficulty is then to know what is to be understood under "to be" when understanding is not orientated on "is" anymore. Therefore, an unresolved tension remains in *SuZ* and in the whole of Heidegger's thought: sometimes being is understood phenomenologically or as phenomenon, sometimes it is orientated on "is".

At the threshold of *SuZ* the question of being is straightaway, and with reference to Plato, determined as a question pertaining to the uses of the verb "to be" and of the verbal participle: *being, seiend*. Heidegger refers again, in § 1, to expressions of the kind like: "the sky *is* blue", "I *am* happy" (p. 4; trans. p. 23) and he lists different uses of the participle *seiend*. But two pages further on, we read this, which is very hard to reconcile with the initial question:

> there are many things which we designate as 'being' ["seiend"], and we do so in various senses. Everything we talk about, everything we have in view, everything towards which we comport ourselves in any way, is being; what we are is being, an so is how we are. Being lies in the fact that something is, and in its Being as it is; in Reality; in presence-at-hand; in subsistence; in validity; in Dasein; in the 'there is'", *ibid*. 6–7 (trans. p. 26).

The list is quite astounding, because the series of terms require rather the distinctions, the differentiations with relation to meanings of "to be" or of being that should be indicated. But Heidegger continues:

> In *which* entities is the meaning of Being to be discerned? From which entities is the disclosure of Being to take its departure? Is the starting-point optional, or does some particular entity have priority when we come to work out the question of Being? Which entity shall we take for our example, and in what sense does it have priority?

In a sense everything is said, or at least decided with this series of questions! The "concrete" elaboration of the question will be "hermeneutico-phenomenological", and not linguistic or logical! The exemplary being from which the "meaning" of being is to be deciphered (*ablesen*) is *Dasein* that becomes thus the focal point, as it were, to which the different meanings of being are lead back. In fact, Heidegger maintains to the end the heavy presupposition of a unitary pole of meanings, as is still attested by the question, recalled in *Mein Weg in die Phänomenologie* (1963): "If beings are called according to their multiple senses, what is the guiding, fundamental meaning?" Yet, one could very well defend, conversely, the idea that we do not need a fundamental meaning of being against which the others would be secondary or derived. The terms could remain equivocal here, or one could find oneself amidst a network of meanings amongst which none is more "fundamental" than the others.

Why does *Dasein* provide a new main theme? Precisely because it is characterised in its being by "understanding of being"; because it is the being that, in its being, relates to its own being; because it is, equally, the one that poses the question of being. It seems to me that Heidegger finds there something like an intensification of the question initially referred to Plato: we are invited to ask ourselves the same question as the one of the Stranger of Elea: "What does 'to be' mean?", but we are also invited to pose ourselves the question: "What does it mean to pose this question?". On the one hand, then, the *Frage nach dem Sinn des Seins* – on the other, the question, completely different, of the *Sinn der Seinsfrage*.

For Heidegger, Greek ontology is essentially "dialectical", in that it inquires about the meaning of being (or of its "concept" as Heidegger also says strangely) by interrogating the *logos*, by taking the *logos* as the main theme. It is, therefore, onto-*logy* in an emblematic sense and, therefore, it contrasts radically with that which Heidegger, for his part, calls "fundamental-ontology"; the latter examines, in fact, another exemplary being, *Dasein*, that is, the being that is itself defined by its opening towards the understanding of being and, even more, by its opening towards the question of being. *Dasein*, as Derrida [18] emphasised quite rightly, is what "we" are from the moment that we know of ourselves only that we have "the power, or rather the possibility to question, we have the experience of questioning". The guiding question could then be formulated as a question of "who?". Who am I, who are we? This being that we are, this "we" who, at the beginning of the existential analysis, may have no other name than *Da-sein*[19], is chosen as exemplary being for the question of being only from the moment of *experience of the question*, the possibility of *Fragen*, in the way in which it fits within the network of the *Gefragte*, being, of the *Erfragte*, the meaning of being, of the *Befragte der Seinsfrage*, that is, the being that we are and that becomes thus the exemplary or privileged being for a *reading* ... of the meaning of being.

The importance of the overturn that has been carried out, since the beginning, could be assessed if on thinks simply for example of the movement of the ontological question in *Metaphysics* Z 1: the question that has always been asked and which leaves us always in an aporia: to *palai te kai nûn kai aei zétoumenon kai aei aporoumenon, ti to on, touto isti, tis hè ousia* (one is clearly tempted to discern here a conscious reference to the Sophist, 244 A), the question: *ti to on?*, is, posed differently and more precisely, the question: *tis hè ousia?*, what is substance or, if one would like to follow an indication by Jacques Brunschwig[20], the question: what is properly speaking and in an exemplary way "substance"?

But now I shall have to conclude: the ambiguity of Heidegger's taking up or repetition of the question of being appears henceforth in all its fullness: Heidegger engages, by his reference to Plato and by the first paragraphs of the Introduction of *SuZ*, in a double question, a question pertaining to the meaning of the verb "to be" and that concerns a "phenomenon, called "being"" (*das Phänomen: Sein*).

---

[18] J. Derrida, *De l'esprit. Heidegger et la question*, Paris, Galilée, 1987, p. 37. *Of spirit: Heidegger and the question*. Translated by Geoffrey Bennington and Rachel Bowlby, Chicago, University of Chicago Press, 1989.

[19] Cf. Thomas Sheehan, "Reading Heidegger's "What Is Metaphysics"", in *The New Yearbook for Phenomenology and Phenomenological Philosophy*, I – 2001, p. 182, n. 2.

[20] Cf. Jacques Brunschwig, "Dialectique et ontologie chez Aristote – A propos d'un livre récent", in *Revue philosophique de la France et de l'Etranger*, 89ème année, 1964, reprint in *Etudes Aristotéliciennes, Métaphysique et théologie*, éd. J.-F. Courtine, Paris, Vrin 1985, pp. 207–228.

To put it differently, Heidegger seems to telescope two heterogeneous questions: the "semantic" question of the meaning of the verb "to be" and the question of the "meaning" of a phenomenon, the phenomenon "being", which becomes the emblematic phenomenon, the phenomenon *par excellence* (according to this sense of the phenomenon it is precisely that which in the first place and most often doesn't show itself!). To elaborate the question "in a concrete way" Heidegger finally identifies an "emblematic" being of which the first trait is precisely the "meaning of the question", the possibility to question according to a "pre-understanding" of being that characterises it before any *logos*.

From the beginning of *SuZ*, Heigger emphasises that the question of being (*die Frage nach dem Sein*) should be posed (*gestellt*), i.e. not only set about haphazardly: "Was ist Sein?" The question should be taught, argued, documented. That is what Heidegger calls: *die Ausarbeitung der Seinsfrage*. But in order to be elaborated as genuine research, the question should already be able to draw from something pre-given, given beforehand, from being; that about which one inquires is therefore the meaning of being, such that "being" which is to be defined is already understood in a certain way. So the question is a *Bestimmungsfrage*, a question of determining/definition, that implies, therefore, a *Vorgegebenes*. There again, the point of departure seems to be "logico-linguistic": The question is therefore posed, starting from the undetermined pre-understanding of this expression "to be". "Was besagt "Sein"?"

For Plato that which is asked about (*das Gefragte*) was the *logos* and the *Hauptfrage* was, therefore, onto-*logy!* For Heidegger that which is asked about is *Dasein*, i.e. also the one that poses the question, but again and more, the one that is defined by the question, in its "who?" and who, by its relation to its being (the one for whom in his being there is question of its being itself), is equally straightaway characterised by the "understanding of being". One has left straightaway – despite the pre-beginning and the epigraph – the *logos*, the main theme of the *logos*, one has left the understanding that E. Tugendhat called "in the form of language" or linguistic.

What remains to be seen – and I shall make no conclusion on this point now – is what the possibilities and promises are concerning onto-*logy* and fundamental ontology as analysis of Dasein.

Karl-Otto Apel

Questioning: The Almost Forgotten Dimension in Traditional Logos-Reflection and its Re-Detection by Hermeneutics

I. Introduction: Exposition of the Topic

The title of my paper is a somewhat complicated indication of the philosophical point and significance of the role of questioning, as it was detected and stressed in the context of "philosophical hermeneutics", e.g. in H. G. Gadamer's work *Truth and Method*. For, if this novel perspective on the role of questioning is appropriately explicated, it turns out, I suggest, that its philosophical point is not restricted to hermeneutics in a narrow methodological sense but amounts to be a revolutionary redetection and revaluation of the function of questioning with regard to the whole range of *episteme* and what I like to call logos-reflection in occidental philosophy. Although this philosophical tradition has one of its origins in the Socratic art of questioning within the framework of the dialogue, this fact with Plato and Aristotle did not become the basic theme of logos-reflection and thereby of understanding epistemic rationality.

With Aristotle reflection on possible questions takes indeed a heuristic role with regard to exploring the categories and other *topoi* in the context of *Topica* (ch. VIII). But even in this preparatory part of dialectics philosophical research is primarily oriented toward the *pragmata* as objects of cognition, whereas the intersubjective dimension of questioning is rather considered only as a matter of teaching.[1] This constellation, I think, is continued by the so called *quaestiones* of medieval scholastics. In this whole context of ancient and medieval dialectics, at least no special problem seems to exist in regard of finding out – through communicative understanding – which really is the meaning of the questions of the partners in a dialogue, say, by asking for the presuppositions of their questions.

Very characteristic, in this context, is the division of the dimensions of the "logos" that by the commentator Ammonius is ascribed to Aristotle's successor Theophrast. It reads: "Since speech (greek: logos) has a twofold relation ..., one to the hearers to whom it means something, the other to the things (pragmata) about which the speaker wants to bring about a belief with the hearers, with regard to the hearers arise poetics and rhetorics ..., but with regard to the things the philosopher primarily has to take care to refute the false and to prove the true."[2] (emphasis K.-O. A.)

---

[1] Gadamer, H.-G., 1965, *Wahrheit und Methode: Grundzüge einer philosophischen Hermeneutik*, Mohr, Tübingen.

[2] Ammonius, in *Arislotelis De Interpretatione* Commentarius (ed. R. Busse, Berlin 1887, 65, 31–66, 19). For a comment see Apel, K.-O., 1963, 1980, *Die Idee der Sprache in der Tradition des Humanismus von Dante bis Vico*, Bouvier, Bonn, 150 ff.

The context of this passage shows that the philosophically relevant dimension of the logos is indeed restricted to the relation to things. For rhetorics is not meant in any philosophically relevant sense but only as an act of using "beautiful" and "emotionally moving" words. Finally, in modern times, reflection on reason as cognitive function of consciousness completely superseded any reflection on the logos as dialogical dimension of intersubjective understanding. From Descartes through Husserl even "methodical" or "transcendental solipsism" was considered the ultimate (transcendental) basis position of thought and cognition.[3]

Hence, in respect to the history of philosophy, one could think that the systematic preconditions for a fresh detection and analysis of the dialogical basis of questioning could only be provided by the so called linguistic-pragmatic turn of philosophy in the 20th century. But, strangely enough, this did not immediately come about where it could be expected: say, in the later Wittgenstein's reflection on "language games" or in Austin's and Searle's "speech act" theory. Rather, I would say, it took place in a novel and challenging way in the context of the hermeneutic-linguistic turn of phenomenology, which was initiated by Heidegger and especially by Gadamer, partly indeed with a retrospective to the English historian and philosopher Collingwood.[4]

One of the main reasons for this surprising fact, I suggest, was provided by the circumstance that only in the context of philosophical hermeneutics the dimension of (historical) time and the problem of bridging the distance of time by the operation of understanding plays an essential role in reflecting on the relationship between question and answer as being the basis of a dialogue. Philosophical hermeneutics indeed has to reflect upon the following fact: Trying to understand the propositions of a historically given text presupposes an understanding of the responsive relationship of these propositions to questions, but not simply of the relationship of responses to questions in general (or to problems), but a double relationship of propositions to questions: one to the questions that, together with unavoidable prejudices, are pre-given in the world-pre-understanding of the hermeneutic interpreter, and, on the other hand, the relationship to those questions that may be really presupposed by the interpretandum, i.e. by the propositions of the text to be understood.

Now, this double relationship between propositions and questions and the interfering gap of historical time constitute the essential problem of logos-reflection that was presupposed by Gadamer as the challenge to hermeneutics. It has to be responded, he suggested, by the conception of a "fusion of horizons", which has to make possible hermeneutic understanding.[5]

---

[3] Cf. Apel, K.–O., 1998, "The Cartesian Paradigm of First Philosophy. A Critical Appreciation from the Perspective of Another (the Next?) Paradigm", *International Journal of Philosophical Studies* 6, 1–16.

[4] Cf. Especially Gadamer, H.-G., 1965, loc. cit. 351 ff., with reference to R. G. Collingwood's project of a "logic of question and answer", pointed out in his *Autobiography* (Clarendon Press, Oxford, 1939).

[5] Ibidem, 289 f., 356 f., 375.

It seems clear, I think, that this hermeneutic account and its underlying problem is different both from the Socratic use and reflection on questioning within an actual dialogue and also from the thematizations of questioning or of interrogative speech acts by language-analytic philosophy of the 20th century.

In the Socratic horizon of our problem the function of the art of questioning was primarily that of mediating between ignorance (or the knowledge of ignorance) and winning possible knowledge. The paradoxical prima facie situation of how to ask the right questions from a starting point of ignorance, this apparent *aporia* was answered by Socrates/Plato by the conception of "maieutic" questioning, i.e. of stimulating a reflective recollection ("anamnesis") of the inborn ideas.[6] This approach meets indeed a special aspect of the method of questioning, which later was taken up as a metaphor for explaining the aprioristic aspect of a rationalistic epistemology. But from the hermeneutic point of view one could ask, if or, respectively, how this Socratic dimension of asking and answering questions in an actual (philosophical) dialogue, which presupposes equal logos-conditions with the partners of the dialogue, can be applied to a hermeneutic dialogue or quasi-dialogue. Can it take into account and be related to the gap of (historical) time between the different logos-conditions presupposed by the interpreter and the interpretandum in such a situation? (I shall come back to this problem.)

On the other hand, the thematizations of questioning in language-analytical philosophy could be called "abstract", if compared with hermeneutic reflection. That is to say: they disregard the fact that all propositions as parts of human speech can be considered as concrete historical responses to concrete historical questions or at least to possible concrete questions. Those interrelations between questions and answers are completely neglected in speech-act theory, where interrogative acts are simply subsumed under the class of acts of requesting an information from one's partner.[7] (The horizon for imagining a hermeneutically relevant interrelationship between historically given or possible questions and propositions as answers to those questions is at best opened up by the conception of the "background" of meaningful use of language in Searle's book *Intentionality* (1983).[8]) Even Strawson's and others' reflection on ("existential" and "rule") "presuppositions" of questions is "abstract" in respect to our problem. This shows up especially if one considers the long-standing debate about "transcendental presuppositions"[9], comparing this debate e.g. with Collingwood's earlier "historical" and "metaphysical" conception of "absolute" and "relative presuppositions" of thought which indeed was embedded in a history-related logic of question and answer.

---

[6] Cf. Plato, *Menon* 81d 4f, *Phaidon* 14 d9–e4.
[7] See e.g. Searle, J. R., 1969, *Speech Acts*, Cambridge University Press, 69.
[8] See Searle, J. R., 1983, *Intentionality*, Cambridge University Press, Ch. 5.
[9] For a comprehensive account see Niquet, M., 1991, *Transzendentale Argumente: Kant, Strawson und die sinnkritische Aporetik der Detranszendentalisierung*, Suhrkamp, Frankfurt a.M.

However, by a confrontation of Collingwood's account of "absolute metaphysical presuppositions" of human questions and the debate about "transcendental presuppositions" of questions in the wake of Strawson's language-analytical reconstruction of Kant's Critique of Reason[10], one can also realize that by the distinction between the "abstract" and the hermeneutic, history-related approach to our problem no definite assessment and evaluation has been reached. For, Collingwood's talk about "absolute metaphysical" presuppositions, which at the same time are considered to be history-dependent and explorable by a metaphysical historian or historicist metaphysician[11], this strange conception obviously exposes an *aporia*. For, which are those presuppositions of questioning that make Collingwood's own approach to history and especially the universal validity claim of his "metaphysics" possible? This latter claim obviously cannot be reduced to one of the "absolute" and "history-dependent presuppositions" he supposes in his doctrine. This *aporia* of Collingwood's approach may already suggest that hermeneuticism or historicism without transcendentalism cannot answer the question concerning the presuppositions of its own fundamental questions and their possible philosophical responses. We will try to confirm this conjecture more closely with regard to the late Heidegger and Gadamer.

On the other hand, the debate about transcendental arguments in language-analytical philosophy is widely considered to have ended with a failure. Transcendental apriorism seemed to be always reducible to the quasi-transcendental particularism of the ad hoc validity of parasitism arguments.[12] But I think that the reason for this result of the debate consisted in the fact that it from the outset was restricted to the task of justifying categorical schemes.[13] These schemes could ultimately be relativized by a holistic questioning of the very distinction between categorical form and empirical content. But the transcendental question as to the conditions of the possibility of valid thought can be asked more radically with regard to the pragmatic dimension of the presuppositions of argumentation, namely with regard to the necessary validity claims of arguments which cannot be denied or disputed without committing a performative self-contradiction.[14] In that case, I think, a transcendental-pragmatic reflection can show up those presuppositions of asking and possibly answering philosophical questions that cannot be relativized by holistic or by historicist arguments.

---

[10] Cf. Strawson, P. F., 1966, *The Bounds of Sense*, Methuen, London.

[11] Cf. Collingwood, R, G., 1940, *An Essay on Metaphysics*, Clarendon Press, Oxford.

[12] Cf. Strawson. P. F., 1985, *Skepticism and Naturalism: Some Varieties. The Woolbridge Lectures 1983*, London, and Rorty, R., 1991, "Verificationism and Transcendental Arguments", in *Nous* 5, and the same, 1972, "The World Well Lost", *Journal of Philosophy* 96, and the same, 1978, "Epistemological Behaviorism and the De-Transcendentalization of Analytic Philosophy", *Neue Hefte für Philosophie* 14.

[13] Cf. Niquet, M., 1991.

[14] Cf. Apel, K.–O., 1975, "The Problem of Philosophical Fundamental Grounding in Light of a Transcendental Pragmatics of Language", in *Man and World* 8, 239–75. reprinted in K. Baynes et al. (eds.), 1987, *After Philosophy. End or Transformation?* MIT Press, Cambridge, Mass., 250–90.

By these considerations, I suggest, we have reached the point in the introduction of our topic where we can try to clarify the relationship between hermeneuticism and transcendentalism with regard to the problem of questioning (and eventually this clarification might show as well, how a novel version of (quasi-) "maieutic" questioning can and must take its place in our day's philosophy). We will begin with a critical reconstruction of Gadamer's and Heidegger's approach to the hermeneutic dimension of questioning or, respectively, understanding questions.

II. The Problem of Hermeneuticism/Historicism versus Transcendentalism in the Logic of Questions and Answers with Gadamer and Heidegger

In the first place, I would fully agree with Gadamer's thesis that all propositions primarily must not be considered as abstract entities in a logical space but as parts of meaningful speech in a dialogue (or in a text as part of an expanded dialogue), and that thus far they must be conceived as answers to questions. Therefore our understanding of the meaning of propositions must take recourse to understanding the pertinent questions. This does not only hold for hermeneutics as art of understanding texts, but in a more basic sense even for understanding the propositional meaning of what the partner in a dialogue says. Or, more precisely: it holds from the moment where, already within the dialogue, our understanding of what the partner says is no longer immediately transparent, for this moment is, as already Schleiermacher suggested, the starting point of "hermeneutic operations". (At this occasion it may be noticed that with regard to the inter-subjective dimension of communication within a dialogue – say between interrogative and responsive speech-acts – we must indeed start out from the presupposition of an immediate mutual understanding; we cannot start out from the supposition that is suggested by Davidson's conception of "radical interpretation"[15], so that our mutual understanding would rest on hypotheses; for, in my opinion, immediate intersubjective, i.e. communicative understanding is a precondition for setting up scientific hypotheses and corresponding questions with regard to nature, or, for that matter, with regard to human "behaviour". Even the initial "hermeneutic operations" within a dialogue and those of interpreting a text are far from being hypotheses in the sense of "radical interpretation". This latter project rather has to be understood as a limiting case of communicative understanding.

Thus I also suppose, with Gadamer, that understanding propositions and corresponding questions is originally a part of communicative understanding. Even the later Dilthey has realized that communicative understanding within a "common sphere of life" is not primarily "reviving" or "reconstructing" psychological

---

[15] Cf. Davidson, D., 1973, "Radical Interpretation", *Dialectica* 27, 313–328.

processes of other persons;[16] it is indeed rather "communicative understanding on something" (in German: "sich verständigen über etwas" or "über eine Sache"). This latter structure, taken as a whole, in my opinion, is also the transcendental-hermeneutic basis of our cognition of something as something; for, it contains – still unseparated – two complementary dimensions of cognition: viz. objectifying cognition, or cognition according to the subject-object relation (which, however, is mediated by language and thus also by communication) and, on the other hand, cognition according to the subject-cosubject relation, i.e. understanding of other persons (which, however, in its turn, is part of communicative understanding on something)[17]. It is by a methodical differentiation of the two complementary dimensions of this integral structure, I suggest, that the typical approaches of human inquiry, viz. scientific cognition and hermeneutic text-interpretation come about.

Thus far, my transcendental-hermeneutic approach and Gadamer's universal-hermeneutic approach, which also presupposes the structure of a dialogue on things ("die Sachen"), are still in agreement, I suppose. But now, with Gadamer, the structure of text-interpretation is characterized, as I already indicated, by the tension between two more or less different kinds of questions: those that must be implied in the world-pre-understanding of the interpreter of the text and, on the other hand, those that may be presupposed by the propositions of the interpretandum. The reason for supposing this difference can be reduced, roughly speaking, to the structure of historical time, which in hermeneutics comes into play as being constitutive for the task of not immediate but reflective understanding. With this supposition I can agree too, but not with the way Gadamer suggests we should or rather would in fact deal in hermeneutics with the deep structure of different horizons of questions conditioned by the (historical) time.

The main response to this situation that is provided by Gadamer's hermeneutics – the conception of a "fusion of horizons" – is either too vague, i.e. without methodological relevance, or, if understood in accordance with Gadamer's methodologically relevant suggestions, it is unsatisfactory. It is too vague in so far as one may concede that a "fusion of horizons" is a factual precondition of understanding, a precondition however that is somehow fulfilled in any case of text-interpretation – be it hermeneutically adequate or not. If, however, we take into account those methodologically relevant suggestions that Gadamer in fact gives, his device of bridging the gap of time-conditioned differences of questions and their presuppositions is seriously one-sided and thus far unsatisfactory, in my opinion. For his device does not do justice to both sides of the postulated fusion of horizons, i.e. to the different priorities or privileges of the interpretandum and the interpreter, which ultimately must be compatible with the reciproc-

---

[16] Cf. Dilthey, H., *Gesammelte Schriften VII*, 84 ff., 147 f.
[17] Cf. Apel, K.-O., 1992, "The Hermeneutic Dimension of Social Science and its Normative Foundation", *Man and World* 25, 247–270.

ity of the transcendental-hermeneutic preconditions of a communicative discourse. Let me try to spell this out in more detail:

First, there is Gadamer's postulate of an "anticipation of perfectness" ("Vorgriff der Vollkommenheit") with regard to assessing the intelligible meaning, the coherence and even the truth of the propositions of the interpretandum. I think, this is a well justified heuristic demand in so far as it corresponds to the cognitive interest of all hermeneutics: viz. the interest in learning as much as possible from the interpretandum. However, this cognitive interest does not include any disposition towards a renunciation of possible critique; it rather should serve to make justified critique possible through excluding misunderstandings.

This viewpoint can shed light on a second demand, or rather suggestion, that for Gadamer is closely connected with the "anticipation of perfectness". I think here of his rehabilitation of the "authority" of texts as parts of a – sometimes "classical" – heritage of the "tradition" of our culture, which anyway has to be handed down, nay even kept in force with regard to its validity claims.[18] Also this demand can be justified, I think, in the sense of well understood value-conservatism, but this means that it can be justified so long as it does not promote (foster) dogmatism by immunizing the validity claims of the tradition against any justified critique.

Thus far we have thematized and partly justified only the hermeneutic priority of the interpretandum, which Gadamer almost treats as a superiority on principle. Now, what does emphasizing the priority of the interpretandum mean, if it is analyzed in terms of a hermeneutics that relates back propositions of texts to presupposed questions and their cultural background? I think it means that the interpreter has to reflectively problematize and possibly correct those questions he or she must presuppose if he or she tries to understand in light of his/her world-pre-understanding the propositions of the interpretandum. The interpreter has to correct his/her own presupposed questions at least heuristically as far as possible in favour of the questions underlying the propositions of the interpretandum. This is of course a one-sided conception of the necessary "fusion of horizons", but it can still be justified as a heuristic device of hermeneutics, I think.

But what about the other side of the whole process of the "fusion of horizons"? Are there also reasons for supposing a possible priority and even cognitive and evaluative superiority of the side of the interpreter, who after all represents the possibility of additional reflection and of progress due to the growth of scientific knowledge of the facts or perhaps even due to new philosophical insights concerning ethical norms? Now this question, on the basis of Gadamer's hermeneutics, can only be answered in the negative. Here, I suggest, one has to supplement or even to correct Gadamer's use of the hermeneutic logic of question and answer.

---

[18] Cf. Gadamer, H.–G., 1965, loc. cit. 256 ff., 261 ff.

In the hermeneutic tradition of the 19th century, e.g. with Schleiermacher, Boeckh and Dilthey, and before already with Fichte and Kant, a well known *topos* can be found that suggests, almost as a matter of course, the possibility also of a superiority of the interpreter's position in hermeneutics. What I mean is the suggestion that an author of a text can, or through hermeneutics even should, be better understood than he could understand himself.[19] Gadamer makes a distinction between two versions of this *topos*, or even between two epochal preferences of accounting for it: one, predominant in the enlightenment of the 18th century, emphasizes the possible superiority of the interpreter's knowledge of things due to scientific progress; the other, predominant in the romantic hermeneutics of the early 19th century, primarily points to the interpreter's chance of making conscious creative unconscious processes of work production, especially in the case of interpreting works of art. Gadamer, in his final judgment (assessment), rejects both versions of the *topos* (the second version he rejects along with his general critique of the Schleiermacher/ Dilthey conception of understanding as identical re-construction or re-enactment of the author's productive thought.) He declares: "Understanding is in truth not understanding better, neither in the sense of objectively understanding better through clearer concepts, nor in the sense of the fundamental superiority of the conscious over the unconscious moment of production. It suffices to say that one understands differently if one understands at all."[20]

Here we have indeed arrived at a central tenet of Gadamer's whole conception of hermeneutics as a counter-position against the Schleiermacher/Dilthey hermeneutics (and beyond that, I think, against any possible conception of a methodologically relevant hermeneutic with a normative dimension). As I understand the quoted passage from its context, it is not only directed against the *topos* of the 18th and early 19th century, but, beyond that, in general, against any supposition of definite progress in hermeneutics as – in a wide sense – a scientific enterprise. Now, from the perspective of a methodologically relevant hermeneutics, I have always considered both meaning claims of Gadamer's tenet to be extremely implausible, since so many examples of understanding the author of a text by way of reflectively overtaking his self-understanding are available, especially in the history of science; and, in general, still today the regulative idea of improving our understanding of texts is a guiding objective of all historic-hermeneutic disciplines.

But let us consider the problem from the point of view of our attempted analysis of the logic of question and answer, which virtually underlies Gadamer's conception of a "fusion of horizons". I think there is no inconsistency between the *topos* of better understanding and the heuristic postulate of first trying to find out and give maximal weight to the underlying questions of the interpretandum, in accordance with the heuristic "anticipation of perfectness".

---

[19] Cf. Ibidem, 180 ff.
[20] Ibidem, 280 (engl. trans. R. Sommermeier, emphasis K.-O. Apel).

For, through trying in this way to make the case of the interpretandum as strong as possible and to learn as much as possible from it, the interpreter can also win an optimal point of departure for bringing to bear his/her own deviating and possibly superior questions and answers; and thereby he/she may be able to overtake the self-understanding of the author of the interpretandum. (At this point one has also to notice that overtaking the self-understanding of an author may be restricted to a certain respect. In other respects the propositions of an interpretandum may still be superior, because even the underlying questions are not yet understood.)

However, on the other hand, the interpreter, who looks for the interrelations between the propositions and the presupposed questions of a text may even find inconsistencies and other deficits in the interpretandum that give good reasons for switching over from the "anticipation of perfectness" to a "hermeneutics of suspicion" (in the sense of Ricoeur[21]) or even to a demasking critique of ideology.[22]

With regard to the more general meaning of Gadamer's rejection of "better understanding", I would claim that there is no inconsistency either between the supposition of the possibility of progress in understanding and the insight that we shall never reach certainty about having definitely improved former interpretations of a text. This is simply an implication of the principle of fallibilism, which does not contradict meliorism. Hence, in this respect, the methodological postulate of "better understanding" can only be refused if one confuses the regulative idea of progress toward the truth with the utopia of – factually to be reached – complete transparency of interpretation – a confusion that, according to my experience, is very fashionable in our day.

But this defence of the good sense of the regulative idea of "better understanding" presupposes – so to speak, on the level of my meta-question with regard to understanding "hermeneutics" – that, as an art of interpretation hermeneutics is at least also methodology and as such implies a normative dimension. Now, precisely this presupposition is not shared by Gadamer, who in *Truth and Method* conceives of hermeneutics as an "ontology"[23]; more precisely, as an ontology in Heidegger's sense of the "clearing" of truth as self-revelation of temporal being in the "history of being". Hence, in order to better understand Gadamer's underlying question in *Truth and Method*, I will at first put in brackets my own, at least partly methodological pre-understanding of "hermeneutics".

As far as I can see, the most important Heideggerian presuppositions of Gadamer's conception of hermeneutics are the following ones: first, the equation of being and time[24], and second, the corresponding conception of truth as his-

---

[21] Cf. Ricoeur, P., 1969, *De l'interprétation. Essai sur Freud*, Seuil, Paris.

[22] Cf. Apel. K.-O. et al., 1971, *Hermeneutik und Ideologiekritik*, Suhrkamp, Frankfurt a. M.

[23] Cf. Gadamer, H.-G., 1965, "Dritter Teil: ontologische Wendung der Hermeneutik am Leitfaden der Sprache", loc. cit. 361 ff.

[24] Ibidem. 243.

tory- and language-related "disclosure" or "uncovering" of being which always at the same time is "hiding" or "concealing" of being.[25] The crucial, but often scarcely noticed implication of Heidegger's conception of truth as disclosure of temporal being lies in the fact that it is no longer connected with the claim to universal validity. (In some statements of the thirties the claim to universal validity for all reasonable beings is even derided by Heidegger.[26] Later, in 1964, Heidegger indeed revoked his early conception of truth in favour of the traditional one, but at the same time he emphasized that history-related clearing of being, i.e. linguistic articulation of the sense of being, is the condition of the possibility of all true and false propositions.[27] Thus even then the pre-eminence of the history-related conception of "clearing" or "uncovering" over the conception of truth as universal validity has been confirmed.)

It is obvious that this history- and language-dependent conception of truth or, respectively, "clearing of being" is the background of Gadamer's "ontological" conception of "hermeneutics" in Truth and Method. And it is clear as well, that the "happening" of "understanding", which in Gadamer's sense is dependent – again and again – on the "fusion of horizons" of world-pre-understanding, can only be considered as "understanding differently" – from time to time. For the dimension of a potentially infinite progress toward a redemption of the claim to universal validity – say, for all possible members of an "indefinite community of interpretation" in the sense of Peirce's and J. Royce's semiotics[28] – is not open on Heidegger's and Gadamer's presuppositions. This seems to follow in particular from Heidegger's supposition that any "clearing" or "uncovering" of the sense of being must at the same time be a "hiding" or "concealing" of other possibilities of the sense of being and hence also of other true and false propositions.

---

[25] Cf. Lafont, C., 1994, *Sprache und Welterschliessung. Zur linguistischen Wende der Hermeneutik Heideggers*, Suhrkamp, Frankfurt a. M.. and Apel, K.-O., 1998, "Sinnkonstitution und Geltungsrechtfertigung. Heidegger und das Problem der Transzendentalphilosophie" and the same, *Auseinandersetzungen*, Suhrkamp, Frankfurt a.M., 505–568, and the same, "Regulative Ideen oder Wahrheitsgeschehen? Zu Gadamers Versuch, die Frage nach den Bedingungen der Möglichkeit gültigen Verstehens zu beantworten", ibidem 569–608 (Engl. Trans., "Regulative Ideas or Truth-Happening?", in Hahn, L. E. (ed.), 1997, *The Philosophy of Hans-Georg Gadamer, The Library of Living Philosophers*, Open Court, Chicago and La Salle, Ill.)

[26] See e.g. the following passage from Vom Ereignis (1936/37), 343: "Wo die Wahrheit sich in die Gestalt der 'Vernuft' und des 'Vernüftigen' hüllt, ist ihr Unwesen an der Arbeit, jene zerstörerische Macht des für Alle-Gültigen, wodurch jedermann beliebig ins Recht gesetzt wird und jenes Vergnügen aufkommt, dass nur ja keiner dem anderen etwas Wesentliches voraus hat. Dieser ‚Zauber' der Allgemeingültigkeit ist es, der die Herrschaft der Auslegung der Wahrheit als Richtigkeit befestigt und fast unershütterlich gemacht hat." (Citation from C. Lafont, loc. cit. 201 f., note 30.)

[27] See Heidegger, M., 1964, "Das Ende der Philosophie und die Aufgabe des Denkens", in *Zur Sache des Denkens*, Tübingen 1969, 76 ff.

[28] Cf. Apel, K.-O., 1973, "Szientismus oder transzendentale Hermeneutik?", in *Transformation der Philosophie*, vol. II Suhrkamp, Frankfurt a. M., 178–219. (Engl. trans., *Towards a Transformation of Philosophy*, Routledge & Kegan Paul, London, 1980, 93–135). See also my essays cited under note 25.

The late Heidegger has even suggested that the whole conception of the logos of occidental metaphysics, and especially the logics or dialectics of ideas (which still works in Kant's conception of "regulative ideas" and thus in the normative conception of progress) is dependent on, and relative to, the historical "event" of the Greek invention of philosophy. And this is not meant as recalling only the "context of discovery" but that of "justification" as well.

Now, what has to be said about this conception, especially from the point of view of the logic of the correlation of question and answer which, as we said, was detected or re-detected by Gadamer's "hermeneutics"?

III. A Transcendental-Hermeneutic Interpretation of the History-Related Logic of Question and Answer

In think that the hermeneutic logic of the correlation of question and answer, which we have introduced in the preceding, can indeed show that there is a point in Heidegger's and Gadamer's connecting the question as to the conditions of the possibility of understanding meaning and the possible answer to this question with the history of being. Yet, I think there is also a point in the universalistic conception of truth and of an indefinite progress in hermeneutic interpretation: a point that can be supported and elucidated by a transcendental-pragmatic and transcendental-hermeneutic application of the logic of the correlation of question and answer. Let us first try to show up Heidegger's point in light of the logic of question and answer.

When Heidegger in 1964 stated that the "clearing" of the meaning of being (and its articulation in language) is the condition of the possibility of true and false propositions he could have made this thesis even more plausible by adding: for, the propositions are always answers (responses) to questions, and specific questions can only be asked in light of a specific history- and culture-dependent "clearing" of the meaning of being. (In this sense, one could e.g. suppose that the fundamental questions of occidental metaphysics, and later of occidental science, could indeed not be conceived outside of this culture and its tradition – e.g. not with the Hopis in Arizona, whose categories of language and world-pre-understanding B. L. Whorf has contrasted with those of the "standard European languages"[29].)

But would this really entail that type of historicism/relativism that is suggested by Heidegger and Gadamer (which, in my opinion, is much more radical than that to be found e.g. with Dilthey)?

Against the later Heidegger's conception of "language" as "the house of being" the following objection has been directed with good reasons, I think: Heidegger has hypostatised language (more exactly: the intensional dimension of meaning) according to his corresponding conception of the "ontic-ontological

---

[29] Cf. Whorf, B. L., 1963, *Language, Thought and Reality,* MIT Press, Cambridge, Mass.

difference". He thereby completely ignored any possible impact (influence) of the empirical exploration of the "ontic" dimension of meaning, say, of the reference and extension of concepts, on the epochal changes of the history of being and language.[30] If this hypostatisation of the intensional meaning of being could be corrected by a more holistic conception of semantics, it would be possible to correct, or at least to modify, also Heidegger's thesis that the "clearing" of the meaning of being is the condition of the possibility of true and false propositions, for these propositions may also be the result of scientific learning processes with regard to the reference and extensional meaning of concepts, and as such they may very well also be conditions of the possibility of even "epochal" – or paradigmatical – changes of language as the "house of being". Thus these epochal changes would no longer appear as the result of an irrational "fate of being", as they in fact are characterized by Heidegger (in a similar way as the changes of "incommensurable paradigms" of science with T. Kuhn[31]).

This holistic conception of the history of the meaning of being, which as a structural pattern has some similarity with the "hermeneutic circle" of text-interpretation, would by no means nullify (abolish) the insight that possible questions – especially categorically relevant questions – are made possible somehow by the whole background of the semantic world view of a language. But this insight may be concretized, I suggest, by the conception of a logic – so to speak – of questions and propositional presuppositions of questions. For it is not only true that understanding propositions may be deepened by understanding presupposed questions but also that understanding questions can be deepened by finding out which presuppositions make the questions meaningful or relevant.

By such an investigation we may find existential presuppositions, rule-presuppositions and also such a thing as cognitive interests, e.g. those very different cognitive interests that constitute the meaning of the typically different "why"-questions in causally explanatory natural science (or, for that matter, behavioural social science) on the one hand, and hermeneutically reconstructing "Geisteswissenschaften", asking for good or bad reasons, on the other.[32] I cannot go into the details of such a logic of questions and presuppositions of questions, but I finally want to apply this logic to those questions and presuppositions of questions that lie at the ground of the whole enterprise of a hermeneutic reconstruction of the human intellectual history.

I have already suggested that, in order to understand the conditions of the possibility of philosophical hermeneutics itself (as a scientific enterprise), one has to look for those questions and underlying presuppositions that somehow transcend the holistic hermeneutic circle of intra-historical text-interpretation. I

---

[30] Cf. Lafont, C., 1994, loc. cit., part II.
[31] Cf. Kuhn, T., 1962, *The Structure of Scientific Revolutions*, Chicago.
[32] Cf. Apel, K.-O., 1979, *Die Erklären-Verstehen -Kontroverse in transzendentalpragmatischer Sicht*, Suhrkamp, Frankfurt a. M. (Engl. trans., *Understanding and Explanation. A Transcendental-Pragmatic Perspective*, MIT Press, Cambridge, Mass., 1984).

would call the conditions I have in mind the transcendental-pragmatic or transcendental-hermeneutic preconditions of hermeneutics. How can they be identified and explicated?

To be sure, Heidegger and Gadamer could argue that they indeed have supposed and partly analysed the so called "pre-structure" of "being-in-the-world" in the way of understanding being, and that by this supposition they have in fact brought down "hermeneutics" of "Dasein" to its transcendental ground in being itself. (In *Sein und Zeit* Heidegger called this ground of his investigation "existential-ontological" or "fundamental-ontological".) But Heidegger also called this ground the "apriori of facticity" and of "historicity", and he characterized its structure as that of a "thrown project" (as "geworfener Entwurf"). This is the reason why he – and Gadamer – later could totally subject the apriori of being-in-the-world through understanding the world to the history of being and – as a consequence – deny any universal validity claim of the truth of hermeneutics.

Now, this tenet, which we refused already with regard to the truth-claims of empirical science (including empirical hermeneutics), obviously must be fallacious *a fortiori* with regard to its self-understanding as a philosophical tenet. For, if it would be true with regard to its own truth claim it would abolish the propositional meaning of this truth-claim. For, by reflectively comparing its propositional meaning (viz. that the validity of all philosophical truth-claims is relative to the history of being) with its performative truth-claim (viz. that this truth is universally valid) we would come to ascertain a performative self-contradiction.

The reason for this *aporia*, I suggest, lies in the fact that the so called "pre-structure" of "being in the world" as "thrown project" of (pre-) understanding the world is not the transcendental ground of philosophical hermeneutics; or, to use another way of clarifying this point: The "pre-structure" of "being in the world as thrown project" is not the "pre-structure" of the philosophical analysis of that existential pre-structure (although the philosopher of course as a human being also underlies existential conditions). (It is almost taboo in our day to ask the question as for the conditions of the possibility (presuppositions) of the specifically philosophical truth-claim, nay even to recognize the peculiar status of this truth-claim.[33] Thus, not only Heidegger and Gadamer ignore this kind of transcendental reflection. Also Wittgenstein never asked the question as to the status of his own philosophical language game, through which he – from time to time at least – says something with a universal validity claim about the structure of language games in general, their belonging to "forms of life", being "interwoven with activities" etc. (This abstinence, I think, is a sequel of the paradox of the philosophical para-language in the Tractatus and before in Russell's "theory of types" and Tarski's theory of (meta-)languages.[34])

---

[33] Cf. Apel, K.-O., 2002 (forthcoming), "Transzendentale Intersubjektivität und das Defizit einer Reflektionstheorie in der Philosophie der Gegenwart".

[34] Cf. Apel, K.-O., 1995, "Rationalitätskriterien und Rationalitätstypen", in Wüstehube, A. (ed.), *Pragmatische Rationalitätstheorien*, Königshausen & Neumann, Würtzburg, 65–84.

The "pre-structure" of argumentation which makes specifically philosophical questions and answers possible, in my opinion, is characterized by universalistic validity claims that cannot be denied without committing a performative self-contradiction (or, in other words, finding out, which presuppositions belong to the pre-structure of philosophical argumentation can be achieved by asking the test-question as to whether candidates of philosophical validity claims – those of theoretical philosophy or those of ethics – can be denied without committing a performative self-contradiction. This test-question, I would claim, can be considered to be the quasi-maieutic self-reflective way of philosophy by which the transcendental apriori presuppositions of philosophical argumentation can be discovered.[35]

Now, what, after all, is the relation between the transcendental presuppositions of philosophical argumentation, which imply e.g. universal validity claims, and the presuppositions of hermeneutic understanding, which doubtlessly imply a bridging of historical time through a "fusion of horizons"?

Since the apriori presuppositions of philosophy are also presuppositions of (philosophical) hermeneutics there must be an internal relationship between them and hermeneutic understanding of texts. What I mean here is not simply the relationship between empirical cognition and transcendental preconditions of cognition. What I mean is a consequence of the fact that the transcendental conditions of philosophical hermeneutics have become a fact of history by their being fulfilled by the factually given enterprise of hermeneutic reconstruction of intellectual history, in which all hermeneutics is involved. Therefore, every attempt at hermeneutic understanding is not only dependent somehow on the history of being; it is moreover committed to contribute to the reconstruction of that course of history that has made possible as its result the factual realization of the preconditions of hermeneutic reconstruction of history. In short: every case of hermeneutic understanding underlies the normative principle of self-catching up or self-recuperation (in German: "Selbsteinholungsprinzip").[36]

An example of following the normative principle I have in mind has been provided, I think, by I. Lakatos in his controversy with T. Kuhn: Lakatos has demanded that correct interpretation in the history of science presupposes the tentative construction – to be repeated again and again – of an "internal history" of good science, i.e. of progress in science. This approach should only then be supplemented by "external" (say, psychological or sociological) explanations, if, or respectively, when the limits of a maximization of the scope of the "internal history" have been reached.[37]

---

[35] Cf. Kuhlmann, W., 1985, *Reflexive Letztbegründung,* Alber, Freiburg, München.

[36] Cf. Apel, K.-O., 1992, loc. cit., and the same, "Das Selbsteinholungsprinzip der kritisch-rekonstruktiven Geisteswissenschaften", in Académie Intern. de Philosophie de l'Art (ed.), *L'Art, La Science et la Métaphysique. Festschrift für A. Mercier,* Peter Lang, Bern, 1993, 53–66.

[37] Cf. Lakatos, I., 1974, "Die Geschichte der Wissenschaft und ihre rationalen Rekonstruktionen", in Diederich, W. (ed.), *Theorien der Wissenschaftsgeschichte,* Suhrkamp, Frankfurt a. M., and Apel, K.-O., 1996, "Kann es eine normative Begründung einer hermeneutischen Rekonstruktion

This conception, which, I think, can be generalized with regard to all hermeneutic reconstruction of intellectual history, in my opinion would be the transcendental-hermeneutic alternative to Gadamer's conception of "philosophical hermeneutics". It would be even in better accordance with a logic of questions and answers, since it would not leave the "fusion of horizons" between the interpretandum and the interpreter's questions to the "fate of being".

---

der Geschichte geben?", in Johannessen, K. S. et al. (eds.), *Wittgenstein and the Philosophy of Culture,* Hökler-Pichler-Tempsky, Wien, 18–31.

PART IV

QUESTIONING AS AN EPISTEMOLOGICAL AND SCIENTIFIC METHOD

Vladislav Lektorsky

Questions in Philosophy, Science and Education

The widespread opinion according to which questions in philosophy, science and education are principally different is contested. It is shown that both philosophers and scientists deal with questions that exist in a framework of a definite theory or intellectual tradition. In certain cases solutions to these questions can lead to formulating principally new theories and they can also turn out to be answers to new kind of questions which could not be put in the old theory. In such cases answers, being connected with new questions, change their meaning. It is shown also that the character of education should be changed in such a way that questions in it begin to be similar to those in philosophy and science, and searching answers to them can be considered a kind of inquiry.

* * *

There is an opinion according to which questions in philosophy, science and education are principally different.

Questions in science stimulate research of problems and tasks and indicate directions of research. Each question obtains a definite answer, and this creates a new question, which also obtains an answer as a result of new research. All the history of science can be interpreted as a constant change of questions and answers. The analysis of the nature of questions and ways of giving answers can give a clue to the understanding of the logic of scientific discovery. According to this opinion the situation in philosophy is different. Philosophers constantly deal with the same eternal questions concerning being, knowledge, consciousness etc., which they discuss, try to answer, but the answers are always unsuccessful.

But questions in philosophy and science presuppose the absence of ready answers and a process of search. Meanwhile in education questions have ready answers. The aim of questions in this case is not finding something unknown, but only testing a pupil's knowledge. H.-G. Gadamer wrote that pedagogical questions are not genuine ones, because "…it is a question without a questioner" (Gadamer).

In this paper I will try to defend the following thesis. It is true that questions and answers in philosophy and science are different to a certain degree. But their resemblance is more important. As to education there is an active group of theoreticians and teachers who think that it is now necessary to change the character of education, to transform it from the process of learning knowledge and skills into the process of creating ability to solve new problems. I share this position. But in such a case questions in education begin to be similar to those in philosophy and science, and searching answers to them can be considered as a kind of inquiry.

* * *

First of all I would like to distinguish between general and specific questions. It is possible to interpret the development of science as searching answers to the same questions, for example: is space finite or not, what was there before the beginning of time, or has time neither beginning nor end etc.? (Heisenberg 1963). According to such interpretation, as W. Heisenberg wrote, scientific problems seem to be eternal, and answers to them transient, because they loose their significance as a result of the extension of our knowledge (Heisenberg 1958). Under such interpretation of scientific questions and answers they don't differ from those in philosophy. But in reality such questions don't determine scientific investigation. A scientist deals with questions that exist in a framework of a definite theory. Such questions have definite answers: finding new facts, explanations of theoretical or empirical results, proofs of certain statements, discoveries of conceptual relations between different theoretical constructions etc. It is very important that scientists who share a definite theory have means to learn if an answer to a certain question is obtained or not. Only if we write history of science is it possible to interpret it in artificial mode as dealing with the same questions: the nature of the Universe, of space and time, of life etc. But the situation in philosophy is similar. In specific cultural and cognitive situation in history general philosophical questions are specified in a framework of a definite philosophical theory. For example, it is doubtful that philosophers always discussed the same question of the nature of mind. Because the understanding of mind by Plato and Aristotle is hardly the same as that by Descartes and post-cartesian philosophy which dealt with the questions about relations between mind and body, mind and the external world, my mind and other minds (Rorty).

Philosophers sharing a certain theoretical framework not only deal with the same questions, but can come to agreement concerning what can be considered an answer to a question and can acknowledge in any case some answers as satisfactory. As far as we are in the framework of a certain philosophical system we can think that in any case some problems are solved. Some questions can be common for different philosophical systems, although criteria of answers can be different. For example, J. Locke shared the Cartesian formulation of the question about mind, but did not accept the criteria of answering the question that the Cartesians shared. The real difference between philosophy and science is not in principally different relations of questions and answers. It is in the abundance of philosophical systems and approaches, which sometimes deal with the same questions, sometimes with different ones. These questions often don't have common criteria of what can be considered an answer to a certain question. So the history of philosophy can be interpreted as the history of questions, but not answers. L. Wittgenstein once wrote that there was the possibility of a philosophy that would only consist of questions. But in the history of philosophy each question was given a certain answer, and without a possible answer a question had no sense.

* * *

Now I would like to discuss a problem about which there are different opinions. I said that usually scientists deal with questions arising in the framework of a certain theoretical system or intellectual tradition. But in such a case it is natural to ask how a theoretical system arises. There is a view that it arises as an answer not to specific questions that exist within a certain theory, but to a general question about a theory as a whole. This is what K. Popper, for example, thought. According to him a new theory arises as an answer to a problem (question), which in its turn appeared as a result of a contradiction between the consequences of a previous theory and facts (Popper). According to K. Popper the history of science is a succession not of theories, but of problems. It seems that from this point of view something like that takes place in the history of philosophy.

But according to investigations of some Russian specialists in the philosophy and history of science in most cases (maybe in all) the real situation in science is different. Scientists as a rule deal with problems within already existing theories and intellectual traditions. In the process of searching answers to these questions some unexpected results can arise. In ancient science there was a notion of porism. It is a statement that arises in a process of the proof of a theorem or of the solution to a task as an unexpected consequence or an intermediate result. If a scientist tries to understand the significance of a porism, he can come to ideas that lead outside the framework of an old theory and make it possible to create a principally new conceptual system. In such a case a question concerning a theory as whole doesn't precede its creation and doesn't direct investigation, but is formulated only when a theory already exists. Its function is understanding of an existing theory.

I will try to illustrate this thesis with the use of the results of some Russian scholars. Boris Grjaznov has reconstructed the history of the creation of the heliocentric system by Copernicus. According to Grjaznov Copernicus didn't deal with the problem of the structure of the Universe. He tried to solve the problem of determining the point of the spring equinox and the causes of its displacement. It was a task of an old Ptolemean theory. At the beginning of the XVI Century the Catholic Church was worried about determining the day of Easter. This day is dependent on the day of the spring equinox: the day of Easter is the first Sunday after the first day of a full Moon that is after the day of the spring equinox. Meanwhile at the beginning of the XVI Century there was an error equal to 10 days in the determining the day of the spring equinox. If one considers the Earth as motionless, as it was according to the Ptolemean system, it is impossible to explain the displacement of the points of equinox. To solve the task Copernicus had to choose a motionless system of reference. It was natural to choose a system of motionless stars as such a system, because during the whole history of astronomical observations which was known to Copernicus no changes in mutual locations of stars had been found. But when Copernicus stopped the heaven he, if only theoretically, had to make the Earth revolve on its axis, as only so one could explain an apparent rotation of the heaven. But even this innovation didn't explain the displacement of the point of the spring equinox. In the framework of the picture of motionless stars and the revolution of the Earth on its axis the displacement of the point of the spring equinox could only be a result of the revolution of the Earth around the Sun. Copernicus had to admit also this movement (Grjaznov).

When Copernicus was solving a task of an old Ptolemean theory he introduced into the theory such additions which he first understood as serving this solution. And only later were these additions recognized as foundations of a new theory with principally new questions.

The Russian specialist in the philosophy and history of science Michael Rozov has shown that many principally new ideas in science arise as a result of intersection of different intellectual traditions. A question that directs investigation is put in the framework of a certain tradition. But a result that is obtained in this investigation can be reinterpreted in the light of another tradition and begins to answer another question. As an example M. Rozov has investigated the history of discovering the law of interaction of electrical charges by Ch. Coulomb. Usually this discovery is described as follows. Coulomb did research in the framework of the theory of electricity which was accepted at that time, and tried to answer the question: what are the forces in the interaction of electrical charges? In order to answer the question he invented a new device – a turning balance. After a number of measurements with the help of the device Coulomb discovered the law of the interaction of electrical charges. But according to M. Rozov Coulomb didn't do research in the framework of the theory of electricity. He tried to answer questions arising in the theory of elasticity. In his research he managed to learn the dependence of the angle of a thread's turn on quantity of acting force. But when he discovered this dependence he could reinterpret the obtained result as answering another question: what is the quantity of force if we know the angle of turning a thread? In other words he obtained a method of measuring forces on the basis of which he made a corresponding device – a turning balance. He began to use the device for measuring forces in different fields, including interaction of electrical charges. So the discovery of Coulomb's law was not a result of searching an answer to a question about the character of the interaction of electrical charges but an unexpected consequence of the solution of a different task (Rozov).

At last, I would like to give one more example. In his famous "Dialogues concerning the two main systems of the world" Galileo showed that under certain conditions answers to some questions in the framework of Aristotelian physics can lead outside this framework and allow formulating the main statements of a principally different understanding of the nature – classical mechanics. One of the participants of the "Dialogues...", Simplicio, a follower of Aristotelian physics, has to admit that an ideally hard ball put on an ideally smooth inclined plane will go down endlessly and with constant acceleration. It corresponds to the principle of Aristotelian physics: such movement has to take place as a result of the action of Aristotelian causality – striving of heavy bodies for the center of the Earth, their "natural place". In the case of going up an inclined plane motion would constantly decelerate, as it would be contrary to the striving of a body for its "natural place". As a result of these "ideal experiments" Simplicio has to admit that a movement of a body along a plane that is parallel to the surface of the Earth, in other words, without descent and ascent, would continue endlessly and without acceleration and deceleration. So the famous Galilean principle of inertia, one of the main principles of the new mechanics, is introduced, as a result of answering questions formulated in the framework of Aristotelian physics. On the face of it one can think that during this "ideal experimenting" there were no deviations from the ideas of Aristotle. As a matter of fact such deviations were made because a movement down an inclined plane can't be endless according to Aristotle: it has an end – its "natural place", the center of the Earth. But even in this case there is a way of reconciling Aristotelian physics and the new mechanics. This is possible if we identify a movement along an endless direct line with a movement along an endlessly large circle. In this case a movement corresponds to Aristotle: it leads to the center of a circle, but the center is endlessly far away. But then a circular motion according to Aristotle coincides with inertial motion according to Galileo (Galileo). So answers to questions in the framework of Aristotelian physics lead to formulating a principally new theory and turn out to be answers to other questions (Bibler 1991).

One can think that this relation between certain questions and answers in science can't exist in philosophy, as philosophers deal not only with questions within a certain theory but also with those about a theory as a whole. One of the special features of philosophy is that it constantly doubts general presuppositions of philosophical conceptions. But I think that in philosophy also situations arise rather often, when questions to which a philosopher first tries to answer are not those which he formulates later as the main questions of his philosophical system. "The Critique of Pure Reason" by Kant is an answer to a question: how are synthetic judgements a priori possible? This main question has three subquestions: how is pure mathematics possible? How is pure natural science possible? How is metaphysics possible? But the analysis of the history of creating Kant's conception shows that Kant first tried to answer other questions. His understanding of reason and sensual experience as completely excluding each other was formed in the framework of the philosophical tradition of Leibniz and Wolff. When Kant got to know the ideas of Hume concerning causality he understood the latter one as a challenge to the tradition to which he adhered. He could not see an answer to the challenge if nothing is changed in that tradition. In order to preserve the main principle of the tradition to which he then adhered and at the same time to refute Hume Kant had to elaborate his conception of time as a priori form of pure sensitivity, of schematisms, to give a new understanding of experience etc. But this gave rise to a new philosophical conception with new questions which were impossible for Leibniz and Wolff.

* * *

I will now discuss the problem of questions in education. It is evident that education without questions is impossible. But usually their aim is to inquire what a pupil has learned. A teacher can ask a pupil, for example, when a certain event took place, how to do a sum by means of a method that a pupil must have learned etc. A teacher knows the answers to his questions. Such kind of questions depends on the nature of education that exists now in most schools in the world. In the past many theoreticians of education, beginning with Jan Amos Komenski, said that a genuine education presupposes the activity of a pupil, his ability not only to find ready answers, but also to put questions to others and to himself. In this connection they referred to Socrates and his question and answer method of a dialogue. But if the main aim of education is the appropriation of knowledge and skills, as it takes place in most systems of education now, it is impossible to change the nature of education and, in particular, the type of questions in education. Meanwhile there is an opinion, which I share, that contemporary civilization creates a lot of unexpected situations and demands of a person not only knowledge and skills, but also critical and creative thinking. But if this is true, the type of education should be changed. Teaching creative thinking to pupils should occupy a significant place in education. But a teacher can teach creative thinking only if a pupil is involved in solving a problem with an unknown answer. Such education begins to resemble inquiry in some respects, and questions in education begin to be like questions in science and philosophy. I will briefly analyze three attempts to include the elements of inquiry in education, made recently in the USA and Russia. These attempts are different, but they have common features. The followers of these pedagogical innovations interpret the latter ones as the future of education.

First of all it is a program which has been elaborated by Mattew Lipman and other scholars from the USA and which is called "Philosophy for children" (Lipman). The program has been realized in the practice of education for two decades in the USA and many other countries, including Russia. The main thesis of Lipman is that it is necessary to teach creative and critical thinking in school, and that the best way of doing it is teaching philosophy in a special form for many years. Because according to Lipman philosophy, to a higher degree than any scientific discipline, liberates thinking and affords to doubt statements that are usually considered evident. It is important that pupils should not study philosophical texts and discuss already existing philosophical conceptions, but should be involved in philosophical thinking, should try to give their own answers to some problems that can arise in ordinary life, but which have a philosophical nature. Pupils, with the help of special texts and a teacher, are involved in the discussion of problems that have no generally accepted solutions. A discussion, something like a Socratic dialogue, arises between pupils. The participants of a dialogue put questions to each other, answer them, formulate arguments against given answers, give counter-arguments, put new questions etc. The class of pupils becomes the inquiry community (this is a key notion for Lipman). The participants of such a dialogue acquire not only the ability to reason, to argue, but also the abilities to view analogies, to take into consideration a context, formulate hypotheses, and to give non-trivial solutions. They are taught an ability to ask such questions that presuppose non-trivial answers. Questions of participants to each other help to find such presuppositions in their reasoning which were not clear to them before a dialogue. A teacher organizes a dialogue. He asks questions that don't suppose a single and known answer but stimulate a discussion and direct it.

In Russia there are also attempts to develop creative thinking of pupils by means of introducing elements of inquiry into education. One of such attempts is so called program of "the school of the dialogue of cultures" which was elaborated by a philosopher, a theoretician of culture and education Vladimir Bibler (Bibler 1998). The followers of the program think that creative thinking can be taught not at special lessons (as it takes place according to Lipman's program), but through changing teaching in all school disciplines, beginning from mathematics and physics and finishing by history and literature. In this connection a teacher can put such questions, including ones about the main notions of mathematics, physics, biology etc., which in any case admit several answers. Pupils come to be involved in a discussion with each other. Certainly, they are inclined to be guided by a teacher's authority. It is natural and important. Without this education is impossible. But this inclination should be supplemented by a pupil's striving to ask non-trivial questions and answer them. This is possible if a pupil interacts not only with a teacher but with other similar pupils, because in the latter case the equality of positions exists. A pupil can't participate in a dialogue with a teacher in equal terms, to ask and object him. He can do this with his classmates. The realization of the program helped to find an interesting fact. Usually a child comes to school with a readiness to learn and striving for studying. But after the first or the second year of learning many children don't want to learn any more: their learning motivation drastically decreases. The explanation of this fact is as follows. The aim of the traditional education as giving a pupil knowledge and skills doesn't help to create a striving for understanding and to form a learning motivation. Forming motivation that gives sense to study is a special and difficult problem for the traditional school. But this problem doesn't exist for the program of "the school of the dialogue of cultures". It turned out that creative thinking motivates itself.

At last one pedagogical program with the aim of developing the creative thinking of a pupil. It is a program of the so-called developmental teaching, elaborated by the Russian specialist in pedagogical psychology Vasilii Davydov (Davydov). He and his followers have created, in particular, a method of applying a special game by a teacher. The teacher plays the part of a pupil and pretends not to understand some questions and answers. A teacher specially makes mistakes and provokes a pupil to doubt and make mistakes. A teacher shows to a pupil the possibility not to understand a question, to ask a question again, to ask for proof. A teacher creates "points of amazement" and the condition of a dialogue between pupils. A pupil finds the existence of different points of view and as a result of this he first has a certain feeling of discomfort. There is not only his own position, which is self-evident for him, but there are also other ones (of a teacher, of other pupils). A pupil learns to understand a position of another pupil, to asses it, to doubt it, to put questions to another pupil, and so to begin to realize his own position, to be able to distinguish it from another one, to defend it, to answer questions concerning it.

* * *

The "school of the dialogue of cultures" of Vladimir Bibler and the theory of the developmental teaching of Vasilii Davydov have used some ideas of the outstanding Russian philosopher and theoretician of culture Michail Bakhtin (Bakhtin). Studying the structure of F. Dostoevski's novels, M. Bakhtin discovered that they are polyphonic, in other words, they can be interpreted as dialogues, as interaction of different voices, representing different conceptual positions. This dialogue includes questions, answers, arguments and objections, elucidation and the development of a position, new questions and answers etc. As a result of the analysis of the pre-history of polyphonic novels by F. Dostoevski M. Bakhtin came to study the Socratic dialogues as a genuine source of polyphonism. Later he elaborated the dialogical conception of all cultural phenomena, beginning from language. Every statement according to M. Bakhtin can be interpreted as a part of a certain dialogue: a question, an answer, an objection, an elucidation of a position etc. He suggested similar interpretation for literature, philosophy, science. From his point of view a certain culture can be interpreted as an obvious or a hidden dialogue with other ones. The consciousness of a person can't be understood out of the context of its dialogue, including questions and answers, with consciousness of other people and with itself. M. Bakhtin's ideas have influenced a lot of studies in the theory of literature, art, culture, philosophy, psychology and the theory of education in Russia and other countries. I think that

M. Bakhtin's ideas about the dialogical nature of philosophy, science and education can help us to understand not only our past, but also our current state and possible ways for developing it.

Russian Academy of Sciences, Moscow, Russia

REFERENCES

Bakhtin, M. M., 1986, *The Aesthetic of Creativity in Writing*, Iskusstvo publishers, Moscow, pp.281–307 (in Russian).
Bibler, V. S., 1991, *From the Logic of Science to the Logic of Culture*, Politizdat publishers, Moscow, pp. 185–200 (in Russian).
Bibler, V. S. (ed.), 1998, *Philosophical and Psychological Presuppositions of the School of the Dialogue of Cultures*, Rosspan publishers, Moscow, pp. 13–87 (in Russian).
Davydov, V. V., 1996, *The Theory of the Developmental Teaching*, Intor publishers, Moscow, pp. 366–393 (in Russian).
Galileo, G., 1964, *Selected Writings in 2 vol.*, Mysl publishers, Moscow, Vol 1, pp. 186, 188, 228 (in Russian).
Grjaznov, B. S., 1982, *Logic, Rationality, Creativity*, Nauka publishers, Moscow, pp. 115–116 (in Russian).
Gadamer, H.-G., 1985, *Truth and Method*, Crossroad Publishing Company, New York, p. 327.
Heisenberg, W., 1958, "Planck's Discovery and Main Philosophical Questions of the Atomic Conception". *Voprosi filosofii*, No 11, p. 61 (in Russian).
Heisenberg, W., 1963, *Physics and Philosophy*, Mysl publishers, Moscow, p. 97 (in Russian).
Lipman, M., 1991, *Thinking in Education*, Cambridge University Press, Cambridge, pp. 7–100.
Popper, K. R., 1975, *Objective Knowledge*, Clarendon Press, Oxford, pp. 118–122.
Rorty, R., 1980, *Philosophy and the Mirror of Nature*, Princeton University Press, Princeton, pp. 17–79.
Rozov, M. A., 1981. "The ways of scientific discoveries", *Voprosi filosofii*, No 8, pp. 139–143 (in Russian).

Gerhard Schurz

Models of Abduction – From An Interrogative Viewpoint

1. Abduction and Interrogation

In this paper I will discuss models of abduction from an interrogative viewpoint. However, my interrogative viewpoint will not be as radical as the *interrogative logic of inquiry* developed by Jaakko Hintikka and his collaborators. Hintikka's interrogative logic (1998, Hintikka et al. 2000) starts from the assumption that all *newly acquired* information in scientific discovery must be obtained from a reliable information *source*. This source is abstractly viewed as an *oracle* which gives answers to our questions. In scientific discovery, the ultimate oracle is *nature itself* – as it presents itself in observations or controlled experiments. Therefore, in Hintikka's interrogative theory of inquiry only *two* basic and irreducible steps of inquiry are needed: (1) logico-deductive inference steps, in which one acquires information from other previously acquired information, and (2) interrogative moves, i.e. question-answer steps, where one puts questions to nature in form of experiments and obtains certain answers from these experiments. *Non-deductive* or *ampliative* inference steps such as *induction* or *abduction* do not literally exist in Hintikka's interrogative theory of inquiry: they are reduced to interrogative steps, to question-answer-steps.

In the following paper, I will not pursue this radical line. I do not think that every piece of information either comes from logical deduction or from an information source which is located in nature. I think that there always remains an irreducible inferential step in inductions or abductions which is not dictated by nature's answers but is performed by us, by the *subject* of inquiry. Nevertheless, I fully agree with Hintikka's program in that induction and especially abduction are closely connected with *strategies of interrogation*. Such strategies of interrogation correspond very closely to what computer scientists call *search strategies*, and it will emerge from this paper that the function of abductions as strategies of interrogation constitutes the most important aspect of abductions which by far exceeds the significance of their inferential roles.

Following Charles Sanders Peirce (e.g., 1878, 1903) there are three basic kinds of inferences: deduction, induction and abduction. In *deduction*, the conclusion-information which we draw from the given premises follows from these premises with *certainty*, and *independently* from the facts of the world. No questions to nature are involved in deductive inferences: their character is *purely inferential*, so to speak. In this respect, deductions are the most harmless and indubitable kind of Peirce's triad of inferences.

For inductions and abductions the situation is very different, because these inferences are *ampliative*. We first consider *inductive generalizations* of the form

All As so far observed have been Bs
==============================
(Conjecture:) All As are Bs

That an inductive generalization is ampliative means that its conclusion is not contained in its premise(s): even if the truth of the premises is taken for granted, the conclusion remains conjectural and its acceptance is only *preliminary* and subject to *further testing*. In this way, the conclusion of an ampliative inference gives rise to further interrogative activity, to further experimental questions in which we test the truth of the conjectured conclusion.

In the case of simple inductive generalizations, however, there is not much strategy involved in these further questions since they all point into the same direction – for the reason that, unlike abductions, inductive generalizations are not *creative* but merely transfers observed regularities to unobserved cases. All questions stimulated by an inductive generalization concern the preparation of representative samples of the same kind, and the interrogative strategies involved in this task belong to the well-established area of *empirical testing*. So the role of inductive generalizations as interrogative strategies is not of special significance – what counts is their role as inferential moves.[1] At this point I depart from Hintikka who has argued that inductive inferences are never needed because inductive generalizations are direct output of controlled experiments and hence entailed by nature's answers (cf. 1998, 509; Hintikka et al. 2000, §§ 6–7). On the contrary, I think that Hume was basically right in that nature's direct answers are always particular *sample results*, finite sets of observations or measurements, and the move from sample results to generalizations about unobserved cases will always be an *irreducible* inductive step.

We have seen that in inductive generalizations their function as interrogative strategies is of marginal importance. In *abductive inferences*, however, this function becomes really crucial. Peirce described abduction during his lifetime in different ways; the most general form of abduction is described by him as follows (1903, CP 5.189):

---

[1] Hintikka (1998, 523) has emphasized that the late Peirce characterizes induction as the operation of empirical testing, but I agree with Niiniluoto (1999a, S439) that this does not imply that the late Peirce has denied the inferential aspect of induction.

F: An observed (singular or general) *fact* F which is in need of explanation
B: *Background knowledge* which implies that the hypothetical situation R would be a reason (cause, or explanation) of F
==
R: Conjecture that the hypothetical reason R is in fact the case.

So, abduction is reasoning from given facts or effects to conjectured reasons or causes. Prototypical examples are detective stories, where the detective reasons from the various traces which (s)he finds in the vicinity of a murdered person to conjectures about the murderer (cf. Niiniluoto 1999b). In distinction to the situation of induction, we are confronted here with thousands of theoretically possible causes – everyone in the village might be the murderer. As Peirce put it, abductive hypotheses are prima facie not even probable, like inductive hypotheses, but merely possible (1903, CP 5.171). The important point about an abductive hypothesis is that it points to a series of *questions* in which we put our conjecture to further empirical test. Only upon being confirmed in further tests may abductive hypotheses become probable or be finally accepted. So the essential role of rules of abduction is to figure as interrogative strategies which tell us which among the multitude of possible questions we should address first. Or in more general terms: what would presumably be the shortest series of experiments, of conjectures and refutations, the shortest path through the *search space* of possible reasons, which will take us to the true reason of the fact to be explained?

Peirce did not confine abduction to simple retroductive inferences from effects to causes. He claimed that the scientific importance of abduction consists in its ability to introduce new theoretical hypotheses and theoretical concepts (1903, CP 5.170). For example, from the refraction and bending of light Huygens abduced that light consists of waves. In the abductive inference to new theories and concepts the problem of the *combinatorial explosion* of the number of possible conjectures is even stronger. Peirce once remarked that there are myriads of possible hypotheses which would explain the experimental phenomena, and yet scientists usually have managed to find the true hypothesis after only a small number of guesses (cf. CP 6.5000). But Peirce did not tell us any abductive rules for conjecturing new theories; he rather explained this miraculous ability of the human minds by their *abductive instincts* (CP 5.47, fn. 12; 5.172; 5.212).

Indeed, the crucial epistemological question is whether there exists anything like a 'logic' of discovery. This question is hotly debated but cannot be discussed in this paper – instead, I confine myself to the following remark: the true observation of the logical positivists that the justification of a hypothesis is independent from the way it was discovered does not imply that it would not be *desirable* to have in addition good heuristic rules for scientific discovery – if there only *were* such rules. The real question is whether there exist reasonable rules or schemata for abduction.

2. INFERENCE TO THE BEST EXPLANATION OR LOGIC OF DISCOVERY?

There are two opposite ways of looking for schemata of abduction. The *first way* tries to establish the most general schema of abduction which matches every particular case. The *second way* establishes various particular schemata of abduction, each fitting a particular conjectural situation. The majority of recent literature on abduction has gone along the first route. I will argue in this paper that this route is not very fruitful, because general schemata of abduction are usually worthless vis-à-vis their purpose as *strategies* of finding promising conjectures.

Let me first clarify here what I mean by a *good (interrogative or search) strategy*. It is not enough for a good strategy to be truth-conducive, i.e., to lead in most cases to the true answer within a finite but arbitrary time span. If the space of possible hypotheses is finite, this aspect of truth-conduciveness is already provided by the operations of deduction and induction by which we put the conjectured hypotheses under successive empirical tests (cf. Peirce CP 5.171). What is also essential for a good strategy is that it leads us to the truth *in a reasonable time*, and exactly this is the task of abduction. In other words, a good abductive (or interrogative) strategy takes us to a small part of the large search space in which the true hypothesis lies in most cases, so that we may find the true hypotheses with just a small number of interrogative steps, without the need of travelling through all *nodes*, i.e. possible hypotheses, of the search space and without testing all of them.[2] The most important general schema of abduction is what Gilbert Harman (1965) has called *inference to the best explanation*, in short *IBE*. In this formulation of abduction, the strategic element is completely missing. Asking which explanatory conjecture we should choose for further investigation among myriads of possible conjectures, IBE just tells us: "find out the best conjecture and then choose it". This sounds like a joke. If you don't see the joke, think about someone in a hurry who asks an IBE-philosopher for the right way to the railway station and receives the following answer: "Every way which starts were you are right now and ends at the railway station is possible. Find out which is the shortest way among all of them and then choose it". Hence, IBE is more a rule of justification than one of discovery. What IBE merely reflects is the inferential aspect of abduction, the inference from the belief that a certain explanation is the best one to the belief that its premises are acceptable as true.

Note that this criticism of IBE is valid *even if* one assumes that there exists a unique and clear definition of the *goodness* of an explanation (which is a problem of its own; cf. Niiniluoto 1999a, S443ff). As long as such a definition does not entail any search heuristics but requires from us the explicit evaluation of all possible hypotheses, it does not serve any strategic function. So viewed as a rule of discovery, IBE it is almost worthless, because the number of possible explanations is much too large (if not potentially infinite) to be explicitly assessed.

---

[2] Search strategies are most important in *AI* research (cf. Nilsson 1980, ch. 2–3).

Moreover, if we perform abduction at the level of theoretical explanation then we never have access to all *possible* explanations because the 'space' of theoretical innovations is unbounded and our cognitive capacities are limited.

Therefore, what one usually has in mind is not IBE but *inference to the best available explanation, in short* IBAE. However, IBAE is unacceptable as a rule for scientific discovery. Rather, IBAE is the leading rule of what one may call *rational speculation* because it amounts to the following: for whatever phenomenon you encounter, try to find an explanation for it and however speculative your explanation may be, accept it as long it is the best one you can imagine. For example, when people of early cultures had no idea at all about why the sun was moving above the horizon every day, their best available explanation was that the sun is an intentional agent, a God, with intrinsic plans like human beings. In other words, IBAE was also the leading rule of the spiritual and animistic wordviews of early stages of human mankind. More formally, IBAE admits all abductions of the following form:

From E_a infer: C_a, and for all x: if C_x, then E_x

This schema allows all sorts of empty speculations such as that the weather is bad because God is angry and whenever God is angry the weather turns bad. Let me emphasize that I do not want to diminish the value of rational speculation by these remarks. In fact, rational speculation is the predecessor of scientific inquiry. I just want to point out that not every possible explanatory story, even if it is the best available explanation for a person, is *good enough* to count as a scientific explanation. *Scientific abductions* have to satisfy certain constraints which distinguish them from arbitrary speculations. The most general and I think the most promising constraint is the requirement of empirical *unification* or *coherence*, which has been elaborated by various authors[3]. This is the requirement that theoretical hypotheses must predict or explain a multitude of empirical phenomena by a few theoretical principles. Speculative explanations which introduce for each empirical phenomenon a new hidden intentional plan or story do obviously not have such unificatory power, nor do they have any predictive power. However, if we consider unification from the strategic viewpoint, this criterion is still much too weak to give us effective rules for the discovery of hypotheses. Criteria of unification or coherence tell us in what goodness of explanations consists, but usually they don't tell us how to *find* the best, i.e. most unifying explanatory hypothesis in a reasonably short time.

In the rest of this paper I will pursue the second route to schemata for abduction – I will suggest various particular schemata of abduction. I do not think that there is just one optimal strategy of abduction. Abduction is an open family of

---

[3] The list includes Friedman 1974, Kitcher 1989, Thagard 1988, 1992, Bartelborth 1996, and myself in Schurz/Lambert 1994 and Schurz 1999.

heuristic schemata for generating explanatory hypotheses, a resemblance family in Wittgenstein's sense, which cannot be delimited by ultimate rules because abduction is ultimately a matter of creativity. Nevertheless there are some prototypical patterns of abduction, each fitting particular situations, which usually lead rather quickly to most promising hypotheses. Variants of these particular patterns of abductions are performed again and again in ordinary thinking as well as in science.

3. Factual Abduction

One may classify kinds of abduction along three dimensions (cf. the classification at the end of the text) – (1.) along the kind of hypothesis which is abduced, i.e. which is produced as a conjecture, (2.) along the kind of *evidence* which the abduction intends to explain, and (3.) according to the beliefs or cognitive mechanisms which *drive* the abduction. Factual abductions are always *driven* by known laws, and both their evidence and their abduced hypotheses are *singular facts*. Depending on the methodological nature of the abduced hypothesis, one may distinguish between the following subgroups.

3.1 Observable-Fact-Abduction

This kind of abduction may also be called 'retroduction' or 'the official Peirce schema' and it has the following structure:

Known Law: If Cx, then Ex
Known Evidence: Ea has occurred
===
Abduced conjecture: Ca could be the reason – where Ca is *observable*.
Stimulated question/experiment: find out whether Ca is in fact true.

This kind of abductions reasons from observed effects to observable reasons or causes in the background of known laws. Prototypical examples are the already mentioned detective stories, or more generally, all sorts of *causal analyses of traces.* As an example, assume Ea says that there is a foot print in the sand at the beach, and Ca is the conjecture that somebody was recently walking here. In examples of this sort, the space of theoretically possible abductive conjectures is potentially infinite, at least at the level of empirical description. Classical physics allows for myriads of ways of imprinting footprints into the sand of the beach. Nobody would seriously try to classify these possibilities which reach from cows wearing sandals on their feet to footprints which are drawn into the sand, blown by the wind, or caused by radioactive decay of foot-shaped portions of the sand, etc. The majority of these physically possible abductive conjectures will never be considered by us because they are extremely improbable. So I think the major strategic rule which we use in factual abduction cases of this sort is a *probabilistic elimination technique* which usually works in an unconscious manner: our mind quickly scans through our large memory store containing millions of memorized possible scenarios and only those which have minimal plausibility pop up in our consciousness. The importance of probabilistic elimination in Bayesian abduction has also been emphasized by Earman (1992).

We have seen that the probabilistic evaluation of a conjectured hypothesis plays an important role in factual abduction. Fumerton (1980) has gone further and has argued that factual abduction can be *reduced* to ordinary inductive-statistical inference. More precisely, he argues that the inferences pattern at the left can be reduced to the inference pattern at the right (592f):

Abductive inference: *Inductive-statistical inference:*
$\forall x(Fx \rightarrow Gx)$ Fumerton's $p(Fx/Gx) = high$
Ga reduction: Ga
================== 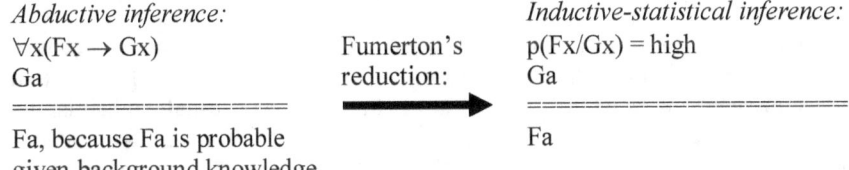 =======================
Fa, because Fa is probable   Fa
given background knowledge

Although Fumerton may be right in some cases, I see two reasons why his argument is not generally correct. *First*, the abductive hypothesis is not merely evaluated in the light of the evidence Ga, but in the light of the entire background knowledge. Fumerton may reply, of course, that the inference pattern at the right may be appropriately extended so that it includes background knowledge. But *second*, and more importantly, Fumerton's proposed transformation neither corresponds to psychological reality nor would it be strategically recommendable. Usually, human minds do not explicitly store probabilistic conditionals going from effects to possible causes. Every individual case is 'different' (the slogan of philosophers of history), and hence, only a small fraction of possible cause-effect-scenarios are actually encountered in a human life-time and can be explicitly stored by Fumerton-like conditionals. For example, if you are not a turtle expert and you observe the trace of a turtle in the sand, then the only way in which you may arrive at the right guess that there was a turtle robbing here is by careful backward reasoning combined with elimination. Only if you are a turtle hunter may you have explicitly stored the typical sand-traces of turtles with a corresponding forward conditional of Fumerton's sort. The importance of backward reasoning is also emphasized by all experts of detective stories (Niiniluoto 1999b).

Peter Lipton (1991, 61ff) has argued that in abduction or IBE we do not infer to the *likeliest* explanation (i.e., the most probable hypothesis in the light of background knowledge), but to the *loveliest* explanation, i.e., to the best *potential* explanation – that explanation which has strongest explanatory power, maximal simplicity, etc. I think that Lipton is right insofar as high loveliness of an explanation is itself something which increases the probability of the explanatory premises. Often, therefore, the loveliest will be at the same time the likeliest explanation. But generally, I think, Lipton is wrong, and what we ultimately prefer is always the likeliest explanation. For example, assume you have observed foot-prints on the Himalaya which look like the footprints of Yeti. The loveliest explanation of this fact would clearly be that there was indeed a Yeti walking there. But your background knowledge tells you that the existence of Yetis is extremely improbable. In such a situation you will clearly prefer the less lovely but more likely explanation that the Yeti-traces were faked in order to attract tourists.

3.2 Logical and Computational Aspects of Factual Abduction.

In the case of foot-prints at the beach, there are only a few possible conjectures of minimal plausibility, while in the case of detective stories, the initial space of plausible scenarios which led to the death of the VICTIM is usually much larger. If we assume that the background knowledge does not contain general theories but only a finite set of empirical causal laws, then the set of possible abductive conjectures is finite and can be generated by *backward-chaining* inference procedures.[4] This form abductive inference has been studied in detail in AI research (Josephson/Josephson 1994, Flach/Kakas 2000) as follows. Given a knowledge base K = <L[x],F[a]> in form of a finite set L[x] of monadic implicational laws of the form $A_i(x) \rightarrow B_i(x)$, and a finite set F[a] of facts about the individual case a. Given is moreover a certain fact Ga (the 'goal') which is to be explained. One is not interested in just any hypotheses which (if true) would explain the goal Ga given K, but only in those which are not further potentially explainable in K, i.e. which are *basic* or ultimate causes with respect to K (Paul 1993, 133; Console et al. 1991). Hence formally, candidates for abducible hypotheses are all singular statements of the form A(a) such that A(a) is neither a fact, nor is A(x) the consequent ('head') of a law, i.e., A(a) cannot possibly be further explained by other laws; the set of these possible abductive conjectures A(a) for arbitrary abduction tasks in K is called the set of *abducibles* H[a]. The *abductive task* for goal Ga is then defined as follows: find all possible explanations, i.e., all *minimal* sets E[a] of singular statements about a such that (i) E[a]⊆F[a]∪H[a], (ii) L[x]∪F[a]∪E[a] is consistent and (iii) L[x]∪E[a] ⊢ Ga. The sets E[a] are all possible explanations if Ga and the elements of E[a] which are abducibles are the abductive hypotheses for Ga. Solutions of abductions of this sort of task can easily be implemented, for example, in the programming language PROLOG in the form of a backward-chaining procedure with backtracks on all possible solutions. This kind if abduction problem is graphically displayed in figure 1 in the form of the

---

[4] Or by task-equivalent algorithms, such completion & deduction (Console et al. 1991) or resolution-refutation towards dead ends (Paul 1993, 3.1.1).

so-called *And-Or-tree*. The nodes of the Or-tree are sets of literals (atomic facts or their negations) (cf. Nilsson 1980, 99ff). The nodes of an And-Or-tree correspond to literals which carry certain computationally relevant information; the directed edges (arrows) correspond descriptively to laws in L[x], and procedurally to one layer in the search-depth. Arrows connected by an *arc* are And-connected, otherwise they are Or-connected; + indicates facts, * indicate possible abductive hypotheses.

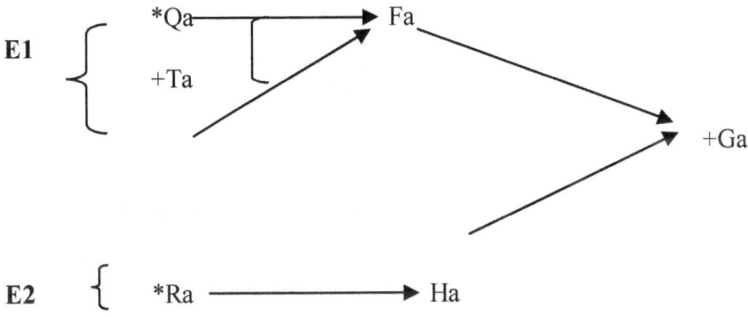

Figure 1: A simple abduction-to-facts problem.

Following from the above, the laws underlying figure 1 are $\forall x(Fx \to Gx)$, $\forall x(Hx \to Gx)$, $\forall x(Qx \land Tx \to Fx)$ and $\forall x(Rx \to Hx)$, and the only fact is Ta. Qa and Ra are the two possible abductive conjectures found by a PROLOG-backward reasoner; Qa explains Fa together with the known fact Ta, Ra explains it by itself. Our presentation is slightly more refined than standard AI presentations of logic-based abduction insofar as we allow possible explanations to contain not only hypotheses but also facts (such as 'Ta' in fig. 1; cf. Christiansen 2000, 200, as an exception who admits this possibility). This assumption is certainly more realistic. For example, think about a murder case where one knows at the start that Peter is the son of the murdered person John, and this fact makes part of the later explanation of John's murder (who was murdered by Peter in order to inherit John's property).

Figure 2 shows the corresponding presentation of the abduction problem of fig. 1 in Hintikka's interrogative tableau logic. Abducibles are again marked by *. In formal comparison, the tableaux-presentation of an abduction problem is slightly more complex than the And-Or-representation. On the other hand, logical tableaus are more general. For example, if we do not confine ourselves to monadic predicates but allow arbitrary relations, then the nodes of And-Or-trees may contain elementary quantified sentences; they cause no further problems in tableau logic but require subtle additional conventions in And-Or-trees (see Schurz 1996b, Prendinger 1998, 101; cf. also §3.3).

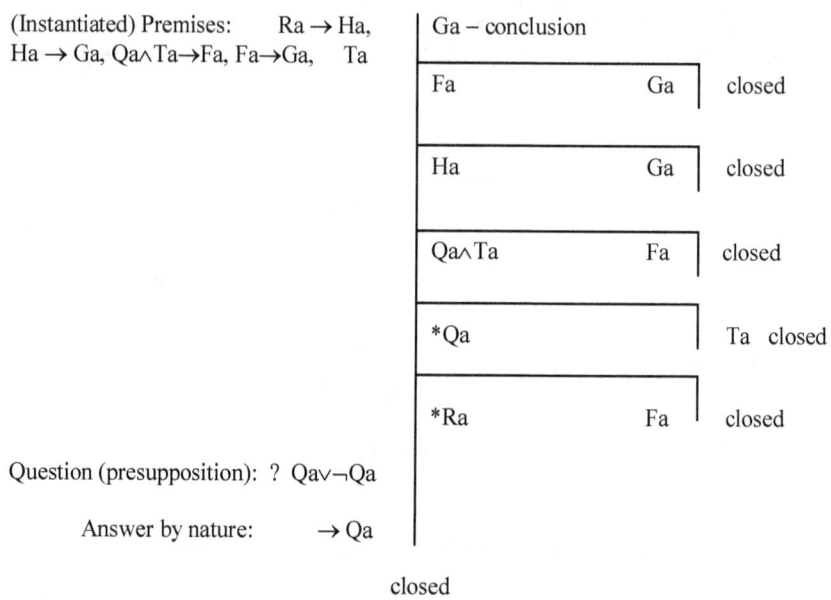

Figure 2: *Abduction problem of fig. 1 in interrogative logic.*

In interrogative logic, the original why-question "why Ga?" is called the *principal* question of the inquiry, while the questions corresponding to abductive conjectures are called *operative* questions (Hintikka et al. 2000, §14). The main difference of interrogative logic compared to simple AI abduction algorithms is that tableau logic also incorporates the *questions* which correspond to abductive conjectures as well as nature's answers. This is illustrated in fig. 2: the truth-value of the first abductive conjecture, Qa, is put to nature (this is formally displayed by writing the presupposition of this question at the left side) and nature's answer (which we assumed to be Qa) is *introduced* as an additional premise (indicated by →). Insofar interrogative logic allows the introduction of new premises obtained by nature's answer, it should be regarded as a tool which simultaneously captures abductive hypothesis formation *and* belief revision. In the AGM-terminology (Alchourrón/Gärdenfors/Makinson 1985), adding an answer which does not contradict previously accepted premises is a case of mere *expansion*, while adding an answer which contradicts previously accepted premises is a case of (non-trivial) *revision* which is handled in interrogative logic by *bracketing* previously accepted premises (Hintikka et al. 2000, §8). There are also some AI-abduction systems which incorporate question-asking modules. For example, the RED-system (designed for the purpose of red-cell antibody identification based on antigen-reactions of patient serum) asks question to a data-base (Josephson/Josephson 1994, 72f), or the system DENDRAL asks questions to nature in form of spectra-predictions based on abductive conjectures (see section 3.3 below). But while question-modules of this sort are designed to particular cases, interrogative logic is a far more general method than what has been developed in these areas of AI research.

And-Or-trees may quickly become complicated. Possible explanations of an And-Or-tree will be subsets of its leaves, but in the case of iterated And-Or-nesting the literals making up a possible explanation will not lie nearby but will be spread over the leaves. One way to handle this is to transform the formula corresponding to the leaves of the And-Or-tree into a disjunctive normal form whose elementary disjuncts will corresponds to all possible explanations of the given goal (see Console et al. 1991, 22, def. 4). Another way, suggested in Schurz (1996b, 209), is to pick out all distinct And-subtrees of an Or-tree. Alternatively one may present the search space as a pure Or-tree with nodes consisting of sets of literals and with leaves corresponding to possible explanations – on the cost that this Or-tree will no longer be procedurally transparent insofar its edges will not correspond to single law-applications but to the simultaneous effect of several law-applications.

Constraining the search space for possible explanations by the method of probabilistic elimination explained in the previous section means for an And-Or-tree that whenever a node is encountered which has less than a minimal threshold probability, the entire subtree below this node gets ignored. Figure 3 shows the search path (depth-first and right-first) constrained by probabilistic elimination; nodes who's plausibility is below the minimal threshold are marked with "–". Note that if only one successor of an And-node has negligible plausibility, then the entire And-node is ignored; this is motivated by the probabilistic consideration that $p(X \wedge Y) \leq p(X)$.

Finding all possible explanations, i.e. abductive hypotheses, will be exponentially costly with the size of the constrained search space (cf. also Josephson/Josephson 1994, ch. 7). Finding just one explanation will, under certain conditions, have only polynomial costs. Here, a simple heuristic strategy is *best-first* search: for each Or-node one determines the successor with highest plausibility value and processes just this successor-node. More complicated procedures update the plausibilities or costs of chosen paths at each node (cf. Brake 1986, ch. 12; Hobbs et al 1993).

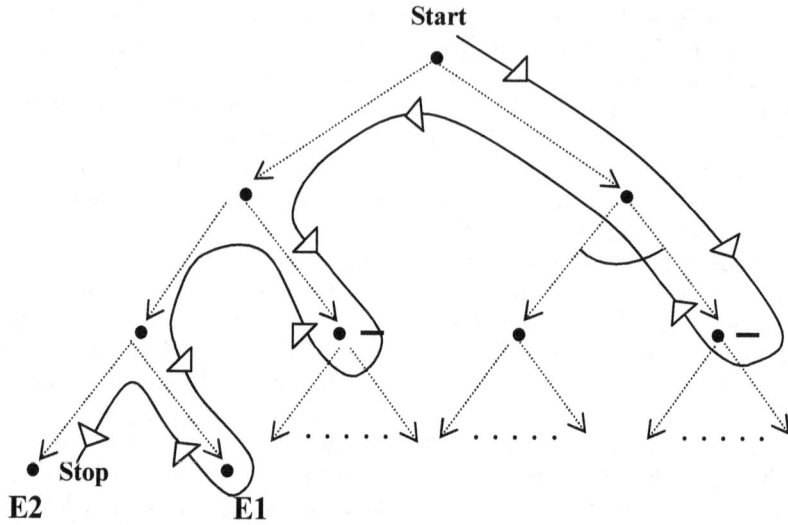

Figure 3: Depth-first right-to-left search restricted by probabilistic elimination: finds possible explanations E1 and E2 ("-" for "below plausibility threshold")

Usually, the data to be explained in abduction problems do not consist of a single fact but of a set of facts. Here we have a *goal set* containing several literals. This situation makes abduction more complicated. Because of the format of the laws in L[x], the goals of the goal set will be processed one by one. Let the goal set be G[a] = {G1a, G2a} and assume that for G1a explanation F1a was found, and for G2a explanation F2a. Then the set of abductive hypotheses E1 = {F1a, F2a} is clearly a possible explanation of G[a]. However, it maybe a *redundant* one because it may turn out that F2a also explains G1a, or that F1a also explains G2a, via some other paths of the search space which so far have not been checked. This problem is of particular importance for the RED-system, where a *set of* reactions of the patient's serum with red-cell antigens has to be abductively explained, and each reaction can be explained by several possible red-cell antibodies in the patient's serum. The problem that RED does to overcome is this: if GS_i is the current goal set, ES_i the current explanation set found for GS_i, and G_{i+1} a new goal for which the explanation (set) E_{i+1} was found, then the new explanation set $ES_{i+1} = ES_i \cup E_{i+1}$, which explains the new goal set $GS_{i+1} = GS_i \cup \{G_{i+1}\}$, is made non-redundant before the procedure continues. This means that for each element E_j of ES_{i+1} (in arbitrary ordering) it is tested whether the contracted explanation set $ES_{i+1} - \{Ej\}$ still explains GS_{i+1}; if yes the element Ej gets removed from ES_{i+1}, until one arrives at a non-redundant subset of GS_{i+1}, and the next goal can be processed. If finding some explanation for a literal is assumed to be polynomial in complexity, the task of finding some non-redundant explanation will still be polynomial, while the task of finding the (or just some) best minimal explanation is NP-hard (for details cf. Josephson/Josephson 1994, ch. 7).

Besides probabilistic elimination, the second major technique of constraining the search space is, of course, interrogation. Not only do the ultimate conjectures, the leaves of the tree, correspond to questions – let us call these questions the *ultimate questions*. We may also ask a question at every intermediate node in the search tree, provided the corresponding 'intermediate conjecture' corresponds to an observable fact. Let us call the corresponding questions *intermediate questions*. In criminal cases, for example, intermediate questions will play an important role. We investigate the footprint of the murderer and infer from its seize that it must have been a large man, and this reduces the entire search space to a small fraction of suspects, etc. In figure 3, the same reduction of search space may be effected by asking a question at every node marked by "–" and obtaining "no" as an answer. While reduction by plausibility considerations is only of heuristic value, reduction by intermediate questions is safe to the extent the answers to intermediate questions are reliable. This decreases the possibility that the right answer is not found in the preferred part of the search space and that backtracking to previously ignored parts becomes necessary.

3.3 1st Order Existential Abduction

This is a special case of factual abduction (Thagard 1988, 57f, calls it simply 'existential abduction') which occurs when the antecedent of laws contains so-called *anonymous* variables, i.e. variables which are not contained in the consequent of the law. In the simplest case, the formal structure of 1st order existential abduction is the following:

$\forall x \forall y (Ryx \rightarrow Hx)$ or equivalently: : $\forall x (\exists y\, Ryx \rightarrow Hx)$
Ha
================
Conjecture: $\exists y Rya$

Instantiating the law-consequent in the law and backward chaining yields a law-antecedent in which one variable remains uninstantiated ("Rya"); the weakest and most reasonable abductive conjecture will be the one in which we existentially quantify over this variable (provided the background knowledge gives us no clue as to which individual has actually instantiated this variable). We have already discussed an example of this sort in §3.1: from the footprint in the sand we abductively infer that *some* man was walking at the beach. Existential abductions also play an important role in science. For example, the perturbations of planet Uranus were explained by Adams and Leverrier by a hypothetically postulated planet called Neptune which was later observed in telescopes. In some cases we will be satisfied with the existential conjecture – e.g., *some* turtle was robbing here in the sand. In other cases, e.g. criminal cases, everything depends on finding out *which* individual is the one who's existence we conjecture – who was the murderer? This gives rise to further questions and experiments.

In interrogative logic, this case is of particular importance. The existential hypothesis $\exists yRya$ is at the same time the presupposition of the corresponding which-question ?yRya. There is just one subtlety involved in this point. According to Hintikka's tableau rules, a which-question may be asked if its presupposition appears at the left side of the tableau (Hintikka et al. 2000, §3). However, the abductively conjectured presupposition $\exists yRya$ will appear at the right side of an open and completely developed branch of the tableau (cf. fig. 2). To move it to the left side we would first have to ask the whether-question $\exists yRya \lor \neg\exists yRya$? and then have to obtain the answer "yes" from nature. In practice, however, one asks the which-question immediately. If the 'culprit' individual is found, the presupposition is confirmed at the same time; otherwise the presupposition is rejected. This motivates the suggestion to extend tableau logic by the following rule: *If the presupposition of a which-question appears at the right side of an open and completely developed branch, the corresponding which-question may be asked and the answer to it may be added to the left side.* (If the answer is a proper answer, the branch gets closed; if the answer consists in the rejection of the question-presupposition, the branch remains open.)

In observable-fact-abduction the abduced hypothesis may at later stages of inquiry be confirmed by direct observation, in other words, it may be directly obtained as an answer by nature – for example, when we later meet the man who had walked at this beach the day before, or when we observe Neptune by a telescope. In this case, the abductive move gets indeed fully replaced by an interrogative move – abduction has played only a strategic but not an inferential role. This is different, however, in all of the following schemata of abduction, where the abductive hypothesis is not directly observable, but only indirectly confirmable via its empirical consequences.

3.4 Unobservable-Fact-Abduction

In the simplest case, this kind of abduction has the same formal structure as observable-fact-abduction, with the only difference that the abduced fact is unobservable, either because it is located in the past, or because it is unobservable on principal reasons. So we have important subcases.

3.4.1 Historical-Fact-Abduction

This kind of abduction is of obvious importance for all historical sciences (this is also emphasized by Niiniluoto 1999a). Assume for example that biologists discover marine fossil records, say fish bones, in the ground of dry land. They conjecture abductively, given their background theories, that some geological time span ago there was sea here. Is this hypothesis true? The hypothesis cannot be directly verified by observations; only indirectly. So the biologists look for further empirical consequences which follow from the abduced conjecture plus background knowledge – for example, further geological indications such as calcium deposits, or marine shell fossils, etc. If the latter findings are observationally verified, the abductive conjecture is confirmed.

In other words, unobservable-fact-abduction performs a combination of abductive backward reasoning and deductive or probabilistic forward reasoning to consequences which can be put to further test. This is graphically displayed in figure 4. Nature's answer does not directly inform us about the truth-value of the abductive hypothesis but only about the truth value of its empirical consequences. In such a case, there remains an irreducible inferential aspect in abduction, the move from nature's direct answers (E*a) to the acceptance of the unobservable hypothesis (Ha). Note also that the confirmation of the unobservable abductive hypothesis through the verification of its independent empirical consequences is at the same time a means of achieving empirical unification.

Testing the unobservable abductive conjecture by predicted consequences is also performed by a well-known AI abduction system – DENDRAL (Buchanan et al. 1969). This system has been designed to find the chemical structure of an organic

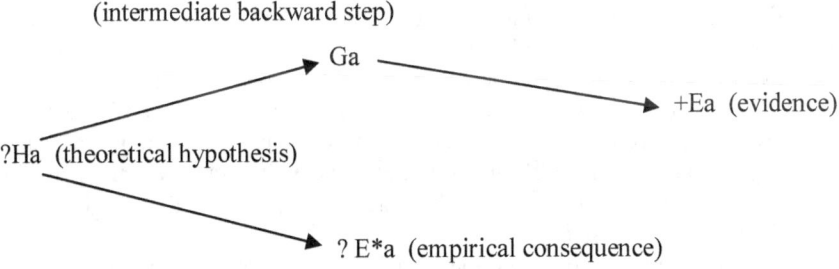

Figure 4: Unobservable-fact-abduction

molecule given its mass spectrum and its empirical formula. In a mass spectrometer an organic substance is broken in different ways; the higher the frequency of a fragment, the higher its peak in the spectrum. When DENDRAL searches for the most plausible abductive conjectures it only uses the most salient peaks of the spectrum (and moreover, it eliminates conjectures by the absence of peaks), but it does not use all peaks of the spectrum, especially not the peaks with lower intensity. To test its conjecture, DENDRAL then derives what the entire spectrum would be like if its conjecture were true. This prediction is matched against the full spectrum and if it turns out to be true the abductive hypothesis gets accepted (234ff).

The preceding considerations have an important consequence for interrogative logic. They tell us that if an abductive hypothesis is about something unobservable, an interrogative move consists of the following four distinct steps:

1. Abducing a conjecture: finding the direction of questions – initiating an interrogative programme.
2. Deriving empirical consequences from it: finding operative questions.
3. Testing the consequences: obtaining nature's answer (belief expansion).
4. Re-evaluating the hypothesis in the light of nature's answers (belief revision).

3.4.2 Theoretical-Fact-Abduction

Here the abductive hypothesis is about something unobservable because it contains theoretical terms. Usually, what drives a theoretical-fact-abduction is not a couple of low-level laws but a *quantitatively formulated theory* – usually a differential equation describing the dynamics of a system in a state space (cf. Schurz 2004). The empirical phenomenon to be explained is a reproducible experimental phenomenon, and the abductive task consists in finding *theoretical initial and boundary conditions* which describe the phenomenon in the theoretical language and which allow the mathematical derivation of the phenomenon from the theory. As an example, consider Archimedes' law of buoyancy force. Here one searches for a theoretical explanation of the fact that certain substances like stones or metals sink in water while others like wood or ice swim on water, *solely in terms of mechanical and gravitational effects*. Archimedes' ingenious abductive conjecture was that the amount of water which the swimming or sinking body supplants tends to lift the body upwards, with a force which equals the weight of the supplanted water – if this force is greater than the weight of the body the body will swim, otherwise it will sink.

We see that this kind of abduction, which is of highest important for theoretical physics, is tantamount to the formation of *theoretical models*. In contrast to the previous cases, here we usually don't have a large multitude of possible theoretical models or conjectures. In theoretical abduction cases of this sort, the empirical phenomenon under investigation is usually well-known and experimentally reproducible; so the relevant variables are known in principle. In the Archimedean case, we know that the ultimate causes are only contact forces and gravitational forces – other ultimate causes such as invisible water creatures etc. are excluded. In this respect, the situation of theoretical abduction in physics is fundamentally different from factual abduction. The real difficulty here is not to eliminate possible explanations but to find *at least one* theoretical model which allows the quantitative derivation of the explanandum. Successes in such tasks are usually celebrated by the community of physicists.

A special area of theoretical fact abduction is *interpretation*. Here the abduced facts are the beliefs and intentions of the speaker, given the evidence of his utterances or written words. It all depends on *what* the speaker says and *how* (s)he says it, whether there will be many possible interpretations, with the difficulty of their elimination, or whether it will be hard to find just one coherent interpretation. The investigation of interpretation as abduction is a growing area in AI (Hobbs et al. 1993).

3.5. Law-Abduction

This kind of abduction can already be found in Aristotle – it corresponds to what Aristotle has called the mind's power of *hitting upon the middle term* of a syllogism (*An. Post.*, I, 34). The evidence is an empirical law, the abduced hypothesis is a law and the abduction is driven by a background law:

Background laws:	$\forall x(Cx \to Ex)$	Whatever contains sugar tastes sweet
Emp. law to be explained:	$\forall x(Fx \to Ex)$	All pineapples taste sweet
Abduced conjecture:	$\forall x(Fx \to Cx)$	All pineapples contain sugar.

According to my knowledge, it is not clear whether this pattern fits more Aristotle's *epagoge* or his *apagoge*.[5]

Often, law-abductions produce conjectures of theoretical hypotheses concerning unobservable characteristics of objects. For example, a common abduction pattern in chemistry is this:

All substances of empirical kind S have certain empirical properties E.
All substances which contain molecular groups of the form X have property E.
———
Conjecture: Substances of kind S have molecular characteristics X.

Here is a particular example of this pattern:

If salt is held in a hot flame it turns the flame intensely yellow.
Substances which contain sodium turn flames intensely yellow.
———
Conjecture: Salt contains sodium.

---

[5] Cf. Niiniluoto (1999b, 241), and in particular Rocha (1998); according to her discussion law-abduction is in Aristotle (but in different places) conceived both as apagoge and as epagoge.

Flach and Kakas (2000, 21f) have proposed reducing law-abduction to the following concatenation of fact-abduction and inductive generalization.

Background law:	$\forall x(Cx \to Ex)$
Observed facts:	$Fa_i \wedge Ea_i$ $1 \leq i \leq n$ $\Rightarrow$ *Induction basis* for: $\forall x(Fx \to Ex)$

Abduced hypotheses:	Ca_i $1 \leq i \leq n$
hence:	$Fa_i \wedge Ca_i$ $1 \leq i \leq n$ $\Rightarrow$ *Induction basis* for $\forall x(Fx \to Cx)$

Their decomposition, however, is somewhat artificial. Law-abduction is usually performed in one single conjectural step. We don't form the abductive hypothesis of containing sugar for each observed pineapple one after the other and then generalize it, but we form the law-conjuncture "pineapples contain sugar" at once.

So far we have only discussed schemata of abduction which cannot introduce *new concepts*. This is the most delicate case, to it we turn in the next section.

4. SECOND ORDER EXISTENTIAL ABDUCTION.

Here we abduce an at least partly new general property or natural kind concept altogether with an at least partly new theoretical law. The underlying evidence consists of empirically observed regularities, so-called *phenomena* – not just of particular facts. Let me first mention two simple cases:

4.1 Micro-Part-Abduction

In this most harmless case of 2nd order existential abduction we generate abductive hypotheses about the microscopic composition of observable substances: the prototypical example is the *atomic hypothesis* in the form in which it was conjectured already in antiquity by Leucippus and Democritus. Based on various empirical phenomena[6], these philosophers have abduced a new natural kind term: atoms, which are too small to be observable but which otherwise obey the *same* mechanical laws as macroscopic bodies. So what we do here is extrapolate from macroscopic concepts and laws into the microscopic domain – hence we may also speak here of *extrapolative* abduction.

4.2 Analogical Abduction

In analogical abduction we abduce a partially new concept and at the same time new laws connecting that concept with other (empirical) concepts. The concept is only partly new because it is analogical to familiar concepts, and this is the way

---
[6] E.g., dissolution of sugar in water, or re-sublimation of salt from 'salty air' at the sea, etc.

in which this concept was discovered. So analogical abduction is *driven* by analogy. We first consider Thagard's (1988) example of sound waves.

Background knowledge: Laws of propagation and reflection of water waves.
Phenomenon to be explained: Propagation and reflection of sound.
==

Abductive conjecture: Sound consists of atmospheric waves in analogy to water waves.

According to Thagard (1988, 67) analogical abduction results from a *conceptual combination:* the observational concepts of wave and sound which we already posses are combined into the unobservational (only indirectly testable) concept of a sound-wave. However, this analysis is too simple because it does not distinguish analogical abduction from simple conceptual combinations such as the conjunctive combination of "table" and "metallic" into "metallic table". In my view, what is crucial for analogical abduction is *conceptual abstraction* based on *isomorphic* (or homomorphic) *mapping*. What is abduced by this analogy is not only the theoretical concept of sound-wave, but at the same time the theoretical concept of a *wave* in abstracto.

In fact, Holyoak and Thagard (1989) explain abduction as a morphism between structures. A very clear analysis of analogy based on mapping and conceptual abstraction has been given by Gentner (1983; cf. also Falkenhainer et al. 1989/90). According to his analysis, an analogy is a *partial isomorphic* mapping m between two relational structures, the *source* structure $<D, F_i\ (1\leq i\leq m), R_i\ (1\leq i\leq n)>$ and the *target structure* $<D^*, F^*_i\ (1\leq i\leq m), R^*_i\ (1\leq i\leq n)>$, where the F_i are monadic predicates and the R_i are relations. Gentner argues very convincingly (158f) that an analogical mapping preserves only the *relations* of the two structures, and 2nd order relations such as "causes", while monadic predicates are not preserved. This is what distinguishes an analogy from a literal similarity. For example, our solar system is literally similar to the star system X^{12} in the Andromeda galaxy insofar the X^{12} central star is bright and yellow like our sun, and surrounded by planets similar to our planets. On the other hand, an atom (according to Rutherford's theory) is merely analogical to our solar system: the positively charged nucleus is surrounded by electrons just as the sun is surrounded by planets, governed by a structurally similar force law, but concerning its monadic properties, the nucleus is very different from the sun, the electrons are very different from the planets, and the force is different in its nature (gravitational versus electrical force). Formally, then, an analogical mapping isomorphically maps (subsets of) D into (subsets of) D*, and (some of) the relations R_i into (some of the) R^*_i such that $aR_i b$ iff $m(a)R^*_i m(a)$. In this sense, the Rutherford-analogy maps "sun" into "nucleus", "planet" into "electron", "gravitational attraction" into "electrical attraction", "surrounding" into "surrounding", etc. It follows from the existence of such a partial isomorphic mapping that all explanatory laws holding for the source structure which are solely expressed in terms of mapping-preserved relations will hold in structurally similar way for the target structure. In this way, explanations can be transferred from the source to the target structure (which is of particular importance for Thagard 1992).

Every partial isomorphism gives rise to a *conceptual abstraction* by putting together just those parts of both structures which are isomorphically mapped into each other, and interpreting them in an *abstract* system-theoretic sense. In this way, the abstract model of a *central force system* arises, from the concepts of a *central body, a peripherical body, a central force, etc.* (160f). Since finding an abductive analogy consists in finding those theoretically essential features of the source structure which can be generalized to other domains, the procedure goes hand-in-hand with the corresponding process of conceptual abstraction. For example, the analogical transfer of water-waves to sound-waves only makes sense if the theoretically essential features of (water-) waves have been identified, namely, that waves are produced by *coupled oscillators*. The abductive conjecture of sound-waves then says that also sound should consist of coupled oscillations. Immediately, this gives rise to the further question of what the *medium* of coupled sound oscillators *materially* consists in. The abductive conjecture says: the medium here is the air, with the air molecules moving back and forth, thereby bouncing against each other.

It is after the formation of this theoretical model of sound-waves that a *theoretical* explanation of propagation and reflection of sound-waves becomes possible. Another example of analogical abduction which is extensively discussed by Thagard (1992, 131ff) and which I only mention in passing is Darwin's hypothesis of evolution by natural selection. Darwin abductively conjectured this hypothesis as an explanation of various records of similarities between living species and extinct species inferred from fossil records, thereby drawing upon the analogy with *artificial selection*, i.e., breeding of domestic plants and animals.

4.3 Missing-Link Common Cause Abduction (Reichenbach, Salmon)

Here we know that two event types Fx and Gx are strongly correlated, but our causal background knowledge tells us that they cannot be directly causally connected because there exists no direct causal mechanism which connects them – the 'link' is missing. An example is the correlation of lightning and thunder; we know by experiments that light does not produce sound. Another example is provided by simultaneously correlated events at a distance, such as the simultaneous ringing of clocks. In these cases, we abductively conjecture a common cause Cx which produces both Fx and Gx. Of course, the common cause hypothesis is subject to further test.

This kind of abduction differs from what we will call fundamental common cause abduction in the next section in that we assume here just *one* regularity or correlation to be explained. The first and most parsimonious conjecture in this case would be that one of the two event-types causes the other one – it is only because our background knowledge tells us that this cannot be that we postulate a 'hidden' common cause. It should be noted, however, that Salmon (1984, 213ff) understands his account of common-cause explanation in a much broader way which seems to include fundamental common cause abduction.

4.4 Fundamental Common Cause Abduction

The most fundamental kind of conceptual abduction is illustrated by cases where we abductively conjecture a new unobservable property together with laws connecting them with observable properties, without drawing on analogies with concepts with which we are already familiar. This kind of abduction (also discussed in Schurz 1996a) does not presuppose any background knowledge except knowledge of those phenomena which we intend to unify. So what drives fundamental abduction is the pure search for unification. The facts to be explained are various empirical regularities. We already know from section 2 that it would not meet the scientific constraint of unification if we could explain *every* regularity by a special unobservable causal power. In other words, the following abduction schema belongs to rational speculation but not to science:

Observed effect: If Fx then Gx (where F, G are observable properties)
==
Conjecture: If Fx, then x has causal power $P_{F/G}x$, which produces Gx.

However, the situation changes drastically if we observe many regularities of this kind which are themselves *correlated* in a way which allows to explain all of them by one and the same hypothetically postulated causal power or common cause as follows:

4.4.1 Theoretical Property Abduction

Assume we have a set of empirical regularities manifesting themselves at some but not all objects x:

$\forall t(C_i(x,t) \leadsto E_i(x,t))$ $1 \leq i \leq n$

where $\leadsto$ is an implication stronger than material one, e.g. a counterfactual or lawlike implication. Assume that these nomological regularities are abbreviations for certain empirical dispositions, such as solubility, elasticity etc. Now assume that all these empirical laws are themselves correlated in the following way:

$\forall x(\ \forall t(C_i(x,t) \leadsto E_i(x,t))\ \leftrightarrow\ \forall t(C_j(x,t) \leadsto E_j(x,t))\ )\ 1 \leq i < j \leq n$

In words: whenever an object exhibits one of these empirical laws (or empirical dispositions), it also exhibits all the others. In sum, we have $n + n.(n-1) = 2n$ elementary regularities.

For example, whenever an object exhibits conductivity of heat it also exhibits conductivity of electricity, characteristic flexibility and elasticity, hardness, and characteristic glossing. We then abduce that there is a really existing material characteristics which is the common cause of all these empirical dispositions or regularities. We call this characteristics *metallic character* Mx. In this way, chemical scientists have abduced natural kind terms for chemical kinds of substances.

From the viewpoint of unification, we thereby reduce the n^2 elementary empirical laws to the following n theoretical laws

$$\forall x(Mx \leftrightarrow \forall t(C_i(x,t) \leadsto E_i(x,t)))\ 1 \leq i \leq n$$

which is a polynomial reduction from n^2 to n.

Instead of counterfactual conditionals we may also use Carnap's *reduction sentences* to characterize empirical dispositions, which are n 'partial' definitions of the form $\forall x \forall t(C_i(x,t) \rightarrow (D_i x \leftrightarrow E_i(x,t))$ ($1 \leq i \leq n$). We then have the following $n.(n-1)$ empirical correlations: $\forall x \forall t(\ C_i(x,t) \land E_i(x,t) \rightarrow (C_j(x,t) \rightarrow E_j(x,t))$ ($1 \leq i < j \leq n$). In this setting, we abductively replace the n^2 empirical laws by the following 2n theoretical laws: $\forall x \forall t(\ C_i(x,t) \land E_i(x,t) \rightarrow Mx)$ and $\forall x(Mx \rightarrow \forall t(C_i(x,t) \rightarrow E_i(x,t))$ ($1 \leq i \leq n$).

4.4.2 Abduction to Reality

The same schema of abduction underlies the most elementary form of abduction: abduction from introspective evidence to the conjecture of an external reality as the common cause of our introspective evidence (cf. Schurz 1996a). Our instinctive and unconscious inferences from our sensory experiences to the hypothesis of external objects which cause these experiences are based on the same pattern of mutually correlated regularities. First, there are intrasensory correlations: the visual images of a given object systematically vary with the angle at which we look at the objects, and these variations in visual appearances are strictly correlated. Identification of three-dimensional objects based on two-dimensional projective images from various angles is an important abductive task in the AI field of visual object recognition. But more importantly, there is the correlation between the visual perceptions and the tactile perceptions. If I have a certain perceptual appearance in my visual field when I look in a certain direction, then I will also be able to walk to the visually identified position of the appearing object and touch the object. The correlation between visual and tactile senses is the major fundament of our common-sense belief in the existence of an outer reality. Visual impressions which do not correlate with tactile ones are, on the other hand, a central source of the imagination of the *unreal* – from ghosts and haunted masons to spiritual powers. This shows that abduction to hidden common causes based on correlated regularities is of fundamental epistemological importance.

I conclude this paper with a final classification of kinds of abduction.

Universität Düsseldorf, Germany
E-Mail: gerhard.schurz@phil-fak.uni-duesseldorf.de

Kind of Abduction	Evidence to be explained	A. produces	A. is driven by
Factual Abduction:	Singul. emp. facts	New facts (reasons/causes)	Known laws or theories
Observable-fact-A	"	Factual reasons	Known laws
Unobservable-fact-A	"	Unobs. reasons	"
Historical-fact-A	"	Facts in the past	"
Theoretical-fact-A	"	New initial or boundary conditions	Known theories
1st order existential A.	"	Factual reasons postulating new unknown individuals	Known laws
Law-Abduction	Empirical laws	New laws	Known laws
2nd order existential-Abd.	"	New laws/ theories with new concepts	Theoretical b(ackground) k(nowledge)
Micro-Part-Abduction	"	Microscopic composition	Extrapol. of b.k.
Analogical Abduction	"	New laws/ theories with analogical concepts	Analogy with b.k.
Missing-link Com.-cause-A.	"	Hidden common causes	Causal b.k.
Fundamental Com.-Cause A.	"		
Theoret.-property A.	"	New theoretical entities	Unification of b.k.
Abduct. to reality	Introspect. laws	External entities	Unification of b.k.

Figure 5: Classification of kinds of abduction.

References

Alchourrón, C. E., Gärdenfors, P., Makinson, D., 1985, "On the Logic of Theory Change", *Journal of Symbolic Logic* 50, 510–530.
Bartelborth, T. , 1996, *Begründungsstrategien*, Akademie Verlag, Berlin.
Bratko, I., 1986, *Prolog Programming for Artificial Intelligence*, Addison-Wesley Publishing Company, Reading/Mass.
Buchanan, B., Sutherland, G., Feigenbaum, E A., 1969, "HEURISTIC DENDRAL: a Program for Generating Explanatory Hypotheses in Organic Chemistry", *Machine Intelligence* Vol. 4 (ed. by B. Meltzer, D. Michie; Edinburgh University Press), 209–254.
Christiansen, H., 2000, "Abduction and Induction Combined in a Metalogical Framework", in Flach/Kakas (eds., 2000), 195–211.
Console, L. et al., 1991, "On the Relationship between Abduction and Deduction", *Journal of Logic and Computation* Vol. 1, No. 5, 661–690.
Earman, J., 1992, *Bayes or Bust?*, MIT Press, Cambridge/MA.
Falkenhainer, B., Kenneth, D.F., Gentner, D., 1989/90, "The Structure-Mapping Engine: Algorithms and Examples", *Artificial Intelligence* 41, 1989/90, 1–63.
Flach, P. and Kakas, A. (eds.), 2000, *Abduction and Induction*, Kluwer, Dordrecht.
Friedman, M., 1974, "Explanation and Scientific Understanding", *Journal of Philosophy* 71, 5–19.
Gentner, D., 1983, "Structure-Mapping: A Theoretical Framework for Analogy", *Cognitive Science* 7, 155–170.
Harman, G. H. 1965, "The Inference to the Best Explanation", *Philosophical Review* 74, 173–228.
Hintikka, J., 1998, "What is Abduction? The Fundamental Problem of Contemporary Epistemology", *Transactions of the Charles Sanders Peirce Society*, Vol. XXXIV, No. 3, 503–533.
Hintikka, J., Halonen, I. and Mutanen, A., 2000, "Interrogative Logic as a General Theory of Reasoning", in R. H. Johnson and J. Woods (eds.), *Handbook of Practical Reasoning*, Kluwer, Dordrecht.
Hobbs, J. R., Stickel, M., Appelt, D., Martin, P., 1993, "Interpretation as Abduction", *Artificial Intelligence Journal* 63(1–2), 69–142.
Holyoak, K., and Thagard, P., 1989, "Analogical Mapping by Constraint Satisfaction", *Cognitive Science* 13, 295–355.
Josephson, J. and Josephson, S. (eds.), 1994, *Abductive Inference*, Cambridge University Press, New York.
Kitcher, P, 1989, "Explanatory Unification and the Causal Structure of the World", in Kitcher, P. and Salmon, W. (eds.), *Scientific Explanation*, University of Minnesota Press, Minneapolis, 410–505.
Lipton, P., 1991, *Inference to the Best Explanation*, Routledge, London.
Nilsson, N. 1980, *Principles of Artificial Intelligence*, Tioga Publications, Palo Alto.
Niiniluoto, I., 1999a, "Defending Abduction", *Philosophy of Science* 66 (proceedings), S436–S451.
Niiniluoto, I., 1999b, "Abduction and Geometrical Analysis. Notes on Charles S. Peirce and Edgar Allan Poe", in L. Magnani, N. J. Nersessian, P. Thagard (eds.), *Model-Based Reasoning in Scientific Discovery*, Kluwer, Dordrecht, 239–254.
Peirce, C. S., 1878, "Deduction, Induction, and Hypothesis", in *Collected Papers* 2.619–2.644 (ed. by C. Hartshorne and P. Weiss, Harvard University Press, Cambridge/Mass., 1931–35).
Peirce, C. S., 1903, "Lectures on Pragmatism", in *Collected Papers* 5.14–5.212 (ed. by C. Hartshorne, P. Weiss, Harvard University Press, Cambridge/Mass., 1931–35).
Prendinger, H., 1998, *Approximate Reasoning*, dissertation, University of Salzburg.
Rocha, M., 1998, "Abduktion und Intuitive Induktion bei Aristoteles", in P. Weingartner et al. (eds.), *The Role of Pragmatics in Contemporary Philosophy,* Hölder-Pichler-Tempsky, Vienna.
Salmon, W., 1984, *Scientific Explanation and the Causal Structure of the World*, Princeton University Press, Princeton.
Schurz, G., 1996a, "Die Bedeutung des abduktiven Schließens in Erkenntnis- und Wissenschaftstheorie", in A. Schramm (ed.), *Philosophie in Österreich 1996,* Hölder-Pichler-Tempsky, Vienna, 91–109.

Schurz, G., 1996b, "The Role of Negation in Non-monotonic Logic and Defeasible Reasoning", in H. Wansing, *Negation. A Notion in Focus*, W. de Gruyter, Berlin, 197–231.
Schurz. G., 1999, "Explanation as Unification", *Synthese* 120, No. 1, 95–114.
Schurz, G., 2004, "Explanations in Science and the Logic of Why-Questions", to appear in *Synthese* 2004.
Schurz, G./Lambert , K., 1994, "Outline of a Theory of Scientific Understanding", *Synthese* 101/1, 65–120.
Thagard, P, 1988, *Computational Philosophy of Science* MIT Press, Cambridge/MA.
Thagard, P., 1992, *Conceptual Revolutions*, Princeton University Press, Princeton.

MATTI SINTONEN

THE TWO ASPECTS OF METHOD: QUESTIONING FELLOW INQUIRERS AND QUESTIONING NATURE

To observe is to detect the actions of nature; but we shall not advance far in this path, unless we have a notion of its character. To make experiments is to lay questions before nature; but he alone can do that beneficially who knows what he should ask. (Christian Oersted, *On the Spirit and Study of Universal Natural Philosophy*, London 1852).

1. IN THE BEGINNING THERE WAS A QUESTION

Man by nature desires to know, as Aristotle noted in *Metaphysics*. This desire finds expression in wonder and perplexity, but what counts as fulfilment of such desire, and how is wonder and perplexity to be dissipated? The most natural view is the one which has been the favourite through millennia: wonder and perplexity give rise to questions of various sizes and shapes; refining these questions as well as searching for answers to them is a method of inquiry; and arriving at and possessing conclusive answers to the questions counts as fulfilment. Both the notions of method and of science have of course gone through a multitude of conceptual upheavals, and similarly philosophy has meant a multitude of intellectual endeavours. Yet any sort of inquiry, into one's own soul or into the world out there, can be couched in interrogative terms. Questioning and answering are also primordial types of speech acts, indeed complementary aspects of a language game deeply rooted in the human cognitive capacity. If there is anything, then, that deserves the title of *the* method in philosophy or in science it surely is the method of questions and answers.

In this paper I shall examine some of the forms which the interrogative perspective has been given in knowledge acquisition and especially scientific inquiry. Some aspects can only be mentioned in passing, and some others are left out completely, for lack of space. To mention just one, I shall not deal with the use of the interrogative notion as the methodological backbone of many specific methods in the social sciences. There are two areas of focus in this paper. The first one concerns the transition from the epistemology of the ancients and the medievals to the idea that the proper partner in questioning is Nature. The very existence of the so-called Scientific Revolution has been questioned (Shapin 1996). Yet it is undeniable that the 17th Century witnessed rising social and epistemological individualism, the emergence of experimental and mathematical philosophy, the birth of a new notion of evidence and the rise of probability, as well as the erosion of the ideal of metaphysical or philosophical certainty under the pressure to settle for the less demanding moral certainty (Hacking 1975, Shapin 1994, Shapin and Schaffer 1985).

The modern epistemological and metaphysical scene has been variously described, and no account is universally accepted. But there is an underlying development which bears on interrogation as philosophy and as method. As has been documented, the ancient and medieval notion of experience as a ground of justification amounted to something like received knowledge and common acceptance, and hence something which was in no particular need for justification. The modern notion of experience shifted allegiance to what could and actually had been witnessed by reliable individuals in particular circumstances. And since these witness reports were reports on what Nature had to say in contrived experimental circumstances, reliable witnessing became the epistemological crux. The claim that I would like to advance is that there is a direct link between this shift of allegiance to witness reports and the far-reaching changes in the aims and scope of science or natural philosophy. On the interrogative agenda these changes can be seen as changes in the *types* and *scope* of questions one can address. Nature can only be called on to give evidence on something She has witnessed – and these are particulars. There is no way to address general questions to Nature – in fact Nature does not understand grand theoretical questions in general, and explanation-seeking why-questions in particular. One cannot, then, derive general truths from Nature's answers – or indeed from the naturalists' eyewitness reports on what Nature says. And if direct interrogation of Nature is what the experimental method boils down to there can be no metaphysical certainty on the principles of Nature.

I shall also address a related issue in the transition from the Aristotelian and medieaval notion of dialogue conducted within a community to a Baconian or modern dialogue conducted with Nature. The main complaint of Francis Bacon and other advocates of the New Philosophy against the old logic was, briefly, that it was inadequate in the acquisition of new knowledge. Dialogue between two inquirers or within a wider community can teach respect for logic and give guidanc in the preservation of truth. Dialectics is also eminently suitable for the purpose of detecting and destroying inconsistencies and possible weaker forms of incoherence. Rhetorics in turn is efficient in spreading and marketing available notions. Although dialectics and rhetorics have these admittedly important services in safeguarding epistemic integrity and inheritance, they are insufficient if the goal is to explore new terrains and unexplored depths, and to discover truths that are news not just to a particular inquirer but to all members of the inquiring community. On the face of it, they share a drawback which many naturalists detected in the grand theory of natural selection proposed by Charles Darwin. As Darwin's much appreciated mentor Charles Lyell wrote, the theory of evolution through natural selection could well serve the functions of two of the members of the "hindu trinity", Visnu the sustainer and Siva the destroyer. But Lyell could not understand how it could serve as Brahma the creator – and without its creative power "we cannot conceive the others having any function" since... "nothing new w.^{d} appear if there were not the creative force."

What was called for was, to use the analogy with natural selection, variation, food for thought, grist to the communal mill called natural philosophy. One should trust one's own reason and senses as well as the testimony of Nature, and not rely on the tradition arising from the interpretation of authorities. The novelties to be found "must be sought from the light of nature, not fetched back out of the darkness of antiquity," Bacon wrote.

All this rhetoric seems to imply that the dialectical and rhetorical tradition and the questions-to-Nature idea differ in that one represents inquiry as a social affair and the other one in terms of a solo inquirer who confronts Nature with his reason and senses as tools. This would be an oversimplification. Both views are at bottom social, though in different ways. The differences manifest in differing views of what is efficient as well as whom (or what) one should trust. To illustrate that the two dialogues are two sides of the same interrogative coin I shall take an example from 19th Century biology. Charles Darwin was an avowed Baconian who in his own words advocated the method of induction and who, "without any theory collected facts on a wholesale scale..." On the face of it this sounds like one more case of mistaken methodological identity, due to scientists' understandable need to tally their practices to the prevailing ideals of what science is supposed to be. And so it is if by Baconianism we mean the image of Bacon propagated in early 19th Century. But somewhat ironically this reading would gain in credibility if we were to locate it in the actual context in which Bacon's views were formed. I shall in fact suggest more than this. The real Bacon based his methodological ideal, including the notion of induction, in lists of questions or *interrogatories* modelled after the emerging legal practices of the day. Now Darwin was the interrogator *par excellence* of his days. Just like Bacon, he equated experiments with questions put to Nature. However, where Bacon eloquently spoke against relying on others' testimony, Darwin explicitly addressed his interrogatories to fellow naturalists. When questions to nature, i.e. experiments, were too time-consuming or costly, and when trustworthy friends and gentlemen were available, he readily addressed his questions them – and to laymen.

2. "Finding the Right Questions to Ask"

The interrogative view loomed large in early modern science as well as in 19th Century German philosophy, in the discussions about the comprehensiveness of the logic and psychology of judgment. It has been used in epistemology and methodology but equally well within attempts to understand perception and observation, or language, meaning and communication. R. G. Collingwood (1939, 30–31) summed up the philosophical insight of the interrogative view well: Francis Bacon's *Novum Organum* and René Descartes' *Discourse de la Méthode,* he wrote, anchored the idea of a method (*the* Method) on the "principle that a body of knowledge consists not of 'propositions', 'statements', 'judgments' or whatever name logicians use in order to denote assertive acts of thought". As Collingwood saw it, knowledge rather consists of propositions "together with the questions they are meant to answer; and that a logic in which the answers are attended to and the questions neglected is a false logic". If we add to this Gadamer's (1989) insight that the questions themselves emerge against the background of the moving horizon of expectations we get view of inquiry as a dynamic process of questions and answers.

How should one, then, proceed in knowledge acquisition if this is a correct characterization of the goal, knowledge? It was typical of the turn to the modern to see this as a methodical procedure in which Nature is subjected to interrogation directly. Bacon insisted that science begins where man begins 'putting nature to the question'. And, as Collingwood added, this insight was taken over by Kant who made up his mind "that scientific technique meant simply the skilful asking of questions" (Collingwood 1940, 238–239). The roots of this understanding of the interrogative method go to the writings of those who made the preparation work and to those who carried out the Scientific Revolution. Indeed, the 17th Century could well be called the Age of Method.

If the crucial inquiry skill is that of finding the right questions to ask, how does one find the right question? Where do questions come? Does the interrogative view imply anything constructive with respect to the most obvious difficulty in our motto: to be able to raise the right question one would already have to know what one is looking for? This is the interrogative variant of Meno's problem, but what would be the solution? By the interrogative lights this question is ambiguous between two distinguishable readings. What we desire to know determines the goals of inquiry, i.e., what is worth knowing for cognitive or practical purposes. These goals manifest in and give rise to what I call *big* questions. But a closer look at Kant's proposal reveals another role for questions and answers. The paths to answers to these big questions are paved by *small* questions. Both types of questions can be graded with respect to their importance or weight, the intrinsic cognitive value an answer has for the edifice of knowledge, or the instrumental value an answer has in bringing inquiry closer to the goal. The distinction is, of course, highly contextual. Someone's big question can occupy a more modest place on another one's cognitive map. And a small question, once motivated by its role as stepping stones to big questions, can lead a life of relative independence.

With this caveat in mind, let us look at big questions first, those that trigger an inquiry. Roughly, they seem to arise in two ways. First, there are the discrepancies between theory-laden expectations and the results of observations and experiments. Secondly, to the extent a body of knowledge, theory, model or paradigm specifies what its intended applications are, questions emerge as unfinished business: questions are gaps in the existing body of belief, crying out for a filling of the right size and shape.[1] A now classic proposal which adopts this point of view is Thomas Kuhn's account of scientific discovery. According to Kuhn (1977, 173–174), episodes of discovery seem to have two requisites. First, there are the individuals, or the individual, who have the "skill, wit, or genius to recognize that something has gone wrong in ways that may prove consequential". Thus it is clear that on Kuhn's view talent is crucial and, moreover, that it manifests in the ability to explore the ramifications of the wayward phenomena. And secondly, he notes that genius is not enough. Anomalies can only be seen for what they are if experimental equipment, most notably instruments and concepts, "have been developed sufficiently to make their emergence likely and to make the anomaly which results recognizable as a violation of expectation."

However, I shall take three explicitly interrogative accounts into a closer scrutiny, Sylvain Bromberger's predicament view, Nicholas Jardine's account of the local and absolute reality of questions, and Scott Kleiner's account of problem choice (see also Sintonen 1989). All three are accounts of what prompts questions to arise, adopting the stance that in the beginning of inquiry there is a question. All three also agree with R. G. Collingwood's insistence on the logical primacy of questions over assertive acts of thought. Sylvain Bromberger (1965, 1966 and 1971) has attempted to construct a comprehensive interrogative model of inquiry, addressing both the logic and the methodology of question-answer analysis in the philosophy of science. The guiding intuition was that one should aim at stating the "principles which govern the acceptability of any alleged contribution to science" (Bromberger 1971, 49). This general aim covers not just the developing of an erotetic logic for the various types of questions, but also the characterization of what the question-answer relationship is, of how scientific questions arise, and of how answers are sought (by search algorithms). The ambitious programme was not carried to completion, but it did provide useful criteria of adequacy.

How are questions generated? Bromberger's interrogative construal starts with the assumption that questions arise from a structured form of curiosity, from a combination of knowledge and ignorance. Ignorance is "not one big undifferentiated glop, one huge unstructured nothingness" (ibid, 51). A particularly hoary but important type of questions are why-questions arising from such structured from of curiosity. According to Bromberger (1966, 91), why-questions arise when a person is either in a p-predicament or a b-predicament concerning some fact. The former is the case when a person thinks that a why-question admits of a right answer but she or he can think of no non-objectionable one. The

---

[1] The problem has earlier been treated in connection of the problem-solving model of inquiry. Thus for instance Hattiangadi (1979) has argued that all scientific problems have the form of an inconsistency, whereas Laudan (1977), Leplin (1980) and Nickles (1980) have tried to find room for a wider notion of a scientific problem. Both Laudan and Nickles have maintained that a mere logical compatibility of a phenomenon with a theory counts as a problem if there is a "premium" for solving it (Laudan) or if the phenomenon falls in the domain of the theory.

latter is the case if the question "admits of a right answer, no matter what the views of the person, but that answer is beyond what that person can think of, can state, can generate from his mental repertoire". In these cases the question is unanswerable relative to person's set of propositions and concepts. Essentially, Bromberger writes, explanation is "search for and discovery of answers to questions that are unanswerable relative to prevailing beliefs and concepts". Both types of predicaments thus give rise to why-questions, as the label "predicament" suggests.

A question may, however, fail to arise for two intuitively speaking different reasons. Bromberger, and later van Fraassen (1980, but see also Belnap and Steel 1976) groped for a way to distinguish between questions which fail to arise simply because the inquirer has made a factual mistake, and questions which are, by the lights of an inquirer or community of inquirers, not of a type which admit of direct answers. The latter type of failure is more radical. A question which flouts the fundamental ontological and methodological commitments of the accepted view borders on nonsense.

Scott Kleiner (1970) has expanded on the question of question choice by suggesting that scientific theories provide vocabularies which make some kinds of questions admissible. Kleiner criticizes e.g. Kuhn (1970) and Laudan (1977) for embracing notions of a paradigm or research programme which refer to progress as puzzle or problem solving – without giving an account of how problems or questions are chosen. His own proposal is to give principles which grade problems in accordance with their epistemic importance or weight. Thus problems concerning the core or theories or research programmes or about the principles governing the fundamental processes are to be given high priority (see also Sintonen 1996). For instance the languages of classical and relativist mechanics render different questions well-motivated or illegitimate. He (1993, 122) has continued this theme in his logic of discovery in which choices of questions are justified locally against a relatively stable background consisting of ontological, conceptual, metascientific and empirical assumptions. For instance the Darwinian research context (the Darwinian paradigm) ruled out, through its built-in presupposition that organisms always have natural parentage, creationist questions. On his view scientific inquiry indeed is a problem solving or question answering process. For him the logic of discovery is not a special form of inference from observation to theory, but rather a theory of the rationality of research which includes, as one of its most crucial objectives, the study of the principles bearing upon "the rational choice of problems, or epistemic objectives, and heuristics, or means to solving the problems."[2]

---

[2] In much the same way Gary Gutting (1980) has proposed that processes of discovery proceed along question-answer lines: discovery always starts with a question, and it "derives many of its most important characteristics from a set of empirical, theoretical, and methodological givens" which Gutting calls the question-context. Now this context consists of three types of elements: empirical facts, theoretical concepts, laws and (non-propositional models) which "previous inquiry has shown

More importantly still, Kleiner (1993) distinguishes between questions which give the goal and questions which serve as means. Some questions are a means of answering another and more important question: thus the question arising from the fudamental problem of evolution, "Do species transmute?", was approached by the subquestion "Are these specimen (of mockingbirds) distinct species or distinct varieties" and the subsubquestion "Do the variations in observable specimen correspond to variations among mockingbird species." Clearly, these subquestions obtain their importance and studying them their motivation from the initial question.[3]

This way these approaches focus on how questions emerge against the background of accepted theory and methodology, available experimental apparatus etc., also opens a new way to see history of science. Michel Foucault (1970) has suggested that biology, in the modern sense, was a result of a change in the *episteme* which structured thought on living things. Natural history and its classificatory schemes gave way to a perspective in which organisms were seen in the light of what they had to cope with in their environment. Changing scenes in the emerging biological sciences were witnessed by new *types* of questions.

3. There Is More to a Question than Meets the Ear

It can also happen that an innocent-looking question *sentence* in two different mouths carry a different force. This is to refine Collingwood who maintained (1939, 38) that a sentence (or a proposition) and its negation, abstracted from their interrogative contexts, can not contradict one another. In fact, sentences or propositions are not truth-bearers in isolation but only in what he called question-answer complexes. For a contradiction to arise the potential answers need to belong to the same question-and-answer complex. In addition, these answers

---

to be relevant to the description and explanation of the empirical facts (of the question context), and of methodological strategies for developing an answer to the questions" (Gutting 1980, 38) These elements are a motley crew, and they comprise "heuristic tricks" (e.g. oversimplifications and analogies), mathematical and experimental techniques (such as use of partial differential equations or linear accelerators), and, most importantly, "directives derived from very general substantive assumptions about the nature of the world and of scientific inquiry." As examples of such assumptions Gutting mentions the search for conservation laws, the presumption that biological systems can be understood in chemical terms, preferences for hypotheses exhibiting certain sorts of simplicity or for certain types of explanation.

[3] He therefore joins those who doubt that the logic of questions could be turned into a logic of inquiry sufficient to deal with actual historical cases. In like manner Sintonen (1984) argues that scientific questions have both logical presuppositions (statements which must be true for the question to have direct answers at all) and pragmatic presuppositions which narrow down the set of admissible answers. The so-called structuralist theory notion, Sintonen (1989, 1990, 1996) suggests, gives a pragmatic account of centrality or importance: a paradigmatic theory which consists of a fundamental theory-element and a set of intended applications is essentially a hierarchically organized structure which both guides and constrains the search for answers to detailed questions within an application as well as for special laws for so-far unconquered applications. The logic of questions, then, has to be augmented with a rich enough notion of a theory to narrow down the set of possible answers.

must be, within this complex, sensible and not a silly. One way to put this is to adapt Shakespeare: there usually is more to a question than meets the ear. As an example take the Tinbergen-inspired question of stickleback fish ethology (Tinbergen 1963, Kuipers and Wisniewski 1994). Stickleback fish sometimes exhibit a particular behavioural pattern of fanning with their pectoral fins. One can raise the question "Why do male sticklebacks fan with their pectoral fins?" This question is open to several more precise readings, as Ernst Mayr (1961, 1502–1503) pointed out in a classical paper. This, and others like it, is a request for a causal account, but the cause queried can a *proximal* or an *ultimate* one. A proximate cause can refer to an intrinsic physiological cause (possibly having to do with the male's hormonal state etc.) or to an extrinsic physiological cause (such as water temperature or oxygen level in the nest's vicinity etc.). An ultimate question could refer to an ecological cause (whatever is required for sticklebacks to make it in the particular habitats) or a genetic cause: there is a historical account as to why and how sticklebacks have acquired a genetic constitution which causes them to respond in a certain way to environmental stimuli. The way Mayr drew the distinction was in terms of types of question: proximal causes are the business of functional biologists and they are phrased in terms of *how* an organism functions. Ultimate questions belong to the province of evolutionary biologists and they give a historical account as to *why* sticklebacks developed the fanning pattern (as well as why the pattern has survived).

It has been claimed (see Mayr 1975, Sober 1994) that the Darwinian revolution in biology was in the shift of focus on populations instead of individual organisms. Prior to Darwin, evolution was seen as resulting from growth and perfection of individuals towards their ideal types, and of passing these newly acquired features to the offspring. Darwin initiated another Copernican revolution: the changes individual organisms undergo during their lifetime are inessential. The driving force of evolution is heritable variation coupled with blind variation and selective retention rather than individual growth. In fact the theory of evolution through natural selection requires stability.

Foucault and Mayr differ on the details of how biology as a discipline came about, but they agree on the results of changes of episteme or paradigmatic theory: new domains of questions became open to investigation. There was remarkable progress in this sense: equipped with the ideas of common ancestry and natural selection the new generations of naturalists would have an endless array of possible questions to ask, concerning biogeography, paleontology, embryology, anatomy, physiology etc. Mayr's account is, in an interesting sense, continuation of the pluralistic line initiated by Aristotle. According to Julius Moravcik (1974) the popular Aristotelian doctrine of four causes really is "a theory about the structure of explanations." Instead of talking about *aitiai* as causes we should really talk about explanatory factors in a wider sense. (For refinements, see e.g. Mayr 1997.)

In his penetrating outline for a programme for a new historiography Nicholas Jardine (1991) suggests, following Collingwood and elaborating on Foucault (amongs others), that the time is ripe for turning attention from answers to questions. Jardine's example is early German *Naturphilosophie*, and especially Lorentz Oken's puzzling *Lehrbuch*. Oken was not a nobody but a highly respected naturalist and canoniser of natural philosophy who gave an extraordinary detailed classification of the three orders of nature. Yet, writing just some 200 years ago he had, by our lights, bizarre questions to raise and things to say of natural history: "The organic must be a vesicle because it is the image of the planet"; "The animal kingdom is but a dismemberment of the highest animal, man" (quoted from Jardine 1991, 51). According to Jardine these pronouncements are so far removed from our way of seeing the world that Oken's questions are, for us, unreal and not just uninteresting. The interesting question is: how come Oken's books were so widely discussed and taken seriously? Jardine's short answer is that from the perspective of the then prevailing Blumenbach–Kant view of natural history these opinions were well within the mainstream thought – it takes *us* some deconstruction and reconstruction of the past scenes to see this. The lesson to learn is that these questions were locally real – *then*. The Kant–Blumenbach way of tallying empirical laws with the grand teleological requirements of reason and understanding opened up an entire range of new questions (and excluded others as illegitimately metaphysical), and resulted, through a series of transformations, to the scene on which Oken acted. From this perspective there can hardly be a universal measure for the right questions to ask.

To understand how sciences have evolved it is important to focus, not on the doctrines that are answers but on the "the ways in which new questions are brought into being and old ones dissolved" (Jardine 1991, 3). Jardine's is a historically rich account of how questions surface as candidates for serious pursuit and examination within particular scientific communities and specific times. He sees the changing scenes of inquiry as formation, transformation and dissolution of scenes of inquiry: questions which in one scientific and cultural setting are locally real may be incomprehensible in another one. But what is the driving force that occasions changes in scenes of inquiry? Jardine offers a pluralistic account in which cultural contexts, social, institutional and technological factors, grand logical and epistemological principles, appeals to authority and particularist interests all have a say. The crucial explanatory engine behind the visible scene is, however, the constellation of methodological commitments considered appropriate and legitimate within local contexts. They to a large extent determine what questions are real.

4. THE METHOD OF DISCOVERY: FRANCIS BACON'S *VIA ET RATIO*

Bromberger's and Jardine's views try to capture the way questions emerge against the horizon of expectations. Yet this manner of interrogating is, in an important sense, a passive affair. You perceive or infer that something does not fit and ask what and why – but this asking belongs to the province of the cognition rather than conation. There is a sense in which taste for good big questions can be honed, viz., by focusing on the cognitively central, and by exploring the consequences of this core. There is also a sense in which Nature can feed questions to the inquiring mind, and in which tradition is a subject of inquiry as Hans-Georg Gadamer's makes clear in his *Truth and Method*.[4] There is this much truth in the saying that innovative ideas frequent the prepared mind, and these chances can be improved by using various routines and heuristics.

Both Bacon's and Kant's sided with the activist epistemological camp, as against seeing the mind as a spectator. For them interrogation as method in inquiry was more akin to seeking and searching which culminates, through deliberation, in rational acceptance. Consider again Bacon's *venatio*. Bacon was a man of action and both his criticism of Aristotelianism and his own positive proposal advocated utility and intervention with the ordinary course of events. Bacon himself presented his *Novum Organum* as an improvement or, rather, a replacement for Aristotle's *Organon* which he thought was inadequate. In the words of the Lord Chancellor (*Novum Organum*, Book I, Aphorism 12), "current logic is good for establishing and fixing errors (which are themselves based on common notions) rather than for inquiring into truth":

Bacon's theory of scientific method, *via et ratio*, was part of a larger project, *The Great Instauration*, whose purpose was to collect and order all empirical knowledge by the new inductive and experimental method. These methodological ambitions were, in their turn, part of a more encompassing legal and political agenda. Bacon was above all else a high-ranking politician and lawyer. As Julian Martin (1993, 75) has shown Bacon's 'philosophic method' aimed at harnessing philosophers to the Crown's purposes, not (or not just) at showing them the way out from the "darkness of antiquity." Nor was Bacon's grand plan for the advancement of knowledge exactly a constitution for a society of disinterested truth-seekers. True, Solomon's House was based on collaboration within a clear-cut division of labour, but more than anything else it was an institutionalised and hierarchical solution for collecting and processing useful facts. All participants had to take an oath of secrecy, and everything was directed towards maintaining

---

[4] Hans-Georg Gadamer's views of the logic of questions go all the way to Socratic questioning, via the German logic of questions and especially Edmund Husserl's *Logical Investigations*, to the ontological turn Heidegger. Husserl (1973) was concerned with the pure logic of science as well as with the phenomenology of experiencing. Gadamer's claim is that questioning indeed has ontological bearing for the *Geisteswissenschften*: *all* (human) experience shares this question-answer structure. Gadamer (1989, ibid., 299) continues the line of thought that the driving force in questioning is the opening up of possibilities, but emphasizes that all questioning and understanding begins when "something addresses us": "We now know what this requires, namely that the fundamental suspension of our own prejudices. But all suspension of judgment and hence, a fortiori, of prejudices, has the logical structure of a question." However, space does not allow a more thorough treatment of Gadamer's insightful account of the properly *philosophical* method.

the sovereign's (James I's) authority as well as political stability and public order.

But what does the idea that one should approach nature directly, in a methodical fashion, amount to? For Bacon (and, later, Kant) this amounted to the view that Nature was to be forced to reveal her secrets. As Julian Martin demonstrates, not only did Bacon's philosophical ideas reflect 17th Century social and political upheavals. Bacon was a lawyer and his proposal for method in natural philosophy was modelled on the legal practices of his day, especially on the emerging science of common law. A court (such as the Court of Chancery) was usually called on to deal with an "issue of fact" (who had done what, etc.), and the most important part of this was to collect evidence. This was done along formally set "schedules of interrogatories", i.e., questions put to the witnesses. These questions and the answers to them were made available to the barristers on both sides. In exceptional and important cases of possible treason the accused could be subjected to torture – and possibly to a refined schedule of interrogatories if the answers of the accused were found to be contradictory.

But who can be called in as witness? Bacon's very terminology and the proposal for the reformation of natural philosophy was based on a parallel between interpretation of law and interpretation of nature. This was not implausible at the time. The idea of putting questions to Nature was coupled with the notion that natural philosophers were in the business of reading the great book of Nature. These two books did not have exactly the same status in Bacon's thought, for Bacon wished to distance himself from the emblematic tradition as well as from the allegoric readings of the Bible (Rossi 1996, 32). Natural philosophy was in the business of inspecting the works of God, and it was left to theologians to examine what God's will was. But it did follow, of course, that word and world could not possibly be in conflict. For similar reasons it was no wonder that the law which guided civil government was at bottom just one side of the grand design established by the great Author.

As to the interrogation of witnesses, in this case natural bodies, Bacon was not a shallow empiricist who would take the deliverances of naked observation at face value. Nature is not keen on giving up Her secrets and indeed is not likely to succumb to the interpreter's wishes without effort. Rather, Nature must be forced to reveal Her secrets in a process analogous with the schedules of interrogatories in courts of law. The way to do this is through "vexing questions" – indeed torture, that is, intervention and contrived experiments. When properly conducted, and with ironing out of incoherences and inconsistencies, an experienced interrogator could make reluctant natural bodies talk.

Interrogating Nature was, for Bacon, just the first step in the interpretative process. Again, the emerging legal science of common law gives the clue. As Martin (ibid., 80–81) points out, not just "facts" but also "issues of law" could be raised in courts. The latter concerned what exactly the highly complex and hidden but in principle complete legal system was. As sources in the search for so far undiscovered and unexpressed "maxims" or "rules" or "principles" the practitioners of the science of common law, authorities on legal dogmatics, had not just the statutes and the earlier decisions but also "law reports" and "Year Books" based on lawyers' and judges' notes. Once these rules and maxims were appended with an account of the reasoning that had led into making particular judgments, *rationes decidendi*, more general principles underlying the judges' reasoning could be formulated. To the extent the legal order was complete to start with, new principles thus obtained were genuine discoveries.

On this view of legal decision making judgments were not based on *brute* facts, to use John Searle's useful coinage, but rather on *reasoned* facts. The same was true, and this is more obvious, of "issues of law". Both were, as Martin puts it, artefacts of the legal process, and needed a professional hand to turn them into entities which had the right ontological and epistemological shape. What the witnesses reported could be contradictory and incomplete, so that they could not be taken at face value. And how legal issues were resolved by help of higher maxims of law was up to the digestive labour of the lawyers.[5]

Legal dogmatics starts by collecting cases and by registering them in reports of law. In the same fashion, true interpretation in natural philosophy begins when man puts Nature to question, and when Her answers, in the form of observations of the deeds of natural bodies and especially experiments put to Nature, are recorded in natural histories. And just as legal decision making is not directly based on brute facts, available to the untutored mind, brute facts collected by fact hunters do not provide a sufficiently firm foundation for natural history and natural philosophy. Bacon was a realist or a moderate constructivist at bottom. True causes might be beyond actual reach but they nevertheless existed. However, Nature's answers, even though confined to particular "natures", could not be trusted. Or rather, since interrogating Nature is, at bottom, just a metaphor (see the next section), observations can give rise to errors. This is all the more so because man in general is prone to see in Nature more law and order than there actually is, and in particular because he is under the spell of the variety of Idols – of superstition in particular. This is an ailment for which method, not of direct interrogation of Nature but of induction, is the best and only workable antidote.

As regards being of service to the enterprise of knowledge, Bacon rated his contemporary Empiricists lower than the sophistic Schoolmen. The Empiricists of course did make experiments. But, using the catchy image later resorted to by Kant, these haphazard experiments were blind and stupid (see Rossi 1996, 28–

---

[5] Needless to say, top legal interpreters were invested with great power – so much so that Bacon feared this constituted a threat to the authority of the King. To prevent excessive legal power-wielding Bacon suggested that Year Books and reports be reduced and digested in to officially sanctioned law reports, and eventually, turned into an expanding body of law, *De regulae juris*. Such an officially sanctioned sources would include high order maxims and rationalise decisions. The practical benefits of so using *regulae juris* would include decrease in idiosyncracies, possibilities of settling indeterminacies and hence of deciding issues of laws (indeed, filling in gaps!), as well as increase in coherence and predictability. See Martin 1993.

29). The Empiricists, whom Bacon likened (somewhat unjustly) to industrious but unimaginative ants, would advocate aimless interrogation. Presuming that science is a single-shot affair, they would labour on the assumption that there are no depths beyond the answers so obtained. The Reasoners in turn have ample time but they spend it neither on reading nor on first-hand fact hunting. They commit the error opposite to that of the Empiricists, of locking themselves up into splendid isolation, and of not consulting Nature at all. Bacon made it plain that both views would be one-sided: "the true business of philosophy", he wrote, is between that of the ant and the spider, viz. of the bee: "for it neither relies solely or chiefly on the powers of mind, nor does it take the matter which it gathers from natural history and mechanical experiments and lay it up in the memory whole, as it finds it, but lays it up in the understanding altered and digested" (Bacon 1878, Book One, Aphorism XCV). And only someone equipped with knowledge of the deeper principles could discover the secrets of Nature. As in politics and law, he who knew these principles would have an extremely powerful tool in his hands. This is why knowledge for Bacon was power.

Bacon's counsel for the advancement of knowledge was indeed much the same as Kant's, that of combining the strengths of the Empiricists and the Reasoners, (with the notable exceptions that it was expressly social at bottom, and that Bacon acknowledged the virtues of dialectics and rhetorics as well; see Vickers 1996). Although not a shallow empiricist his *via et ratio* advocated a view of inquiry as a process which started with particular facts. He contrasted this view with the Aristotelian syllogism which had a crucial shortcoming. Syllogisms with the major and the minor premises are no good as tools for acquiring new knowledge since reaching the conclusion presupposes that one knows that the major premise is true. And this can only be known through knowledge of the type laid down in the conclusion. Bacon's point – and here he echoes the criticisms advanced by others before – was that the proper direction of movement is from knowledge of particulars to knowledge of generalizations. This is what induction was for Bacon. He was keen to point out that responsible inquiry is not anticipation but interpretation of Nature. Anticipation amounts to rushing into generalization in the direction the mind finds agreeable, without due respect to empirical checks, whereas interpretation consists of ascending, little by little and with caution, to increasingly encompassing generalizations.

5. Putting Questions to Nature: A Troubled Metaphor

Although direct interrogation of Nature was, for Bacon, subordinate to the hermeneutic pattern of interpretation within the community of lawyers or philosophers, he got one aspect of inquiry essentially right. If questions to fellow inquirers, within a community, were sufficient, inquiry would be too easy. There had to be a way an inquirer come to terms with Nature, by putting questions to Her.

However, precisely because direct interrogation of Nature has this limited role it is a troubled metaphor – and potentially a misleading one. I submit that Bacon and Kant who adopted the metaphor, clearly saw why. Bacon advocated observation and experiment as the only true means for the interpretation of nature, and indeed these can be construed as situations or set-ups in which the inquirer attempts to force Nature to say either "Yes!" or "No!" to his queries.

But of course putting questions to Nature, direct interrogation of natural bodies, is a metaphor, because Nature does not have beliefs, wants or intentions. Answers, literally construed, are linguistic expressions intended to effect the interlocutor in a certain way, and it is illegitimate animism to think that She says (or tells) anything, or intends by Her utterings to get us to know (understand) true answers to our questions. Nature does respond to vexation in experimental and observational contexts, but such commerce can only be described in causal and not communicative terms.

The metaphor of putting questions to Nature started to break down already in the hands of Bacon (and Kant). Consider the objective of forcing Nature to give unambiguous answers to our questions. Bacon was already familiar with the difficulty, and envisioned the possibility of "Instances of the Fingerpost", crucial experiments, only in cases "which exhibit the nature in question naked and standing by itself". But since the seminal work of Pierre Duhem it has been clear that natures are never exhibited naked and standing by themselves. And as Willard Van Orman Quine, the companion to the often misunderstood Duhem–Quine thesis (is taken to have) said, hypotheses face the tribunal of experience in corporate bodies. This means, in interrogative terms, that hypotheses exhibit natures in rather promissory terms. Nature's answers to such questions, in observational and experimental contexts, always are amenable to conflicting interpretations. There are no crucial experiments here and, if we still insist on playing along with the metaphor, we must learn to live with Nature's tendency to answer "Yes *and* no!"

But there is serious further fault in the metaphor which gives rise to a related worry. If Nature is an authoritative source and a full-blown partner in communication there should be no reason not to try and solicit from Her answers to explanation-seeking questions. But this would be to misplace the onus of inquiry, as Kant already made clear. Consider his transcendental method and what he referred to as the Copernican Revolution. The Revolution consisted in the acknowledgement of the active contribution of the mind, when approaching Nature. How does and should Reason approach Nature? Kant's ingenious answer was to follow in Bacon's footsteps. For him interrogation was the very same thing as experimentation, that is, causal interaction with Nature's ordinary course of events. For one, the legal nomenclature carries the day also for Kant. And secondly, there is also textual evidence for the identity of interrogation and experimentation, in the very *Preface* itself Kant alludes to such founders of modern natural science as Galileo, Stahl and Torricelli. These were the scientists, he wrote, who made it plain "that reason has insight only into that which it produces after a plan of its own." But when he elaborates on this idea it becomes obvious that the mind not just anticipates but also commands Nature. The Copernican quotation continues, namely, as follows: Reason "must not allow itself to be kept, as it were, in nature's leading-strings". Rather, when it approaches Nature it must do so, not "in the character of a pupil who listens to everything that the teacher chooses to say, but of an appointed judge who compels the witnesses to answer questions which he has himself formulated." (B xiii–xiv).[6]

But there are still unaddressed problems with the questions-to-Nature metaphor. We saw that theoretical yes-no questions are beyond Her reach but the situation is worse than this. The real challenge is that the metaphor, even when stripped from animism and anthropomorphism, is helpless when we come to some of the most interesting questions in inquiry, i.e., explanation-seeking questions. These questions often have the form of a why-question (or a how-question), and they take as answers hypotheses which go beyond descriptive accounts to explanatory factors. Such questions do not offer Nature a ready-made list of alternatives to choose from. There is no way we can put explanation-seeking questions to Her. If we still choose to play along with the catchy, we must conclude that Nature simply does not understand why-questions.

This conclusion has a consequence for the task of explicating the aims of inquiry, viz., that a crucial part of what it is to give an adequate explanation seems to fall outside the purview of logic. And this shortcoming in the logic of questions in turn gives us one clue as to what the turn towards the modern was. This is the notion that Nature can only witness to something She has seen herself. But what is it that Nature can be called on to witness? The answer, canonised by David Hume, was that Nature's answers only reach so far as particular facts, or particular bodies and their properties, while generalizations are beyond her reach. The turn toward's Nature's answers also highlights the difference in the aims of knowledge. Whereas the Aristotelians knowing was tuned to giving explanations based on the first principles of any particular science, the problem for Bacon and the moderns was how to find and justify these principles in the first place (Dear 2001). The syllogism, useful for the former task, was singularly helpless in the latter. In interrogative terms the dilemma is pressing and highly consequential. Resorting to current opinion, however probable, was out of question. The problem, though, was that they could not be derived from Nature's answers either. Putting to Nature a grand theoretical question literally was an illegitimate move As Hintikka (1999) has argued, begging the question, for Aristotle and the later tradition, amounted to putting to the oracle the big initial question.

---

[6] It must be added, though, that there was an interesting difference in the legal procedures of Elizabeth's and James I's England on one hand and Kant's Prussia on the other. In the latter, the appointed judge did not have the inquisitory role judges had in the former. But Kant's philosophical point of emphasizing the ineliminable role of the inquirer in the interpretation of nature remains.

6. Darwin's Interrogative *Venatio*

There has been an ongoing debate about the nature and even existence of any particuclar method Darwin used when discovering or justifying his theories in the *Origin of Species* and elsewhere. The proposals have ranged from the hypothetico-deductive method to Baconian inductivism and the inference-to-best explanation view (Sintonen 1989). The difficulty in the first proposal is that so much of the detail was missing at Darwin's time (and still is, some would say) that the deductive theory notion or hypothetico-deductive notion of theory support simply does not apply. The standard defence is that deductive closure is an ideal, and that actual theories are mundane and imperfect approximations of this ideal. However, naturalists do not even seem to display an interest in the construction of deductive theories, nor does theory-testing seem to fit the view.

As to the inductivist view, the time when the *Origin* was published coincided, roughly, with the peak of Baconian methodology, or what was taken to be Baconian methodology. Darwin had to take it seriously, and indeed claimed in his autobiography (Darwin 1903) that he proceeded in the true Baconian spirit: "I worked on true Baconian principles, and without any theory collected facts on a wholesale scale..." He was also critisized for not living up to this, then exacting standard. William Whewell, who had helped the young but already recognized naturalist to get the necessary funds to publish the results of the *Beagle* voyage, was among those who complained that Darwin's theory of descent through natural selection could not be established by true Baconian principles.

Both Darwin's method and his own view of his method are gratifying objects of study, for rival reconstructions can be substantiated by reference to his publications and notes. Darwin kept extensive record of the emergence of his ideas in his Journal, Notebooks, memoranda, and loose pieces of paper. Whether or not Darwin was a Baconian very much depends on what Baconianism is. Indeed, I shall suggest that although Darwin did not amass facts in a mindless way he came closer to the original intent of Bacon's inductive-interrogationist method than just about anyone else in science. Darwin was an interrogationist *par excellence*, in just about all senses of the term. He organized his work along hierarchically nested series of questions; his early entry into the world of science proceeded along the interrogative lines, he was constantly addressing questions to members of the scientific community; and although he was an explorer more than exposer of knowledge, he frequently phrased his arguments in traditional question-answer terms.

Where did Darwin get the notion that inquiries could be set out in question-answer terms? Without giving too much weight to Darwin's early exposures to science, it is noteworthy that he expressly mentioned, in his Autobiography, one of the most influential science education publications around the turn of the 18th Century, viz. was Samuel Parkes's *Chemical Catechism* (1818). As the title suggests, the book, along with many others serving the same or similar purpose, is fleshed in terms of questions and answers. In Chapter VII, "Of Acids", Parkes writes:

What is an acid?

Most of the acids are substances which produce that sensation on the tongue which we call sour; but some substances are classed with the acids which have not this characteristic–though they possess some of the other properties of acids

What are the properties of acids?

Acids change the blue, green, and purple juices of vegetables to red; and combine with alkalies, earths, or metallic oxides, so as to form those compounds called salts.

What is the origin of acids? How is it known that oxygen imparts acidity?[7]

Parkes also praises the pedagogical virtues of the interrogative method of exposition and instruction, writing that it "has been found to possess at least all the advantages that any other mode of instructing youth in chemistry can claim". He also makes his allegiance to Bacon plain: if knowledge is power (and doubting this was not an option), then it is of utmost importance that a love of knowledge and a taste for accurate investigation are given the chance to flourish. Parkes's example of good experimental science was chemistry, for focusing on it "gives the habit of *investigation*, and lays the foundation of an ardent and inquiring mind".

Darwin thought this was better than the school had to offer, and engaged in experimentation with zeal that earned him the nickname "Gas". He wrote, in his Autobiography:

Towards the close of my school life, my brother worked hard at chemistry, and made a fair laboratory with proper apparatus in the tool-house in the garden, and I was allowed to aid him as a servant in most of his experiments. He made all the gases and many compounds, and I read with great care several books on chemistry, such as Henry and Parkes' 'Chemical Catechism.' The subject interested me greatly, and we often used to go on working till rather late at night. This was the best part of my education at school, for it showed me practically the meaning of experimental science.

If the interrogative mode was Darwin's pattern of learning, the way he worked was organized along several big questions. Just before he was about set

---

[7] Parkes (1818, 15–16) In the introduction Parkes writes about the benefits of thus organizing inquiry: It may also be remarked, that the catechetical form, which was first chosen for this work, has been found to possess at least all the advantages that any other mode of instructing youth in chemistry can claim, the work having already been introduced with benefit into several of the most eminent seminaries in the kingdom; and, that, if the author's original intention be followed, the progressive improvement of the student will be pleasant, rapid, and correct. He also praises the advantages of studying chemistry: If "knowledge is power", surely the *love* of knowledge, and a taste for accurate investigation, are the most likely means of conducting him into that path which leads to opulence, respectability, and rational enjoyment...Moreover, it is the necessary consequence of an attention to this science, that it gives the habit of *investigation*, and lays the foundation of an ardent and inquiring mind. If a youth has been taught to receive nothing as true, but what is the result of *experiment*, he will be in little danger of ever being led away by the insidious arts of sophistry, or of having his mind bewildered by fanaticism or superstition. The knowledge of *facts* is what he has been taught to esteem; and no reasoning, however specious, will ever induce him to receive as true what appears incongruous, or cannot be recommended by demonstration or analogy."

out to sea on the *Beagle*, Darwin entered the following note in his Diary (p. 14): "I am afraid I shall be quite overwhelmed with the number of subjects which I ought to take into hand..." The context indicates that Darwin thought he needed knowledge from Meteorology to Latin and Greek. He proved right; his first papers were on Geology, and these papers already showed the question-answer model in work. He and his son Francis have both described his procedure in regard to his working papers. Initially and at least until 1839, Darwin jotted his notes and thoughts on his readings in small bound notebooks. In his Autobiography, Darwin explained: 'I keep from thirty to forty large portfolios, in cabinets with labelled shelves, into which I can at once put a detached reference or memorandum' (p. 137). Thus for example his assembled notes and correspondence containing useful facts on the struggle for existence are still together in volume 46(i) of the Darwin Papers at Cambridge. Notes for other chapters of his evolution book are similarly grouped together. Finally he resolved even to select, separate, and sort out the many pages of his early evolution notebooks which had material he might use in planned species book.

The most important one of Darwin's interrogative agenda was the "mystery of mysteries" presented by John Herschel in his letter in 1836 to the geologist Charles Lyell. Darwin refers to Big Question in his notes (Darwin 1986, Notebook E, 59) and in the opening passage of the *Origin* (Darwin 1859/1964):

WHEN on Board H.M.S. 'Beagle,' as naturalist, I was much struck with certain facts in the distribution of the organic beings inhabiting South America, and in the geological relations of the present to the past inhabitants of that continent. These facts, as will be seen in the latter chapters of this volume, seemed to throw some light on the origin of species – that mystery of mysteries, as it has been called by one of our greatest philosophers. On my return home, it occurred to me, in 1837, that something might perhaps be made out on this question by patiently accumulating and reflecting on all sorts of facts which could possibly have any bearing on it.

These big questions were developed into more manageable subquestions and subsubquestions. In this masterplan the mystery of mysteries, "How is that extinct species have been replaced by others?" is approached via subquestions concerning the nature and extent of variation, generation and inheritance, and along the subsubquestions of variation, generation and heredity on domestic and wild animals, and ditto for flora. Howard Gruber (1980) has described the execution of this masterplan as goal-directed activity in which the agenda consists of three subsystems, of organization of knowledge, of purpose, and of affect. Scientific thinking is a series of structural transformations, at all stages of inquiry. Not just the facts but also Darwin´s theoretical agenda expanded as a result of such transformations. Starting with the initial notions of natural theology and catastrophism, but facing the facts, he ended up embracing the uniformitarian view that nature is subject to gradual transformations. In Gruber's account questions arise from such transformations as well as from perceived similarities and analogies. The new theoretical horizon, together with the flow of facts, answered some questions but created new ones: "If organisms are perfectly adapted to the milieu for which they were created, what becomes of this adaptation when the milieu changes?" Such questions create disturbances and disturbances create new questions.

However, Baconian (and Whewellian) scruples prevented him from rushing to the conclusion without adequate empirical backing. So, before making the sweeping selectionist claim public he needed information about the extent of variation, and about the possibilities of selection in domestic and natural populations. The uncertainty was not so much about the existence of variation and selective forces, but about their strength and manner of operation. The way Darwin set out to hunt for facts was through strategically organized series of questions. His notes and manuscripts are littered with questions from issues of metaphysics (for Darwin this was philosophy of mind rather than metaphysics in our sense) to nitty-gritty details concerning, say, pollination by species of insects, or the habits of varieties of bees. Sometimes, when reviewing his notes, Darwin highlighted an important point in pencil with a capital encircled Q.

And it is a remarkable that Darwin explicitly equated questions with experiments: in his unpublished notes there is a set of questions with the title "Questions" crossed over, and the word "Experiments" written in its place. Once he had become convinced *that* transmutation and hence common descent was possible and a likely explanation of the many classes of facts from systematics to paleontology, he was ready to tackle the how and why, that is, the search for an explanatory theory of transmutation. As he says above artificial and later natural, selection emerged as candidates for this role, sometime in 1936–37.

7. RHETORICS AND PERSUATION

The way of questions and answers not only manifested in the discovery of the theory, for Darwin also used it in presentation and persuasion. The first chapters of *Origin,* and the famous passage in which its results are summed up, are phrased in question-answer terms. The discussion begins with singular and general questions concerning variation in animal breeding, and then proceeds to establish its analogue in nature. The preliminary fact-exposing arguments then turn to establishing the principles of the struggle for existence and heredity. And Chapter IV opens with the questions "How will the struggle for existence, briefly discussed in the last chapter, act in regard to variation? Can the principle of selection, which we have seen is so potent in the hands of man, apply under nature?" The result, an interrogative account for the principles of Variation, Inheritance, Variation in Fitness and Struggle for Existence, were then pooled into an argument for the Principle of Natural Selection in Chapter IV, represented below as conclusion (20). An edited reading goes like this (for further discussion, see Sintonen (1990):

(1) Is there variation in domestic animal breeds?
(2) Yes there is.

(3)   Are some of these variations inherited?
(4)   Yes they are.
(5)   Are some of these variations useful for the breeders?
(6)   Yes they are.
(7)   Is there competition between variations for food and sexual partners.
(8)   Yes there is.
(9)   Are these variations more likely to survive and leave offspring?
(10) Yes they are.
(11) Is there variation in nature?
(12) Yes there is.
(13) Are some of these variations inherited?
(14) Yes they are.
(15) Are some of these variations useful for the beings?
(16) Yes they are.
(17) Is there competition between natural variations for food and sexual partners?
(18) Yes there is.
(19) Are these variations more likely to survive and leave offspring?
(20) Yes they are.

Darwin also used rhetorical question-answer sequences in his rebuttals of the main rival to common descent, special creation, pointing out that they left important questions unanswered. Chapters VII and VIII of *Origin* deal with the particular problems of instincts and sterility: how is it possible that natural selection has given birth to such amazingly fine structured instincts as those which take care of bee-hives? Why does interbreeding of species result in sterility, while the offspring of variants are usually fertile? The question of the eye bothered Darwin a lot, but in his reply he relies on the credentials of the theory established elsewhere. Reason ought to conquer imagination: once we have been able to explain such a large class of facts, we should feel confident that the transitional forms of the eye, whatever they are, have been of some evolutionary advantage at least. And he couples this with a comparison with the Creationist story on which they eye makes no sense at all. Also, in this chapter Darwin deals with such trifling organisms as giraffe's tails which are inexplicable on the creationist assumption. In answer to the bee-hive issue Darwin again leans on the power of the theory elsewhere, adding that there is a general principle which supports this view, namely, the universal constraint *Natura non facit saltum*. As a response to the question of sterile hybrids, Darwin denies the presupposition: sometimes interbreeding results in fertile offspring, and occasionally varieties are sterile. This answer of course relieves, in part, Darwin of the obligation to give a direct answer to the question (although there is the different question as to what determines sterility in the general). As to the main explanatory principle itself, Darwin sums up the facts by writing (1859, 63–64)

> Can the principle of selection, which we have seen is so potent in the hand of man, apply in nature? I think we shall see that it can act most effectually. Let it be borne in mind in what an endless number of strange peculiarities our domestic productions, and in a lesser degree, those under nature, vary, and how strong the hereditary tendency is. Under domestication, it may be truly said that the whole organisation becomes some degree plastic. Let it be borne in mind how infinitely complex and close-fitting are the mutual relations of all organic beings to each other and to their physical condi-

tions of life. Can it, then, be though improbable, seeing that variations useful to man have undoubtedly occurred, that other variations useful in some way to each being in the great and complex battle of life, should sometimes occur in the course of thousands of generations? If such do occur, can we doubt (remembering that many more individuals are born that can possibly survive) that individuals having any advantage, however slight, over others, would have the best chance of surviving and procreating their kind? On the other hand, we may feel sure that any variation in the least degree injurious would be rigidly destroyed. This preservation of favourable variations and the rejection of injurious variations, I call natural selection

8. Questions To Professionals – And Amateurs

The outcome of all this is pretty much Baconian: the facts to be gathered were *informed* facts, organised along natural histories, and these were then processed into inductive generalizations. Darwin emphasised, again in true Baconian spirit, adequate care when drawing conclusions, lest the outcome be anticipation rather than interpretation. He was a voluminous reader as well as an astute observer and experimenter. Herbert and Kohn (1987, 9) have suggested that Darwin's way or organizing his research along these interrogative lines suggests that he employed a special discourse logic. But as Silvain Schweber notes, there is a simple key to Darwin's success, viz., his "uncanny ability to pose right questions, and of his extraordinary communion with nature".[8] If there ever was a Baconian *venatio*, sparked by persuasive interrogation, Darwin's twenty-odd years from the conception of the idea to its publication in 1859 was one.

Methodwise, there are two remarkable further features of his work worth noting. First, Darwin had no scruples about relying on the testimony of others, *if* the informant was reliable. In the autobiographical note where he claimed to have worked along Baconian principles he said he collected facts "on a wholesale scale ... *by printed enquiries, by conversation with skilful breeders and gardeners*, and by extensive reading" (emphasis added). Where Bacon had dreamed of armies of fact gatherers and interrogators, Darwin made this happen by establishing *ad hoc* workshops at Downe house and by resorting to the world-wide community of amateur and professional naturalists – to provide specimens and scientific information. Again, in the words of Silvain Schweber, this was the pattern for Darwin followed all his life. The key to his success was "not only the skill with which he organized and carried out the in-house anatomical dissections, but also the impressive managerial talents he exhibited in creating the scientific network which made these activities possible." (Schweber 1985, 59.)

---

[8] Herber and Kohn 1986, 9. "Every known biological fact, generalization and law would be confronted and the question posed of how to account for it or how to fit it into an explanatory scheme based on descent and natural selection. Every branch of botany and zoology (anatomy, morphology, embryology, physiology etc.) and of natural history (biogeography, habits and instinct of animals, classification etc....) was combed for this purpose. That the facts considered were always of relevance several enterprises, was the result of Darwin's uncanny ability to pose the right questions, and of his extraordinary communion with nature. The answer or putative answers to questions from one field became transferred to others to raise new questions or as checks for consistency."

But this is not, yet, all there is to the interrogative method. One could object to using the interrogative idea as a methodological pattern by arguing that it is heuristically suggestive but not terribly interesting. Isn't it just the problem solving idea in another guise? I suggest that this is not quite all there is to it, for there are questions and questions. Darwin's correspondence clearly shows that he was aware of what we now know as the logic of questions. Furthermore, this logic is the clue to the epistemological shift of allegiance to the testimony of Nature – and fellow inquirers. In a nutshell, yes-no -questions (and sometimes wh- questions) were put to Nature, in the form of experiments, and to breeders and gardeners. However, the whys and hows he addresses to himself and, occasionally, his trusted fellow naturalists. The reason for this was – trust!

The theory Darwin spelled out in the *Origin*, one long argument for common descent as he put it. During his lifetime Darwin had a number of trusted colleagues who provided needed information, and his correspondence is full of these letters. But the remarkable thing was that he engaged not just his network of fellow naturalists but also animal breeders, missionaries, country doctors, and acquaintances in consulates outside Britain. The very idea of the theory of natural selection builds on the parallel between man's intentional artificial selection and Nature's blind but much more effective natural selection. But who else but those who had been involved in artificial selection would have known the extent and limits of variation? Darwin understood better than anyone else that the communities of poultry and livestock breeders, pigeon and rabbit raisers, practical horticulturalists and gardeners all had practiced artificial selection for ages. To make the most of this insight he joined breeders' clubs, established personal connections with pigeon raisers, and often send requests for varieties he needed for his purposes. (See especially Secord 1985 and 1992.) These men of practice also had a number of advantages over his usual circles of fellow naturalists or academics. As Secord (1985) notes, domesticated animals and cultured plants provided a new realm of facts, facts which would not be available through established channels. And secondly, related to this, these facts were organized differently, with an eye on potential practical utility and economic gain to be obtained from useful varieties. The outcome of all this was that Darwin managed to establish an unprecedented network of informants and collaborators whom he sent personal written questions, or engaged in informal discussions, or published "lists of interrogatories".

There are a number of publications through which Darwin explicitly uses an organized questioning method. He sent queries to professional journals, such as the *Journal of Horticulture*, asking whether there is "any sensible difference between the bees kept in different parts of Great Britain" (see Secord 1985, note 7), or to the *Annual Report of the Board of Regents of the Smithsonian Institution* where he published "Queries about Expression for Anthropological Inquiry", asking 17 detailed questions about the expression of emotions in man. He already had experimented (interrogated) with his own children (sometimes causing them to burst into tears, a practice that was not approved by all members of his family), and he had collected natural histories of facial expressions from his sources. What he wanted to know was whether these observations and experiments on the expression of emotions in his own culture could be survived evidence from other cultures. Before rushing to conclude, say, that astonishment was universally expressed "by the eyes and mouth being opened wide, and by the eyebrows being raised" (Query 1), or if shame excites blush "when the color of the skin allows it to be visible" (Query 2), he wanted to have reliable observations from other cultures. He ended his list of queries by explaining what would be most valuable and interesting to him (Darwin 1977, 136–137):

Observations on natives who have had little communication with Europeans would be, or course, the most valuable, though those made on any natives would be of much interest.

General remarks on expressions are of comparatively little value. A definite description of the countenance under any emotion or frame of mind would possess much more value.

An answer to any single one of the foregoing questions would be gratefully accepted.

Memory is so deceptive on subjects like these that I hope it may not be trusted to.

These instructions are interesting for a number of reasons. The entire project can be seen as Baconian induction with the notable exception that interrogation was directed to the relevant community of anthropologists, through a written appeal. Darwin was aware that European influences might have tainted or coloured native reactions and wanted to make sure that these natural histories reflected untutored reactions. This can be seen as an appeal to the informants' expertise, although such care must have been a professional virtue amongst anthropologists in any case. Finally, the reference to general remarks, and the reminder on deceptive memory, point to the idea that although Darwin here relied on the reports from others, these reports themselves should be based on direct interrogation of nature!

The most impressive notebook in this respect was the notebook marked *Questions & Experiments* (Darwin 1987), commenced in all probability in 1839. It consists of a systematic series of questions to ask and experiments to carry out on plant crossing and animal breeding. As Darwin editors Paul Barrett, Sydney Smith and Sandra Herbert note in their *Introduction*, here "the questions and experiments are grouped together into a programme of research". It is remarkable that almost exactly twenty years before the publication of the Origin Darwin had "a masterplan for his treatment of variation in the Origin, ad later in the massive two volumes on *Variation of Animals and Plants under Domestication* (1968)". The questions were no idle shots but leading questions, designed to solicit as comprehensive as possible answers, to some important subquestions. They are of interest because they indeed develop initially rather big questions into more manageable ones by suggesting more specific questions. I can only take some samples by way of illustration (All italics except on the last line are mine):

1. If the cross offspring of any two races of birds or animals, be interbred, will the progeny keep as constant, as that of any established breed; or will it tend to return in appearance to either parent? *Thus* if a cross from the Chinese and common pig be interbred, will the offspring have a uniform character during successive generations, *that is*, as uniform a character, as the pure-bred English or Chinese ordinarily retains? *Thus, again*, if two mongrels, (*for instance* of shepherd dog and pointer) which are like each other, be crossed, will the progeny, during the succeeding generations retain the same degree of constancy and similarity, which might have been expected from pure-bred animals? Is it known by experience, that when an attempt has been made to improve any breed by a cross with another, that the offspring are apt to be uncertain in character, and that unusual care is required in matching the descendants of the half-bred among themselves in order to keep the character of the first cross? – Always please to give as many examples as possible, to illustrate these *and the following questions*.

5. What would the result be, in the foregoing respects, in crossing a wild animal with a highly domesticated one of another species, supposing the half cross to be fertile? Thus if a fox and hound were crossed with pointer-bitches, what would the effect be both in the first litter and in the successive ones of the half-bred animals? To form a judgment on this latter point, the subsequent crosses in each case should be relatively the same; thus the half-bred fox and half-bred hound should be recrossed with the pointer, or with some other, but the same breed.

16. What are the effects of breeding in-and-in, very closely, on the males of either quadrupeds or birds? Does it weaken their passion, or virility? Does it injure the secondary male characters,– masculine form and defensive weapons in quadrupeds, or the plumage of birds? In the female does it lessen her fertility? does it weaken her passion?...

This questionnaire was not much of a success, although some responses have been documented. To improve on the catch Darwin changed his strategy and returned to customizing his questions, just as he had done before. But perhaps the most interesting aspect of Darwin's strategy in these interrogatories is the nature of the questions submitted to the informants. Not all the questions are leading yes-no -questions. There are wh-questions with the force "What would happen if...?", "What are the effects of ...?" and "Can you give an account or history of ...?" But they are invariably made more specific, thus giving the questioner alternatives at least by way of examples, as well as further instructions as to what would amount to an adequate answer. However, there are no explanation-seeking why-questions or theoretical how-questions. Sometimes Darwin refrained from explaining his informants why he puts the questions that he does. This no doubt is the interrogative equivalent of the cautious methodological stand he shared with Joseph Hooker and practically all British naturalist: explaining why he chose certain questions might have influenced the informants, and therewith the questions might have become theoretically tinted.

Darwin most trusted informant was Hooker the botanist, whom Darwin was able also to enlist as a midwife in soliciting answers from others.[9] He wrote, in a

---

[9] Thus Hooker wrote: "I do not know Owens opinion upon these subjects, nor do I like to ask him, for I never propose such subjects to these master minds without being soon convinced of the feebleness of my own reasoning in such matters: indeed my own opinion is wholly formed upon the arguments of others & I shall be quite content to be a gatherer of facts for you to work with." (Hooker, Letter to Darwin, 23.3. 1845)

letter dated 10.2.1846: "I am very glad to hear that you mean to attack this subject some day: I wonder whether we shall ever be public combatants: anyhow, I congratulate myself in a most unfair advantage of you, viz., in having extracted more facts & views from you than from any one other person." His correspondence with Hooker is remarkable for a number of reasons. That he refers not just to facts but also to views indicates that in Darwin's view Hooker was an increasingly trustworthy botanical oracle and friend. But even more interestingly, when Darwin's inquiries progressed Hooker became a fellow transmutationist. As a result, Darwin no longer feeded Hooker mere yes-no and wh -questions concerning *particulars* but let him read his theories and hypotheses. Hooker is addressed also how and why-questions. This trust is clearly visible in, e.g., Darwin's account of speciation.[10]

---

[10] To indicate the extent of correspondence, and the way e.g. the transmutation question was dealt with, I shall give an extract of a long letter by Hooker to Darwin (23...3. 1845): Hooker first discusses Forbes's glacier theory, and then writes:

"With regard to Morphology (Vegetable) the best work I know is St. Hilaire's "Lecons de Botanique comprenant principalement la Morph. Veg. &c" Paris 2 Parts. – P. J. Loss. 10 Rue Hautefeuille – 1841." The long letter indicates that many of the alternative explanations of the species question are alrady around. Hooker writes: "By the bye, Decaisne of Paris wrote to Lindley asking him about the transmutation of Cerealia, & the latter wrote back word that he did not believe in the change at all.. this rather surprzed me I must confess, for though Lindley has never actually avowed himself a believer, the tenor of his communications apparently shewed him to be one, & this full recantation to a foreigner makes me think him not very candid to us his country men. From all that I heard at Leyden, the Indian Islands seem not only to be peculiarly rich in species, but also to present many curious facts regarding the distribution of the individuals & species in the different localities. I talked much with Schlegel, who appears a very nice fellow, he is strongly in favor of a multiple creation & against migration, & as he drew most of his arguments from Zoological grounds, I could not follow him well, he says he has long studied the subject & has come to that conclusion after a full consideration of the number of cases, in which a species is common to two narrow areas separated by large tracts equally capable to all appearance of supporting the said species: from what I know of the Botany of these regions I incline decidedly to the migration principle, the number of dispersed species being very great & belonging to very transportable orders. Blume told me that the Bos (bubalus?) of Java is decidedly the same as that of India, but that the species is nowhere found (not even fossil) in Sumatra, the high road to Java if it migrated: this is to me startling but Blume may be mistaken, or Bos may have been imported by the Javanese, a very different & more energetic people I suppose than the Sumatrans: I did not think of this latter explanation when with Blume, but Horsfield would doubtless solve the difficulty.

The Holland Botanists are Miquel of Rotterdam, a most agreeable person & accomplished Botanist, Blume of Leyden who has published a most beautiful work & knows the plants of Java well, & de Vriese of Amsterdam, all these, & to first I attach some importance, are strong anti-migrationists. I do not think however that the subject has engrossed much of their attention – I have set Miguel to collect facts for you, which will probably lead to the modification of his opinions as a similar course did of mine.

I add the subject with great trepidation to Brown the other day, & found him a migrationist, he quoted Schouw & shewed the folly of his reasoning by adducing the opposite characters of the vegetation of the temperate regions of the 2 hemispheres, though the momenta cosmica were similar, whilst at the same time there were so many species common to the two as to render it probable that had their appearance been owing to such a cause the whole vegetation naturally have followed the impulse

9. THE MODERN CONDITION: WHOM DO YOU TRUST?

We started with the view that questioning as method of inquiry falls within two traditions, to the dialectic-rhetorical one in which the interlocutors are members of a truth-seeking community, and the tradition in which questions are put to Nature directly. This shift in the metaphor, and the shift in allegiance from received and common notions to direct testimony, took place around the time of the Scientific Revolution, so-called. The timing and even the very existence of an identifiable series of events amounting to the Scientific Revolution has been contested (Shapin 1996). Questioning received wisdom was not alien Renaissance humanists and, rhetorics notwithstanding, much of early 17th Century natural philosophy made use of unmistakable Aristotelian methodological and substantial assumptions. But although the Scientific Revolution cannot have started from a clean table, the early modern natural philosophers' message came out so loud and clear that there must have been *something* to it.

What was this something? We have explored the idea that the news was in the trust on one's own reasons and senses instead of reliance on tradition and authority. From this perspective the key to the Revolution was the epistemological (and social, and religious) individualism, as against the communitarian epistemology of the ancients and the medievals. This, we saw, needed qualification, but yes, it is part of the picture. Another important change concerned the goals of inquiry, with the moderns emphasizing discovery of new facts as against mere systematization and elaboration of already available knowledge. The third feature in the Revolution also relates to the diminished interest in explanation: the moderns were far more interested in producing useful knowledge. Causes remained of interest but not for purely contemplative. Rather, knowledge of causes was worth pursuing to the extent it enable effective intervention and hence enhanced chances of obtaining practical aims. Again Bacon was the most outspoken advocate of this view, insisting that contemplation as an aim in itself was epistemologically inane and morally deplorable.

Supposing that all these features were on the agenda and contributed to the birth of modern science, there is, I suggest, still something to add. There is a deeper connection between the diminishing importance of explanation, the aim of inquiry in the Aristotelian sense, and the interrogative procedure. The connecting link – or difference – is in the way the dialectical-rhetorical and the questions-to-Nature tradition understood experience. As has been claimed, and more or less accepted in standard accounts, up until the 17th Century experience referred to something that was commonly known and accepted. For the moderns experience came to refer to itemized and particular experiences of individuals. This understanding more or less began with Robert Boyle's experimentation with the "spring of air", that is, the air-pump, and was adopted by the Royal Society (Shapin and Schaffer 1985). Natural philosophy was to be advanced by observations and experiments, but these had to be properly recorded and witnessed by the society of fellows, gentlemen with credibility.

Under the standard reading Baconianism was a species of narrow inductivism that advocated a mechanical discovery procedure, a procedure that did not depend, for its success, on individual skill and insight. This, as we saw, is an oversimplification. But there is another and more important misreading of Baconianism and the entire new natural philosophy of the 17th Century. It is the idea that giving up the Aristotelian *endoxa* as an accepted basis of explanation seeking, that is, giving up the socially sanctioned home-base of knowledge, amounted to *direct* interrogation of Nature. In this image the experimental philosopher has no need for, and therefore can not seek comfort from, the company of his peers. No doubt this was the image of Descartes in particular, and the rhetorics of the other moderns carried the same force. Nevertheless, this way of contrasting the two epistemological modes is a non-starter. Both are utterly social from the start, albeit in a very different way, and one reason why Darwin and the Victorian science more generally is a useful example is that both Nature and fellow inquirers are in the picture, on equal footing. This is why it is more appropriate to speak of the two aspects of the interrogative method.

To see how the epistemological tenor shifts between the two aspects, consider the novelty in the questions-to-Nature metaphor. Aristotelian science was essentially geared to explanation, since what needed to be known, by way of general explanatory principles at least, was already known. The standard complaint of the new natural philosophy was that this procedure is question begging, since the issue is how it is that we come about these first principles to begin with. Now, by the lights of the moderns, the starting points, given in Nature's pronouncements and endorsed by gentlemen and possible other members of the enquiring community, were particular facts. But this being so there was a dilemma – indeed a dilemma which created a great deal of epistemological havoc for it paved the way down the slippery road to skepticism. One could not rely on what tradition had to say about the first principles. But equally little could one rely on the sayso of others, at least on matters that surpassed the range of reliability of the witnesses. The dilemma was that even if one could rely on witness reports concerning particular things and events, these reports could not serve as a demonstrative foundation for generalizations. Not only does this reverse the order of inquiry. It makes explanation in the Aristotelian sense an impossibility. And as became clear in the Boyle–Hobbes controversy over the credentials of the air-pump as evidence for vacuum (or anything), Hobbes vehemently denied that principles which could not be established with philosophical certainty could play an explanatory role.

REFERENCES

Bacon, F., 1878, *Novum Organum*, Oxford.
Bacon, F., 1996, *A Critical Edition of the Marjor Works*, Oxford, Oxford University Press.
Bromberger, S., 1965, "An Approach to Explanation", in R. J. Butler (ed.), *Analytical Philosophy*, 2nd Series, Oxford, Basil Blackwell.
Bromberger, S., 1966, "Why-Questions", in R. Colodny (ed.), *Mind and Cosmos*, pp. 86–111, Pittsburgh, Pittsburgh University Press.
Bromberger, S., 1971, "Science and the Forms of Ignorance", in Ernest Nagel, Sylvain Bromberger and Adolf Grunbaum (eds.), *Observation and Theory in Science*, pp. 72–103, Baltimore, MD, Johns Hopkins Press, pp. 45–67.
Bromberger, S., 1992, *On What We Know We Don't Know: Explanation, Theory, Linguistics, and How Questions Shape Them*, Chicago, London, Stanford, University of Chicago Press.
Collingwood, R. G., 1939/1967, *An Autobiography*, London, Oxford University Press.
Collingwood, R. G., 1940, *An Essay on Metaphysics*, Oxford, Clarendon Press.
Darwin, C., 1859/1964, *On the Origin of Species*, Cambridge, Massachusetts, Harvard University Press.
Darwin, C., 1987, *Charles Darwin's Notebooks, 1836–1844*. Trascribed and edited by P. H. Barrett, P. J. Gautrey, S. Herbert, D. Kohn and S. Smith, Cambridge, Cambridge University Press.
Darwin, C., 1977. *The Collected Papers of Charles Darwin, Vol. 2*, edited by P. H. Barrett, Chicago and London, The University of Chicago Press.
Dear, P., 2001, *Revolutionizing the Sciences. European Knowledge and its Ambitions, 1500–1700*, Basingstoke, Palgrave, Macmillan.
Foucault, M., 1970, *The Order of Things*, London, Tavistock Publications.
Gadamer, H.-G., 1989, *Truth and Method*, London, Sheed and Ward.
Gruber, H., 1980, "The Evolving Systems Approach to Creative Scientific Work: Charles Darwin's Early Thought", in T. Nickles (ed.), *Scientific Discovery: Case Studies*, pp. 113–130, Dordrecht, D. Reidel.
Gutting, G., 1980, "Science as Discovery", *Revue Internationale de Philosophie* 131 (32), 26–48.
Hacking, I., 1975, *The Emergence of Probability. A philosophical study of early ideas about probability, induction and statistical inference*, London, Cambridge University Press.
Hattiangadi, J. N., 1978, "The Structure of Problems II". *Philosophy of the Social Sciences* 9, 49–71.
Herbert, S. and D. Kohn, 1987, "Introduction" to *Charles Darwin's Notebooks, 1836–1844*, Cambridge, Cambridge University Press
Hintikka, J., 1999, *Inquiry as Inquiry: A Logic of Scientific Discovery*, Selected Papers 5, Kluwer Academic Publishers.
Husserl, E., 1973, *Experience and Judgment*, translated by J. Churchill and K. Ameriks, Evanston, Northwestern University Press.
Jardine, L., 1974, *Francis Bacon: Discovery and the Art Discourse*, Cambridge University Press, New York.
Jardine, N., 1991, *The Scenes of Inquiry. On the Reality of Questions in the Sciences*, Oxford, Clarendon Press.
Kant, I., 1968, *Critique of Pure Reason*, translated by Norman Kemp Smith, New York, St Martin's Press, 1968. (Published in 1787.)
Kleiner, Scott A., 1970, "Erotetic Logic and the Structure of Scientific Revolution", *British Journal for Philosophy of Science* 21, 149–165.
Kleiner, Scott A., 1988a, "The Logic of Discovery and Darwin's Pre-Malthusian Researches", *Biology and Philosophy* 3, 293–315.
Kleiner, Scott A., 1988b, "Erotetic Logic and Scientific Inquiry", *Synthese* 74, 19–46.
Kleiner, Scott A., 1993, *The Logic of Discovery: A Theory of the Rationality of Scientific Research*, Kluwer Adademic Press, Boston, MA.
Kuhn, T., 1970, *The Structure of Scientific Revolutions*, 2nd ed. Chicago, University of Chicago Press
Kuhn, T., 1977, *The Essential Tension*, Chicago, University of Chicago Press.

Kuipers, T. A. F. and A. Wisniewski, 1994, "An Erotetic Approach to Explanation by Specification", *Erkenntnis* 40, 377–402.
Laudan, L., 1977, *Progress and Its Problems. Towards a Theory of Scientific Growth*, London and Henley, Routledge & Kegan Paul.
Leplin, J., 1980, "The Role of Models in Theory Construction", in T. Nickles (ed.) 1980a, pp. 267–284.
Malherbe, Michel, 1996, "Bacon's method of science", in M. Peltonen (ed.), *The Cambridge Companion to Bacon*, pp. 75–98, Cambridge, Cambridge University Press.
Martin, J., 1993, "Francis Bacon, Authority, and the Moderns", in T. Sorell (ed.), *The Rise of Modern Philosophy. The Tension between the New and the Traditional Philosophies from Machiavelli to Leibniz*, Oxford, Oxford University Press.
Mayr, E., 1961, "Cause and Effect in Biology", *Science* 134, 1501–1506.
Mayr, E., 1975, *Evolution and the Diversity of Life*, Cambridge, Mass., Harvard University Press,
Mayr, E. 1997, *This is biology: the science of the living world*, Cambridge, Mass., Belknap Press of Harvard University.
Moravcsik, J. M. E., 1974, "Aristotle on Adequate Explanation", *Synthese* 28, 3–17.
Nickles, T. (ed.), 1980, "Introductory Essay: Scientific Discovery and the Future of Philosophy of Science", in T, Nickles (ed.), *Scientific Discovery, Logic, and Rationality*, Boston Studies in the Philosophy of Science, Vol. 56, D. Dordrecht-Holland/Boston-U.S.A./London-England.
Nickles, T., 1981, "What is a Problem that We May Solve It?", *Synthese* 47, 85–118.
Oersted, C., 1852, *On the Spirit and Study of Universal Natural Philosophy*, London, 1852.
Parkes, S., 1818, *The Chemical Cathecism: with notes, illustrations, and experiments*, London.
Perez-Ramos, A., 1988, *Francis Bacon's Idea of Science and the Maker's Knowledge Tradition*, Oxford, Clarendon Press.
Rossi, Paolo, 1996, "Bacon's idea of science", in M. Peltonen (ed.), *The Cambridge Companion to Bacon*, pp. 25–46, Cambridge, Cambridge University Press.
Secord, J., 1985, "Darwin and the Breeders: A Social History", in D. Kohn (ed.), *The Darwinian Heritage*, pp. 519–542, Princeton, N.J., Princeton University Press.
Schweber, S. 1985, "The Wider British Context in Darwin's Theorizing", in D. Kohn (ed.), *The Darwinian Heritage*, Princeton, N.J., Princeton University Press, pp. 35–69.
Shapin, S., 1996, *The Scientific Revolution*, Chicago, The University of Chicago Press.
Shapin, S., 1994, *A Social History of Truth: Civility and Science in Seventeenth-Century England*, Chicago, The University of Chicago Press
Shapin, S. and S. Schaffer, 1985, *Leviathan and the Air-Pump: Hobbes, Boyle, and the Experimental Life*, Princeton, Princeton University Press.
Sintonen, M., 1989, "Explanation: In Search of the Rationale", in P. Kitcher and W. C. Salmon (eds.), *Scientific Explanation*, Minnesota Studies in the Philosophy of Science, University of Minnesota Press, Minneapolis.
Sintonen, M., 1990, "How to Put Questions to Nature", in Knowles, D. (ed.), *Explanation and Its Limits*, Cambridge, Cambridge University Press, pp. 267–284.
Sintonen, M., 1996, "Structuralism and the Interrogative Model of Inquiry", in W. Balzer and C. Ulises-Moulines (eds.), *Structuralist Theory of Science*, Walter de Gruyter, Berlin, New York, pp. 45–74.
Sober, E., 1994, *From a Biological Point of View: Essays in Evolutionary Philosophy*, Cambridge, Cambridge University Press.
Tinbergen, Niko, 1963, "On aims and methods of ethology", *Zeitschrift für Tierpsychologie* 20, 410–430.
Vickers, B., 1996, "Bacon and rhetoric", in M. Peltonen (ed.), *The Cambridge Companion to Bacon*, pp. 200–231, Cambridge, Cambridge University Press.
Wallace, A. R., 1905, *My Life*, 2 volumes, New York, Dodd, Mead & Co.

LUC BOVENS AND WLODEK RABINOWICZ

DEMOCRATIC ANSWERS TO COMPLEX QUESTIONS – AN EPISTEMIC PERSPECTIVE

1. TWO VOTING PROCEDURES

Suppose a committee has to take a stand on a complex issue, where the decision presupposes answering a number of sub-questions. The committee agrees which sub-questions should be posed. All questions are of the yes-or-no type and the main question is to be given the yes-answer if and only if each sub-question is answered with "yes". After discussion, the committee proceeds to a vote in which the majority rule is being applied. Two different voting procedures can be used. On one procedure, the committee members vote on each sub-question and the voting results then determine the committee's conclusion on the main issue. In other words, the vote is on each premise and the conclusion is accepted if and only if each of the premises is supported by a majority of the members. This premise-based procedure (or pbp, for short) can be contrasted with the conclusion-based procedure (cbp). On that procedure, the members directly vote on the conclusion, with the vote of each member being guided by her views on the relevant sub-questions.

To illustrate, suppose a company is considering purchasing a new item of equipment and the board is willing to approve the purchase if and only if the item meets certain safety standards and the purchase is economically feasible. The board can follow the premise-based procedure: it can separately vote on each factor (safety and feasibility, respectively) and then decide for the purchase if the item has got a majority with respect to each of the factors. On this procedure, the board never gets to vote on the conclusion, but only on the premises. Or the conclusion-based procedure can be followed: Each board member votes for the purchase if and only if she thinks all the requirements are met. The majority in this vote on the conclusion determines whether the purchase will be made. No vote is conducted on the premises.

These procedures are by no means equivalent. Within legal theory, this has been noticed in connection with jury votes (cf. Kornhauser and Sager 1986, 1993, Kornhauser 1992a, 1992b, and Chapman 1998a, 1998b). There may be a majority of voters supporting each premise, but if these majorities do not significantly overlap, there will be a majority against the conclusion.

Pettit (2001) connects the choice between the two procedures with general political theory, in particular, with the discussion of deliberative democracy. (This connection is also made in Brennan 1999. For a general characterization of deliberative democracy, cf. Elster 1998.) Pettit mentions three requirements that are essential for a deliberative democratic regime. (i) All members of the group should vote. (ii) In voting, each person takes a considered stand on what decision is reasonable from the point of view of the goals of the group (rather than from the point of view of her personal goals). (iii) Voting is preceded by a process of deliberation that takes place in an open dialogue between the group members. Furthermore, an important desideratum is that the collective decisions be contestable: It should be possible for the citizens to criticize democratic decisions by questioning their underlying reasons. The premise-based procedure makes such contestability much easier, as Pettit points out, since it gives the premises of an argument a democratic imprimatur and thus places them in a public arena. It thereby allows for the contestation of the conclusion by questioning the premises. The conclusion-based procedure, on the other hand, keeps the premises out of the public arena and hence the democratic regime dodges accountability for the reasons behind its decisions. To this observation of Pettit, one might also add another consideration: Deliberative democracy puts a premium on collective deliberation and reasoning. A group that follows a premise-based procedure may be said to reason as a collective: it takes as a whole a stand on the premises and from there it moves to the conclusion. The conclusion-based procedure also contains or at least allows for some collective elements: it does involve reaching a collective decision and it may be preceded by some collective deliberation. Still, in contrast to the premise-based procedure, it lets the reasoning from the premises to the conclusion proceed on the individual level. Thus, even in this respect, the premise-based procedure more closely approximates the ideal of deliberative democracy.

However, the problem we here want to examine concerns the relative advantages and disadvantages of the two procedures from the *epistemic* point of view. In some cases one can assume that the question before the committee has a right answer, which the committee is trying to reach. Is one of the two procedures better when it comes to tracking the truth? As it turns out, the answer to this query is not univocal. On the basis of Condorcet's jury theorem we shall show that the premise-based procedure is clearly superior if we want to reach truth for the right reasons, i.e. without making any mistakes on the road to the conclusion. However, if the goal instead is to reach truth for whatever reasons, right or wrong, there will be special cases in which using the conclusion-based procedure turns out to be more reliable. But, for the most part, the premise-based procedure will retain its superiority. In this respect, our results disconfirm the tentative conjectures that have been put forward in Pettit and Rabinowicz (2001).

2. The Condorcet Jury Theorem

It need not always be the case that there exists an independent truth, which can be tracked by a democratic voting procedure. In some contexts, the right decision is simply the decision that is reached by a legitimate political procedure. Still, it seems that such a purely "procedural" reading of right and wrong would quite often be inappropriate. For example, in many cases, the voters on the losing side might well consider the majority decision to be wrong, even if they are prepared to abide by it. What they object to is not the legitimacy of the decision-making process but its outcome. And the objections need not be framed in terms of their personal interests; they might well appeal to the goals of the collective. The minority voters might argue that the decision, however legitimate, was an incorrect decision for the collective to take. If such views can be justified, then it is meaningful to evaluate collective decision procedures from the epistemic perspective and compare their capacities as truth-trackers. "Epistemic" democrats take democracy to be especially valuable from such a truth-oriented perspective. (Cf. Estlund 1990, 1993, 1997, 1998, and List & Goodin 2000. The label itself, "an epistemic theory of democracy", comes from Cohen 1986.) Rousseau is often seen as a founding father of this approach to democracy. It is central in Rousseau's theory that voters express their views on the "general will" rather than their individual preferences. (See Rousseau 1762, book 4, ch. 2. In a modified version this idea is retained by the deliberative democrats, who require the voters to express their opinions as to which decision is best from the point of view of the common goals of the collective.) At the same time, another French Enlightenment figure, marquis de Condorcet, is given credit for the theorem that is meant to clarify democracy's epistemic advantage (cf. Condorcet 1785, 279ff; for an English translation of the relevant passages, see McLean and Urken 1995). This Condorcet Jury Theorem (CJT), in one of its versions, can be formulated as follows:

> (CJT) Suppose there are n voters, with n being odd and greater than 1. For some p such that $1 > p > .5$, let each voter have a chance p of correctly assessing whether a proposition is true or false and let this chance be independent of whether the other voters' assessments are correct or not. Then the probability that the majority vote is a correct assessment of whether this proposition is true or false (i) is greater than p and (ii) converges to 1 as the number of voters increases to infinity.

If, on the other hand, each voter's chance p of being correct is lower than .5 (but still higher than 0), then the chance of the majority being correct is lower than p and decreases to 0 as the number of voters increases. If $p = .5$, the chance of the majority being correct will be .5, however much we increase the number of voters. Still, as long as the voters are even slightly reliable, i.e., if their opinions are worth more than a prediction made by a random coin flip, the Condorcet Jury Theorem says that the majority view will be more reliable than the opinion of a single voter.

There are three assumptions in this statement of the theorem that can readily be relaxed. There is (a) a constraint on the number of voters; (b) a symmetry assumption; and (c) an independence assumption.

(a) The number of voters is odd. The consequence (ii) in CJT also holds for even-numbered voters, but not the consequence (i). To see that (i) does not hold for even-numbered voters, set their number at 2. Then, given the other assumptions of the theorem, the chance that the majority of voters, i.e. both voters, are correct is p^2, which is smaller than p for $0 < p < 1$. However, for all even numbers $n > 2$, there exists a number $p(n) \in (.5,1)$ such that (i) holds for any $p \in (p(n), 1)$. Furthermore, $p(n)$ is a decreasing function of the even numbers n and approaches .5 as n approaches infinity. (See appendix 1.)

(b) The voters are equally competent. Each voter has the same chance p, where $.5 < p < 1$, of correctly assessing whether the proposition is true or not. The requirement that this level of competence is the same for all can be relaxed by assigning to each voter i a chance p_i so that their average competence of correctly assessing whether the proposition is true or not is contained in (.5, 1). (Cf. Borland 1983, Grofman, Owen and Feld 1983, Owen, Grofman and Feld 1989.)

(c) The voters are independent as far the correctness of their assessments is concerned. For any voter i, the chance that i's assessment of some proposition is correct is independent of whether any of the other voters' assessments of this proposition are correct or not. Suppose we learn about some subset of the remainder of the voters whether they are or are not correct in their assessments, without learning anything about what votes they have cast. Then this newly acquired information is not supposed to affect the probability of voter i being correct. It is easy to see that the theorem does not hold when the voters are voting en bloc: Suppose that one person casts an autonomous vote and has a chance p of being correct, while all the others simply duplicate his vote. Then the chance that the majority vote is correct is still precisely p. In general, the chance that the majority is correct decreases as the committee members are more influenced by how other members vote. However the Condorcet Jury Theorem still stands as long as the influence of opinion leaders is not too overwhelming (cf. Estlund 1994).

To avoid computational complexity, we will conduct our investigation under the assumptions of an odd number of voters, equal competence and independent voters. Essentially the idea behind the Condorcet Jury Theorem is simple. The theorem is a special case of a more general principle. For any odd number of individuals i, if each i's chance to have a property F is p, where $.5 < p < 1$, and there is no dependence between the individuals as far as that property is concerned, then the chance for the majority of the individuals to have F is higher than p and converges to 1 as the number of individuals increases. In the case of the Condorcet Jury Theorem, the property F is being correct in one's assessment of a given proposition, but in general F may be any property whatsoever.

3. THE BASIC MODEL

To introduce our methodology, let us construct a function that measures the probability of the majority vote providing a correct assessment for different values of $p \in (.5, 1)$ and $n = 3, 11, 101$. We number the voters from 1 to n. The probability that the first k voters are correct for $k = 1, ..., n$ is:

(1) $\quad p^k$

The probability that the first k voters are correct and the remaining $n - k$ voters are incorrect is:

(2) $\quad p^k(1-p)^{n-k}$

There are $\binom{n}{k}$ ways to pick out k individuals out of a group of n voters. Hence, the probability that precisely k out of n voters are correct is:

(3) $\quad \binom{n}{k} p^k (1-p)^{n-k}$

For k voters to be the majority of n voters for odd n, it must be the case that

(4) $\quad k$ is an integer contained in $[\frac{n+1}{2}, n]$.

So, letting M be the statement that a majority among n voters, is correct (for odd n), the probability of M is:

(5) $\quad P(M) = \sum_{k=(n+1)/2}^{n} \binom{n}{k} p^k (1-p)^{n-k}$.

In figure 1 we have plotted this function for p ranging from 0 to 1 and for $n = 3, 11, 101$. Clearly, the greater the number of voters, the more confident we may be that the majority gets it right for any particular value of p in the interval $(.5, 1)$.

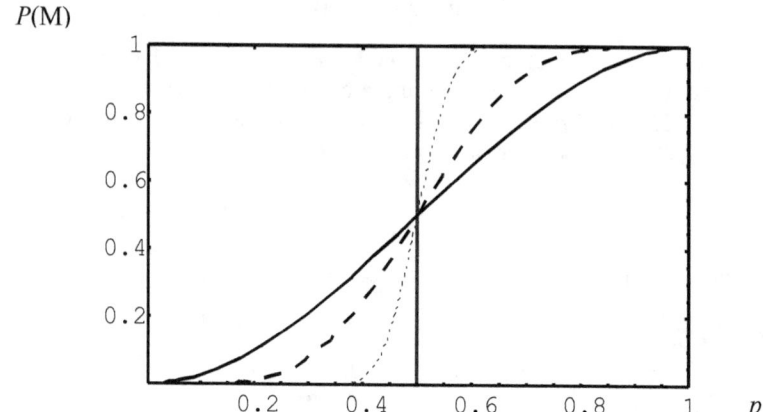

Figure 1: The chance that the majority is correct for different levels p of voter competence and for the number of voters n =3 (full line) , n = 11 (dashed line) and n = 101 (dotted line).

One might be curious to learn how much the chance that the majority vote is correct improves upon the chance that an individual voter is correct. This difference function is defined as follows:

(6) $\quad \Delta = P(M) - p$

and is plotted in figure 2. At first, when p increases above .5, the advantage of relying on the majority vote rather than on a single voter very rapidly increases, and the more so, as the number of voters increases. But then, as p comes close to 1, this advantage decreases for the obvious reason: Since $P(M)$ cannot be higher than 1, the difference between $P(M)$ and p must decrease to 0.

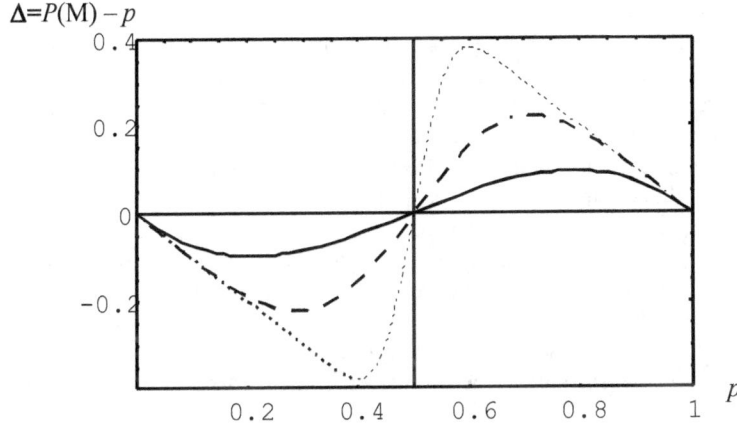

Figure 2: The difference between the chance that the majority is correct and the chance that a single voter is correct for the number of voters n =3 (full line), n = 11 (dashed line) and n = 101 (dotted line).

4. A COMPLEX SOCIAL DECISION

So far, we have just considered voting on a single proposition. Let us now turn to the more complex decision that is involved in the purchase of the item of equipment. Consider the following three propositions:

(S) The item of equipment meets safety standards;
(F) The item of equipment is economically feasible;
(C) The item of equipment should be purchased.

In the circumstances, the proposition C is equivalent to the conjunction S & F: The item should be purchased if and only if it meets the safety standards and is economically feasible. For each voter i in the committee that decides the issue, we assume that (i) i has a definite opinion with respect to each of the propositions S, F, and C – she either accepts it or rejects it; (ii) i's opinions with respect to S, F and C are internally consistent; and (iii) i recognizes that, as things stand, C is equivalent to S&F. By (i), (ii) and (iii), i accepts C if and only if she accepts each of S and F, and she rejects C otherwise.

From the previous section we adopt the assumption (a) concerning the number of voters and we also adopt the symmetry assumption (b) and the independence assumption (c) for each of the propositions S and F. Furthermore, we make two additional symmetry assumptions, (d) and (e), and four additional independence assumptions, (f), (g), (h) and (i):

(d) There is an equal chance that an arbitrary item of equipment meets safety standards and is economically feasible. Consequently, we let $P(S)$ and $P(F)$, the ex ante probabilities of S and F, be equal to q, where $0 < q < 1$. Needless to say, this might not be the case: The chances that an item meets the safety standards and is economically feasible may differ. To avoid computational complexity, we shall ignore this complication. We will distinguish between stringent contexts, in which fewer items of equipments meet the safety standards and are economically feasible (low q), lenient contexts in which more items pass the bar (high q), and intermediate contexts that are in between the stringent and the lenient ones.

(e) There is an equal chance that a voter is correct in her assessment of safety standards as in her assessment of economic feasibility. The parameter $p \in (.5, 1)$ is the common measure of competence of each voter's assessment of S as well as of F.

(f) Safety features and economic feasibility are independent factors. Learning that S does not teach us anything about the chance of F nor vice versa.

(g) Whether a voter is correct in her assessment of safety is the same whether the item of equipment is safe or not (and similarly for economically feasibility)). Each voter has a chance p of correctly saying of what is that it is, and an equal chance p of saying of what is not that it is not: We conceive of the reliability of a voter in the same way as of a medical test that yields the same proportion of false positives and false negatives.

(h) Whether a voter is correct in assessing safety is independent of whether she is correct in assessing economic feasibility, and vice versa. One might make the following objection with regard to this assumption: Learning that a particular voter is correct, say, in assessing economic feasibility may give us reason to think that she is an intelligent committee member, which may in turn increase our confidence in her assessment of safety. This is a reasonable objection, but we will assume a certain modularity of competence here: We conceive of assessing safety and economic feasibility as unrelated areas of expertise; one's competence in one area does not reflect on one's competence in the other.

(i) Whether a voter is correct in assessing safety is independent of others being correct in assessing economic feasibility, and vice versa. Learning about others being correct in assessing one factor does not change the chance that a particular voter is correct in her assessment of other standards.

At certain junctions, our argument will require certain conditional independences that are entailed by our independence assumptions. Using graphical models of conditional independence structures we will show in appendix 2 that these entailments hold.

5. MODELING THE PREMISE-BASED PROCEDURE

The committee members vote on S and on F separately and the item will be purchased if and only if a majority casts a positive vote on S and a majority casts a positive vote on F. We need to distinguish between four different situations that are defined by the truth-values of the propositions S and F:

(C1) S & F
(C2) not-S & F
(C3) S & not-F
(C4) not-S and not-F.

The item ought to be purchased in situation C1, but not in situations C2 through C4. On grounds of assumptions (d) and (f):

(7) $P(C1) = q^2$;
(8) $P(C2) = P(C3) = q(1-q)$;
(9) $P(C4) = (1-q)^2$.

We need to assess the chance that the premise-based procedure will yield a correct assessment in each of these situations, i.e. $P(M^{pbp}|Ci)$ for $i = 1, ..., 4$. Consider C1: the only way that the premise-based procedure will yield a correct assessment is when the majority is correct on S and the majority is correct on F. In appendix 2 (Fact 1) we show that the majority being correct on S is independent of the majority being correct on F given that a particular situation C1, ..., C4 obtains. Hence,

(10) $P(M^{pbp}|C1) = P(M)^2$.

Consider C2. S is false but F is true. There are three mutually exclusive ways in which the committee can reach the correct decision that the item should not be purchased: (i) The majority is right in their assessment of S and is right in their assessment of F; (ii) The majority is right in their assessment of S, but wrong in their assessment of F; (iii) The majority is wrong in their assessment of S and in their assessment of F. Hence,

(11) $P(M^{pbp}|C2) = P(M)^2 + P(M)(1 - P(M)) + (1 - P(M))^2$.

Note that in case (i) the right decision is reached for the right reasons, while in cases (ii) and (iii) the right decision is reached for the wrong reasons. C3 is analogous to C2:

(12) $P(M^{pbp}|C3) = P(M^{pbp}|C2)$.

Consider situation C4. S and F are both false. There are three mutually exclusive ways in which the committee can reach the correct decision that the item should not be purchased: (i) The majority is right in their assessment of S and is right in their assessment of F; (ii) The majority is right in their assessment of S, but wrong in their assessment of F; (iii) The majority is wrong in their assessment of S and is right in their assessment of F. Hence,

(13) $P(M^{pbp}|C4) = P(M)^2 + 2P(M)(1 - P(M))$.

Again, note that in case (i) the right decision is reached for the right reasons, while in cases (ii) and (iii) the right decision is reached for the wrong reasons.

The chance that the premise-based procedure will yield a correct assessment of whether the item ought to be purchased is:

(14) $P(M^{pbp}) = \sum_{i=1}^{4} P(M^{pbp}|Ci)P(Ci)$

This is the chance that the premise-based procedure yields a correct assessment, whether the decision will be reached for the right or for the wrong reasons, i.e. for whatever reasons. But one might want to know what the chance is that this procedure will yield a correct assessment for the right reasons (rr) only. In each of the four situations Ci, this chance is $P(M)^2$, and hence $P(M^{pbp\text{-}rr})$, unlike $P(M^{pbp})$, is independent of the situation:

(15) $P(M^{pbp\text{-}rr}) = P(M)^2$.

6. MODELING THE CONCLUSION-BASED PROCEDURE

We turn to the conclusion-based procedure. Let $P(V)$ be the chance that a particular voter is correct in her vote on whether the item ought to be purchased. To determine $P(V)$, we will need to consider each situation. In situation C1, to cast the correct vote, the voter will need to be correct on both S and F. In appendix 2 (Fact 2) we show that a particular voter being correct on S is independent of her being correct on F, in each of the situations C1, ..., C4. Following the same reasoning as for entries (10), ..., (13),

(16) $P(V|C1) = p^2$.
(17) $P(V|C2) = P(V|C3) = p^2 + p(1-p) + (1-p)^2$.
(18) $P(V|C4) = p^2 + 2p(1-p)$.

We calculate the chance that the majority reaches the right decision on whether the item ought to be purchased for each situation C1, ..., C4. In appendix

2 (Fact 3) we show that a particular voter being correct on whether the item ought to be purchased is independent of other voters being correct on this issue, given that a particular situation C1, ..., C4 obtains. Following the same reasoning as for entries (1), ..., (5):

(19) $\quad P(M^{cbp}|Ci) = \sum_{k=(n+1)/2}^{n} \binom{n}{k} P(V|Ci)^k (1-P(V|Ci))^{n-k}$

Subsequently, we calculate the chance that the majority will reach a correct decision on whether the item ought to be purchased tout court:

(20) $\quad P(M^{cbp}) = \sum_{i=1}^{4} P(M^{cbp}|Ci)P(Ci)$

This is the chance that the conclusion-based procedure leads to a correct assessment for whatever reasons, right or wrong. But once again, one might want to know what the chance is that this procedure will lead to a correct assessment for the right reasons only (rr), i.e. what the chance is that a majority among the voters makes the right assessment of the conclusion for the right reasons. In each of the four situations Ci, the chance that a particular voter casts a correct vote for the right reasons is p^2 and hence, following the same reasoning as for entries (1) to (5):

(21) $\quad P(M^{cbp-rr}) = \sum_{k=(n+1)/2}^{n} \binom{n}{k} (p^2)^k (1-p^2)^{n-k}.$

7. THE TWO PROCEDURES COMPARED WITH THE COMPETENCE OF A SINGLE VOTER

In the last section, we calculated the competence of a single voter to reach the correct complex decision in each situation, i.e. $P(V|Ci)$ for $i = 1,..., 4$. This allows us to calculate the competence of a single voter tout court:

(22) $\quad P(V) = \sum_{i=1}^{4} P(V|Ci)P(Ci).$

In this section we will consider whether the probabilities that the majority is correct in respectively the premise-based and the conclusion-based procedures exceed the probability that a single voter is correct. We let n range over odd numbers from 3 through infinity and p over the open set (.5, 1).

We start with the premise-based procedure. It is not surprising that the probability that the majority is correct on this procedure always exceeds the probability that a single voter is correct. To show this we calculate $P(M^{pbp})$, using entries (7) through (14), and we calculate $P(V)$, using entries (7) through (9) and (16) through (18) and (22). Subsequently we calculate the difference $P(M^{pbp}) - P(V)$. We first consider the special case of $q = .5$: Given assumptions (d) and (f), we are considering a case in which $P(S\&F) = (.5)^2$, i.e. one out of four items is worth purchasing. Some algebraic manipulation yields:

(23) $P(M^{pbp}) - P(V) = 1/2(P(M)^2 + 1) - 1/2(p^2+1) = 1/2(P(M)^2 - p^2)$,

which is larger than 0, since $P(M) > p$ for the relevant values of p and n. In the general case, some algebraic manipulation yields:

(24) $P(M^{pbp}) - P(V) = (P(M) - p)((2 - P(M) - p)(1 - q)^2 + q^2 + (P(M) + p - 1)(1 - (1 - q)^2)$,

which again is larger than 0, since $P(M) > p$ and $0 > q > 1$ for the relevant values of p and n. Hence, we can conclude in general that the premise-based procedure is a better truth-tracker for complex social decisions than a single person in the constituency of voters.

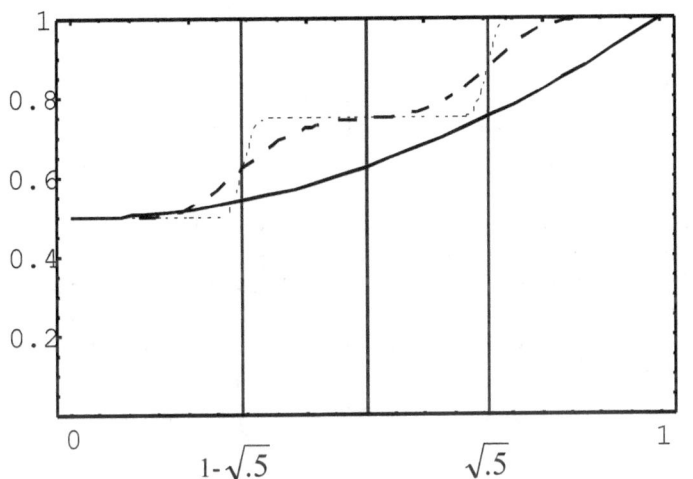

Figure 3: The chance that the majority vote is correct on the conclusion-based procedure for 51 voters (dashed line) and for 501 voters (dotted line), along with the chance that a single voter is correct (full line), for q =.5

We now turn to the conclusion-based procedure. Here the results are more surprising: As we shall see, in lenient contexts (high q), the probability that the majority is correct on this procedure may not exceed the probability that a single voter is correct. But let us consider the intermediary context first. In figure 3, we plot $P(M^{cbp})$ for $n = 51$ and $n = 501$ along with $P(V)$, both times for $q = .5$. As n converges to infinity, the function $P(M^{cbp})$ converges to a step function: In the limit, (i) for all $p \in (0, 1 - \sqrt{.5})$, $P(M^{cbp})$ tends to $2q(1 - q) = .5$, (ii) for all $p \in (1 - \sqrt{.5}, \sqrt{.5})$, $P(Mcbp)$ tends to $2q(1-q)+(1q)^2 = .75$, and (iii) for all $p \in (\sqrt{.5}, 1)$, $P(M^{cbp})$ tends to 1. Let us explain these results for each step:

Step 1: $p \in (0, 1 - \sqrt{.5})$. If we plug in values for p in this range in (16) to (18), then we notice that $P(V|C2)$ and $P(V|C3)$ exceed .5, but $P(V|C1)$ and $P(V|C4)$ fall below .5. Hence, by the Condorcet Jury Theorem, $P(M^{cbp}|C2)$ and $P(M^{cbp}|C3)$ converge to 1, but $P(M^{cbp}|C1)$ and $P(Mcbp|C4)$ converge to 0 as n approaches infinity. By (8) and (20), $P(M^{cbp}) = 1 \times P(C2) + 1 \times P(C3) = 2q(1 - q)$.

Step 2: $p \in (1 - \sqrt{.5}, \sqrt{.5})$. We follow the same reasoning as in step 1. For the values of p in this range, $P(V|C2)$ through $P(V|C4)$ exceed .5, but $P(V|C1)$ falls below .5. Hence, by the Condorcet Jury Theorem, (8), (9) and (20), $P(M^{cbp}) = 1 \times P(C2) + 1 \times P(C3) + 1 \times P(C4) = 2q(1-q) + (1-q)2 = 1 - q^2$.

Step 3: $p \in (\sqrt{.5}, 1)$: Again, we follow the same reasoning as in step 1. For the values of p in this range, $P(V|C1)$ through $P(V|C4)$ exceed .5. Hence, by the Condorcet Jury Theorem and (20), $P(M^{cbp}) = 1$.

For lower values of n, e.g. for $n = 51$, the curve for the $P(M^{cbp})$ is increasing in two waves. As the value of n rises, e.g. for $n = 501$, the curve flattens out into three horizontal plateaus, which continue to broaden, converging to the critical values as n approaches infinity.

How does $P(M^{cbp})$ compare to $P(V)$ for $q = .5$? From (16) through (18) and (22), it follows that $P(V) = 1/2(p^2 + 1) = .75$ for $p = \sqrt{.5}$. But we have just learned that $P(M^{cbp})$ converges to .75 as p approaches from below. Hence, $P(M^{cbp})$ converges to $P(V)$ for $p = \sqrt{.5}$ as n approaches infinity. This is a curious result: As the number of voters approaches infinity, the chance that the majority of the voters is correct tends to the same value as the chance that a single voter is correct, provided that the competence p of each voter is $\sqrt{.5}$.

The results are even more surprising when we relax the assumption that $q = .5$. As n approaches infinity, the central plateau for $P(M^{cbp})$, i.e. the horizontal curve for that function over the p-interval $(1 - \sqrt{.5}, \sqrt{.5})$, has the height $1 - q^2$. $P(V)$ is an increasing function of p which takes on the value of $2q(1-q)$ for $p = 0$, and 1 for $p = 1$. As we increase the value of q to, say, $q = .65$, then the central plateau of $P(M^{cbp})$ moves down and drops below the curve for $P(V)$ for certain values of p (figure 4). That is, there are certain levels of competence p for which the vote of a single voter on a complex decision is more likely to be correct than the majority vote following the conclusion-based procedure. This phenomenon occurs (i) for higher values of q, i.e. for more lenient contexts, (ii) for relatively low $p > .5$, but not necessarily for those values of p that are only slightly over .5, as we can see in the figure 4, and (iii) for higher n, since the central plateau of $P(M^{cbp})$ flattens out and then broadens as the value of n increases.

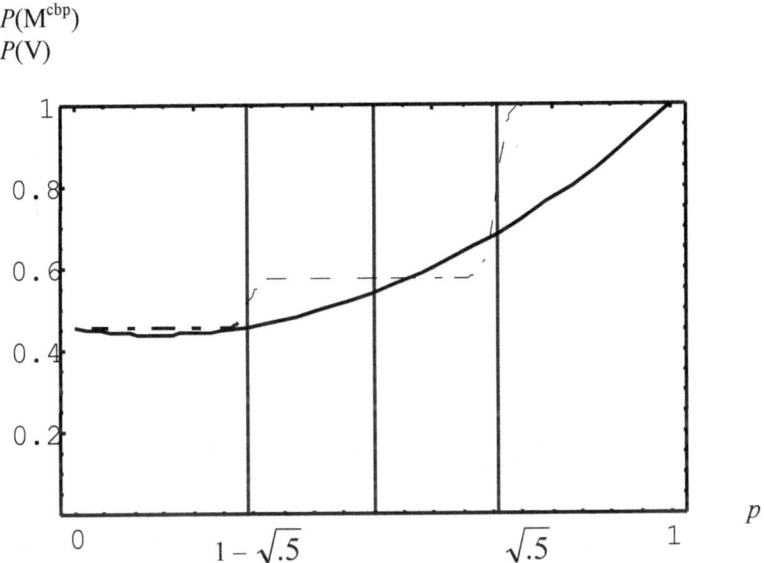

Figure 4: The chance that the majority vote is correct on the conclusion-based procedure for 501 voters (dashed line) and the chance that a single voter is correct on a complex decision (full line), for q =.65,

8. IF OUR OBJECTIVE IS TRUTH FOR WHATEVER REASONS, HOW DO THE TWO PROCEDURES COMPARE TO EACH OTHER?

We already know that the premise-based procedure will perform better for certain values of n, p and q, since $P(M^{pbp}) > P(V)$ for all values of these parameters and $P(V) > P(M^{cbp})$ for some values of these parameters. But are there any values of n, p and q for which $P(M^{cbp}) > P(M^{pbp})$? Let us set q once again at .5. We notice that $P(M^{cbp})$ starts rising for lower values of p than $P(M^{pbp})$, but its slope decreases sooner for $n = 3$ in figure 5 or it reaches a plateau for $n = 101$ in figure 6. Thus, $P(M^{cbp})$ is higher than $P(M^{pbp})$ for lower values of p. Furthermore the range of values of p for which $P(M^{cbp})$ exceeds $P(M^{pbp})$ is broader for a lower value of n in figure 5 than for a higher value of n in figure 6.

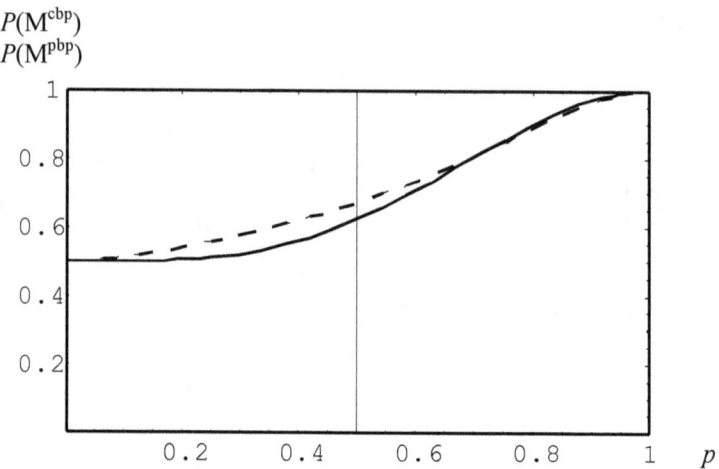

Figure 5: The chance that the majority vote is correct on the conclusion-based procedure (dashed line) and on the premise-based procedure (full line), for 3 voters and $q = .5$

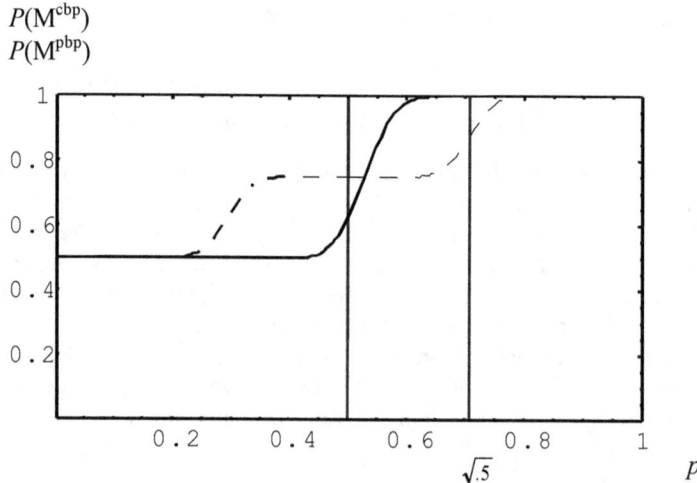

Figure 6: The chance that the majority vote is correct on the conclusion-based procedure (dashed line) and on the premise-based procedure (full line), for 101 voters and $q = .5$.

Finally, we know from the previous section that we can raise the platform of $P(M^{cbp})$ by lowering the value of q: As we pull up the platform, the range of values of p for which $P(M^{cbp})$ exceeds $P(M^{pbp})$ will broaden. In figure 7 we have plotted phase curves that indicate for what values of q and p the conclusion-base procedure does better than the premise-based procedure for $n = 3, 11, 101$.

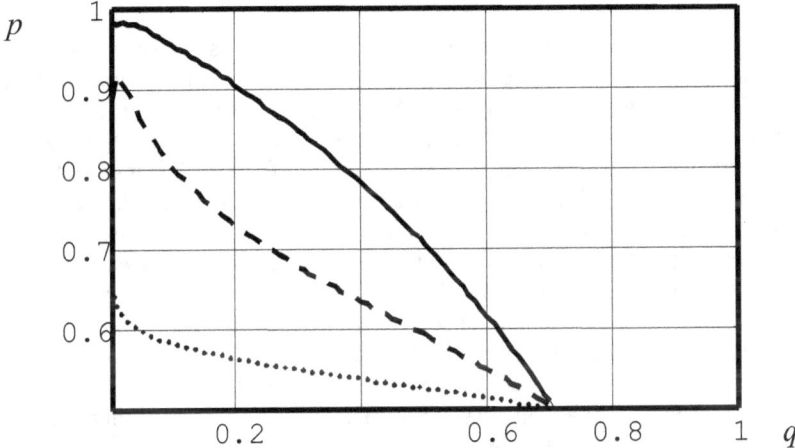

Figure 7: Phase curves for $n = 3$ (full line), 11 (dashed line), 101 (dotted line), for p between .5 and 1, and for q between 0 and 1. Underneath the phase curves, the conclusion-based procedure is a better truth-tracker; above the phase curves, the premise-based procedure is better.

This graph confirms our comparisons of the behavior of the functions $P(M^{cbp})$ and $P(M^{pbp})$ for different values of p, q and n: The conclusion-based procedure tends to do better as we decrease the size of the committee, the competence of the voters and the leniency of the context.

The following reasons account for these facts: (i) Truth about a conjunction can be reached by mistake, i.e. for the wrong reasons, only when the conjunction is false. It is easy to see that, in such cases, the conclusion-based procedure reaches truth about the conjunction (i.e., rejects it) whenever the premise-based procedure manages to do likewise. But the opposite is not the case. Consequently, the conclusion-based procedure does better than the premise-based procedure when it comes to reaching truth by mistake. At the same time, less competent voters are more prone to commit mistakes, and room for truth by mistake is larger in less lenient contexts, in which the probability of the conjunction being false is higher. (ii) As we shall see in the next section, as n increases, with less competent voters the premise-based procedure does increasingly better than the conclusion-based procedure, when it comes to reaching truth for the right reasons. But for small numbers of voters, this advantage of the premise-based procedure is smaller and thus it cannot outweigh its disadvantage as regards reaching truth by mistake.

9. IF OUR OBJECTIVE IS TRUTH FOR THE RIGHT REASONS, HOW DO THE TWO PROCEDURES COMPARE TO EACH OTHER?

Concerning the capacity of the two procedures as regards truth-tracking for the right reasons, it is easy to see that the premise-based procedure is superior in that respect. This procedure yields the correct assessment based on the right reasons whenever (i) there is a majority that correctly assesses one premise and also (ii) a majority that correctly assesses the other premise. The conclusion-based procedure, on the other hand, correctly assesses the conclusion for the right reasons if and only if (iii) there is a majority that correctly assesses both premises. Obviously, (iii) entails (i) and (ii), but not vice versa. Therefore, whenever the conclusion-based procedure makes the right assessment for the right reasons, the premise-based procedure would do so as well. At the same time, there are possible cases in which the premise-based procedure would make a right assessment for the right reasons but the conclusion-based procedure would fail. Such cases (in which (i) and (ii) hold, but (iii) does not) have non-zero probability as long as the voters' competence with respect to one premise is at least partly independent of their competence with respect the other premise. And we have assumed that these competences are fully independent for each other.

Still, it is one thing to know that premise-based procedure is superior as a truth-tracker for the right reasons, but yet another to determine the extent of this superiority. We now proceed to this task. We calculated the $P(M^{pbp\text{-}rr})$ in (15) and $P(M^{cbp\text{-}rr})$ in (21). In figure 8 we plot both $P(M^{pbp\text{-}rr})$ and $P(M^{cbp\text{-}rr})$ and in figure 9 we plot their difference. $P(M^{pbp\text{-}rr})$ always exceeds $P(M^{cbp\text{-}rr})$, but the difference is particularly large for values in the range (.5, $\sqrt{.5}$), and the more so for greater numbers of voters. It is easy to see why this is so. By the Condorcet Jury Theorem, $P(M)$ tends to 0 for $p < .5$ and to 1 for $p > .5$ as the value of n approaches infinity, while $P(M) = .5$ for $p = .5$. Hence, $P(M^{pbp\text{-}rr}) = P(M)^2$ will tend to 0 for $p < .5$ and to 1 for $p > .5$, while it equals .25 for $p = .5$. On the other hand, by the Condorcet Jury Theorem, the expression in (21) will tend to 0 for $p^2 < .5$ and to 1 for $p^2 > .5$ as the value of n approaches infinity, while it will equal .5 for $p^2 = .5$. Hence, $P(M^{cbp\text{-}rr})$ will tend to 0 for $p < \sqrt{.5}$ and to 1 for $p > \sqrt{.5}$ as the value of n approaches infinity, while $P(M^{cbp\text{-}rr}) = .5$ for $p = \sqrt{.5}$. We can conclude that as n approaches infinity, $P(M^{pbp\text{-}rr}) = P(M^{cbp\text{-}rr}) = 0$ for $p < .50$, $P(M^{pbp\text{-}rr}) = 1$ and $P(M^{cbp\text{-}rr}) = 0$ for $p \in (.5, \sqrt{.5}$), and $P(M^{pbp\text{-}rr}) = P(M^{cbp\text{-}rr}) = 1$ for $p > \sqrt{.5}$. For lower values of n, the curves are less steep and, as a consequence, the differences between $P(M^{pbp\text{-}rr})$ and $P(M^{cbp\text{-}rr})$ are smaller for $p \in (.5, \sqrt{.5})$, but there is a broader range of values of p for which $P(M^{pbp\text{-}rr})$ exceeds $P(M^{cbp\text{-}rr})$.

So if what we are after is truth for the right reasons, the truth-tracking potential of the premise-based procedure is never worse than that of the conclusion-based procedure. It tends to be substantially better for voters whose assessments are slightly better than random. For small committees, the difference is small, but the range of competence levels for which the premise-based procedure exceeds the conclusion-based procedure is wide. For larger committees, the difference is larger but the range of competence levels for which the premise-based procedure exceeds the conclusion-based procedures is smaller: It converges to the p-interval $(.5, \sqrt{.5})$.

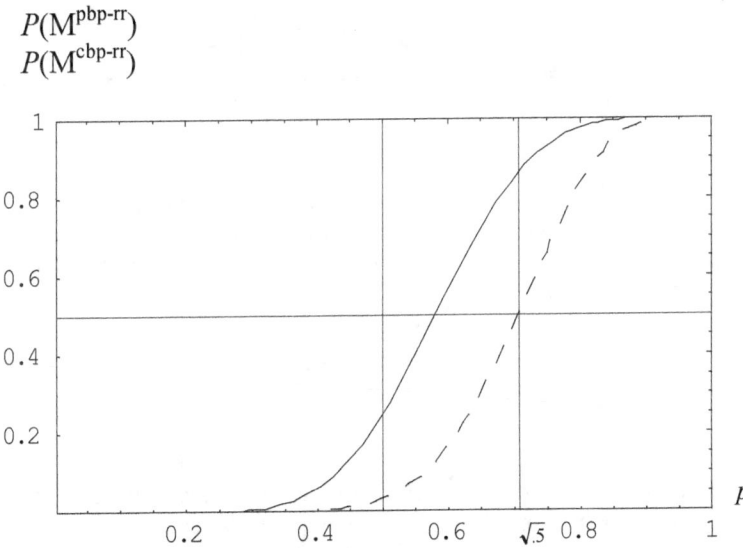

Figure 8: The chance that the majority vote is correct for the right reasons for the premise-based procedure (full line) and for the conclusion-based procedure (dashed line), for 11 voters.

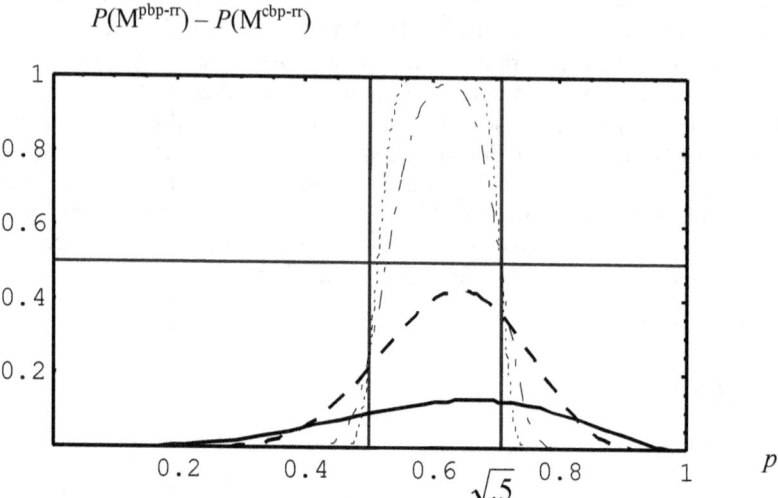

Figure 9: The difference between the chances that the majority vote is correct for the right reasons for the premise-based procedure and for the conclusion-based procedure, for n = 3 (full line), n = 11 (dashed line), n = 101 (dot-dashed line) and n = 501 (dotted line)

10. DISCUSSION

Independence

Our model is constructed under a series of idealizations of independence. These idealizations may be more or less realistic in particular empirical situations. It is an open question how robust our results are if we relax various combinations of idealizations, by substituting positive or negative relevance for independence, as the case may be. This exercise needs to be undertaken relative to a particular empirical situation.

An interesting application of our model is the tenure vote in north-American institutions of higher learning. In many institutions, both the teaching and research skills of the candidates are deemed to be relevant to the decision and the candidates are required to meet certain standards on both skills. The dean's decision is informed by a faculty vote in the home department of the candidate. Either the dean might ask each faculty member to assess the candidate on teaching and research and cast a yes vote for tenure if and only if she deems the candidate to be worthy on both teaching and research. Tenure will be granted just in case there is majority support for the candidate. Or the dean might ask each faculty member to cast a vote on whether the candidate is worthy of teaching and to cast a vote on whether the candidate is worthy on research. Tenure will be granted just in case there is majority support on teaching and there is majority support on research. This decision has the same structure as the decision to purchase a new item of equipment. One might therefore be tempted to conclude that the conclusion-based procedure is a better truth-tracker than the premise-based procedure as fewer candidates meet the mark on teaching and research in a particular school, as the faculty members are less qualified in their assessment and as there are fewer voters in the department.

However, the independence assumptions are somewhat less plausible in this case than in our example. For instance, one might object to independence assumption (f): Typically there is some connection between the candidate's research and teaching skills. One might argue that there is positive relevance, since teaching typically involves research and vice versa. But one might equally argue that there is negative relevance, since time devoted to research is time taken away from teaching, and vice versa. Or one might object to independence assumption (h): Typically there is a connection between the assessment skills of senior faculty members on teaching and research. One might argue that there is positive relevance, since both assessments will be influenced by the degree of bias, the level of expertise and the care invested in the evaluation process. On the other hand, one might argue for negative relevance: faculty members typically profile themselves either as good teachers or as good researchers, and this dichotomy might carry over in the quality of their assessment of tenure candidates.

We mentioned earlier that the Condorcet Jury Theorem still stands even if assumption (c) is to some extent violated, e.g. when opinion leaders have a limited influence. As an analytical exercise, we relaxed the assumption of independence (f) in the direction of positive relevance and in the direction of negative relevance. (Results are omitted.) As it turned out, our general results proved to be quite robust under these relaxations. Of course, the idiosyncrasies of every situation will need to be examined and modeled accordingly, but there is at least some reason to believe that our general results are not an artifact of unrealistic independence assumptions.

The Cost of Error

We have shown under what conditions the conclusion-based procedure is a better truth-tracker than the premise-based procedure. The conclusion-based approach gains its advantage because it is better at reaching truth for the wrong reasons. Truth for the wrong reasons can only be reached when the conjunction is false. Hence, the conclusion-based account gains its advantage from providing a more accurate assessment of non-acceptable items of equipment or of non-acceptable candidates for tenure. Now, a company or an institution of higher learning may be more concerned about the danger that non-acceptable items or unqualified candidates would be incorrectly accepted rather than about the opposite danger that acceptable items or qualified candidates would be incorrectly rejected. Hence, they will be somewhat more favorable to the conclusion-based account. Under other circumstances (when there is a shortage of available alternatives), the preferences of the committee may be different: the danger of incorrectly rejecting an acceptable alternative may be deemed to be more serious than the opposite mistake. Our model rests on the assumption that one cares about truth per se and does not make any distinction between the kinds of errors that are committed. If the cost of incorrect acceptance differs from the cost of incorrect rejection, then the balance in the evaluation of the premise-based procedure and the conclusion-based procedure will shift. In order to give a precise answer as to whether we should favor the premise-based procedure or the conclusion procedure when the types of error committed carry different costs, we would need to introduce utility values into the model and develop a more complex decision-theoretic approach.

Deliberative Democracy and Reliabilism

In section 1, we have seen that the premise-based procedure is much more congenial to the ideal of deliberative democracy. As we have shown in section 8, however, in some types of cases (with fewer voters, lower competence levels, and in more stringent contexts) the conclusion-based procedure is a more reliable truth-tracker. Should this observation be worrisome for the adherents of deliberative democracy? Pettit (2001) denies this. What is decisive for the deliberative democrat is a procedure's potential when it comes to reaching truth for right reasons and in this respect the premise-based procedure is definitely superior. As Pettit puts it:

When a person or community makes a correct judgment that A for the wrong deliberative reasons, then we deny that they understand why it is the case that A, or that they know that A. But the ideal of deliberative democracy, as that has been articulated on all sides, is closely bound to the alleged prospect of an increase of understanding and perhaps knowledge on the part of individuals in the community, and the group as a whole; there is no suggestion that it merely increases the likelihood of serendipitous error. The ideal supposes that in relying on deliberation to guide them towards a collective judgment, people will be guided by right reasons: that is, by reasons that are sound as well as supportive. (Pettit 2001; quoted with small changes in the notation)

In other words, what deliberative democrats are after are not simply true beliefs but increased understanding and knowledge, i.e., true beliefs for the right reasons. This applies, in particular, to the beliefs of the group as the whole. Obviously, the premise-based procedure is especially helpful in this respect. However, leaving the issue of understanding aside, we should point out that Pettit's argument rests on a contested concept of knowledge. The classical analysis of knowledge as true belief based on right reasons does not appeal to epistemologists of externalist persuasion. An especially popular externalist view takes knowledge to be a true belief arrived at by reliable methods (e.g. Goldman,

1979). Thus, it is the truth-tracking potential of the methods used that determines the epistemic status of the true belief under consideration. The epistemic status of a belief increases with the reliability of the methods by which it has been reached. On this externalist view then, the conclusion-based procedure would confer a higher epistemic status to the assessments of the group in all those types of cases in which that procedure is a better truth-tracker. Consequently, the superiority of that method in certain types of cases should be worrisome for deliberative democrats of an externalist bent. There is a tension between the epistemological commitment to externalism and the political commitment to deliberative democracy. In certain cases, the former commitment pulls one in the direction of the conclusion-based procedure, while the latter commitment always pulls one in the direction of the premise-based procedure.

Other Inference Patterns and the Problem of Instability.

In this paper, we have only considered a very simple type of case, one in which a group takes a stand on a conjunction on the basis of the voters' views concerning the conjuncts. What can be said about complex social decisions in which premises lead to the conclusion via inference rules other than conjunction introduction? Being right in the assessment of the truth-value of a proposition is equivalent to being right in the assessment of the truth-value of its negation. Since the negation of a conjunction is equivalent to the disjunction of its negated conjuncts, our results concerning conjunction introduction extend to disjunction introduction just as well: We can apply them mutatis mutandis to those social decisions in which the conclusion is a disjunction that is being accepted if at least one of the disjuncts gets a majority of votes (the premise-based procedure) or if the voters who accept one or the other of the disjuncts are in the majority (the conclusion-based procedure). But what about other inference rules, such as modus ponens, disjunctive syllogism, etc.?

And what about the inference patterns in which the conclusion could be reached by a series of steps rather than in just one move? It is important to note that, in such cases, the premise-based procedure may be applied in different ways. We could either let the voters vote on the propositions from which the main conclusion immediately follows, or instead ask them to vote on the premises that lie farther back in the inference chain. As it turns out, the premise-based procedure may deliver different results depending on the level at which it is applied. In other words, unlike the conclusion-based procedure, the premise-based procedure is unstable, as shown by the following example:

Suppose that, in a given group, there are majorities against each of the propositions A, B, C, D, but also (ii) majorities for $A \vee B$ and for $C \vee D$. Suppose the group needs to take a stand with respect to the following proposition:

(X) $(A \vee B) \& (C \vee D)$.

If the premise-based procedure is applied at level (i), i.e., if the vote is conducted on each of the propositions A, B, C and D, then the group will reject each of the conjuncts in X and then move on to reject X itself. But if that procedure instead is applied at level (ii), i.e., if the vote is be conducted only on A ∨ B and on C ∨ D, then the group will accept X. How serious is this instability problem?

APPENDICES

Appendix 1

For k voters to be the majority of n even-numbered voters, it must be the case that k is an integer contained in $[\frac{1}{2}n+1, n]$. Following the methodology outlined in section 3, the probability that a majority among n even-numbered voters is correct is:

$$P(M_{even}) = \sum_{k=\frac{1}{2}n+1}^{n} \binom{n}{k} p^k (1-p)^{n-k}.$$

$\Delta_{even} = P(M_{even}) - p$

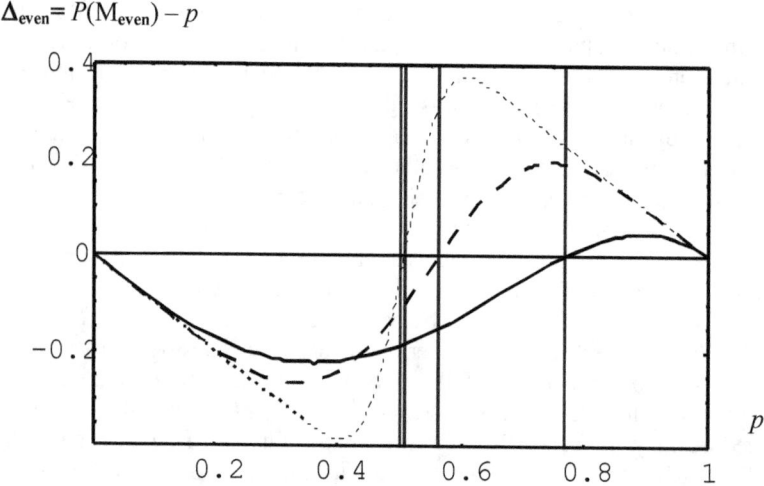

Figure 10: The difference between the chances that the majority judgment is correct and that a single voter is correct, for n=4 (full line), n = 12 (dashed line) and n = 102 (dotted line) voters. For n = 4, $\Delta_{even} < 0$ for $p < .77$; for n = 12, $\Delta_{even} < 0$ for $p < .56$; and for n =102, $\Delta_{even} < 0$ for $p < .5056$.

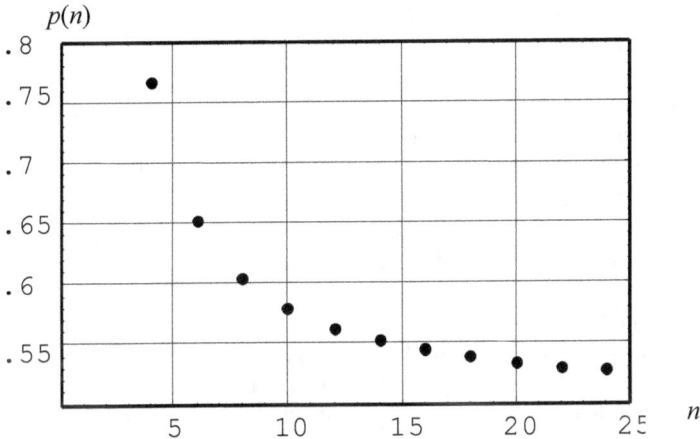

Figure 11: p(n) is the value of p beyond which the probability that the majority is correct exceeds the probability that an individual voter is correct for n = 4, 6, ..., 24

We calculate the difference function, $\Delta_{even} = P(M_{even}) - p$, for $n = 4, 6, 8,...$ In figure 10, we plot the difference function for $n = 4$, $n = 12$ and $n = 102$: The probability that the majority is correct exceeds the probability that a single voter is correct if and only if the competence of each voter exceeds $p(4) \approx .77, p(12) \approx .56, p(102) \approx .5056$. We have plotted the critical values $p(n)$ as a function of n in Figure 11. Notice that the values of $p(n)$ tend towards .50 as n grows larger: The more even-numbered voters there are, the less competence is required from each voters for the probability that the majority is correct to exceed the probability that an individual voter is correct, subject to the constraint that $p > .5$.

Appendix 2

We will show by means of graphical models of conditional independence structures (see e.g. Pearl 1988, 77–141) that the three conditional independences in Facts 1, 2 and 3 below hold. The arrows in a Directed Acyclical Graph (DAG) represent direct influences between variables, with conditional independence being understood in terms of the shielding-off condition: Parents shield off their children from all the non-descendants in the graph. Or, in other words, the DAG respects the Parental Markov Condition:

(PMC) A variable represented by a node in a Bayesian Network is independent of the variables represented by its non-descendant nodes in the

Bayesian Network, conditional on all variables represented by its parent nodes.

We define the following variables:
- S states whether the item of equipment is safe;
- F states whether the item of equipment is economically feasible;
- C states what combination of the values of S and F obtains;
- Fi states whether voter i is correct about F;
- Si states whether voter i is correct about S;
- Vi states whether voter i is correct about the conjunction of S and F (i.e., about C);
- M^F states whether the majority is correct about F;
- M^S states whether the majority is correct about S;
- D states whether the committee's decision to either purchase or not purchase the item of equipment (i.e., its assessment of C) is correct.

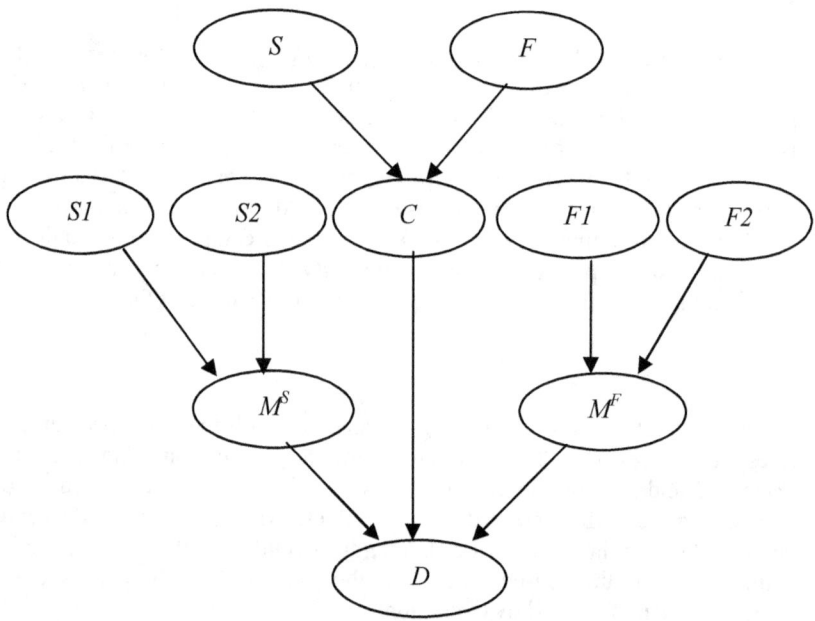

Figure 12: Graph for the Premise-Based Procedure

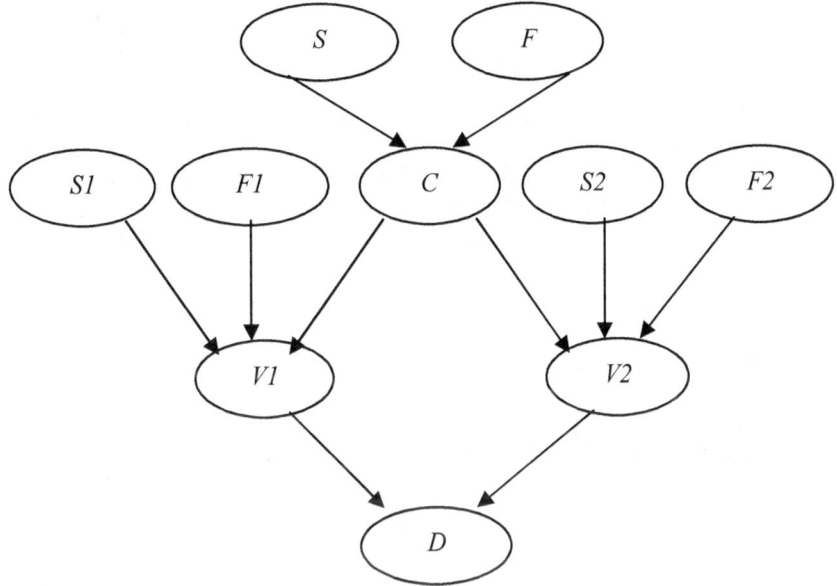

Figure 13: Graph for the Conclusion-Based Procedure

We have presented the DAGs for $n = 2$ voters in figure 12 for the premise-based procedure and in figure 13 for the conclusion-based procedure. It is clear how these arrows track direct influences in both procedures, except maybe for the arrows leaving the nodes with the variable C. We explain: Note that for the premise-based procedure, if S & F obtains, it is much more difficult for the committee to draw the correct conclusion about whether the conjunction of S and F obtains, than if S & not-F, not-S & F or not-S & not-F obtain. If S & F obtains, then the committee needs to be correct about both S and F to be correct about the conjunction, but if any of the other combinations obtains, being incorrect about some combinations of S and F will also get the committee to the correct truth-value for the conjunction. The same argument holds mutatis mutandis for the conclusion-based procedure. For individual voters to be correct about the conjunction is much more difficult if both conjuncts are true. For any sets of variables α, β, and γ, let $\alpha \perp\!\!\!\perp \beta$ and $\alpha \perp\!\!\!\perp \beta \mid \gamma$ stand, respectively, for the claims that α is independent of β and that α is independent of β given γ. Since the parents of S, F, Si and Fi are the empty set in both graphs, we can read off the following independences in both graphs (or, more precisely, in the generalizations of these graphs for n voters) by means of the (PMC):

$S \perp\!\!\!\perp F$
$Si \perp\!\!\!\perp S1,..., Si-1, Si+1,..., Sn, S, F, Fi, F1,..., Fi-1, Fi+1,..., Fn$, for $i = 1,..., n$
$Fi \perp\!\!\!\perp F1,..., Fi-1, Fi+1,..., Fn, S, F, Si, S1,..., Si-1, Si+1,..., Sn$, for $i = 1,..., n$

The first independence corresponds to assumption (f) and the latter two independences correspond to assumptions (c), (g), (h) and (i). The standard method to check whether a particular conditional independence holds in the graphical model is to appeal to the d-separation criterion. By means of this criterion, we can read off the following conditional independences in the graph in figure 12:

Fact 1: $M^S \perp\!\!\!\perp M^F \mid C$

and in the graph in figure 13:

Fact 2: $Si \perp\!\!\!\perp Fi \mid C$ for $i = 1,..., n$.
Fact 3: $Vi \perp\!\!\!\perp V1,..., Vi-1, Vi+1,..., Vn \mid C$ for $i = 1,..., n$.

REFERENCES

Brennan, Geoffrey, 1999, "Collective Coherence?", manuscript.
Borland, P. J., 1989, "Majority Systems and the Condorcet Jury Theorem", *Statistician* 38, 181–189.
Chapman, B., 1998a, "Law, Incommensurability, and Conceptually Sequenced Argument", *University of Pennsylvania Law Review* 146, 1487–1582.
Chapman, B., 1998b, "More Easily Done than Said: Rules, Reason and Rational Social Choice", *Oxford Journal of Legal Studies* 18, 293–329.
Cohen, J., 1986, "An epistemic conception of democracy", *Ethics* 97, 26–38.
Condorcet, J. A. de, 1785, *Essai sur l'application de l'analyse à la probabilité des décisions rendues à la pluralité des voix*, l'Imprimerie Royale, Paris; partly translated into English in McLean and Urken (1995).
Elster, J. (ed.), 1998, *Deliberative Democracy*, Cambridge University Press.
Estlund, D., 1990, "Democracy Without Preference", *Philosophical Review* 49, 397–424.
Estlund, D., 1993, "Making Truth Safe for Democracy", in *The Idea of Democracy*, ed. by David Copp, Jean Hampton and John E. Roemer, Cambridge University Press, New York, 71–100.
Estlund, D., 1994, "Opinion Leaders, Independence and Condorcet's Jury Theorem", *Theory and Decision* 36, 131–162.
Estlund, D., 1997, "Beyond Fairness and Deliberation: the Epistemic Dimension of Democratic Authority", in *Deliberative Democracy*, ed. by James Bohman and Willian Rehg, MIT Press, Cambridge, Mass., 173–204.
Estlund, D., 1998, "The Insularity of the Reasonable: Why Political Liberalism Must Admit the Truth", *Ethics* 108, 252–275.
Goldman, A. I., 1979, "What is Justified Belief?", in *Justification and Knowledge*, ed. by G. S. Pappas, Reidel, Dordrecht, 1–23.
Grofman, B., G. Owen and S. L. Feld, 1983, "Thirteen Theorems in Search of the Truth", *Theory and Decision* 15, 261–278.
List, C., and R. E. Goodin, 2000, "Epistemic Democracy", Working Papers in Social and Political Theory, Working Paper 2000 – W9, Australian National University.
Kornhauser, L. A., 1992a, "Modelling Collegial Courts. I. Path-Dependence", *International Review of Law and Economics* 12, 169–185.

Kornhauser, L. A., 1992b, "Modelling Collegial Courts. II. Legal Doctrine", *Journal of Law, Economics and Organization* 8, 441–470.
Kornhauser, L. A., and L. G. Sager, 1986, "Unpacking the Court", *Yale Law Journal* 82.
Kornhauser, L. A., and L. G. Sager, 1993, "The One and the Many: Adjudication in Collegial Courts", *California Law Review* 81, 1–59.
McLean, I. and A. B. Urken (translators and editors), 1995, *Classics of Social Choice*, Ann Arbor, University of Michigan Press.
Owen, G., B. Grofman and S. L. Feld, 1989,. "Proving a Distribution-Free Generalization of the Condorcet Jury Theorem", *Mathematical Social Sciences* 17, 1–16.
Pearl, J., 1988, *Probabilistic Reasoning in Intelligent Systems: Networks of Plausible Inference*, 2nd ed. Morgan Kaufmann, San Francisco, CA.
Pettit, P., 2001, "Deliberative Democracy and the Discursive Dilemma", *Philosophical Issues* (supplement 1 of Nous) 11, 268–295.
Pettit, P. and W. Rabinowicz, 2001, "The Jury Theorem and the Discursive Dilemma", *Philosophical Issues* 11 (supplement 1 of Nous 35); appendix to Pettit (2001), 295–299.
Rousseau, J.-J., 1762, *Du Contrat Social ou Principes de Droit Publique*; translated into English by G. D. H. Cole , se http://www.constitution.org/jjr/socon.htm

Jaakko Hintikka

Presuppositions of Questions – Presuppositions of Inquiry

1. Presuppositions as the Crucial Limitation of Inquiry

Socrates was right. All rational knowledge-seeking can be conceptualized as a questioning process, with question-answer steps interspersed with logical inference steps. "Rational" means here "capable of epistemological evaluation". This is what I have shown in an earlier paper. (See Hintikka 1998.) I will not review here the arguments for this view of "inquiry as inquiry", as I have called it, but instead examine some of its implications. In any case, I am not the first philosopher to defend the omnipresence of questioning in our knowledge-seeking. Aristotle modeled both his methodology and his logic on the different aspects of the Socratic questioning process or *elenchus*. One of the better known – albeit not the better appreciated – later representative of similar views is R. G. Collingwood who went even farther and asserted that

Every statement that anybody ever makes is made in answer to a question. (Collingwood 1940, p. 23.)

Or is Collingwood perhaps merely echoing Aristotle according to which all the propositions used as dialectical premises originate from questions? (See Topica I, x.) In any case, Collingwood had something of an ulterior motive in conceiving of all propositions as answers to questions. This ulterior motive is a legitimate one. He wanted in this way to subject to philosophical examination the limitations that characterize a certain line of inquiry or the thought of some one thinker or even the intellectual stance of an entire era. These limitations are according to Collingwood due to the presuppositions of questions. As he puts it,

Every question involves a presupposition. (Op.cit. p. 25.)

A question can be meaningfully asked only if its presupposition is available. Hence the need of a presupposition limits our questions and consequently, since all propositions are answers to questions, limits the propositions we can propose.

Whatever one may say of the details of Collingwood's ideas, his main conception is correct if I am right in construing all rational inquiry as inquiry as an interrogative procedure. For then the limits of inquiry are determined by the presuppositions of questions and answers. (The qualifications this statement needs are discussed below.) It follows that all doctrines concerning the limitations of scientific or other kinds of knowledge-seeking will have to be discussed by reference to the presuppositions of questions and questioning. In particular, all relativistic epistemologies must be defended or criticized in terms of the logic of interrogative presuppositions.

But where do we get the presuppositions of our questions that enable us to raise them? This question can be raised either apropos Collingwood or absolutely. In some cases, the presupposition of a question can be an answer to an antecedent question. That antecedent question must have its own presupposition. But according to Collingwood such a regress of presuppositions will come to an end. Thus at the far end of a Collingwoodean hierarchy of presuppositions there are what he calls ultimate presuppositions. They are not answers to any prior questions. They determine the character of the thinker who presupposes them. They are therefore crucial according to Collingwood's way of thinking to any study of how a thinker's thought is restricted by his or her own assumptions. Hence, they are among other things crucial to any understanding of the entire issue of epistemological relativism.

Thus configurations of Collingwoodean ultimate presuppositions are not entirely unlike Kuhnian paradigms. However, Collingwood is one up on Kuhn in this department, the reason being that presuppositions of questions can – and should – be made a part of a systematic theory of questions and answers, whereas paradigms are such wild and woolly animals as not to allow much rational discussion. Indeed, Collingwood in so many words called his study a "logic of questions and answers" whereas Kuhn has all but abandoned his notion of paradigm in favor of an almost equally mysterious "disciplinary matrix". Collingwood's approach thus exhibits a much greater promise than Kuhn's. For instance, I believe that a careful study of the logic of questions and answers in the same spirit as Collingwood has a much better chance of eliciting the actual conceptual presuppositions of different inquiries and inquirers, including the presuppositions of our own discourse, than any kind of "paradigm research".

Needless to say, Collingwood's "logic" is nevertheless not an adequately formulated logic in a sense that would have satisfied a Tarski. This is not merely a matter of cosmetic exactness or architectonic organization. It will turn out that some of Collingwood's explicit statements are not exceptionlessly true. For instance, *pace* Collingwood, there are questions without nontrivial presuppositions, as will be pointed out below. For another instance, one and the same statement can be an answer to more than one question. Collingwood is not free from confusion, either. I cannot help suspecting that when he speaks of presuppositions of questions he is sometimes in effect thinking of what might be called presuppositions of answers but which I have (perhaps unfortunately) called the conclusiveness conditions of answers. (See sec. 7 below.) All these shortcomings affect the evaluation of Collingwood's idea of the ultimate presuppositions of questions as determining the limits of our thinking.

In the logic of questions and answers we do in fact have an instructive example of how bright and shiny logical tools can help to understand and master important epistemological and other philosophical problems. But in order to make full use of the logic of questions and answers for epistemological purposes, we must also consider how sequences of questions and answers contribute to – and almost constitute – a line of inquiry. This is spelled out by setting up what I have called an interrogative model of inquiry. In principle, this model at first looks exceedingly simple. It is like a deductive argument, except that at any time new premises may be introduced in the form of answers to questions – assuming that the questions in question are answerable.

As a book-keeping device we can use a semantical *tableau* in the sense of E. W. Beth (1955). It turns out to be advisable to rule out any traffic between the left-hand and the right-hand side of any *tableau* (or *subtableau*). A question can be raised only if its presupposition is on the left side, and if an answer is forthcoming, it will likewise be added to the left side.

Such an inquiry can be thought of as a game against nature in the sense of the mathematical theory of games. A play of such a game starts from a number of *initial premises* on the left side and the conclusion to be established on the right side. If the inquirer manages to close the *tableau* he wins and his opponent ("nature") loses. The precise determination of payoffs is in most cases not crucial. Also and importantly, the set of available answers will have to be specified.

Speaking more generally, a word on answers and answering might be appropriate here. The first modern philosopher to have compared scientific inquiry to questioning seems to have been Francis Bacon. He gave the likeness a nasty turn, however, comparing as he did an experimentalist with an inquisitor who forces a prisoner to reveal the truth. For the analysis undertaken here, we do not need to assume the role of a torturer, but we have to postulate a minimal consistency on the part of the answerer. We will simply assume that in each inquiry a certain set of potential answers is given. (We can call this the answer set.) When a question is asked, the respondent will provide an answer to it as soon as there is one in the answer set. This may be considered as a generalization of the repeatability of scientific experiments. It might be of interest to ask whether certain closure conditions should be imposed on the answer set. We will not discuss that question here, however.

This stipulation of a fixed store of available answers can nevertheless be relaxed. If we are thinking in game-theoretical terms, we can allow the inquirer to "purchase" the right to ask certain questions, in the sense that asking them will reduce the potential payoff resulting from the outcome eventually reached. This is not unnatural. For instance, improved (but more expensive) experiments can extend the range of answers a scientist can receive from nature.

As Collingwood's case shows, many questions concerning the presuppositions of questions, and more generally the presuppositions of inquiry are relevant to the larger philosophical and methodological questions about the intrinsic limitations of inquiry, including the problem of relativism, and even more generally to the problem of historical understanding and its limitations. This is because Collingwood is essentially correct in considering any rational inquiry as a questioning process.

2. KNOWLEDGE STATEMENTS

But what can be said of the presuppositions of questions? First I have to explain what the true logic of questions and answers is, which in practice means showing how questions and answers are treated in the right kind of epistemic logic. In using this logic, the ingredients of one's language include the resources of some fixed first-order language plus a sentence initial epistemic operator K. Since the particular knower we are talking about is largely irrelevant, for the purposes of this paper this operator K can here usually be thought of as expressing an impersonal "it is known that". Its meaning can be captured by thinking of it as a universal quantifier ranging over the scenarios (courses of events) left possible by what is known. In game-theoretical semantics, K mandates a choice by the falsifier of one of those epistemically possible scenarios.

For simplicity, in what follows, our formulas are always assumed to be in a negation normal form, that is, in a form where the logical constants are $\sim$, &, $\vee$, $(\exists x)$, $(\forall x)$, = and where all negation-signs $\sim$ occur prefixed to an atomic sentence or an identity.

The novel ingredient in my epistemic logic is the independence indicator / (the slash). Its meaning can be seen from an example or two. The sentence

(1) $K (\exists x) S[x]$

says that in every possible scenario compatible with what is known there exists among its members an individual, call it x, such that $S[x]$. What this amounts to is to say that it is known that there exists an x such that $S[x]$.

But what does it mean to assert the following?

(2) $K(\exists x/K) S[x]$

Here the independence of $(\exists x)$ of K indated by the slash / means that the individual x satisfying $S[x]$ must be chosen independently of the choice of any particular scenario compatible with what is known. Hence the choice of x might as well be made before the choice of a scenario signaled by K. In other words, there is some one and the same individual x which in all those scenarios satisfies $S[x]$. In other words, (2) means that it is known of some particular individual x that $S[x]$. And this is unmistakably what it means *to know who or what* satisfies $S[x]$. In brief, if the variable x ranges over persons, (2) says that it is known who (call him or her x) is such that $S[x]$.

Ordinary language examples of (1) and (2) might be:

(3)   It is known that someone murdered Roger Akroyd.
(4)   It is known who murdered Roger Akroyd.

Here the difference between (∃x) and (∃x/K) is essentially that between *someone* and *who* (in other examples some other wh-word, such as *what, where, when,* ....). The same difference can be said to separated knowledge of propositions from knowledge of objects (of any logical type). In other words, knowledge of entities which perhaps could also be called knowledge of id-entities.

Similar remarks apply to subordinate propositional questions. Consider the following propositions:

(5) $K(S_1 \vee S_2)$
(6) $K(S_1(\vee/K)S_2)$

The former says that it is known that S_1 or S_2. The latter says that it is known whether S_1 or S_2. Thus the relation of $\vee$ to $(\vee/K)$ is like the relation of *that* to *whether*.

These concepts and distinctions can be generalized. Excluding nested interrogative constructions (as well as constructions with *why* or *how*) any knowledge statement can be said to be of the form

(7) KS

where S is like a first-order sentence (in negation normal form) except that some existential quantifiers (∃x) have been replaced by (∃x/K) and some disjunction signs ∨ by (∨/K). These slashed expressions constitute the question ingredient in our formal (but interpreted) language. The propositional question indicator (∨/K) expresses knowledge of propositions while (∃x/K) expresses knowledge of objects (entities, in this case individuals).

3. PRESUPPOSITIONS OF QUESTIONS

This explains the nature of knowledge statements. But what do they have to do with questions? The answer is very simple. Semantically speaking, a question is at bottom a request for information. To specify this information is to specify the epistemic state that the questioner wants to be brought about. Any first-person knowledge statement can serve this purpose. A knowledge statement corresponding to a direct question is called its *desideratum*. For instance, the desideratum of the question

(8) Who murdered Roger Ackroyd?

is

(9) I know who murdered Roger Ackroyd.

This is of the form (2) when K is taken to say "I know that".

Different questions correspond to nonequivalent desiderata and equivalent questions to equivalent desiderata. One way in which the notion of desideratum helps our analysis of interrogative inquiry is that it enables us to deal with ways of answering questions by means of questions. In the original explanation of inquiry by questioning some fixed conclusion was postulated as being given at the outset of the inquiry. This might seem to restrict the applicability of interrogative inquiry tremendously, for only in the case of why- and how-questions do we know at the outset of an inquiry what its conclusions will be. This apparently restrictive assumption can be disarmed by assigning the desideratum of a question to the role of the "conclusion". The entire inquiry will then amount to our attempt to answer this "big" or *principal question* with the help of answers to several "small" or *operative questions*.

A question can thus play two different roles in inquiry. Answering it may be the aim of the entire game, viz. in the case of a principal question. But answering an operative question is merely one step in the process of hopefully answering the principal question. Again, the distinction between principal and operative questions is not recent news. For instance, as Richard Robinson (1971) has shown, Aristotle's injunction against the fallacy of *petitio principii* was originally a warning against asking ("petitioning") the principal question when asking a number of the operative ones is in order.

In general, the desideratum of a question determines its logical behavior and its logical properties. An important example is offered by the very notion of presuppositions we are interested in here. The presupposition of (8) is

(10) I know that someone murdered Roger Ackroyd.

More generally, the presupposition of a question whose desideratum is of the form (2) is (1).

The general characterization of the presupposition of a question is now easy. As you can see, the presupposition (1) of the question whose desideratum is (2) is obtained from (2) by leaving out the slashed /K. This holds in general. If the desideratum of a question (7), its desideratum is obtained from (7) by omitting all expressions of the form /K. This is a good example of how the independence (slash) notation enables us to carry out a simple and uniform treatment of most of the different kinds of questions.

This analysis of the presuppositions of questions deserves a few comments. First, it is perhaps in order to note that many linguists use a notion of presupposition that pertains only to the existential presuppositions of different kinds of sentence or utterances. In a way, presuppositions of questions also vouchsafe existence, as one can see from such presuppositions as (1). But the existence in question is not so much the existence of individuals or of objects of some other sort, but the existence of answers to a question. If Roger Ackroyd was not murdered, there does not exist be a satisfactory answer to the question as to who murdered him.

Of course people actually do ask questions whose presuppositions have not been established. If so, the if presupposition is not in fact satisfied, no answer to the question will be available. Hence the asking of such a question on purpose must have a purpose other than finding an answer to it. Accordingly, the interpretation of a presuppositionless question is a pragmatic matter rather than a logical or semantical one.

One important thing that the interrogative model of inquiry shows is that the presuppositions of such questions as play a role in an inquiry cannot be combined into one super-presupposition, whether we call it an ultimate presupposition, paradigm or an interdisciplinary matrix. They do not depend on each other in the way that would enable us to integrate them in the kind of way in which the premises used in a branch of science can typically be integrated into an axiom system – if we are to believe Hilbert. One reason is that presuppositions of questions do not depend only on presuppositions of earlier questions, but also on answers to earlier questions and ultimately also on the initial premises. I will return to this matter below in sec. 7.

What has been found out helps to put into perspective Collingwood's idea of ultimate presuppositions. Naturally many questions need a presupposition, but this presupposition does not typically come from an earlier presupposition. This means that presuppositions do not form a simple hierarchy, as Collingwood seems to assume. Of course there can also be (and sometimes must be) a number of initial premises of the entire inquiry. But if the presuppositions of the actual operative questions cannot be traced back to these initial premises, it is not clear that they can play the role of Collingwood's ultimate presuppositions. Admittedly, they can provide presuppositions to the inquirer's initial questions, but they also serve as premises for the deductive steps of the inquiry.

Be this as it may, it is instructive to compare Collingwood's ultimate presuppositions with the initial premises of an interrogative inquiry, no matter how Collingwood's idea of presuppositions is to be interpreted in detail. Are they perhaps what Collingwood thinks of as ultimate presuppositions? If so, we are dealing with presuppositions of inquiry, not of isolated questions. Furthermore, we are then dealing with two different kinds of presuppositions here. If Collingwoodean presuppositions are conceptualized as initial premises of inquiry, they do not in a real-life situation constitute an insurmountable obstacle to inquiry. For what can be established by the interrogative depends on two different parameters, not merely on the initial premises but also – and more importantly – on the totality of available answers. A restriction on initial premises can be compensated by widening the class of available answers. Indeed, this is virtually a fact of life for a historian of science. The rise of empiricism, that is, abstention from a priori assumptions, has gone hand in hand with the development of an improved technology of observation and experimentation. Conversely, arguments for the need of a priori assumptions in science and in learning theory are sensitive to the range of questions that are answerable. For instance, Chomsky (1959) has argued that presuppositionless learning models cannot account for the speed at which a child learns his or her first language and that we must therefore postulate innate grammatical ideas. This argument depends heavily on the assumption that the input into the learning process (that is, in effect, the language community's answers to the learner's tacit questions) consists of particular data. Chomsky's argument does not go through if these "answers" can be conceptualized as including general laws or regularities. This illustrates the way in which an extension of the range of available answers enables an inquirer or learner to dispense with initial premises.

But if the limitations imposed on inquiry by the initial premises can be overcome by such means, these premises cannot be ultimate presuppositions in Collingwood's sense in that they do not restrict inquiry in the way he obviously thought.

Another consequence of these observations is that initial premises of inquiry are also a far cry from presuppositions of inquiry of the kind Thomas Kuhn wanted us to consider. In order to overcome limitations of inquiry due to a given set of initial premises we do not have to be converted to a new overall "paradigm" or a new way of thinking and arguing. In some cases, what is needed for such liberalization are better techniques of observation and experimentation. In philosophy of science what is needed might be a realization that scientific inquiry can be conceptualized as an inquiry where the answers a scientist receives are often laws of at least partial generality.

4. Presupposition-free Questions?

The most interesting things about the presuppositions for the purposes of this paper are nevertheless the differences between different kinds of questions. Here is a list of the desiderata of some types of questions and their corresponding presuppositions:

(11) Question Desideratum Presupposition
propositional $K(S_1(\vee/K)S_2) K(S_1 \vee S_2)$
simple *wh* $K(\exists x/K) S[x] K(\exists x) S[x]$
complex *wh* $K(\forall x) (\exists y/K) S[x,y] K(\forall x)(\exists y) S[x,y]$
mixed $K(\forall x) (S_1[x](\vee K) S_2[x] K(\forall x) (S_1[x] \vee S_2[x])$

The first kind of question in this list is a propositional or whether-question. As a special case we obtain a yes-or-no question whose desideratum is of the form $K(S(\vee K)\sim S)$ and presupposition $K(S \vee \sim S)$. But $(S \vee \sim S)$ is tautologically true, and yes-or-no questions hence have an empty presupposition. This gives the lie among other things to Collingwood's claim that every question has a presupposition.

But having to fault Collingwood is not the only disconcerting thing here. Consider any question whatsoever, with a presupposition as complex as you can imagine. Suppose you raise it and receive an answer, say S. Now you could have asked, instead of the original question, the yes-or-no question, "Is it the case that S or not?" Since S was available as an answer to the original question, it must also be available as an answer to this yes-or-no question.

For instance, in an experimental question to nature a scientist might ask: How does the observed variable y depend on the controlled variable x? Such a question has a complex presupposition expressible only by a general proposition. An answer to this question will then be a function f such that $y = f(x)$ expresses the intended dependence. But we could have asked instead the presuppositionless question, "Does y depend on x according to the law $y = f(x)$?" If the former answer is correct, then nature must reply to the latter one, "Yes".

But this seems to mean that in an inquiry any question whatever can be replaced by a yes-or-no question. And since yes-or-no question do not have any nonvacuous presuppositions, it looks as if any inquiry can be conducted without resorting to any presuppositions at all. Both Collingwood's project and mine seems to be misconceived.

Or is there a fallacy in the line of thought we have carried out? No, there is not, but we have to put its result in a wider perspective. What does it mean to say, as we did above, that we *could* have asked the presuppositionless yes-or-no question instead of the presupposition-laden original one? It means that there is nothing that prevents us from asking the yes-or-no question, that it is not forbidden by any law, be it logical, natural, human or divine. But such *de jure* possibility does not mean that the question was *de facto* epistemically possible in the sense that we could have known to ask this particular question without already knowing its answer. In my example, we would have not known to ask the yes-or-no question about the particular function f if we had not antecedently obtained it as an answer to the experimental question.

This puts the entire matter of presuppositions of questions to a new light. The source of this light can be taken to be the crucial distinction that can be made in practically any rational goal-directed process, including interrogative inquiry. It is instructive to conceptualize such processes as games. Then, as in a typical game, we must distinguish from each other, on the one hand the rules that define admissible moves, winning and losing etc, and by so doing define the game, and on the other hand the rules (or principles or whatever you want to call them) that tell one how to play the game well. The former will be called *definitory* rules of the game and the latter *strategic* rules. Both can in principle be formulated explicitly. In this sense, strategic rules are not merely heuristic, even though often optimal strategic rules may not be computable or may not be applicable directly for some other reason. For instance, the optimal strategies in the "game" of deductive theorem-proving are not computable, although they are codified by perfectly well-defined mathematical functions, and hence are not always directly applicable. For a different example, since there is a finite upper bound to the length of a chess game, the optimal chess strategies are recursive, even though no one knows precisely what they are and what the outcome would be of a play in which the antagonists use them.

By means of the game-theoretical framework, we can express the insight we have reached. The fact that questions other than yes-or-no questions require presuppositions does not restrict the range of results one can establish (prove by an interrogative argument), but it does restrict one's strategies, in the sense that if we try to dispense with these presuppositions, we are restricted to clumsy and in more complicated cases unmanageable strategies.

Thus the advantage of relying on strong presuppositions in inquiry is a strategic one. Thus is best seen what an inquirer's strategies might be in different types of inquiry. If I am not allowed to use nontrivial presuppositions in asking the question

(12) Who murdered Roger Ackroyd?

I am reduced to asking of one person after another,

(13) Did a_1 murder Roger Ackroyd?
Did a_2 murder Roger Ackroyd?
......

And if you do not think that this is tedious enough, think of what the corresponding procedure would be in the case of an experimental question concerning the dependence of a real-valued variable y on another variable x. Without nontrivial presuppositions we would be reduced to asking the question whose desideratum is

(14) $K(\forall x)(f(x) = g(x))$

for each function f one by one, where y=g(x) specifies the actual (observable) dependence of y on x. Yet this enormous task can be replaced by asking of a simple experimental question if we have at our disposal the appropriate presupposition.

This strategic power of experimental questions can be considered as the epistemological explanation of the success of early modern science. The methodological "secret" of scientists like Galileo and Newton is not their empiricism, but their use of experiments, especially controlled experiments. Such experiments can be thought of, it was seen earlier, as wh-questions with a functional (general) answer.

In sum, in so far as presuppositions of questions (or, rather the unavailability of presuppositions of questions) restricts our strategies of inquiry, not what it is possible in principle to establish interrogatively.

5. SOCRATIC QUESTIONS

As far as the role of yes-no questions is concerned, the history of philosophy offers us an instructive subject for a case study. The name of this subject is Socrates. In construing all rational knowledge-seeking as questioning, we are merely following the precedent of the Platonic Socrates. Socrates claims that he does not know anything. (Indeed, this pretended ignorance is the original meaning of Socratic irony or *eironeia*.) All the conclusions he puts forward and makes his interlocutor aware of – often painfully aware of – he deduces from the interlocutor's answers. Indeed, what we find in a Socratic dialogue are many of the ingredients of the interrogative model outlined here. There is a principal question, usually a definitory one such as "What is knowledge?, "What is piety?" etc. There are operative questions, put by Socrates to his interlocutor. Logical inferences are drawn at the end of a dialogue, sometimes introduced by statements by Socrates like "Let us now add our admissions together." Furthermore, logical conclusions are sometimes also drawn in the form of an answer to a question. Several examples of such inferences-as-answers-to-questions are found in the slaveboy episode of the *Meno*.

One of the most conspicuous features of Socratic questioning is that he uses for the most part only yes-or-no questions. This feature is shared by Aristotle's dialectical method as it is expounded in the *Topics*. It has prompted a lot of commentary. For instance Gilbert Ryle writes (Ryle 1971, vol. 1, p. 90) apropos Platonic questioning games:

The questioner can only ask questions; and the answerer can, with certain qualifications, answer only "yes" or "no". So the questioner's questions have to be properly constructed for "yes" or "no" answers. This automatically rules out a lot of types of questions, like factual questions, arithmetical questions, and technical questions. Roughly it leaves us only with conceptual questions, whatever they may be.

But what was found out above shows that Ryle is wrong. An answer to any question can also be obtained as an answer to a yes-or-no question, which are therefore not restricted to conceptual questions. On the contrary, suitable wh-questions are obviously much more closely related to conceptual matters, such as the definitions of different concepts. Indeed, the principal questions of Socratic inquiry are prima facie requests of definition and as such wh-questions rather than yes-or-no questions.

One reason why Socrates is asking yes-or-no questions is that they do not need presuppositions. They are the only questions that an *eiron* who professes ignorance can consistently ask. But they do not restrict their answers to some particular subject matter. They can therefore be raised at any time, without needing any preparatory argument to establish their presuppositions. Yet there is little that distinguishes formally or materially answers to yes-or-no questions from answers to other kinds of questions.

In any case, it is not true that Socrates asks only yes-or-no questions. We have to be careful here, however, in view of the distinction between principal and operational questions, for it is conspicuous that Socrates' "principal questions" are typically wh-questions in that they are definitional "what" questions. Hence what I am saying is merely that the operative questions Socrates asks are mostly yes-or-no questions.

It is also not true that the Platonic Socrates always asks only yes-or-no questions, even if we restrict our attention to operative questions. For instance, as *Gorgias* 474B and as *Charmides* 159C Socrates asks a propositional question which is not a yes-or-no question. He also asks repeatedly wh-questions. Cases in point are found at *Apology* 20B, *Euthyphro* 5D, *Hippias Major* 304E, *Laches* 192B, and *Phaedo* 105C–D. I would go as far as to assert that much of the knowledge and wisdom that Socrates typically is looking for is obtainable more naturally through a wh-question – if its presupposition were available – than through a yes-or-no question. But precisely for the purpose of avoiding those presuppositions Socrates replaces other kinds of questions by yes-or-no ones, in the way we discussed earlier. In some of the Socratic questions you can as it were capture this transition *in actu*.

For what is being miserable but desiring evil things and possessing them? (*Meno* 78A)

Here Socrates first raises a wh-question viz. "What is it to be miserable?" However, he immediately transforms it into a yes-or-no question concerning the answer he expects to receive, viz. "Is being miserable to desire evil things and possessing them?"

Similar steps from a wh-question to a yes-or-no question concerning the intended answer to it are taken by Socrates elsewhere. For instance, in *Phaedo* 76C Socrates asks,

When did our souls acquire the knowledge of them [recollected things]? Surely not after we were born as human beings.

He receives the answer

Certainly not.

But "not" is not an answer to a wh-question, but to a yes-or-no question.

Other problems concerning Socrates and his method are also to be illuminated by hat has been found. To say that Socrates does not need any presuppositions in his inquiry amounts to saying that he does not need any factual knowledge in his enterprise. He does not need to know anything. Here we have an explanation of Socrates' ironic professions of ignorance. Such professions serve to highlight one of the merits of Socrates' method, namely its freedom from presuppositions.

Otherwise Socrates' pretended ignorance is hard to understand, as witnessed by scholars' contrived comments on it. For instance, Richard Robinson accuses Socrates of moving illicitly back and forth between information-seeking questioning and examiner's questioning. Vlastos tries to defend Socrates by attributing to him a special strict sense of knowledge. There is no direct basis for such views in the text, and in any case all such accounts are dispensable in favor of the one according to which Socrates is highlighting one of the most important features of his questioning strategies, viz. their independence of background knowledge. Socrates' irony illustrates a valid point in epistemic logic.

Of course Socrates had to possess knowledge of a different kind, viz. strategic knowledge. He did not use in his interrogative argument any answers that his interlocutor does not give. He does not have to claim that he knows anything. But he has to know which questions to ask. This is precisely the gist of a good interrogative strategy. But does it not amount to knowing what the answer will be? In the passages quoted above Socrates first raises a wh-question and then moves on to ask the yes-or-no question concerning the very answer he expects. How can he do this without knowing the answer? Isn't Socrates therefore disingenuous when he pleads ignorance? The answer is that all good questioning strategies involve some amount of anticipation of what the interlocutor's answer will be. For instance, in a court of law, a cross-examiner must anticipate what the witness will say or else he or she is likely to be in dire trouble. Yes, Socrates must have knowledge in order to practice his *elenchus* successfully, but *that knowledge is strategic,* not factual knowledge – which is precisely my point. In an epistemological perspective, Socrates' irony is but a way of highlighting the distinction between definitory and strategic rules or perhaps between factual and strategic knowledge.

6. Strategic Knowledge as Logical Knowledge

Now what is this strategic knowledge like? Strategic knowledge will in interrogative inquiry ultimately come down to a method answering questions of the following form: Given a list of the propositions one has reached in a line of inquiry, which question should one ask next? In view of the need of presuppositions, this amounts to asking: Which proposition should one use as the presupposition of the next question? This strategic problem has a counterpart in deductive logic. This counterpart problem is: Which proposition should one use as the premise of the next logical inference? In neither use does there exist a mechanical (recursive) method of choosing the right proposition, that is, the optimal strategy is not mechanical in either case. But in one type of inquiry there obtains a remarkable connection between the two strategic choices. This case is a context of pure discovery. In technical terms, this means a type in which all answers are known to be true or at least can be treated as being true. If so, all we need to do is to find out what the truth is; we do not have to worry in such cases about justifying what we find. Of course this is how Socrates treats his interlocutor's answers, if only for the sake of argument. This is admittedly a special kind of case, but an especially interesting one, the reason being that according to a widespread view contexts of inquiry cannot be dealt with by rational logical or epistemological means.

In this case of pure discovery, there is a remarkable relation between the two strategic choices. *The optimal choice is the same in both kinds of inquiries.* In other words, even though interrogative (question-answer) steps and logical inference steps in inquiry must be sharply separated from each other, they are governed by the same strategic principles, in so far as the inquiry has the character of pure truth-seeking, freed from all worries about the veracity of the answers the inquirer is receiving.

This insight yields an incisive answer to the question of the nature of Socratic strategic knowledge: It is in effect logical knowledge in the sense of knowledge of strategies of logical (deductive) reasoning. More generally, optimal strategies of interrogative reasoning approximate the optimal strategies of deductive reasoning in so far as we can trust the answers we are receiving.

This throws interesting light not only on the character of Socrates' wisdom but on the nature of strategic knowledge in general. In particular, it shows that our strategic knowledge does not have intransgressible limits. In principle, it can be enhanced by learning more about logic, in the sense of knowledge of strategies of logical reasoning.

7. There Are No Ultimate Presuppositions of Inquiry

What has been said does not close all the issues. Among the ones that have to be re-opened, there are the prospects of tracing presuppositions back to the initial premises, the partial parallelism between interrogative inquiry and deduction, and the presuppositionlessness of yes-or-no questions. Let me start from the last question. It is clearly time that a tautological presupposition ($S \vee \sim S$) cannot fail to be true. But can it fail to be known? It can be argued – I would say, can be shown – that interrogative inquiry should be construed as an epistemic enterprise. What this implies for an explicit treatment of interrogative inquiry is not hard to work out. For instance, each initial premise should be prefixed by an implicit or explicit epistemic operator K, and likewise for the ultimate conclusion of the inquiry. This need of epistemification is instantiated by the necessity of using the desiderata of questions as ultimate conclusions of inquiry mentioned in sec. 3 above. Indeed, this epistemification is in keeping with the treatment of questions, their presuppositions and their answers in sections 2–3 above.

But if so, presuppositions of operative questions will have to require that a certain statement is known, not merely that it is true or assumed to be true. And if so, the presuppositions of yes-or-no questions will be of the form K(S ∨ ~S), not of the form (S ∨ ~S). Now there is a viable notion of knowledge according to which one has to be aware of what one knows. If so, even the presuppositions of yes-or-no questions must be assumed as initial premises or derived from them like all other presuppositions. This would appear to vindicate Collingwood, for it would mean that all presuppositions can often all be traced back to the initial premises albeit usually with the help of answers to earlier questions.

However, a closer look at the structure of interrogative inquiry belies this pretty Collingwoodean picture. The talk of tracing propositions figuring in interrogative inquiry back to the initial premises makes obvious sense only if (definitory) rules of the "game" are such as to satisfy the subformula property. What this property means here is that (the nonepistemic part of) each sentence occurring in one's *tableau* of inquiry is a subformula of an earlier one, or else a substitution-instance of such a subformula. The usual *tableau* rules of ordinary first-order deductive logic satisfy the subformula principle. And since they constitute a complete system of deduction in ordinary first-order logic, no rules violating the subformula principle are needed there. Many formulations of first-order logic admittedly employ further rules of inference, rules that do not satisfy the subformula principle. But the result known as Gentzen's first *Hauptsatz* and others like it show the dispensability of those additional rules, exemplified by unrestricted modus ponens, the cut rule of proof theorists, and so on.

It can be shown that the advantages of such other rules are strategic, in the sense that they can be used to shorten and to and simplify proofs. They are dispensable, but at the cost of longer proofs.

It is here that a subtle difference between deductive inquiry and interrogative inquiry emerges. The basic form of the assumptions that violate the subformula property is the introduction of tautological disjunctions (S ∨ ~S) or in its epistemic variant, K(S ∨ ~S) into the left side. But even though such additional rules do not add to the power of deductive inquiry (in the sense of adding to the range of propositions that are provable by deductive means), the do increase the scope of interrogative inquiry. There are ultimate conclusions that can be proved only by means of such additional quasi-tautological assumptions. The reason is obvious on the basis of what has been said. The newly introduced propositions K(S ∨ ~S) are precisely the presuppositions of yes-or-no questions. If they are not subject to any restrictions, the inquirer can ask any yes-or- no question. And any available answer can be obtained as an answer to such a question. (Cf. sec. 4 above.)

It is also clear that the inquirer must be allowed to introduce any such quasi-tautological premises. I may be limited *de facto* as to which tautological premises I can know in the sense that requires awareness of them, but I cannot – and nobody else can – formulate those limits and bring them to my attention without thereby extending them.

Admittedly, we can emulate Quine and use the interrogative model of inquiry purely descriptively for the purpose of accounting for other folk's knowledge-seeking behavior. Part of such a description could be then a delineation of the class of yes-or-no questions that the subject has enough imagination to raise. But I cannot apply such a descriptive model to my own behavior. And even in the descriptive model the game that the subjects are playing will have to be one without restrictions to presuppositionless questions that may legitimately be asked.

But the presuppositions of questions that the freshly introduced knowledge statements $K(S \vee {\sim}S)$ are cannot be traced back to the initial premises. And since they are sometimes indispensable in inquiry, not all presuppositions have a precedent in the initial premises of inquiry. There is no set of absolute presuppositions that would restrict inquiry. Collingwood's notion is not viable.

To return to the main theme of this paper, we have reached an unequivocal answer to the question as to whether rational epistemological inquiry is subject to intransgressable restrictions such as are supposed to be dictated by Collingwood's ultimate presuppositions or by Kuhn's paradigms. The approach used here has so far followed Collingwood in construing limitations of inquiry as presuppositions of questions. What has been found by means of an examination of the presuppositions of questions is that these presuppositions do play an important role in inquiry, but that they restrict strategies and do not impose limits to what can be established by means of the inquiry. Moreover, the effect of the restrictions can be compensated for, not only by liberalizing the restrictions in the sense of assuming stronger initial premises but also by increasing the range of answerable questions. This can be established perfectly naturalistically, for instance through improved experimental and observational techniques. Hence what has been found here tells against all theories of unavoidable restrictions to inquiry, relativistic or not.

We have also seen in this section that there is no way of tracing all the presuppositions relied on in an inquiry to its initial premises. The notion of ultimate presuppositions is unworkable.

8. Presuppositions of Answers

But can all presuppositions of inquiry in the sense intended by the likes of Collingwood be construed as presuppositions of questions in the logical sense used above? This is a pertinent question. On the one hand, Collingwood not only speaks in so many words of the presuppositions of questions but often has obviously in mind the same sorts of presuppositions as have been considered above. He even uses some of the traditional examples of violations of such presuppositions, e.g. examples of the type "When did you stop beating your wife?".

However, on the other hand it seems to me that Collingwood is assimilating to each other presuppositions of questions in the sense used here and what might be called presuppositions of answers. In order to avoid confusion, I have nevertheless called them uniqueness conditions. They have been discussed elsewhere (see especially Hintikka forthcoming (a)), and hence I can be relatively brief here. An example can convey the main point.

As perceptive philosophers from Francis Bacon to Immanuel Kant to R.G. Collingwood have pointed out, one can – and ought to – construe controlled experiments in science as questions put to nature. Such a question has the form, "How does the variable y for a certain quantity depend on another one, say x, for a different variable?" (It is probably the very fact that the experimenter can in fact control one of the variables that prompted Bacon's metaphor of an investigator forcing nature to reveal her secrets.) The experiment succeeds in providing an answer to this question if the function expressing the dependence is known. Technically this means that the desideratum of the question becomes true. This desideratum can be expressed logically in any of the following forms:

(16) $(\exists f) K(\forall x) S[x, f(x)]$
(17) $K(\exists f/K)(\forall x) S[x, f(x)]$
(18) $K(\forall x) (\exists y/K) S[x,y]$

Here "K" is the knowledge operator ("It is known that") and "/" the independence operator. What the experiment ideally achieves is a function-in-extension, that is to say, an infinite list of correlated arguments values and function values. If this function-in-extension is g, then the purely observational components of an experimental answer is

(19) $K(\forall x) S[x, g(x)]$

You can think of (19) as being illustrated by an infinitely sharp curve on a graph paper.

But (19) does not logically imply (16)–(18). This fact has a concrete interpretation. Even if we abstract from all limitations of observational accuracy and of the accuracy with which on can manipulate the controlled variable, still "Nature's response" (17) will not satisfy the experimentalist unless he or she knows or finds out what the function g is, mathematically speaking. In terms of the hypothetical illustration, even if there is an arbitrarily accurate curve on the experimentalist's graph paper, he or she may still fail to know what the function is that the curve represents. Only if the scientist knows or is shown what that function is has he or she reached a conclusive answer to the experimental question.

This additional information is expressed by what I have called the conclusiveness condition. In an example this condition can be expressed in any of the following four forms:

(20) $(\exists f) K(\forall x)(g(x) = f(x))$

(21) $K(\exists f/K)(\forall x)(g(x) = f(x))$
(22) $K(\exists f/K)(g = f)$
(23) $K(\forall x)(\exists y/K)(g(x) = y)$

Even though (19) alone does not entail (16)–(18), it does so in conjunction with (20)–(23). This shows that (20)–(23) constitute a kind of presupposition of answers to an experimental question. Such "presuppositions" (conclusiveness conditions) limit the possibility of answering questions somewhat in the same way as the presuppositions of questions we encountered earlier. Hence they are relevant to the over-arching theme of this paper, which concerns the limitations of inquiry. In that what way does the need of conclusiveness conditions like (20)–(23) limit our quest of information?

What kind of knowledge is it that the presuppositions of answers like (20)–(23) express? This knowledge concerns the identity of certain mathematical objects, viz. functions. It is hence conceptual and a priori in character. Indeed, we have found one of the main gates through which mathematical knowledge enters into the very structure of empirical science. Such knowledge is needed to answer scientific questions, typified by experimental questions. This knowledge does not come to a scientist automatically. It has to be gained. But such knowledge is not uncovered in a laboratory or found codified in a textbook of experimental physics. It is obtained in departments of mathematics or from textbooks and treatises of mathematics and mathematical physics. Hence we have found here a very real constraint on an empirical inquirer's ability to answer experimental questions and indeed a constraint on inquiry in general. Moreover, what is especially interesting here is that this constraint is conceptual rather than factual in nature. In the case of an experimental scientist, the restriction is imposed on him or her by the limit of one's mathematical knowledge. Any particular scientist labors under restrictions on his or her knowledge of the relevant mathematical knowledge. But these personal restrictions are not inevitable or incorrigible. They can be overcome by increasing one's knowledge of the relevant functions or by consulting suitable sources of mathematical information. Hence, once again we are not dealing with absolute limits of inquiry, only epistemic ones.

These limits are nevertheless a very real factor in the history of science and mathematics. Repeatedly the need of knowing what a function is that has been encountered by physicists and other empirical scientists has prompted mathematicians to come to know it better, not to say come to know which function it really is.

All these remarks can be extended from experimental questions to all complex scientific wh-questions.

An interesting feature of our results resolved so far is that the mathematical or other conceptual knowledge that is required to reach conclusive answers to empirical questions is not *knowledge that,* that is, knowledge of facts, propositions, or truths but identificatory *knowledge of* certain kinds of mathematical *objects*, in the first place of functions. This observation can be taken as further evidence of the independence of the identificatory system operative in our semantics of the referential system.

Knowledge of the identity of objects (of different logical types) can be thought of as definitory knowledge, at least in the sense that it answers questions to the form "What is....?" It is scarcely accidental that such questions play an important role in the questioning method of the Platonic Socrates. Their importance is not due merely to the fact that their answers are definitions but first and foremost to their role in all questioning as unavoidable "presuppositions' (conclusiveness conditions) of answers to all questions. More generally speaking, this role of the knowledge of identities helps us to understand the important role of definitions in the thought of Plato and Aristotle. The more important questions and questioning are for a thinker, the more important is identificatory knowledge likely to be for him or her.

The need of knowing the mathematical identity of the function-in-extension g as in (19) has a counterpart in the case of simple wh-questions like (8). There the conclusiveness condition that a response, say "b", has to satisfy can be expressed in any of the following two forms:

(24) $K(\exists x/K) (b=x)$
(25) $(\exists x) K(b=x)$

where the variable ranges over persons. If so, (24)–(25) obviously amount to saying that

(26) I know who b is.

The need of these requirements is obvious. If I do not know who b is, the response "b" to the question (8) will not fully satisfy me.

When "b" is a proper name, (24)–(25) will express semantical knowledge. They do not give anyone any factual information about the bearer of the name "b". It only tells you who is referred to by it. This kind of knowledge is a counterpart to the mathematical knowledge expressed by (20)–(23). This analogy throws some light on the nature of both kinds of knowledge, and raises intriguing questions which I will try to deal with elsewhere. (See Hintikka, forthcoming.)

It can be seen that this kind of identificatory knowledge is needed both when the identity of a particular object is at issue and when the object in question is a universal, for instance a function. Indeed, one of the most interesting results we have reached is the close parallelism between simple wh-questions and complex experimental wh-questions. Such results throw interesting light on the old interpretational problem concerning the *what*-questions of the Platonic Socrates, recently rehearsed in Benson 1992(b), as to whether he was identifying particulars or universals.

Once again we have found genuine presuppositions of empirical inquiry. Once again, they are factors operative in actual scientific inquiry. The restrictions in question are due to the limitations of our knowledge of mathematical functions. But such restrictions are not unavoidable. They can be escaped by means of whatever mathematical research it takes to come to know previously unexamined functions typically resulting from a controlled experiment.

If there are any absolute limitations to empirical inquiry due to the presuppositions of answers, they will have to be due to limitations of our mathematical knowledge, in particular our knowledge of functions. Are there such restrictions? An answer depends on what we take it to mean to know which mathematical function it is that expresses a given mode of dependence, in brief, what it means to know a certain mathematical function.

But even without knowing any detailed answer to this question (sic), it is clear that the scope of one's knowledge of the identity of various mathematical functions can be enlarged and that the knowledge required for the purpose – as well as the knowledge acquired in the process – is mathematical in character, not empirical. Hence the limitations to our knowledge acquisition imposed by the conclusiveness conditions of answers are not eternal and immutable, but can be removed step by step by acquiring more mathematical and other conceptual knowledge.

In sum, limitations to inquiry due to the initial premises can be overcome by making more questions answerable. Limitations due to presuppositions of questions present only strategic difficulties, not barriers to what can be accomplished by inquiry; and limitations due to the "presuppositions of answers" (i.e. conclusiveness conditions) can be overcome by gaining more mathematical and other conceptual knowledge. And there does not seem to be any intrinsic limitations to such quest of mathematical knowledge, either. Even restrictions on available answers can in principle be removed by improved techniques of inquiry.

Acknowledging these limitations does not aid and abet in the least skeptical or relativistic views, including the views of the "new philosophers of science" à la Kuhn. I am even prepared to say more here and to ask: In view of the results reported here, is it any longer intellectually respectable to hold relativistic views or otherwise believe in unavoidable restriction on our knowledge seeking and knowledge acquisition? The answer is, of course: Only if you can provide a better analysis of the presuppositions of questions and answers.

References

Benson, Hugh H., editor, 1992(a), *Essays on the Philosophy of Socrates*, Oxford University Press, New York.

Benson, Hugh H., 1992(b), "Misunderstanding the 'What-is-F-ness' question", in Benson, 1992(a), pp. 123–136.

Beth, E. W., 1955, "Semantic entailment and formal derivability", *Mededlingen van de Koninklijke Nederlandse Akademie van Wetenschappen, Afd. Leterkund.* N.R. vol. 18, no 13, Amsterdam, 309–342.

Chomsky, Noam, 1959, "Review of Skinner", *Verbal Behavior, Language,* vol. 35, 26–58.
Collingwood, R.G., 1940, *An Essay on Metaphysics*, Clarendon Press, Oxford.
Collingwood, R.G., 1993, *The Idea of History*, Revised edition, Clarendon Press, Oxford.
Hintikka, Jaakko, forthcoming, "Why is mathematics indispensable in science?"
Hintikka, Jaakko, 1999, *Inquiry as Inquiry*, Kluwer Academic, Dordrecht.
Hintikka, Jaakko, 1998, "What is abduction? The fundamental problem of contemporary epistemology", *Proceedings of the Charles S. Peirce Society*, vol. 34, 503–533.
Hintikka, Jaakko, 1996, *The Principles of Mathematics Revisited*, Cambridge University Press.
Hintikka, Jaakko, Ilpo Halonen and Arto Mutanen, 1998, "Interrogative logic as a general theory of inquiry", in Hintikka, 1999, pp. 47–90.
Kuhn, Thomas, 1970, *The Structure of Scientific Revolutions*, Second edition, The University of Chicago Press.
Robinson, Richard, 1971, "Begging the question 1971", *Analysis,* vol. 31, no. 4, 113–117.
Robinson, Richard, 1953, *Plato's Earlier Dialectic*, Clarendon Press, Oxford.
Ryle, Gilbert, 1971, *Collected Papers* I–II, Hutchinson, London.
Sentas, Gerasimos Xenophon, 1979, *Socrates*, Routledge and Kegan Paul, London.
Vlastos, Gregory, 1971(b), "The Paradox of Socrates", in Vlastos, editor, 1971(a), pp. 1–21.

Plato is cited in the Loeb Library translations (Harvard University Press)

www.ingramcontent.com/pod-product-compliance
Lightning Source LLC
Chambersburg PA
CBHW060557230426
43670CB00011B/1853